Israel as a Modern Architectural Experimental Lab, 1948–1978

Israel as a Modern Architectural Experimental Lab, 1948–1978

Edited by
Inbal Ben-Asher Gitler and Anat Geva

intellect Bristol, UK / Chicago, USA

Israel as a Modern Architectural Experimental Lab, 1948-1978 is the fourth book in the Critical Studies in Architecture of the Middle East series. The series is edited by Mohammad Gharipour (Morgan State University, Baltimore) and Christiane Gruber (University of Michigan, Ann Arbor).

Critical Studies in Architecture of the Middle East is devoted to the most recent scholarship concerning historic and contemporary architecture, landscape and urban design of the Middle East and of regions shaped by diasporic communities more globally. We invite interdisciplinary studies from diverse perspectives that address the visual characteristics of the built environment, ranging from architectural case studies to urban analysis.

First published in the UK in 2020 by
Intellect, The Mill, Parnall Road, Fishponds, Bristol, BS16 3JG, UK

First published in the USA in 2020 by
Intellect, The University of Chicago Press, 1427 E. 60th Street,
Chicago, IL 60637, USA

A catalogue record for this book is available from the British Library.

Copy-editor: Emma Rhys
Cover designers: Aleksandra Szumlas, Inbal Ben-Asher Gitler and Anat Geva
Cover art: Arieh and Eldar Sharon, Sackler School of Medicine, Tel Aviv University, 1967-1972. Courtesy of the Azrieli Architecture Archive, Arieh Sharon Collection, Yael Aloni Photograph Collection.
Production editor: Faith Newcombe
Series: Critical Studies in Architecture of the Middle East
Series editors: Mohammad Gharipour and Christiane Gruber
Typesetting: Contentra Technologies

Print ISBN: 978-1-78938-064-4
ePDF ISBN: 978-1-78938-066-8
ePUB ISBN: 978-1-78938-065-1
Series ISSN: 2059-3562

Printed and bound by Gomer, UK.

Acknowledgements

We would like to thank the editors of Critical Studies in Architecture of the Middle East series, Mohammad Gharipour and Christiane Gruber, for their guidance throughout the process of publishing this book.

We thank all the contributors for their hard work, which elevated the book's scholarship.

We would like to thank Isabelle Kargon for her diligent work on the book's index.

We also thank Katie Evans and Faith Newcombe from Intellect Books for working with us on editing and production.

Finally, we would like to thank our academic institutions, Sapir Academic College, Israel and the College of Architecture, Texas A&M University, USA, for their funding of the book's index.

Contents

Introduction

Inbal Ben-Asher Gitler and Anat Geva

Historian Roger Adelson has argued, with regard to mid-twentieth-century western international politics, that a 'view of the Middle East gained currency that tended to simplify the region's diversity and complexity'.[1] As Adelson writes, this is a view that persists even today, at least in the media.[2] As architectural historians, we are given the task of unraveling and exposing a region's diversity and complexity, in retracing the physical space of nation building. In the Middle East, physical territories have been deconstructed and reassembled by conflict and war, migration and exile, nations and communities. The contours of this space delineate the similarities and the unique architectural production of each of its nations. By presenting new research on Israeli architecture, we hope to deepen not only our understanding of Israeli architectural culture, but also to contribute to the research on the region's architecture in general and its recent history.

Studies of nineteenth- and twentieth-century Middle Eastern architecture, which have proliferated during the past two decades, have already begun to reveal the intricate connections between architectural practices, as well as the diverse negotiation of tradition and innovation among different places in the Middle East, in its wider geographical definition.[3] Recent scholarship dealing with these shared architectural histories has challenged established dichotomies of modern versus traditional, East versus West, and centre versus periphery.[4] These alternative histories present analyses and discuss the architects who operated within expanding and rapidly transforming 'boundaries' of aesthetic and formal criteria. However, only a few scholars have discussed these issues in regards to Israel.

The compilation presented in this volume seeks to add significant insights to our reassessment of these concepts and to the understanding of Israeli architecture as an experimental laboratory of modern architecture. The essays included in this book discuss the architecture of Israel during its first three decades following the state's establishment in 1948.

The idea of a modern Jewish state in the Land of Israel was already envisioned by Theodor Herzl's Zionist utopia at the end of the nineteenth century. In his book, *Altneuland* ('Old New Land'), written in 1902, he describes an independent, secular, democratic Jewish state, which would follow modern Europe.[5] His Zionism is described by Steven Smith as 'a [technical] idealism of ends with a Machiavellianism of means'.[6] Herzl's contemporary, Achad Ha'am, envisioned a new Zionist-Jewish culture that would promote the core image of a new modern Jew based on western European culture.[7] It should be noted that this ideal did not account for Eastern European Jewish culture or the cultures of Jews from Muslim countries.

Indeed, Zionism, the secular ideology supporting and promoting the return of Jews to Palestine/Eretz Israel, hailed the western system of culture, economics, and politics as the model society upon which a future Jewish nation would be established. The Yishuv – the Zionist settlement of Palestine/Eretz Israel – developed according to this ideology from the middle of the nineteenth century until the end of the British Mandate in Palestine in 1948. It adopted European modernism as its technological, structural, and stylistic building approach.[8] This architecture, which provided the physical space of the sociopolitical structure of Jewish settlement in Palestine, became the basis and foundation for ensuing Israeli architecture. The Yishuv established distinct typologies for both urban and rural settlements, and by the end of British rule and Israel's establishment in 1948, these too were fully developed.

The year 1948 – when Israel was established as an independent nation-state – is the departure point for this book. Its timeframe terminates in 1978. The state's establishment affected new developments in urban and rural planning, as well as in architecture, and reflected social and political transformations. The year 1978 was a turning point, and generally marks two significant events: (1) the rise of the Likud government (1977), which brought about significant political changes in policies and ideologies and signified profound social transformations in the country; and (2) the signing of peace accords with Egypt (1978), which was the culmination of major political developments throughout the region. As several chapters in the present volume demonstrate, these temporal boundaries allow for flexibility, and can be challenged from various critical positions.

In many ways, Israel's built environment was a continuation of pre-state architectural culture that served as a civic vehicle for building the nation-state. Still, architecture during its first three decades was innovative and experimental in character. It presented a reassessment of modernist architectural approaches emanating from Europe and to some extent from the United States, while expressing local sociopolitical ideologies and economic constraints. Three of these ideologies had a profound impact upon Israeli architecture. First, the perception of Israel as progressive, and as home to an advanced new Jewish society that is part of western culture. This was reflected in the adaptation of western architectural culture, along with its technologies. Second, the use of architecture as a means to express the idea of Israel as a 'melting pot' new society. The vast post-World War II Jewish immigration from all over the world was addressed by a national policy of establishing a new, unified, Jewish society. This ideology ignored immigrants' cultural collective memories and often disregarded the Israeli regional local environment.[9] Third, the establishment of Jewish settlements in all regions of the state, which intended to densify Jewish presence in unpopulated regions, as well as in places deserted by Palestinians, or from which they were expelled. This strategy of claiming land vis-à-vis Palestinian displacement was subject to diverse modes of patronage, as well as to ongoing introspection, disputes, and policy changes. Architecture was inherently impacted by all these ideologies and expressed its modernity as a vehicle to address political changes while trying to continue the civic ideal of uniformity.

Accordingly, and following this volume's essays, three periods that influenced architecture and planning can be outlined. First, the period of early development, between 1948 and

1956. At that time, Israel's national master plan was introduced, and the first developments of modular unified mass-housing and governmental public buildings took place.[10] Second, the period between 1957 and 1966. During this phase, a reassessment of the first plans and designs was conducted. The re-evaluation of those concepts, which turned out to be unsuitable for specific cultural and environmental conditions, pushed designers to adopt modernism's shift towards regionalism.[11] The third phase lasted from 1967 until 1978. The architecture of that period coincided with the state's political transformations following the 1967 War, as well as with the development of new regional and city master plans.[12] These affected local interpretations of evolving global trends in modern architecture, while earlier concepts of uniformity were reassessed and gradually abandoned.

In all three phases, national settlement policies significantly impacted architecture as well. Thus, architecture became a testing ground that reflected policies such as

- 'The conquest of the desert': a concept that dictated the appropriation of the Negev desert;
- The settlement of the Galilee – the northern mountainous part of Israel – which initiated the establishment of hilltop settlements;
- The launch of 'development towns' in the periphery;
- The continuation of the Zionist ideology of the kibbutz and the moshav – the collective rural settlements;
- The instigation of the 'communal settlement' in newly occupied territories, such as the West Bank and the Golan Heights, following the 1967 War.

In light of these events and national ideologies, this volume raises a set of interrelated questions with regard to Israeli architecture: what were the transformations that it underwent during the first three decades? In what way were the novel developments of late modernism, or the late International Style, expressed in Israel? What impact did the Israeli civic policy of uniformity have on the architectural experimentation in modernism? And finally, how was Israeli architecture exported and disseminated globally? These questions are addressed in the book within a broader inquiry into modernism and its relation to the nation-state in the context of cultural, social, economic, and technological issues.[13]

As with inquiries dealing with other Middle Eastern countries, postcolonial theory has proved instrumental in researching the architectural history of Israel.[14] However, Kathleen James-Chakraborty's 2014 call to historians of non-western architecture to move 'beyond postcolonialism' is also valid in this case.[15] New research 'answering' this call has begun investigating the role of collective memory and the architecture of commemoration,[16] and has explored issues of gender, as well as additional themes.[17] An investigation that has further broadened the postcolonial lens can be found in recent discussions dealing with architects' experimentation with the idea of 'placelessness' or internationality, and their attempt at reconciling these with the search for locality.[18] In the Israeli case, this process is especially potent and intriguing, as different interpretations of place and locality were recruited during the early years of establishment: did 'place' refer to a general notion of the Mediterranean

Basin? Was a broad Middle Eastern place elicited, or a local Palestinian one?[19] These issues require investigation, especially since the Mediterranean, which includes several countries in the Middle East, was not only impacted by modernism, but also had a central influence upon its evolvement as a novel architectural approach.[20]

By researching fascinating case studies that discuss a wide variety of typologies, the essays brought together in this volume shed new light on many of the questions posed here and on related phenomena. They are addressed in all four sections of the book, including a concluding chapter that illustrates the essays' analyses of the questions posed at the outset of this introduction, and presents the conclusions that can be derived from these new studies.

The book's first section, 'Modern Experiments in Rural and Urban Design', addresses mass-housing neighbourhoods in development towns and communal settlements in the occupied territories, and devotes a chapter to the kibbutz.

In the first chapter, Yair Barak investigates Artur Glikson's mass-housing neighbourhood in the development town of Kiryat-Gat, located in Israel's central-southern part. In his analysis, Barak scrutinizes the sociological research conducted prior to planning this neighbourhood. The neighbourhood's preparatory studies and its plan were intended to achieve successful implementation of the national ideology of social unification. Barak demonstrates how this project served as grounds for the emerging criticality of the idea of the melting pot, and analyses Glikson's innovative approach to private versus communal spaces on an urban scale.

In the second chapter, Oryan Shachar presents one neighbourhood in the northern development town of Hatzor HaGlilit, built for the ultraorthodox Gur Hasidic community in the early 1970s. Conceived by David Reznik more than a decade after Glikson's neighbourhood, the Gur neighbourhood was a segregated urban space for a community defined by its religiosity. In this, it exemplifies the profound transformation that national planning underwent within this period – from the policy of unification to one of a gradual acceptance of the diverse social groups and ethnicities that comprise the nation as a whole.

In the third chapter, Yael Allweil addresses the West Bank settlement initiatives following the 1967 War. As with the Hasidic community, these settlement projects were carried out by clearly defined sociopolitical entities: the Religious Kibbutz Movement and the settlement movement, Elon-More. Allweil analyses the emergence of the communal settlements of the West Bank as a typology grounded in earlier Zionist traditions. She interprets this typology as a merge of urban and rural settlement ideologies, demonstrating how Zionist settling practices were used to justify territorial claims and harness Israeli support of them. Allweil discusses this experiment as one that challenges the widely accepted periodization, which divides Israeli architectural historiography by the change of regime that took place in 1977. She argues that the continuation of this project well into the 1990s, as settlement initiatives 'enacted by citizens in manipulation of state mechanisms', exhibits continuity rather than rupture of the historical timeline.[21]

The last chapter in this section is by Elissa Rosenberg. She researches kibbutz landscape designs, as well as the writings on this subject by kibbutz architect Shmuel Bickels. Her chapter analyses how the kibbutz – the best-known experimental modern rural space designed under the framework of Zionist ideologies – continued to evolve during the first decades of the nation. Rosenberg illuminates Bickels's emphasis on the relationship between the kibbutz garden and its surrounding landscape, an expression of locality that distinguished him from the mainstream of kibbutz planning and constituted a critique of the 'placelessness' of international modernism.

The book's second section, 'Public Architecture as a Testing Ground', includes four chapters dealing with public buildings: exhibition spaces, youth villages, and synagogues.

Eliyahu Keller investigates the Israel Museum in Jerusalem, designed by architects Alfred (Al) Mansfeld and Dora Gad. Keller compares this national monument with Aldo van Eyck's famous orphanage in the Netherlands. This comparison includes van Eyck's structuralist theory, which influenced the architects' approach to the museum's design. These concepts are used by Keller to explain the appropriation of locality through the abstraction of a typical hillside local Palestinian village. Such analysis provides an in-depth understanding of how late modernism was adapted and embedded in regional contexts.

In the second chapter of this section, Sigal Davidi examines architect Genia Averbuch's plans for youth villages intended for Jewish immigrants, built during the mass-immigration waves of early statehood. The villages' functions were geared towards immigrant children's modern secular education, with the intention of transforming them into 'modern Israelis' with a 'love for the homeland and its soil'.[22] In addition to the analysis of the villages' design, this chapter exemplifies the contribution of women architects to modern Israeli architecture.

The third chapter, by Naomi Simhony, addresses three synagogues designed by different architects. These houses of worship represented a redefinition of this typology by using late modernist formal vocabularies, with no relation to particular religious symbols. These synagogues derived their inspiration from contemporary civic and modern sacred architecture in the West, connecting it with local, as well as Mediterranean, traditions. Simhony demonstrates how the use of familiar sacred architectural elements and morphology were linked later in time to religious symbols and, in the case of architects Alfred Neumann and Zvi Hecker, elicited Muslim and Jewish geometric patterns, in an attempt to convey inter-religious and multicultural dialogue.

Jeremy Kargon discusses in the fourth chapter a design competition for the Center for Technological Awareness, called the 'Technodea'. Focusing on the winning entry by Hillel Schocken, Uri Shaviv, and Tsiyona Margalit-Gerstein, Kargon demonstrates how British architectural discourse, taking place during the same period, influenced Israeli architects. Kargon investigates the immediate and reflexive adaptation of this discourse to local climate, topography, materials, and even nascent sustainability. His research analyses isolate the functional and formal shift from late modernist approaches in the planning of exhibition spaces to postmodern concepts in architectural design. The Technodea scheme was among the first to introduce these design ideas into the local architectural scene.

The third section of this book, entitled 'Considering Climate', discusses the architectural experiments intended to adapt modernism to Israel's environmental conditions, including the country's desert regions.

The chapter by Daphne Binder and Theodore Kofman focuses on the Dead Sea region, the lowest place (below sea level) in the world, and its development in the face of extreme hot-arid environmental conditions. They analyze architecture's relation to topography to afford breezes and views; they reveal the importance of shading and density, achieved by covered streets, minimal, well-oriented fenestration, and internal courts. Binder and Kofman further demonstrate how the architecture for this region integrated modern technology with local materials. The use of concrete with extensive earthwork, as well as local stone and gravel, created a sense of locality and contemporaneity while providing thermal comfort.

Isaac Meir, Rachel Bernstein and Keren Shalev's chapter deals with three decades of climatic considerations in planning the desert town of Be'er Sheva. The chapter investigates mass-housing neighbourhoods, campuses, and additional civic projects using empirical measurements. It demonstrates that the desert was considered by architects only for its summer conditions (e.g., heat and glaring radiation), while the other side of the extreme – cold winters – were ignored.

The last chapter of this section by Or Aleksandrowicz traces the evolvement of science-based climatic planning and conducts a comparative analysis of two university buildings: one in the campus of Tel Aviv University, designed by Werner Joseph Wittkower and the other in Haifa University, designed by renowned Brazilian architect Oscar Niemeyer, with Shlomo Gilad as the local architect. Aleksandrowicz demonstrates that despite the accumulated knowledge and guidelines for climatic planning, architects based their designs more on intuition than on facts.

The final section of the book, 'Reflections Abroad', discusses the exportation of Israeli architecture both conceptually and physically.

In the first chapter, Matteo Cassani Simonetti analyses Italian discourse on Israeli architecture as it evolved from Italian political post-war architectural culture, and as grounded in Italian Jewish architectural tradition, or lack thereof. Simonetti highlights the central role of Italian architectural critic and historian Bruno Zevi in this process. Zevi was one of the key figures affecting the relationship between Italian and Israeli architectural culture, viewing Israeli architectural experiments as viable models for Italy. By examining which Israeli projects received attention, Simonetti positions Israeli architecture within the wider modernist discourse in Italy. The prominence of Israeli architecture in Italian media exemplifies the European attention given to modernist ventures outside its borders, and beyond what was geographically considered as 'West'.

In the second chapter, Ayala Levin compares the Israeli parliament building in Jerusalem, the Knesset, with the Sierra Leone parliament. She analyses how architect Ram Karmi, who participated in the planning of the Knesset, designed the Sierra Leone parliament in light of lessons learned from the former project in Israel. She investigates his desire to imbue architectural modernism with monumentality, as well as his approach to creating a distinct national identity tailored to each locale. Here, too, the question of which traditions were appropriated, and how these were related to post-war modernism, surfaces as a major dilemma for architect Karmi. Levin engages this dilemma by probing the concept of 'nativeness' as expressed in both buildings, and as developed by Karmi in light of Team X and Brutalist ideas that he adopted from Europe. She demonstrates that while in Israel the connection to place and origin constituted an important aspect of the policy of cultural unification and sense of rootedness, in Sierra Leone similar aesthetic devices and local materials were harnessed to promote ethnic and religious coexistence.

As a whole, the book's chapters describe the challenges that architects in Israel faced and their achievements, while operating within the framework of building the nation-state and creating a discourse with their clients and the public. Finally, in this volume's conclusion, we demonstrate how each of the case studies provides fresh insights regarding the wide use of modernism and its negotiations and adaptation to Israel.

Bibliography

Adelson, Roger. 'British and U.S. Use and Misuse of the Term "Middle East"'. In *Is There a Middle East?*, edited by Michael E. Bonine, Abbas Amanat, and Michael Ezekiel Gasper, 36–55. Stanford: Stanford University Press, 2012.

Aleksandrowicz, Or. 'Appearance and Performance: Israeli Building Climatology and Its Effect on Local Architectural Practice (1940–1977)'. *Architectural Science Review* 60.5 (2017): 371–81.

Allweil, Yael. *Homeland: Zionism as Housing Regime, 1860–2011*. Oxford, UK and New York: Routledge, 2017.

AlSayyad, Nezar, ed. *The End of Tradition?* London: Routledge, 2003.

Avermaete, Tom, Serhat Krakayali and Marion von Osten, eds. *Colonial Modern: Aesthetics of the Past – Rebellions for the Future*. London: Black Dog Publishing, 2010.

Ben-Asher Gitler, Inbal. 'Some Notes on Applying Postcolonial Methodologies to Architectural History Research in Israel/Palestine'. In *Narratives Unfolding: National Art Histories in an Unfinished World*, edited by Martha Langford, 100–22. Montreal: McGill-Queen's Press-MQUP, 2017.

Elser, Oliver. 'Just What Is It That Makes Brutalism So Appealing? – A New Definition from an International Perspective'. In *SOS Brutalism: A Global Survey*, edited by Oliver Elser, Philip Kurz, and Peter Cachola Schmal, 14–19. Frankfurt and Zurich: Deutsches Architekturmuseum, Wüstenrot Foundation and Park Books, 2017. Exhibition catalogue.

Elser, Oliver, Philip Kurz, and Peter Cachola Schmal, eds. *SOS Brutalism: A Global Survey*. Frankfurt and Zurich: Deutsches Architekturmuseum, Wüstenrot Foundation and Park Books, 2017. Exhibition catalogue.

Epstein-Pliouchtch, Marina and Michael Levin, eds. *Richard Kaufmann and the Zionist Project*. Tel Aviv: Hakibbutz Hameuhad, 2016 (In Hebrew).

Ergut, Elvan Altan and Belgin Turan Özkaya. 'Editors' Introduction: Culture, Diplomacy, Representation: "Ambivalent Architectures" from the Ottoman Empire to the Turkish Republic'. *New Perspectives on Turkey* 50 (2014): 5–8.

Eyal, Gil. 'Between East and West: The Discourse on the "Arab Village" in Israel'. In *Colonialism and the Postcolonial Condition*, edited by Yehouda Shenhav, 201–23. Tel Aviv: Hakibbutz Hameuhad/Van Leer Institute, 2004 (In Hebrew).

Geva, Anat. 'Immigrants' Sacred Architecture: The Rabi Baal Hanes Synagogue in Eilat, Israel'. In *Design and Identity: The Architecture of Synagogues in the Islamic World*, edited by Mohammad Gharipour, 271–92. Edinburgh: Edinburgh University Press, 2017.

Halkin, Hillel. 'What Ahad Ha'am Saw and Herzl Missed – and Vice Versa'. *Mosaic*. October 5, 2016. Accessed March 13, 2018. https://mosaicmagazine.com/essay/2016/10/what-ahad-haam-saw-and-herzl-missed-and-vice-versa.

Herzl, Theodor, *Old New Land* ('Altneuland'), translated by Lotta Levensohn. Princeton: Markus Wiener, 1997. Leipzig: Hermann Seemann Nachfolger, 1902.

Isenstadt, Sandy and Kishwar Rizvi, eds. *Modernism and the Middle East: Architecture and Politics in the Twentieth Century*. Seattle, WA: University of Washington Press, 2008.

James-Chakraborty, Kathleen. 'Beyond Postcolonialism: New Directions for the History of Nonwestern Architecture'. *Frontiers of Architectural Research* 3.1 (2014): 1–9.

Kallus, Rachel. 'The Political Role of the Everyday'. *City: Analysis of Urban Trends, Culture, Theory, Policy, Action* 8.3 (2004): 341–61.

Lejeune, Jean-François and Michelangelo Sabatino. *Modern Architecture and the Mediterranean: Vernacular Dialogues and Contested Identities*. London: Routledge, 2009.

Meyer-Maril, Edina. 'Women Architects Building the Land'. In *Women Artists in Israel, 1920–1970*, edited by Ruth Markus, 139–80. Tel Aviv: Hakibbutz Hameuchad, 2008 (In Hebrew).

Metzger-Szmuk, Nitza. *Dwelling on the Dunes, Tel Aviv, Modern Movement and Bauhaus Ideas*. Paris: Editions De L'Eclat, 2004.

Mshayekhi, Azadeh and Zvi Efrat. 'Middle East'. In *SOS Brutalism: A Global Survey*, edited by Oliver Elser, Philip Kurz, and Peter Cachola Schmal, 189–97, 214–19. Frankfurt and Zurich: Deutsches Architekturmuseum, Wüstenrot Foundation and Park Books, 2017. Exhibition catalogue.

Neuman, Eran, ed. *Arieh Sharon: The State's Architect*. Tel Aviv: Tel Aviv Museum of Art, 2018 (In English and Hebrew).

——— *Shoah Presence: Architectural Representations of the Holocaust*. Abingdon and New York: Routledge, 2016.

Nitzan-Shiftan, Alona. 'Contested Zionism-Alternative Modernism: Erich Mendelsohn and the Tel Aviv Chug in Mandate Palestine'. *Architectural History* 39 (1996): 147–80.

——— 'On Concrete and Stone: Shifts and Conflicts in Israeli Architecture'. *Traditional Dwellings and Settlements Review* 21.1 (2009): 51–65.

Shadar, Hadas. 'Evolution and Critical Regionalism'. *Journal of Urban Design* 15.2 (2010): 227–42.

Shadar, Hadas and Robert Oxman. 'Of Village and City: Ideology in Israeli Public Planning'. *Journal of Urban Design* 8.3 (2003): 243–68.

Smith, Steven. 'Ahad Ha'am and Theodor Herzl: Together at Last?' *Mosaic*. October 19, 2016. Accessed March 13, 2018. https://mosaicmagazine.com/response/2016/10/ahad-haam-and-theodor-herzl-together-at-last/?print.

Sonder, Ines. *Lotte Cohen: Eine Schreibende Architektin in Israel*, 2 vols. Berlin: Neofelis Veglag, 2017.

Warhaftig, Myra. *They Laid the Foundation: Lives and Works of German-Speaking Jewish Architects in Palestine 1918–1948*, translated by Andrea Lerner. Tübingen and New York: Wasmuth, 2007.

Wharton, Annabel Jane. *Selling Jerusalem: Relics, Replicas, Theme Parks*. Chicago: University of Chicago Press, 2006.

Notes

1 Roger Adelson, 'British and U.S. Use and Misuse of the Term "Middle East"', in *Is There a Middle East?*, ed. Michael E. Bonine, Abbas Amanat and Michael Ezekiel Gasper (Stanford: Stanford University Press, 2012), 49.

2 Adelson, 'British and U.S. Use and Misuse of the Term "Middle East"', 55.

3 Sandy Isenstadt and Kishwar Rizvi, eds, *Modernism and the Middle East: Architecture and Politics in the Twentieth Century* (Seattle, WA: University of Washington Press, 2008); Kathleen James-Chakraborty, 'Beyond Postcolonialism: New Directions for the History of Nonwestern Architecture', *Frontiers of Architectural Research* 3, no. 1 (2014): 1–9.

4 Nezar AlSayyad, ed., *The End of Tradition?* (London: Routledge, 2003); Elvan Altan Ergut and Belgin Turan Özkaya, 'Editors' Introduction: Culture, Diplomacy, Representation: "Ambivalent Architectures" from the Ottoman Empire to the Turkish Republic', *New Perspectives on Turkey* 50 (2014): 5–8.

5 Theodor Herzl, *Old New Land*, trans. Lotta Levensohn (Princeton: Markus Wiener, 1997; Leipzig: Hermann Seemann Nachfolger, 1902).

6 Hillel Halkin, 'What Ahad Ha'am Saw and Herzl Missed – and Vice Versa', *Mosaic*, October 5, 2016, accessed March 13 2018, https://mosaicmagazine.com/essay/2016/10/what-ahad-haam-saw-and-herzl-missed-and-vice-versa; Steven Smith 'Ahad Ha'am and Theodor Herzl: Together at Last?', *Mosaic*, October 19, 2016, accessed March 13 2018, https://mosaicmagazine.com/response/2016/10/ahad-haam-and-theodor-herzl-together-at-last/?print;.

7 Halkin, 'What Ahad Ha'am Saw and Herzl Missed'.

8 Much has been written about the architecture of the Yishuv. See, for example, Alona Nitzan-Shiftan, 'Contested Zionism-Alternative Modernism: Erich Mendelsohn and the Tel Aviv Chug in Mandate Palestine', *Architectural History* vol. 39 (1996): 147–80; Myra Warhaftig, *They Laid the Foundation: Lives and Works of German-Speaking Jewish Architects in Palestine 1918–1948*, trans. Andrea Lerner (Tübingen and New York: Wasmuth, 2007); Nitza Metzger-Szmuk, *Dwelling on the Dunes, Tel Aviv, Modern Movement and Bauhaus Ideas* (Paris: Editions De L'Eclat, 2004); Marina Epstein-Pliouchtch and Michael Levin, eds, *Richard Kaufmann and the Zionist Project* (Tel Aviv: Hakibbutz Hameuhad, 2016) (In Hebrew).

9 Anat Geva, 'Immigrants' Sacred Architecture: The Rabi Baal Hanes Synagogue in Eilat, Israel', in *Design and Identity: The Architecture of Synagogues in the Islamic World*, ed. Mohammad Gharipour (Edinburgh: Edinburgh University Press, 2017), 271–929.

10 For a discussion and reassessment of Israel's master plan, see Eran Neuman, ed., *Arieh Sharon: The State's Architect* (Tel Aviv: Tel Aviv Museum of Art, 2018) (In Hebrew and English).

11 Hadas Shadar, 'Evolution and Critical Regionalism', *Journal of Urban Design* 15.2 (2010): 227–42. The later phase of this development is discussed by Rachel Kallus, 'The Political Role of the Everyday', *City: Analysis of Urban Trends, Culture, Theory, Policy, Action* 8.3 (2004): 341–61.

12 See for example the case of Be'er-Sheva as discussed by Hadas Shadar and Robert Oxman, 'Of Village and City: Ideology in Israeli Public Planning', *Journal of Urban Design* 8.3 (2003): 243–68.

13 For additional recent research that addresses this see, for example, Or Aleksandrowicz, 'Appearance and Performance: Israeli Building Climatology and Its Effect on Local Architectural Practice (1940–1977)', *Architectural Science Review* 60.5 (2017): 371–81; Yael Allweil, *Homeland: Zionism as Housing Regime, 1860–2011* (Oxford, UK and New York: Routledge, 2017).

14 Inbal Ben-Asher Gitler, 'Some Notes on Applying Postcolonial Methodologies to Architectural History Research in Israel/Palestine', in *Narratives Unfolding: National Art Histories in an Unfinished World*, ed. Martha Langford (Montreal: McGill-Queen's Press-MQUP, 2017), 100–22.

15 James-Chakraborty, 'Beyond Postcolonialism', 1–9.

16 Eran Neuman, *Shoah Presence: Architectural Representations of the Holocaust* (Abingdon and New York: Routledge, 2016); Annabel Jane Wharton, *Selling Jerusalem: Relics, Replicas, Theme Parks* (Chicago: University of Chicago Press, 2006).

17 Edina Meyer-Maril, 'Women Architects Building the Land', in *Women Artists in Israel, 1920–1970*, ed. Ruth Markus (Tel-Aviv: Hakibbutz Hameuchad, 2008), 139–80 (In Hebrew); Ines Sonder, *Lotte Cohen: Eine Schreibende Architektin in Israel*, 2 vols (Berlin: Neofelis Veglag, 2017).

18 See for example, Tom Avermaete, Serhat Krakayali, and Marion von Osten, eds, *Colonial Modern: Aesthetics of the Past – Rebellions for the Future* (London: Black Dog Publishing, 2010); and Oliver Elser, Philip Kurz, and Peter Cachola Schmal, eds, *SOS Brutalism: A Global Survey* (Frankfurt and Zurich: Deutsches Architekturmuseum, Wüstenrot Foundation and Park Books, 2017), Exhibition catalogue. In the latter volume, see especially, Oliver Elser, 'Just What Is It That Makes Brutalism So Appealing? – A New Definition from an International Perspective', in *SOS Brutalism: A Global Survey*, ed. Oliver Elser, Philip Kurz, and Peter Cachola Schmal (Frankfurt and Zurich: Deutsches Architekturmuseum, Wüstenrot Foundation and Park Books, 2017), 14–19, Exhibition catalogue; Azadeh Mshayekhi and Zvi Efrat, 'Middle East', in *SOS Brutalism: A Global Survey*, ed. Oliver Elser, Philip Kurz, and Peter Cachola Schmal (Frankfurt and Zurich: Deutsches Architekturmuseum, Wüstenrot Foundation and Park Books, 2017), 189–97, 214–19, Exhibition catalogue.

19 Gil Eyal, 'Between East and West: The Discourse on the "Arab Village" in Israel', in *Colonialism and the Postcolonial Condition*, ed. Yehouda Shenhav (Tel Aviv: Hakibbutz Hameuhad and Van Leer Institute, 2004), 201–23; Alona Nitzan-Shiftan, 'On Concrete and Stone: Shifts and Conflicts in Israeli Architecture', *Traditional Dwellings and Settlements Review* 21.1 (2009): 51–65.

20 Jean-François Lejeune and Michelangelo Sabatino, eds, *Modern Architecture and the Mediterranean: Vernacular Dialogues and Contested Identities* (Abingdon and New York: Routledge, 2010), 1–12.

21 See Yael Allweil's chapter in this book, 73.

22 See Sigal Davidi's chapter in this book, 156.

Section I

Modern Experiments in Rural and Urban Design

The Experimental Integrative Habitation Unit as a Modern Experimental Lab in Israel[1]

Yair Barak

In June 1958, the Israeli government decided to initiate an experimental housing project, the Integrative Habitation Unit (IHU). This decision stemmed from physical and social problems, which were a result of the mass wave of immigration, mainly from Muslim countries, that had ended by 1954. The previous housing solutions, which had been either provisional – such as the *ma'abarot* (transit camps) – or permanent – such as the construction of small and uniform flats that were built in blocks – were clearly no longer suitable.

The decision makers were also highly concerned with the social-ideological problems that had developed, since the Israeli vision of the ingathering of Diasporas had collapsed within a few years. The rifts were not necessarily among veteran Ashkenazi Israelis, but among and between all the ethnic groups (*Edot*). The events and the sociological studies clearly proved that it was difficult to turn the vision of integrating people from the different Diasporas into a reality.

Two solutions to both issues were considered. The first solution was to settle the next wave of North African immigrants in the newly developed Lakhish region. They were taken directly from the ships to the villages (moshavim) during 1955–56. This prevented them from seeing the urban centres. The immigrants were settled in villages according to their original clans, replicating what had existed in their countries of origin. There was to be no integration even among the North African (Moroccan) Jews themselves. The other solution was entirely different: to promote the development of the nearby cities. This was more economically efficient than building villages, since construction of the rural infrastructure was much more expensive than developing what already existed.

The IHU was the implementation of this second solution. It stemmed from the urban trend to integrate diverse social and ethnic groups into a well-defined and well-designed quarter of a new town, which would mix different social groups. This was to be an urban, rationally planned site of cement, blocks, walkways, and open spaces, which would serve as a site for the creation of a new social/national brotherhood. This plan further reflected the slogan 'To build and to be built', which had been coined in an optimistic Zionist popular song.

This experiment contained the contradictions that were inherent in the absorption process of the Mizrahi Jewish (i.e., Jews emigrating mostly from Muslim countries) emigration in the nascent, ambitious, Israel. It included modern urban housing and quarters for conservative rural immigrants; individual dwellings of various types and preferences, which aimed to create positive and cohesive social relations between the diverse groups; and open spaces for individuals and children that would serve as casual social meeting points. All these ideas followed Le Corbusier's 'Radiant City' vision of grounds among buildings that would promote communal cohesion.[2] While the initiators and planners of the experimental IHU thought 'individual', they actually meant 'collective'.

The IHU was explicitly planned, built, and settled as an experimental site in order to examine the feasibility of well-defined neighbourhood architecture. Its telos was to eradicate ethnic strife. The IHU was not an experimental project from a historical perspective, but rather a real-time socio-national architectural experiment. In other words, the IHU was the epitome of Israeli architecture as a modern experimental laboratory.

This chapter analyses the problematic social reality that characterized the second half of the 1950s and the architects' motivations to provide a physical response that would alleviate these problems. From a historical perspective, we can relate to the solutions as aspirations of social engineering or for creating a utopia. The IHU in Kiryat-Gat is an ideal case study for tracing such utopian aspirations that were based on a detailed social-political-ideological programme, and which were architecturally realized. It further enables an examination of the human results of such social engineering.

Mass Immigration Causes a Social-Ethnic Rift

During its first decade, more than half a million Jews immigrated to Israel from Iraq, Yemen, Turkey, Morocco, Libya, and other Muslim countries. Within a few years, mass immigration had effected a profound change in Israeli society. It lost its cultural, social, and economic homogeneity, and became a heterogenic population. The historian, Dvora Hacohen, related to the demographic change as being no less than a 'revolution'.[3]

Political leaders, who were aware of the new sociocultural situation, defined Israel as a binational country consisting of two different nations: a veteran nation and a new, immigrant nation. Golda Meyerson (Meir), the Labor Minister, expressed this sentiment in 1950:

> The reality is of two different Jewish nations in the State of Israel. One nation is the veteran one, and another nation, which can be called the newcomers. There is a huge gap between them. This is a huge rift that cannot be bridged.
>
> (July 14, 1950)[4]

The first Prime Minister of Israel, David Ben-Gurion, shared Meyerson's evaluation.[5] Four years later, he said: 'We will not be able to exist for long in a situation comprised of two nations' (June 10, 1954).[6]

The veteran population perceived the cultures, traditions, and behaviours of the newcomers as primitive and inferior, in comparison to the local hegemonic 'western' culture. This was expressed in some media articles and other publications that deepened the mutual hostility: 'The North African Jews are a most primitive nation. They are ignorant and have no aptitude for understanding any intellectual subject.'[7] As historian Orit Rozin concluded, the political leaders and the veteran Israelis developed aversive feelings towards the oriental Mizrahi newcomers.[8]

In July 1959, the increasing social tension – which came after a long period of protests from people who lived in the *ma'abarot* – escalated into a violent clash. A protest rally, organized by North African immigrants living in Wadi Salib (which had been a Palestinian neighbourhood/district in Haifa), escalated into a physical confrontation between the demonstrators and the police, who fired at them and wounded one of the demonstrators. The demonstrators protested against their discrimination and miserable quality of life, which included their housing. The protests spread to other cities, where other Mizrahi newcomers lived.

The event caused public shock, since the incident made it clear that the vision of the 'melting Diasporas', which was the Zionist version of the American 'melting pot', had collapsed. In the collective memory, Wadi Salib became a symbol of a turning point in the social life of young Israel. For the first time, the events raised public scepticism regarding the possibility of realizing the vision (dream? illusion? wishful thinking?) of *Mizug Galuyot* – the ingathering of the Diasporas.

The Uniformity of Public Apartments in the Years 1948–59

It is understandable why there were governmental efforts to supply housing for the immigrant masses; they were an outcome of the political reality. These efforts could be interpreted as being a 'responsibility' that went beyond the physical sphere; they reflected a 'strategy of patronage', or even a pretense to design a new society composed of different elements.[9]

The main permanent housing solution, for both the newcomers and veterans, was the public housing project (in Hebrew – *shikun*), which was directly planned, built, and populated by government authorities. In the beginning, the design of the block houses and apartments was uniform. A publicly financed apartment, built by the Ministry of Housing, had 1.6 rooms and an area of 34 square metres. In 1957, the area of an apartment in a public housing project was enlarged to 69 square metres. The reason for the uniform small size was that there was a limited housing budget that was used to finance the largest possible quantity of equal and homogenous apartments for families of all sizes.

The letter sent to Mrs Haya Siflinger, who lived in the Har-Tuv *ma'abara*, in response to her complaints about housing, provides authentic evidence of the housing policy:

> We have received a copy of the letter you sent to the Minister of Labor regarding your housing conditions in Har-Tuv. We allocate the apartments as follows: a regular apartment with one room and toilet is given to families of up to four persons; an enlarged apartment of one and a half rooms is given to families with five to eight persons; some bigger flats are given families with 9–11 people. It is very clear that these apartments cannot fulfill all housing requirements of the residents, either those who came from the Orient or those who arrived from Occidental countries.
>
> (October 31, 1951)[10]

The official response could be summarized in the following way: the size of the house is minimal for the immigrant, but the maximum size that the state can provide.

Apartments as Agents of Nationalistic-Idealistic Aspirations

By 1959, it was quite evident that one of the issues was how to design individualistic apartments that would satisfy the needs of different residents. The idea was to include several apartment types in one building and to design an integrated neighbourhood. Yaacov Ben-Sira, one of Israel's prominent planners, addressed the uniform–individuality trade-off:

> The most complicated problem is identifying ahead of time the potential residents since they behave differently and have different ways of living, according to their various cultural origins and their family size. Perhaps it would be possible to design for every need, but the budgetary allocations are so minimal and the living areas so small, that it leaves little room for variations.[11]

Awareness of the need to redesign the apartments allocated to newcomers, in order to adjust them to the various families, led to the appointment of an ad-hoc professional committee (financed by the B. Rothschild Foundation for Research and Planning of Low-Cost Housing). The committee members were prominent Israeli architects and included Artur Glikson, Avraham Yaski, and Alfred (Al) Mansfeld. The committee published five directives/proposals that had been given to it as guidelines for the research, and which could be interpreted as a concise summary of the Israeli housing ethos. The houses would be planned according to the average size of the newcomers' family and would 'be used as an educational instrument for proper family life'.[12] As a result, the patron-state became a somewhat invasive force. Additional directives were: 'The cost will be no more than the costs of the previous houses built by the government. The flats will be small, but can be enlarged at the residents' own expense.'[13]

The committee offered six recommendations and proposed three prototypes for low-cost and flexible constructions. The first item in the committee's final report was a unique Israeli requirement, turning the house into an active part in the integrating Diasporas project:

> The house should only be adapted to the family's size. The newcomers' origin should not be taken into consideration, since the preferences of the newcomers and of the absorbing society need to be solidified into a unified Israeli way of life.[14]

This idea that apartments and houses were agents of the realization of nationalistic-idealistic aspirations was the main objective of the IHU in Kiryat-Gat.

Some Housing Problems in New Development Towns and Suburbs

The IHU in Kiryat-Gat, conceived by the architect Artur Glikson, was an important experiment in the planning of Israeli development towns. 'Development town' is a term used to refer to the new urban settlements that were built in Israel during the 1950s, in order to provide permanent housing for the large influx of immigrants. The towns were designated to enlarge the population of the country's peripheral areas and to ease development pressure in its crowded centre. They were a part of the Sharon Plan – Israel's master plan.[15] The majority of such towns were built in the Galilee – Israel's northern region – and in the southern Negev region.[16]

Though Glikson belonged to the architectural establishment, his paper, 'Some Problems of Housing in Israel's New Towns and Suburbs', is a critique of state policies. He criticized the planning, which did not take into consideration 'the identity of the national group or community that would settle in the specific development site'.[17] This critique may have also been aimed at the team established by the B. Rothschild Foundation for Research and Planning of Low-Cost Housing (see above) in which he participated.

Opposed to the team's recommendations, Glikson claimed that 'there was a need to create true urban forms of housing and diversify the forms of dwellings so as to match the requirements of veteran settlers and new immigrants, large and small families, etc'.[18] Planning entire suburbs, he claimed, was more practical.

Glikson had a central role in planning the new developmental area of the Lakhish region. He published the rationale of the plan as a case study that revealed some ideas that contradicted those that guided him in his critique of housing and planning.

The Lakhish Region: Opposite Policies – Separation versus Integration or Pragmatism versus Idealism

The Palestinian population was expelled from the northern part of the Negev after the success of the Israel Defense Forces' Yoav Military Operation in October 1948.

> Within days of the Israel–Egypt Armistice Agreement of 24 February 1949, Israel violated its terms by intimidating some 2,000–3,000 villagers of Faluja and Iraq al Manshia into fleeing the villages, the last Palestinian Arab communities in the Northern Negev.[19]

Five years later, these two sites became the urban core of the well-planned Lakhish region, now empty of Palestinians. As a result, it became an ideal area for expert state planners (agronomists, architects, hydraulic engineers, and sociologists) to plan from scratch.

Jewish settlement in the Lakhish region was intended to guarantee the territory as Israeli land. As immigration from North African countries ceased in 1952, the government chose to populate the region by renewing immigration from Morocco in 1954, as that Jewry remained the biggest available community for such massive immigration.[20] Since it was impossible to move the *ma'abarot* dwellers from their provisional camps in the centre of the country to the peripheral villages, decision makers developed a cunning method: transference of the immigrants directly from the ships that arrived from Morocco (via France) to the new sites

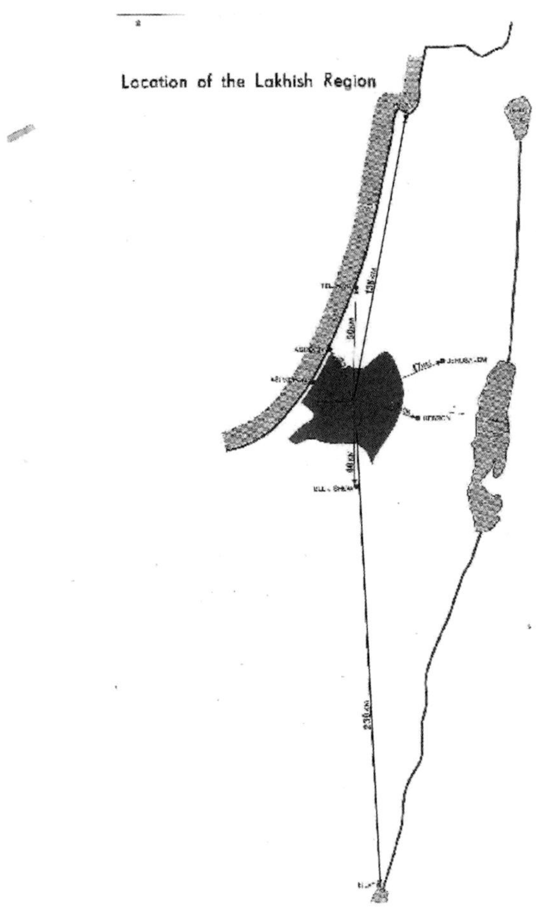

Figure 1: Location of the Lakhish region in Israel. Source: Artur Glikson, 'Integrative Habitation Unit – An Experiment in Planning and Developing', in *Human Being, Region, World – On Environmental Planning, Housing Ministry Quarterly Journal* 3 (1967): 94–95.

in Lakhish [Figure 1]. So, the Palestinians were forced to leave, and the Jewish immigrants were forced to replace them.

The concepts of the Lakhish plan were presented by Glikson at a United Nations seminar on regional planning in 1958:

> The original social unit of the immigrants from African and Asian countries, who settled in the Lakhish region, is the family clan, consisting of 40–60 smaller family units. Such units are kept together from the moment they arrive in the country, and are settled in one village (a moshav). The settlement of two clans of equal size in the same moshav is avoided, as this might lead to internal disorder and strife.[21]

The rationale of that decision is explained in the plan: 'The preservation of communities has proved to be a great advantage for their adaptation and productivity, as well as for maintaining their social and moral stability.'[22]

According to Glikson's plan, five to six villages were grouped in clusters around a main village – the Rural Community Center – that provided services. This centre was designed to be 'a settlement of a privileged class of managers, officials and specialists, mostly of European origin [that would] constitute a foreign body in the midst of the villages of small holders coming from underdeveloped countries.'[23]

Thus, the settlement policy that was enacted in the Lakhish region contradicted the vision of the 'integration of Diasporas' by preferring an efficient and pragmatic 'population dispersal' (including the transfer 'from the ship to Lakhish') in order to gain political advantages. Hence, it also contradicted the social telos of the IHU, put into practice in the same area during the same time. Two opposing policies were implemented simultaneously in the same region: integration versus separation and pragmatism versus idealism.

Artur Glikson's Architectural Ideology

In 2004, the *Journal of Architectural and Planning Research* dedicated an entire issue to Glikson's architectural ideology. It explored the intentions of his architectural and planning projects and his designs of the early years of statehood.

In this issue dedicated to Glikson, Rachel Wilansky writes: Glikson 'embraced a holistic approach to architecture and to the role of the architect. In his outlook, planning and architecture are inseparable: planning is architecture and architecture is planning.'[24] This approach was put into practice in the IHU, as will be demonstrated below. Wilansky further writes that '[t]he study of man's relationship to his environment, based on his sweeping knowledge of basic historical processes, became one of the central issues of regional planning thought on which Glikson concentrated.'[25] However, the Lakhish region plan could not be based on historical knowledge, since its historical inhabitants had been expelled and the new population, which was forced to settle in the region, had no historical connection to it. The Lakhish region was planned as if it was a clean canvas, or *tabula rasa*, on which modernist planners, including Glikson, could operate without any burden or commitment to the real past, or to the legendary or virtual one. James M. Mayo indeed noticed that politics had become Glikson's first priority:

> Glikson's professional beliefs complemented his political ones. He was a Geddes regionalist, committed to local communities having economic, social and political autonomy [...] He had the unique opportunity to consider his regional ideals for planning a new nation, Israel.[26]

The 'clean canvas' concept had been mobilized to meet ideological-political needs, as Rachel Kallus identifies:

> He was faithfully devoted to the modernization of Israel, as a nation state. Thus, although connected to international debates, Glikson was fully committed to local agendas [...] Glikson's work was not only a response to the urgent needs to re-house and re-build, but also an attempt to project a vision for a new society.[27]

Israel was not necessarily a new society, but it was a new nation. Rachel Kallus, who studied Glikson's activity in-depth, claims that 'Glikson's philosophy further revealed the national political program in which housing was made the primary constitutive element for the design of the national landscape'.[28] Was the idea aimed at society building, nation building, or modernization? Kallus further argues that 'Glikson was struggling with the effects of swift modernization. He stated that "the problem of humanization in Israel is how to turn the huge governmental housing 'factories' into human institutions serving the integration of communities and environments"'.[29]

Hubert Law-Yone clarifies and emphasizes the gap (if not the contradiction) between Glikson's universalistic ideology and ideals, and his local activity:

> He faithfully tried to represent the lofty ideas of his theories while attempting to satisfy his patrons [...] Glikson's public works give a concrete meaning to what I have termed official space. Official space that has its genesis on the drawing boards of architects and planners. It is a space that does not adapt to the existing features of the landscape but tries to implement an authoritative structure that resonates with new power. It tells the (new) people that were brought into this space, 'this is your new home. It was built for you by the generosity of the State. Live in it, defend it. And make it your home'.[30]

This insight explains how Glikson bridged the gap created between the Lakhish planning and the IHU: both served the official space, which by definition, included contradictions.

Glikson's Rationale for the Experimental Integrative Habitation Unit in Kiryat-Gat

In 1967, Glikson wrote an article discussing the IHU, titled 'Integrative Habitation Unit – An Experiment in Planning and Developing'.[31] In this article, he described and explained the motivations and the principles of the IHU experimental project, from his point of view. He began by critiquing the housing policy and its results. He did this in order to propose the IHU as a potential alternative to current policy. Mass construction, which was a response to mass immigration, led to uniform suburbs and boring neighbourhoods. The 'average family' flats were equal in size and did not satisfy the various familial types. Both drawbacks caused neglect and instability and the emigration of the more resilient inhabitants.

Most of the towns in young Israel were entirely new. Therefore, Glikson proposed that the way to constitute 'a human urban surrounding is through our scientific and artistic abilities. But we need to prove that this unification of science and art creates a better environment'.[32] The experimental IHU was supposed to supply such proof. Since the creation of the Zionist Organization, science had been a key factor in realizing Zionist visions. The IHU intended to realize one such vision – the idea of integrating Diasporas.

Glikson pointed out that he was inspired by Le Corbusier's idea of the 'Radiant City' as an

> integration of various kinds of inhabitants as neighbors, that live in different kinds of residential blocks and houses. No doubt that there is a special interest in Israel to develop such an IHU since forging ethnic groups together is one of the most important national tasks of Israel.[33]

He defined the IHU as an experiment aimed at

> satisfying the most urgent urban demands, which are merged within a multi-cultural reality. That is an attempt to bypass the rigidity of settlement and the monotonous mass construction by creating a neighborhood, which represents its diverse inhabitants.[34]

Glikson contended that 'it is possible to promote values of urban life by creating an original/innovative environment, by creating proper relations between private houses, aimed at various types of residents'.[35] In other words, Glikson's deep belief was that he could engineer a melting pot of the Diasporas by providing well-designed houses, blocks, and communal services.

In June 1958, the Ministry of Housing initiated the IHU. They termed this step as a research project, noting that its aim was to investigate whether the results of the test case could be implemented on a wider scale. This was a real housing experiment, planned and designed by scientists, sociologists, architects, engineers, and economists, according to the Zionist tradition.

A Well-Designed Scientific Programme

The IHU was designed to be an experimental project for a new way of relating to housing. The detailed study was composed of five studies: demographic, social, economic, construction, and physical design.

It was expected that for ten years the unit would have the following demographic mixture: new immigrants from North Africa – 30%; immigrants from Europe and America – 20%; Kiryat-Gat North African residents – 17%; Kiryat-Gat European residents – 12%; Israeli veterans – 21%. Almost half of the expected population was North Africans. For these future (and anticipated) populations, eight apartment-house types were planned according to five categories: family size, age of the head of the household, ethnic origin, occupation, and length of residency in Israel. The apartment-house types were planned by Glikson as follows:[36]

- 2-room apartments for families of 2–3 persons – 29%
- 3-room apartments (two types) for families of 4–6 persons – 31%
- 2-room houses for families (two types) of 2–3 persons – 9%
- 3-room houses for families of 4–6 persons – 17%
- 4-room houses for families of 7–8 persons – 10%
- 5-room houses for families of 9 or more persons – 4%

In order to undertake a 'real' experiment, the chosen site for the IHU was separated from the town centre by a wadi (river-bed). Glikson wrote: 'The wadi will signify the borders of the experimental unit. Due to such a border, the unit will create a physical unit of its own'.[37] Robert Marans, who collaborated on the project, shed additional light on the motivation to promote the IHU:

> By 1958, the character of new town development began to change. An emphasis on high-density living, economics of scale, and better use of natural landscape marked the beginning of a fresh period of new town design and building in Israel. But while physical planners were concentrating on spatial redistribution of the new towns, little thought was being given to the social and cultural aspects of housing and the new town program.[38]

Hence, the IHU was a test project for two transformations in housing policy. One preferred urban over rural absorption and development, due to the economic advantages of the urban sites. The other – a complementary transformation – was to forgo the policy of settling the new towns, neighborhoods, and villages with inhabitants from the same ethnic origin, so as to create 'ethnic enclaves'. In other words, the programme preferred Kiryat-Gat over Lakhish.

The Social Survey: How Can Diasporas Become Integrated?

Since the main objective of the IHU was to establish a melting pot of Diasporas in the periphery, the core study was the social one, which was conducted in 1959 by the sociologist Judith Shuval. It was entitled "Social Problems in Development Towns – Towards Planning of an Experimental Neighborhood in Kiryat-Gat."[39] The findings demonstrated that in the four development towns in which the research had been conducted – Kiryat-Gat, Ashkelon, Be'er Sheva, and Kiryat-Shmona – there were ethnic tensions. The survey's results led to the following conclusions: all three ethnic groups in these communities – Europeans, North Africans, and Near Easterners – expressed the most hostility towards North Africans as neighbours. Approximately one-third of the total population, and an equal percentage of each of the groups, rejected North Africans as neighbours. This was found even among the North Africans themselves:

> The negative attitude toward North African Jews did not depend on how they are dispersed in the settlements. The same aggression toward them was expressed whether they lived in their own centers or within other populations. This meant that dispersing the North African housing units would not change the hostility toward them.[40]

The sociologist concluded that

> The Europeans in homogenous neighborhoods, in which all their neighbors were ethnic Europeans, were the most aggressive towards the North Africans. It seems that homogeneity reinforces prejudices and stereotypes. It may be that one of the ways to lower the aggression toward North Africans is to entirely refrain from building nuclear neighborhoods populated only by Europeans.[41]

'Nuclear neighbourhoods', an original concept developed by Shuval for her study, referred to an artificially composed unit of three neighbours, comprising one European with another European on the left and a family from North Africa to the right, and so on. Each building would be populated by such engineered trios.

The information, derived from the survey, was to guide family-housing assignment, and it was hoped that the implementation of the survey's results would achieve positive neighbourhood relations and satisfaction. The proposed housing assignment was made according to the following guidelines:

- North African families with high social and occupational levels were to be housed with similar European families.
- European families with low occupational and social levels were to be housed with families from Middle Eastern countries.

- North African families with low occupational and social levels were to be housed with families from Middle Eastern countries.
- One family of North African or Middle Eastern origin was to be housed with two families of European origin.[42]

The first engineered population phase of the IHU was organized and completed during 1964, more or less in accordance with these guidelines. However, the detailed recommendations regarding the nuclear neighbourhood were not implemented.

A Physical Plan Aimed at Creating Societal Cohesion

The IHU was designed to accommodate approximately 1000 families with a total of 3700 inhabitants. Each of the planned six sub-units of the neighbourhood would house 175–200 families, all of them in different sizes of mass-housing. The size of each sub-unit was determined by the optimal capacity of its secondary services, such as a kindergarten; a playground for children between 5 and 8 years old; and a small, well-designed open space that would form the main social area for informal social contact among the families in the sub-unit. The positive social intra-ethnic interactions were planned via these children's venues. These interior spaces would form both the physical and social nuclei of each sub-unit [Figure 2].

Each sub-unit was to include one long central block of three to four storeys, to be built on pillars and constructed on the highest point of the sub-unit. These blocks consisted of the cheap apartments of the IHU. Each delineated the limit of the sub-unit and its inner space, which was important from a social perspective. The second group of houses was built on a square of three-storey houses, built on pillars. One-storey houses were scattered among the buildings. The pillars enabled airflow beneath the houses and opened up the view towards the eastern landscape. This building arrangement enclosed the unit, making it separate and unique.

All the interior spaces would be interconnected through pedestrian walkways, with no motorways inside the site [Figure 3]. This 'green' idea was not necessarily inspired by the garden city idea, since the IHU sought to provide a solution for social problems by offering a well-prepared rational infrastructure. Therefore, it was not conceived as an environmental solution to a motor-vehicle pollution problem. The pedestrian walkways served as connecting links between the interior spaces and the two main pedestrian axes of the quarter. The crossroad of these two axes was designed to form the social and functional centre of the neighbourhood, so that the residents from all the sub-units would have the opportunity to socialize.

The IHU scheme dictated two levels of meeting points. One that would be more intensive, for children's movement and play inside the sub-units; and the other, more purposeful, on the main walkway. The optimistic premise was that in such informal ways, the residents would cultivate positive inter-ethnic relations.

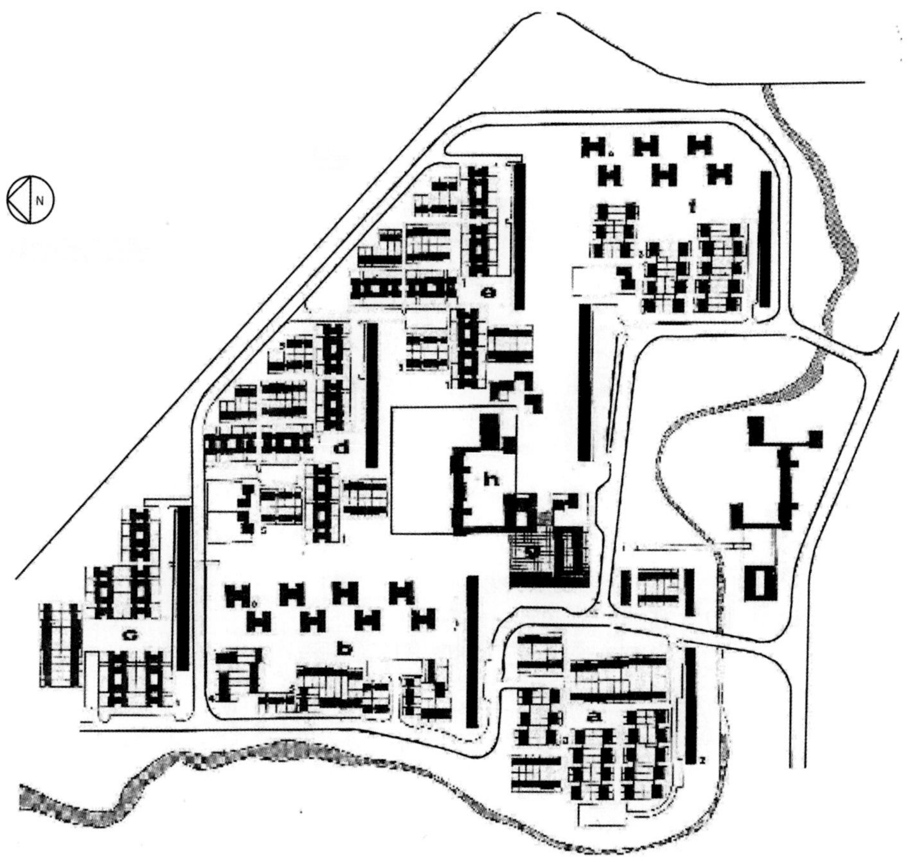

Figure 2: General scheme of the experimental Integrative Habitation Unit (IHU) in Kiryat-Gat: (a–f) six sub-units; (g) the centre; (h) elementary school. Source: Artur Glikson, 'Integrative Habitation Unit – An Experiment in Planning and Developing', in *Human Being, Region, World – On Environmental Planning, Housing Ministry Quarterly Journal* 3 (1967): 94–95.

The south–north axis connected the quarter with Kiryat-Gat and the surrounding landscape. The east–west axis was used as the exit to the main recreational area of the IHU, to an archaeological *tel*, as well as to Kiryat-Gat's most prominent site – Tel Gat. This open area to the east rendered the neighbourhood semi-isolated. The co-architect of the project, Robert Marans, wrote:

> the plan reflects an integrative attempt on four different levels: for residents within any of the sub-units; for residents within the IHU; for residents of the quarter with the town's dwellers; and the unit dwellers with their nearby surroundings.[43]

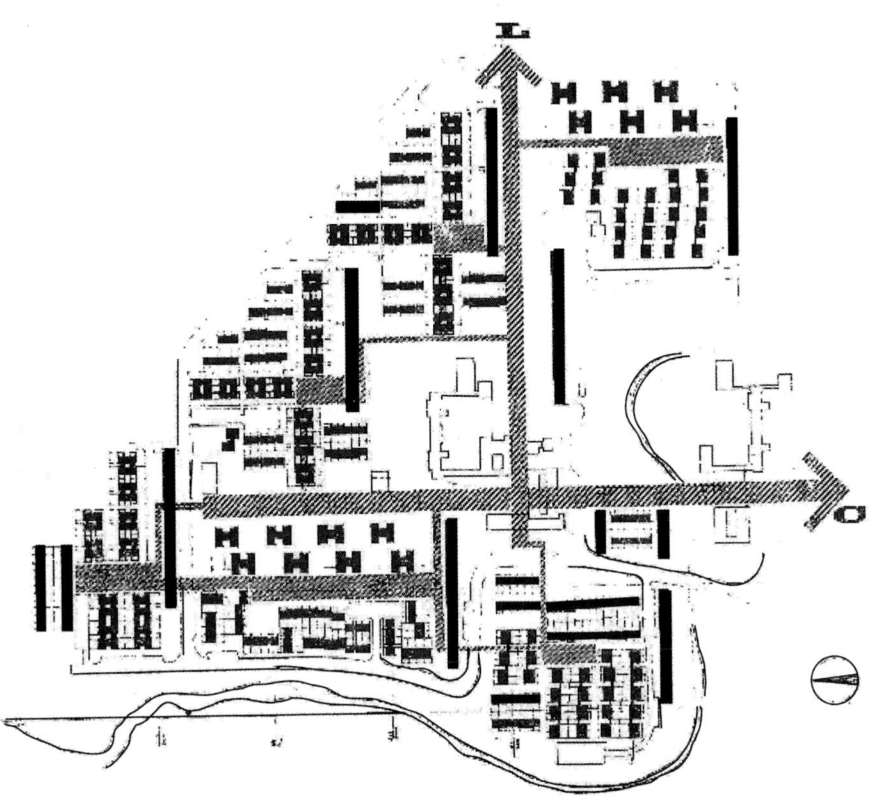

Figure 3: Each of the six sub-units is interconnected through a series of pedestrian walkways, linked to the two main pedestrian axes. The two axes link the neighbourhood to the town centre (C) and towards the recreation area, out of the neighbourhood (L). Source: Artur Glikson, 'Integrative Habitation Unit – An Experiment in Planning and Developing', in *Human Being, Region, World – On Environmental Planning, Housing Ministry Quarterly Journal* 3 (1967): 94–95.

Robert Marans: 'Diversity within Unity or Privacy in Community'

> Glikson was very worried about the success of the neighborhood. He hoped to plan it gradually, step by step. To finish one rung, to consider its results, to conclude, to adjust and then to proceed to the next sub-unit plan, according to the findings.
>
> Robert Marans[44]

Robert Marans, who, for eighteen months, planned the *Beit* (B) and *Gimel* (C) sub-units, told me this in a special interview during a tour through the Glikson neighbourhood on April 27, 2017. He also talked about the six innovative elements in 1960s housing concepts, which were introduced in the IHU.

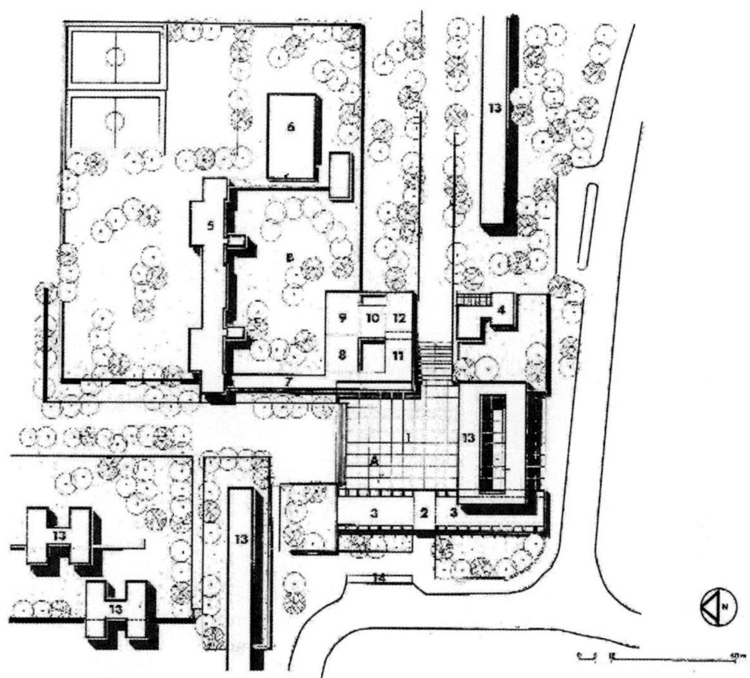

Figure 4: The centre of the experimental Integrative Habitation Unit (IHU) in Kiryat-Gat: (A) the centre; (B) elementary school; (1) plaza; (2) a covered passageway; (3) shops; (4) kindergarten; (5) classrooms; (6) gymnasium; (7) secretariat; (8) dining room; (9) kitchen; (10) social club; (11) library; (12) infant welfare centre (*tipat chalav*); (13) residential block; (14) bus station. Source: Artur Glikson, 'Integrative Habitation Unit – An Experiment in Planning and Developing', in *Human Being, Region, World – On Environmental Planning, Housing Ministry Quarterly Journal* 3 (1967): 94–95.

The first was the unusual and irregular ratio between the open space and the built-up area [Figures 4–5]. Seventy per cent was open space, playgrounds, inner pedestrian paths, public gardens, internal 'tunnels' along the ground floors, and wide public stairs. Thirty per cent was dedicated to buildings for housing, commerce, and public services – schools, kindergartens, and an administration office. The second was the development and construction of the area according to its topography. Construction was adapted to it without any groundwork. This meant that each difference in height, for example, became stairs or even a covered path along the buildings (Figure 6). The third innovation was the roofed passages along the main promenade, which provided shaded and ventilated public paths. The fourth was to adapt the size of the apartments to various family sizes, as opposed to the previous uniformity of public housing.

The fifth was to adapt the flats' locations to ethnic lifestyles and preferences. This meant that the planner assumed that the Moroccan Jews would like to live on the ground floors

Figure 5: *Alef* (A) open space 1963: the vast open space in the first sub-unit – *Alef*. Source: Robert Marans, *Social Integration in Housing: A Case Study in Israel* (Ann Arbor, MI: Institute for Social Research, University of Michigan, 1974).

in order to grow vegetables in a small patch, and that the Europeans (Ashkenazim) would prefer the upper storey [Figure 7]. 'Ashkenazim – up; Moroccans – down,' he ironically added.[45] It was only a premise, since the location preferences were not ethnic-oriented but rather individual-oriented.

The sixth innovation was the introduction of two-storey duplexes [Figure 8]. Each sub-unit contained a block of such duplexes with exterior stairs that reduced construction costs. The staircases of the long central blocks in each sub-unit were exposed as well, in this case, to enable the penetration of light and air into the buildings. The breeze also functioned as natural air conditioning and, hence, lowered temperatures inside the apartments during the hot summers.

The balconies of sub-unit *Alef* (A) faced the inner space of the neighbourhood [Figure 6]. Later on, in sub-units *Gimel* (C) and *Dalet* (D), the apartment balconies faced all public spaces. This provided them with ventilation. The colour of the plastered walls was beige, reflecting the surrounding desert. Part of the upper windows was constructed with bold white frames as aesthetic elements. The original roofs were flat. Roofing tiles were added later and were not part of the original construction.

Figure 6: *Alef* (A) open space 1980: the vast and green open space in the first sub-unit – *Alef*. Source: Robert Marans, *Social Integration in Housing: A Case Study in Israel* (Ann Arbor, MI: Institute for Social Research, University of Michigan, 1974).

Marans' original idea was to plan the sub-clusters of each sub-unit as a traditional Mediterranean unit. A Mediterranean unit is an intimate, small, narrow street that accommodates social interaction. People sit together in the public space, and talk, play, eat, etc., in a familiar atmosphere. In the interview, Marans interpreted and summarized the work he had completed 50 years earlier: 'In this scheme, I integrated the Mediterranean spirit, neighbours' coherence in modern architecture; diversity within unity or privacy in community,' which reflected a certain dialectic approach.[46] The modern architecture designed by Marans catered to a traditional way of life and implemented the idea according to the rationale of the IHU. It was to serve as a melting pot of the Diasporas and to be the ultimate site of *Kibbutz Galuyot* – the integration of the Diasporas.

Figure 7: A shaded pedestrian path under the ceiling of the first floor using the natural ground height differences. Source: Robert Marans, *Social Integration in Housing: A Case Study in Israel* (Ann Arbor, MI: Institute for Social Research, University of Michigan, 1974).

The Neighborhood Centre in the Service of Societal Integration

The quarter's centre was located at the crossroad of the two axes, and it was there that all of the commercial and social services were found. The plan proposed the construction of twelve to fourteen shops, a cafe, a health clinic, a kindergarten, an elementary school, and a community/cultural centre. These were all to be positioned around an interior plaza, which aimed to strengthen social interaction. The same objective led to the idea of encouraging after-school use of the primary-school building and its library, meeting room, dining room, and kitchen. The primary-school complex was an additional site for the creation of informal social gatherings. This demonstrates that ethnic cohesion, or at least tolerant relations, were a top priority in the IHU plan. The architecture and design of the neighbourhood's services centre were very simple and displayed no innovations or unusual features [Figure 9].

Figure 8: Two-storey houses in sub-unit *Gimel* (C). Source: Robert Marans, *Social Integration in Housing: A Case Study in Israel* (Ann Arbor, MI: Institute for Social Research, University of Michigan, 1974).

The network of roads was laid out in such a manner that vehicles first approached the neighbourhood's centre and then moved to the other sub-units via an outer ring road. The maximum distance from the outer ring road to the houses was 140 metres. This was determined after a discussion among the architects and social scientists. When planning the details, the social engineers were also involved. The distance between any resident and a motor vehicle of any type was not to exceed 70 metres. The plan made private transportation more accessible, despite the fact that the motorization rate in Israel was very low at the time.

The neighbourhood's various components, consisting of eight different housing types; the sub-units; the open spaces in each sub-unit; the main playground; the two pedestrian axes; the outer traffic; the social services centre; and the semi-enclosed site, were all used

Figure 9: Courtyard houses. Source: Robert Marans, *Social Integration in Housing: A Case Study in Israel* (Ann Arbor, MI: Institute for Social Research, University of Michigan, 1974).

to establish and maintain a new integrative community. These were the core architectural elements of the experimental Integrative Habitation Unit in Kiryat-Gat. The IHU was therefore perceived as being the epitome of a modern architectural experimental lab in Israel.

Did the IHU Achieve Its Objectives? Follow-Up Studies

Only eighteen months after the initial ground-breaking, the first buildings of the neighbourhood were ready for the first 173 families. After just one year of habitation, the first study, which investigated whether the experimental unit fulfilled its expectations, was conducted by Judith Shuval, who had carried out the preliminary survey.[47] The objectives of the study were twofold: to learn whether the inhabitants were satisfied with the design of their apartments; and to evaluate the mutual ethnic relationships inside the unit. The researchers interviewed 81 per cent of the IHU inhabitants, which were compared to a control group of Kiryat-Gat residents.

The main findings were that the IHU residents were more satisfied with their apartments than the control group. Shuval wrote:

> The experimental quarter shows better inter-ethnic relations than the control group. The reason for this could be the result of the special selection of the residents, reasonable ratios between the ethnic groups and the high level of satisfaction from the flats and the neighbors.[48]

The last sentence reveals two crucial facts that had been concealed in the initial IHU programme and, hence, led to a bias in the research findings. First, that the residents were selected by the project; and second, that the ethnic ratio was manipulated. Therefore, in all likelihood, this ratio did not represent the actual ethnic ratio in the peripheral development town of Kiryat-Gat.

During the same period, the Ministry of Housing conducted seven sociological studies on housing and urban settlements, which investigated different housing schemes and parameters. The study relevant to the IHU was the one conducted in Kiryat-Malachi in 1965. This town, located only 17 kilometres north of Kiryat-Gat, had roughly the same socio-ethnic mixture as the latter.

The first finding was a positive migration balance, i.e., inward mobility greatly exceeded outward mobility. There was an increase of 100 per cent in the size of the local population within five years. The conclusions were that

> the majority of the interviewees expressed a feeling of positive local identification with their community. The number of people employed as skilled workers, who were added to the existing population during the period under review, also greatly exceeded those who left the place.[49]

The positive social results of Kiryat-Malachi were hence not inferior in comparison to the well-designed IHU.

The final study was conducted by Yona Ginsberg and Robert Marans in 1975. Only women who lived in the Glikson neighbourhood – the name given to it after Artur Glikson died in 1966 – were interviewed for this study. The main findings were that two-thirds of the interviewees were satisfied with living in the neighbourhood, although half of them expressed a desire to move. Sixty-eight per cent of the Asian and North African Jews said they were satisfied, while 47% said they wanted to leave. Sixty-four per cent of the European residents said they were satisfied, while 44% indicated a desire to move.[50] Based on these findings and conclusions, Marans summed up the project in 1974: 'The hope that neighborhood residents would interact with each other has been fulfilled.'[51]

In 1991, the Glikson neighbourhood was included in the Neighborhoods Rehabilitation Project that was initiated by the Kiryat-Gat Municipality, together with another neighbourhood. The physical, educational, and social problems that were detailed in the projects' documents were the same in both neighbourhoods. No difference was found between the well-planned and lesser-planned neighbourhood. Both were neglected by the local authorities and their residents.

Conclusions

The IHU can be classified as an architectural utopia based on the premises that well-planned quarters could function as actual melting pots capable of realizing the Israeli dream. Urban designer Alice Coleman described such aspirations in her research of planned housing in Britain as follows: 'In a broad general sense, it was environmental determinism's belief that if the environment is changed, human behavior will also change [...] human behavior will improve and human happiness will increase.'[52]

The scheme used by Glikson relates to the theories of the renowned urban architecture researcher, Lewis Mumford, who recommended adopting utopian ideas and methods in order to design and plan.[53] Glikson's IHU aspired to be a better place within a problematic environment. He aimed to create an isolated utopia, which would generate a better society. Was it an oy-topia (a good place) or an ou-topia (no place)?

By definition, the Glikson neighbourhood was intended to function as an experimental social architectural laboratory in Israel. Most of its innovations had a single aim: to create a new society by building a new neighbourhood. Its planners truly believed in the ability of a well-defined structure to build a well-defined society.

When photographing the neighbourhood in 2004, a young man approached Rachel Kallus and asked her, 'Why are you taking pictures here? The area looks like any poor neighbourhood in any other town in Israel.'[54] My personal impression from my visit to the Glikson neighbourhood in February and April 2017 was the same. It was a neglected, poor site, though some parts have preserved the uniqueness of the neighbourhood and its aesthetic attributes.

The neighbourhood vision could be epitomized by the Hebrew idiom 'a dream and its distress'.

Bibliography

Association of Engineers. 'Typical Immigrant Housing Research Scheme'. *Handasa ve-Adrikhalut – Journal of the Association of Engineers and Architects in Israel* 17.7–8 (1959): 186 (In Hebrew).

Ben-Gurion, David. *Carrier or Mission: A Vision and a Way. Vol. 5.* Tel Aviv: Ayanot, 1958 (In Hebrew).

——— 'Introduction to the "Uniqueness and the Mission"'. *Israel Government Annual.* Jerusalem: Government Publication, 1951 (In Hebrew).

Ben-Sira, Yaacov. 'The Public Housing Problems'. *Handasa ve-Adrikhalut – Journal of the Association of Engineers and Architects in Israel* 17.7–8 (1959): 172–74 (in Hebrew).

Coleman, Alice. *Utopia on Trial – Vision and Reality in Planned Housing.* London: Hilary Shipman, 1985.

Curtis, William J. R. *Modern Architecture Since 1900.* London: Phaidon Press, 1982.

Drabkin-Darin, Haim. *Housing in Israel.* Tel Aviv: Gadish Books, 1957.

——— ed. *Public Housing in Israel.* Tel Aviv: Gadish Books, 1959.

Efrat, Zvi. *The Israeli Project – Building and Architecture 1948–1973.* Tel Aviv: Tel Aviv Museum, 2004 (in Hebrew).

Gelblum, Arie. 'Yemenite Jews and the African Problem'. *Haaretz.* April 22, 1949.

Ginsberg, Yona and Robert W. Marans. 'Social Mix in Housing: Does Ethnicity Make a Difference?' *Journal of Ethnic Studies* 7.3 (1979): 101–12.

Glikson, Artur. 'Integrative Habitation Unit – An Experiment in Planning and Developing'. In *Human Being, Region, World – On Environmental Planning, Housing Ministry Quarterly Journal* 3 (1967): 94–122 (In Hebrew).

——— 'Some Problems of Housing in Israel's New Towns and Suburbs'. In *Public Housing in Israel*, edited by Haim Drabkin-Daein, 93–102. Tel Aviv: Gadish Books, 1959.

——— *Two Case Studies of Rural Planning and Development in Israel.* Jerusalem: Ministry of Labor, 1958.

Goldstein, Joseph. 'Golda Meir as the "Ma'abarot Minister"'. *Kivunim Hadashim* 20 (2009): 157-173 (in Hebrew).

Hacohen, Dvora. *Immigrants in Turmoil – The Great Immigration to Israel 1948–1953.* Jerusalem: Yad Ben-Zvi Publishing House, 1994 (in Hebrew).

——— 'Mass Immigration and the Demographic Revolution in Israel'. *Israel Affairs* 8.1–2 (2001): 177–90.

Israeli Settlement. *Abstracts of Seven Sociological Studies on Housing and Urban Settlements.* Jerusalem: Israeli Ministry of Housing, November 1967 (In Hebrew).

Kallus Rachel. 'Humanization of the Environment: Glikson's Architecture and the Poetic of the Everyday'. *Journal of Architectural Planning Research* 21.2 (2004): 152–70.

——— 'Introduction: Revisiting Artur Glikson's Work'. *Journal of Architectural and Planning Research* 21.2 (2004): 91–98.

——— 'Nation Building Modernism and European Post-War Debates: Glikson's "Integral Habitational Unit" and Team 10 Discourse'. *Architectural Research Quarterly* 18.2 (2014): 123–33.

Katchensky, Miriam. 'The Ma'abarot'. In *Immigrants and Ma'abarot 1948–1952*, edited by Mordechai Naor, 69–86. Jerusalem: Yad Ben-Zvi Publishing House, 1986.

Law-Yone, Hubert. 'Artur Glikson: The Intellectual and the State'. *Journal of Architectural and Planning Research* 21.2 (2004): 102–11.

Marans, Robert, W. Interview with Barak Yair. Kiryat-Gat, April 27, 2017.

——— 'Social and Cultural Influence on New Town Planning'. *Journal of the Town Planning Institute* 56.1 (1970): 60–65.

——— *Social Integration in Housing: A Case Study in Israel.* Ann Arbor, MI: Institute for Social Research, University of Michigan, 1974.

Mayo, James, M. 'The Ideologies of Artur Glikson'. *Journal of Architectural and Planning Research* 21.2 (2004): 99–101.

Morris, Benny. *The Birth of the Palestinian Refugee Problem, 1947–1949*. Cambridge: Cambridge University Press, 1987.

Mumford, Lewis. *The Story of Utopias – Ideal Commonwealths and Social Myths*. London, Calcutta, and Sydney: George G. Harrap Co. Ltd, 1923.

Nitzan-Shiftan, Alona. 'Contested Zionism-Alternative Modernism: Erich Mendelson and the Tel Aviv Chug in Mandate Palestine'. *Architectural History* 39 (1996): 147–80.

Roby, Bryan, K. *The Mizrahi Era of Rebellion – Israel's Forgotten Civil Rights Struggle, 1948–1966*. Syracuse, NY: Syracuse University Press, 2015.

Rozin, Orit. *Duty and Love: Individualism and Collectivism in 1950s Israel*. Tel Aviv: Am Oved Publishers, 2008 (in Hebrew).

Sharon, Arieh. *Physical Planning in Israel 1948–1953*. Jerusalem: Government Publication, 1951 (in Hebrew).

Sharon, Smadar. 'Not Settlers but Settled – Immigrants, Planning and Settlement Patterns in the Lakhish Region in the 1950s'. Ph.D. diss., Tel Aviv University, 2012 (in Hebrew).

Shuval, Judith. 'Social Problems in Development Towns – Towards Planning of an Experimental Neighborhood in Kiryat-Gat'. Jerusalem, October 1959 (in Hebrew).

——— 'Emerging Patterns of Ethnic Strain in Israel'. *Social Forces* 40.4 (1962): 323–39.

——— *Housing Patterns and Social Relationships in the Experimental Neighborhood in Kiryat Gat – A Follow-Up Research*. Jerusalem: Israel Institute of Applied Social Research, August 1966 (in Hebrew).

Tanne, David. 'The Tasks Facing Public Houses in Israel'. In *Public Housing in Israel*, edited by Haim Drabkin-Darin, 5–14. Tel Aviv: Gadish Books, 1959.

Wilkansky, Rachel. 'From Regional Planning to Spatial Planning: The Sources and Continuing Relevance of Artur Glikson's Planning Thought'. *Journal of Architectural and Planning Research* 21.2 (2004): 91–98; 125–39.

Notes

1 All translations from Hebrew to English are the author's own, unless otherwise specified.

2 'In the book *La Ville Radieuse* (1933) Le Corbusier wrote tellingly of the good life lived in the open air and sunlight surveying "a sea of verdure". The Radiant City as a whole was highly centralized and densely populated, yet most of its surface was given over to zones of leisure – parks, playing-fields, etc.' William J. R. Curtis, *Modern Architecture Since 1900* (London: Phaidon Press, 1982), 207.

3 Dvora Hacohen, 'Mass Immigration and Demographic Revolution in Israel', *Israel Affairs* 8.1–2 (2001): 178.

4 Joseph Goldstein, 'Golda Meir as the "Ma'abarot Minister"', *Kivunim Hadashim* 20 (2009), 165 (In Hebrew).

5 David Ben-Gurion, 'Introduction to the "Uniqueness and the Mission"', *Israel Government Annual* (Jerusalem: Government Printer, 1951), 26 (In Hebrew).
6 David Ben-Gurion, *Carrier or Mission: A Vision and a Way. Vol. 5* (Tel Aviv: Ayanot, 1958), 212 (In Hebrew).
7 Arie Gelblum, "Yemenite Jews and the African Problem," *Haaretz*, April 22, 1949, 2.
8 Orit Rozin, *Duty and Love: Individualism and Collectivism in 1950s Israel* (Tel Aviv: Am Oved Publishers, 2008), 200–22 (In Hebrew).
9 Hacohen, 'Mass Immigration', 179–80.
10 Zvi Efrat, *The Israeli Project – Building and Architecture 1948–1973* (Tel Aviv: Tel Aviv Museum, 2004), 980 (In Hebrew).
11 Yaacov Ben-Sira, 'The Public Housing Problems', *Handasa ve-Adrikhalut – Journal of the Association of Engineers and Architects in Israel* 17.7–8 (1959): 172 (In Hebrew).
12 B. Rothschild Foundation for Research and Planning Team, 'Typical Immigrant Housing Research Scheme', *Handasa ve-Adrikhalut – Journal of the Association of Engineers and Architects in Israel* 17.7–8 (1959): 186 (In Hebrew).
13 Ibid.
14 Ibid.
15 The principles of the Sharon Plan were published by Sharon in Arieh Sharon, *Physical Planning in Israel 1948–1953* (Jerusalem: Government printer, 1951).
16 For a discussion of the development towns in the Galilee, see Oryan Shachar's Chapter (1.2) in the present volume.
17 Artur Glikson, 'Some Problems of Housing in Israel's New Towns and Suburbs', in *Public Housing in Israel*, ed. Haim Drabkin-Daein (Tel Aviv: Gadish Books, 1959), 94.
18 Ibid., 96.
19 Benny Morris, *The Birth of the Palestinian Refugee Problem, 1947–1949* (Cambridge: Cambridge University Press, 1987), 243.
20 Smadar Sharon, 'Not Settlers but Settled – Immigrants, Planning and Settlement Patterns in the Lakhish Region in the 1950s' (Ph.D. diss., Tel Aviv University, 2012), 39–49 (In Hebrew).
21 Artur Glikson, *Two Case Studies of Rural Planning and Development in Israel* (Jerusalem: Ministry of Labor, 1958), 27.
22 Ibid.
23 Ibid., 29.
24 Rachel Wilansky, 'From Regional Planning to Spatial Planning: The Sources and Continuing Relevance of Artur Glikson's Planning Thought', *Journal of Architectural and Planning Research* 21.2 (2004): 126.
25 'It is impossible to transfer immigrants from temporary dwellings (*ma'abarot*), situated in the center of Israel, to permanent homes erected later in development areas since [...] the immigrants found some form of employment in the vicinity and were not prepared to move.' David Tanne, 'The Tasks Facing Public Houses in Israel', in *Public Housing in Israel*, ed. Haim Drabkin-Darin (Tel-Aviv: Gadish Books, 1959), 6.
26 James M. Mayo, 'The Ideologies of Artur Glikson', *Journal of Architectural and Planning Research* 21.2 (2004): 100.

27 Rachel Kallus, 'Introduction: Revisiting Artur Glikson's Work', *Journal of Architectural and Planning Research* 21.2 (2004): 94.
28 Rachel Kallus, 'Humanization of the Environment: Glikson's Architecture and the Poetic of the Everyday', *Journal of Architectural Planning Research* 21.2 (2004): 161.
29 Rachel Kallus, 'Nation Building Modernism and European Post-War Debates: Glikson's "Integral Habitational Unit" and Team 10 Discourse', *Architectural Research Quarterly* 18.2 (2014): 127.
30 Hubert Law-Yone, 'Artur Glikson: The Intellectual and the State', *Journal of Architectural and Planning Research* 21.2 (2004): 107.
31 Artur Glikson, 'Integrative Habitation Unit – An Experiment in Planning and Developing', *Human Being, Region, World: Housing Ministry Quarterly Journal* 3 (1967): 94–122 (In Hebrew).
32 Ibid., 94.
33 Ibid., 95.
34 Ibid.
35 Ibid.
36 Ibid., 98.
37 Ibid., 97.
38 Robert W. Marans, *Social Integration in Housing: A Case Study in Israel* (Ann Arbor, MI: Institute for Social Research, University of Michigan, 1974), 8.
39 Judith Shuval, "Social Problems in Development Towns – Towards Planning of an Experimental Neighborhood in Kiryat-Gat," (Jerusalem, October 1959) (In Hebrew).
40 Ibid., 2.
41 Ibid., 3.
42 Ibid., 11
43 Marans, *Social Integration*, 34, 21.
44 Robert Marans, interview with Barak Yair, Kiryat-Gat, April 27, 2017.
45 Ibid.
46 Ibid.
47 Judith Shuval, *Housing Patterns and Social Relationships in the Experimental Neighborhood in Kiryat Gat – A Follow-Up Research* (Jerusalem: Israel Institute of Applied Social Research, August 1966), 73–74 (In Hebrew).
48 Ibid., 73–74.
49 *Abstracts of Seven Sociological Studies on Housing and Urban Settlements* (Jerusalem: Israeli Ministry of Housing, November 1967), 4, 5 (In Hebrew).
50 Yona Ginsberg and Robert W. Marans, 'Social Mix in Housing: Does Ethnicity Make a Difference?' *Journal of Ethnic Studies* 7.3 (1979): 107, 110.
51 Marans, *Social Integration*, 27, 74.
52 Alice Coleman, *Utopia on Trial – Vision and Reality in Planned Housing* (London: Hilary Shipman, 1985), 19.
53 Lewis Mumford, *The Story of Utopias – Ideal Commonwealths and Social Myths* (London, Calcutta, and Sydney: George G. Harrap Co. Ltd, 1923), 268, 281, 299
54 Ibid., 25, 153.

From A-Locality to Locality: The Gur Neighbourhood in Hatzor HaGlilit[1]

Oryan Shachar

Airplane, Three Birds

A pointed plane crushes on
rushes to the northern border.
Tension.
What tomorrow brings.
Below it fly
three birds
in the opposite direction
carefree
sweet worms in their mouths
and beautiful thoughts of a fragile
fledgling in a fragile nest
within a windswept tree on this winter day
in this tiny courtyard in this tiny
neighborhood in the bosom of the Zionist project

Raquel Chalfi[2]

Through the window, the last sunrays are flickering. In the horizon, the cliffs of the Golan Heights are turning gray […] After the evening prayer, the town's festive streets are being filled with families on their way home for the Sabbath dinner. Within a short while, the entire town is drowning in a symphony of voices and melodies rising through the windows in all manner of sounds.

Avraham Farber[3]

In the early 1970s, young leaders of the Gur Hasidic sect, one of the largest ultraorthodox communities in Israel, began calling to move out of the sect's traditional, overcrowded urban centres and settle in rural areas to improve the quality of life of young couples who could no longer afford an apartment in central Israel.[4] With the blessing of their spiritual leader, they began searching for suitable locations for a large group of families to establish a new community. After a prolonged countrywide search, it was decided to settle in the northern town of Hatzor HaGlilit, which received the community with open arms. The Prominent Israeli Architect David Reznik was commissioned to plan the community settlement.[5] In

Figure 1: The New Gur Neighborhood inauguration ceremony, August 11, 1976. Courtesy of Rabbi Asher Neuhaus, private archive.

August 1976, the town celebrated the inauguration of the new neighbourhood [Figure 1] amid praises for this enterprise in the ultraorthodox press.[6]

The Gur Hasidic thought adheres to the exegetic principle of 'rule and detail and rule', meaning that sentences in the Bible or rabbinical text should first present a rule of conduct, followed by an example, and then a reiteration of the rule. Similarly, Avraham Farber's opening quote, along with Reznik's plan, flesh out this principle in the structure of the neighbourhood. Both refer to a process whereby the first rule refers to a structural unity where the details are unknown, and the second closes the circle and rejoins the various details together, with each being representative of the entire structure.

The planning of the Hasidic neighbourhood was grounded in an architectural model that hierarchically organized the systems that mediate between private and public premises, individual and community, and the apartment and the neighbourhood as a whole. The uniqueness of this pattern owed much to the informal contact between the architect and the Gur community in the course of the planning process.[7]

This dialogue between the architect and the Gur community contained four major issues. The first was the unique encounter between a community whose way of life retained diasporic characteristics on the one hand, and Reznik, whose biography, views, and works embody a secular Zionist ideology, on the other. Second, the informality of this dialogue represented a paradigm shift for the Ministry of Housing, which had been accustomed to acting as a mediator between the architect and anonymous residents. Third, the neighbourhood's planning represented a critique of the harsh and uniform architectural language of Israel's first decades. Finally, the chosen location lay deep in Israel's socio-geographical periphery.

In addition to these practical issues, the neighbourhood's planning also embodied an ideological aspect of a new search for Israeli locality, initiated simultaneously and somewhat paradoxically by both the Hasidic sect and secular, modernist architects. While ultraorthodox Judaism emphasized the spiritual consecration of the land and refused to consecrate its mundane and local elements,[8] modernism became identified with Zionism, remaining in touch with current trends and preferring new generic planning over adherence to local cultural concepts.[9]

Thus, in the planning of the neighbourhood in the early 1970s, two transformation processes emerged from the younger ultraorthodox and architectural generation, expressing a new interest in the Israeli place. Through an analysis of this process, this chapter examines the development of a local sentiment of belonging and identification with the place.[10] This case study thus sheds light on the complex physical and spiritual journey of the ultraorthodox community and the modernist architect from a-locality to locality. In this context, a-locality means spiritual consecration of the timeless land and a reserved approach to state institutions and the Zionist locality they embody – the mundane and tangible consecration of the land as a national territory existing in the present.

Place and Time

> The Israelis love Dizengoff [iconic street in Tel Aviv], but we went the other way, from the center to the periphery.
>
> Rabbi Neuhaus[11]

Hatzor HaGlilit was founded in 1953, five years after Israel became independent, as part of a nationwide trend of building 'new towns' for Jewish immigrants in unpopulated peripheral areas. The government planning policy of redesigning the country's space sought to modernize it using a top-down planning model of progress and development, producing a 'uniform and productive' society.[12] The planning and settlement process almost completely ignored both the remaining traces of the Palestinian place and the cultural diversity of the massive post-1948 Jewish immigration,[13] aiming at a cultural melting pot.[14]

Like other new towns, Hatzor HaGlilit was considered by the early 1970s as a symbol of the failure of the early national settlement policy. Populated mainly by immigrants from

North Africa, the town suffered severe unemployment due to its distance from central Israel and the lack of stable sources of income.[15] Contemporary press reports presented it as a backward and impoverished town that the younger generation sought to leave.[16]

The failure of the policy of settling so-called 'national priority' areas was criticized by young architects as early as the late 1950s.[17] At the same time, government planning authorities began discussing the Judaization of the Galilee, given the growing Palestinian population in this area. Theoretically speaking, this would ensure government support of new settlers and the development of industries and income sources in the new towns in the north, but the heavy recession of 1965–67 and the 1967 War delayed these plans.[18] After the war, the national impetus was to build new settlements and neighbourhoods in East Jerusalem and the rest of the occupied territories.

In its search for a neighbourhood site in the early 1970s, the Hasidic community hoped to find in the Galilee a suitable residential area with government-subsidized employment, in proximity to the holy Jewish cities of Tiberias and Safed.[19] As noted, however, the Galilee was far from the government's attention at that time, and the process of approving the plan ran into bureaucratic foot-dragging.

The community's turn to the periphery, described in the quote above by one of its leaders – Rabbi Neuhaus – as contradictory to the general Israeli trend, attests to an identification with the new settlement movement of the 1970s. At the same time, it demonstrates a stable and self-confident community identity, open to a process of joint planning and integration in a foreign and problematic environment, populated mostly by the North African Jews who had been the first to be settled in the new towns and who suffered economic hardship and social isolation.[20]

In the days when the first principles for the planning of the neighbourhood were outlined, the Israeli architectural field was undergoing an ideological and stylistic transformation influenced by the criticism of modernism, which began in the early 1950s in the West in the form of groups such as Team X and the New Brutalism.[21] These architects and critics argued that architecture was not designed to dictate a way of life, but to be a direct product of life.[22] Their values were translated in Israel into a demand to localize the modern Israeli architecture and to abandon the coercive and rigid settlement strategy of the planning authorities.[23]

The encounter between global criticism and the spatial and social transformations in post-1967 Israel provided local architects with an excellent opportunity to articulate belonging, identity, and an emotional and physical attachment to the local landscape and heritage. For the young architects of the 'statehood generation',[24] the adoption of this critical model was combined with the motivation of determining the character of 'the national home'.[25] By the late 1960s, Israel was no longer a sublime and distant ideal, or a *terra nullius* awaiting redemption in the form of architectural planning. The reality faced by the planners was one of a concrete existence, culturally diverse and often tormented. As suggested by one of the leading representatives of the new generation, architect Ram Karmi, new architectural planning required 'solutions that liberate the resident and empower him to suit them to his needs and use them to express himself'.[26] In the process, architects were called upon to adopt a historical perspective that exposed local and cultural values that had been marginalized in the name of relentless modernist innovation, and integrate the heritage of the past with the needs of the future: 'Our generation will learn from the past, and through the past predict the future'.[27]

The search for architectural elements able to establish the sought-after attachment between individuals and their cultural heritage, by highlighting signifiers of unique identity and community values, led critical architecture to examine the native vernacular as representing the authenticity of human values and behaviours and expressing local intimacy. In the Israeli case, the return to the vernacular was also related to the geopolitical situation that transformed the settlement map during those years. The historic return to the Old City of Jerusalem, occupied in 1967, emphasized the internal split of identities in Israeli society, mainly by exposing the othernesses that had been excluded or voluntarily eschewed by the Israeli collective, including the ultraorthodox one.[28] This return also awakened a longing for the physical land and for spatial 'authenticity', as well as for Jewish cultural origins, repressed in the attempt to forge a new national identity.[29]

Against this transformative background, Israeli planning authorities were faced with the challenge of designing a community space in Hatzor, posed paradoxically by the largely a-local ultraorthodox community. The distinctly different authenticity embodied by this community, its unique identity and cultural markers, as well as its close-knit social structure, were highly relevant to the emerging architectural discourse, for which it formed a distinct test case. However, the community's tendency to segregate itself from Israeli secular and Zionist society, and its indifference, if not hostility towards the Israeli place and culture that prioritized modernity over the ultraorthodox lifestyle seen as diasporic and outdated, turned the process of planning the neighbourhood into an even more complex challenge.

The choice of Reznik added yet another layer of complexity. Like many of his elite colleagues from the 'statehood generation architects' group, Reznik was preoccupied with the attempt to integrate modernist values with local materials, especially concrete and stone; local typologies such as alley, inner courtyard, and gate; as well as more communal and mixed uses. However, unlike most of his peers, he was not an Israeli native.[30] In Brazil, where he was born and raised, Reznik apprenticed under renowned architects Oscar Niemeyer and Lúcio Costa, whose plan for Brasilia is considered the epitome of modernist and socialist urbanism.[31] In 1949, while still in his twenties, Reznik immigrated to Israel based on Zionist and socialist motives, and commenced independent practice during the late 1950s. The difference between him and his peers, most of whom were forged in the melting pot of Zionist education and military service, was articulated in a unique combination between a diasporic longing for the Holy Land and concrete Zionism. This enabled concepts such as 'homesickness', 'excitement', 'symbolism', and even 'pathos' to be articulated in his projects.[32] Reznik's ability to identify with an external-diasporic perspective his empathy towards a sense of being 'out of place' and his awareness of the importance of the Jewish community, likely contributed to the unique relationship and resulting productive collaboration between the architect and the Gur sect.

Architectural Dialogue

> I suddenly felt my roots, an excellent rapport with them, with their plans and with the new neighborhood. Heredity? My genes suddenly began to be very active, probably. Is there such a thing as a spiritual gene?
>
> David Reznik[33]

For Reznik, the planning process offered an opportunity to develop an architectural concept grounded in the values of place and community, out of the belief that building for a community with a strong and homogeneous identity is a recipe for shared living as well as integration with its surrounding heterogeneous fabric. In a 1976 interview, Reznik talked about the relation between the Jewish-Hasidic community and the attempt to structure a local Israeli identity using architectural means: 'As an Israeli, I do not want to reproduce the diasporic Jewish town here, but I do want to [...] express that community spirit [...] in the Upper Galilee.'[34]

Reznik's first impression upon arriving in Hatzor HaGlilit was that the town was in great distress, finding it difficult to attract new residents but possessing a planning logic that could enable a meaningful encounter between different populations. According to Reznik, the traditional-religious infrastructure of the town could assimilate the Gur Hasidim.[35]

Following his preparatory tours, Reznik recommended that the neighbourhood be built on two violin-shaped mountain ranges located on the northern edge of the town. This choice reversed the town's direction of expansion to the uninhabited area to the north, facilitating the formation of a segregated area by using a ring road that enabled the community to remain inward facing, without demarcating a physical boundary [Figure 2].[36] This decision engendered a planning concept grounded in the local topographical conditions and enabled the neighbourhood's expansion from the 7 acres originally requested by the community to about 70 acres. This expansion led to a much more spacious planning, made according to the deconstructed cluster model, as opposed to the crowded modern blocks model, and leaving an 'open green margin'.[37]

The neighbourhood took shape at a time when an alternative urban planning model was being formulated by government planning authorities. Beyond the growing interest in new technology, pioneering engagement with old-new sites in East Jerusalem and the rest of the occupied territories, and the yearning for the vernacular, the new model had a social purpose: forming a mixed and locally grounded residential community. The new neighbourhood model was made up of enclosed neighbourly clusters located around an internal open space. Many such systems, representing variations on the same fundamental principles, began appearing in new neighbourhoods.[38] The new construction was characterized by distancing the residential clusters from the main traffic arteries, and by the use of materials and elements such as concrete, stones, and prefabricated elements that interpret building traditions identified as local.[39]

While his peers sought to apply their new critical principles and realize the community ideal by reference to the local vernacular architecture, Reznik found an ideal 'specimen', a

Figure 2: The town plan of Hatzor HaGlilit and the Gur Neighborhood in the north, as published in a marketing brochure for the New Neighborhood. Courtesy of Rabbi Asher Neuhaus, private archive.

readymade prototypical community. Thus, his task was the exact opposite: out of an existing, powerful sociocultural force, he had to cast an architectural image that structured local belonging, and forge with and for the community an architecture identified as both 'Jewish and Israeli'.[40] The task of translating 'Israeli' or 'Jewish' into an ultraorthodox-community format required him, as he put it, to undertake a historical study of traditional residential environments, whose cultural uniqueness was preserved due to their spatial-social segregation: from Jewish towns in Palestine in the late Roman and Byzantine periods, built around spiritual centres, to Jewish towns and neighbourhoods in the European Diaspora.[41]

In addition, Reznik examined innovative urban schemes devised by planners such as Lewis Mumford, which had been prevalent in Europe and North America in the 1930s and 1940s. These schemes eventually inspired concepts realized in Israel in the early years following statehood, such as the 'neighbourhood unit'. This planning solution was designed to ensure high quality of life as an alternative to the bustling metropolis, preserving the structure of the small quasi-Medieval town based on the autonomous existence of neighbourhoods developing around a single urban centre, with open spaces in between.[42] These principles guided the planners of the new towns in the early 1950s, and influenced the way that Reznik perceived the community concept in planning, despite the fact that one could not ignore the problems derived from their decontextualized realization in Israel.[43] Another, subsequent source of inspiration, based in part on acknowledging the problems of the previous model, was Serge Chermayeff and Christopher Alexander's 'subcultural mosaic' of units, which interpreted and relied on old, traditional neighbourhoods as models. These units' segregation was not designed to prevent integration and did not affect the functioning of the urban centre; rather, they were designed to preserve the unique community atmosphere, without becoming ghettos.[44]

According to Reznik, the vision for the neighbourhood aspired for coherence between the architectural plan and the community using it and the local physical and residential landscape. To achieve a deeper understanding of community needs, the architect worked jointly with a planning committee representing the Gur sect. Early on, the community sought to create an urban residential space composed of housing blocks similar to those in the town of Bnei Brak. . The demand was not to return to the courtyard buildings, however, perceived as old-fashioned and which 'remind[ed] them of the ghetto and its overcrowding'.[45] But while the community sought to reconstruct a Bnei Brak-like standard urban housing complex, Reznik suggested a closed neighbourhood perimeter with a rural character, which would prevent internal vehicle traffic yet enable pedestrian flow. He believed that this would allow the required separation between the neighbourhood and the rest of Hatzor HaGlilit and meet the community's demand to prevent vehicles from

Figure 3: Houses and environmental development. Courtesy of the David Reznik Archive at the Central Zionist Archives.. Source: Penny Maguire, 'An Eye on Israel: Reznik at Kirya'. *Architectural Review* (June 1979), 359–60.

entering on the Sabbath [Figure 3].[46] The separation between pedestrians and vehicles was a prevalent planning trend at the time.[47] The abandonment of the joint stairwells and the provision of a separate entrance to each apartment emphasized the need for privacy and led to a planning of the communal space so as to allow a gradual transition from the houses to the neighbourhood courtyards and squares, converging through alleys and footpaths into two main arteries leading to the neighbourhood centre. This centre, in turn, was uniquely planned as a spiritual rather than a commercial one, with the religious schools and a synagogue as hubs of community interrelations.[48]

Immediately after selecting the site and deciding to build some 600 housing units, the actual planning began, with a focus on balancing the need for a separate existence and the desire to maintain a degree of openness to the town and its veteran residents. The main indicator of separation was the segregated education system, which allowed one-way integration only: the local townspeople could integrate in the community system under certain conditions, but not vice versa. Similarly, the synagogues and other religious services were kept separate.[49]

The Plan

> Instead of the barren hill, the neighbourhood now flourishes, bestowing its residents with its grace.[50]

Once the plans were ready, a public meeting was held in Bnei Brak and they were presented to potential residents, some 700 women and men. The meeting commenced with an introduction that emphasized the profound meaning of settling the Galilee near the holy cities of Safed and Tiberias; the advantages of living in the mountain air in autonomous housing units; the prospects for the neighbourhood's development; and the benefits for the younger generation. Next, the plans themselves were presented by Reznik. Following the meeting, a committee of women of different ages and stages in their family life was set up to exactify all the interior-design requirements to be presented to the architect. Thus, the apartments' floor plans were delegated to the women, while the planning of the neighbourhood and community institutions was allocated to the men.[51] According to Reznik, working on the programme with the future residents was a rare intellectual experience given the issues raised by the planning partners and the solutions Reznik had to provide.[52]

The final plan reflected the residents' specific needs and the 'glue of the community', which according to Reznik need not have been invented as it 'was already there'.[53] The planning principles reflected the worldwide trend of the search for the vernacular, combined with a study of local and Mediterranean building styles. According to Reznik, the neighbourhood was planned so as to seem like a building planted in and growing out of the land, inspired by the Arab houses he saw in the villages of the Galilee, which are integrated in the natural landscape. Figure 8 shows Reznik's version of this local connection, which uses a hybrid of modern, Mediterranean, and local styles to create new affinity with the surrounding

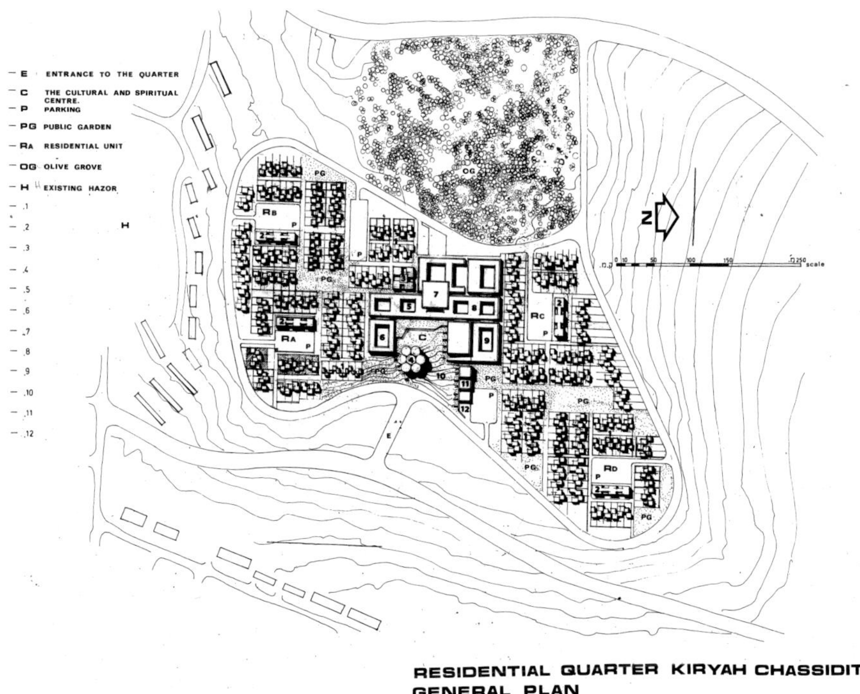

Figure 4: David Reznik, general plan of Gur Neighborhood. Courtesy of the David Reznik Archive at the Central Zionist Archives.

space. Together, these inspired a rethinking of the public space serving the community as a substitute, to a certain degree, for the urban street.[54]

The Hasidic neighbourhood was divided into four sub-neighbourhoods: two southern ones bordering the town and two northern ones opening out into the natural landscape [Figure 4]. Each of the four was planned as a separate complex and all converged on a public space with preschools and meeting areas.[55] The public gardens were located in the communal spaces between the sub-neighbourhoods, and the spiritual centres were located in the central section of the 'violin'.

The fact that the neighbourhood was built on a hill dictated the planning of three main systems. First, *the housing system*, which was divided into an upper level for spiritual functions (religious and educational), and a lower level for 'secular' functions (stores, an event hall, a nursing home and a hostel – non of which were built in the end). These two public planes were planned as interrelated, forming a central space surrounded by public buildings and open to the main access road and panoramic views. Each sub-neighbourhood or cluster contained 80–100 housing units. The units were planned in groups of six, with each group occupying a 300 m^2 plot. The six-unit groups were planned in a pyramid-like

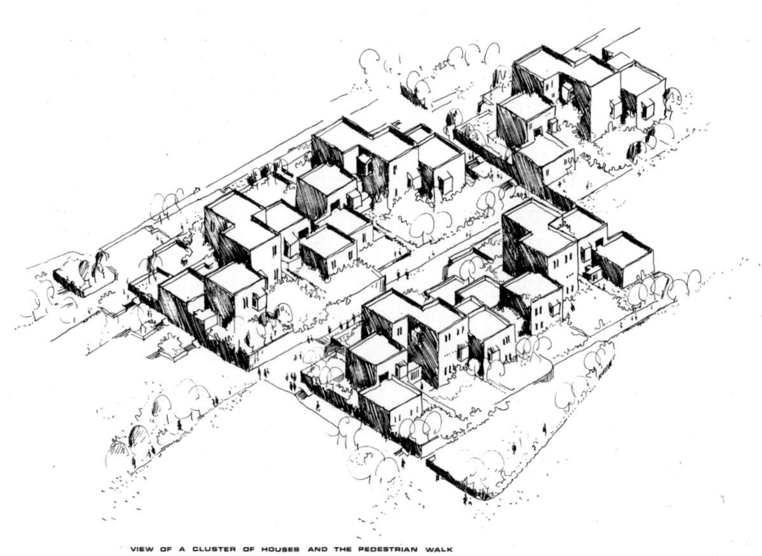

Figure 5: David Reznik, perspective, view of a cluster of houses, gardens and the pedestrian walk :. Courtesy of the David Reznik Archive at the Central Zionist Archives.

configuration: three apartments on the ground floor, two on the second, and one on the top floor – providing the option for future expansion of each unit.[56] Each apartment had its own stairwell that led to the neighbourhood squares and alleys. These squares and alleys were designed to provide a social substitute for the joint stairwell [Figure 5].[57] To this day, these alleys tie the clusters to each other and to the centre. The flat roofs and external staircases; the inner courtyards surrounded by houses, and the alleys leading to them; the white plaster and rough, black natural basalt-stone terraces framing the gardens, all contributed to creating a space that conveyed a sense of intimate locality that blended with the local landscape. The basalt terraces, in particular, became a prominent characteristic, rendering the neighbourhood a black exterior reminiscent of the surrounding rocky Galilee mountains and typical of the Golan Heights on the eastern horizon.

Second, *the pedestrian system*, which was based on two internal axes connecting the neighbourhood with the rest of the town. The vertical axis was connected to the existing centre of Hatzor, to the south, and to the north to a hotel and residential area planned on the slopes of the northern mountain range. The horizontal axis connected the public buildings in the east to the olive grove in the west. The main square was located at the two axes' point of intersection.

Finally, *the road system*, which was the most concrete embodiment of the boundary between the Hasidic neighbourhood and the rest of Hatzor. A ring road enveloped the main residential area and connected to the existing road system at two points: at the main entrance route to the town and at its existing commercial centre [Figure 4]. From the ring road, parking bays extended deep into the residential areas and its centre.

In the early 1970s, these plans were rejected by the Ministry of Housing and the Ministry of Trade and Industry, as the programme seemed too spacious and uneconomic according to accepted standards.[58] Only with the appointment of Avraham Ofer as Minister of Housing, in June 1974, did the government prioritize Jewish settlements in the Galilee again. According to Ofer, 'after Jerusalem – which is always our first priority – the next priority is to settle the Galilee, to increase the population in the Galilee, to enlarge the cities in the Galilee.'[59] This allowed for the realization of Reznik's plan, and already in August of that year the cornerstone was laid in an opulent ceremony.

Eventually, only the south-eastern cluster was built according to Reznik's programme, with 90 housing units. Towards the mid-1980s, the south-western cluster was built using prefabricated construction under standards determined by the Ministry of Housing. According to locals, these new buildings were unsuited to the community's needs and were considered an 'eternal eyesore'.[60] Subsequently, another group of houses was built in the area designated for the north-eastern cluster, and the final row of houses was built about a decade ago in the north-eastern area. The final buildings were planned with emphasis on the needs of the nuclear family, and their design reflects an attempt to return to Reznik's principles – in both their cube-like structure and their external, separate staircases. However, their deployment did not reflect due consideration of their integration in an overall neighbourhood fabric, as intended by Reznik.

House and Courtyard

> More than for the architecture, I felt proud for having returned them to the land.
>
> David Reznik[61]

The residential buildings planned by Reznik were of two main types: the vast majority were pyramid-like buildings for families; only two buildings were rectangular with one- or two-bedroom apartments for newlyweds. Unlike the former, these apartments could not be enlarged.[62] The family apartments were planned so that their ground floor could be expanded towards the courtyard, while the upper floor could expand upon the roofs below them. To maintain separation between visitors and the family, a separate entrance space of 5.5 m^2 was planned, leading to the kitchen, living room, or bedrooms area. All apartments were divided into two sections. The first included the kitchen and living room (35 m^2). The former was larger than the Ministry of Housing standard, as it required double systems for strict observance of kashrut rules. The second section usually included three bedrooms (9–10 m^2 each), with each of the children's bedrooms often intended for three and even four children. The total area was no more than 96 m^2, with the terrace and potential expansion space offering an additional 40 m^2 [Figure 6].

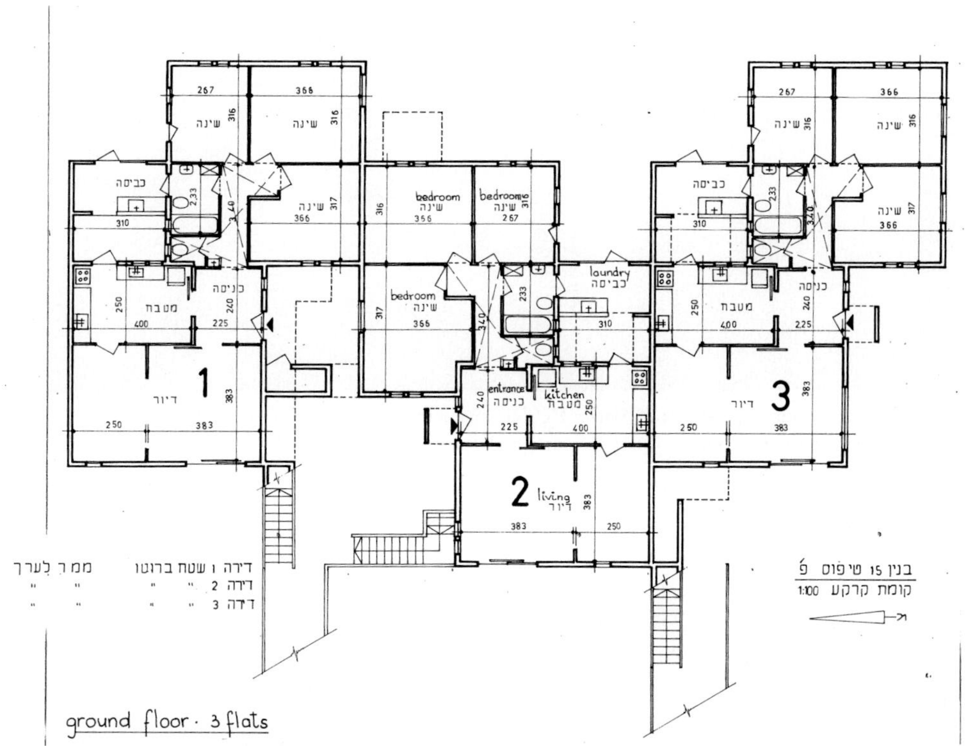

Figure 6: Plans of the apartments' interior: the ground floor. Courtesy of the David Reznik Archive at the Central Zionist Archives.

One of the main innovations in planning the neighbourhood was the community's transition from the overcrowded city to the wide spaces of the Galilean landscape [Figure 7]. This was seen as a significant improvement in the quality of community life, and indeed was one of the declared goals of the entire initiative. Accordingly, Reznik insisted on preserving and developing the olive grove to the west of the neighbourhood. In addition, construction was spacious, allowing green spaces to extend between the houses, a value Reznik saw as important also in building high-risers. On the other hand, he wanted to avoid excessive open spaces between the buildings, since they are liable to remain neglected, as seen in the neighbourhood expansions of recent years. On the other hand, most homeowners tend their ground-floor gardens, with visible results. For Reznik, this newfound passion for gardening in the neighbourhood courtyards during the neighbourhood's early years, vindicated his concept of attachment to the land, and he considered it as his greatest achievement [Figures 8–9].[63] It was also celebrated in various community publications and by leading architects, who viewed it as an example of the desirable transformation in local planning trends.[64]

Figure 7: View of the Gur neighbourhood, Hatzor HaGlilit, end of the 1970s. Courtesy of the David Reznik Archive at the Central Zionist Archives. Source: Penny Maguire, 'An Eye on Israel: Reznik at Kirya'. *Architectural Review* (June 1979), 359–60.

Figure 8: Courtyards, house structure and area development. Courtesy of Rabbi Asher Neuhaus, private archive.

Figure 9: The private courtyards, 2006. Photograph by Oryan Shachar.

Postscript: Body-Boundary

> The buildings were very bright while the paths and fences were made of [the local] black basalt stone. Rabbi Neuhaus asked me, 'Why did you make it black like that, I hate black.' I said, 'But you're wearing black all the time.' And he answered: 'Black is my boundary.'
>
> David Reznik[65]

The Gur neighbourhood project was born out of the community's desire to improve quality of life for young families, at a time of renewed Zionist settlement initiatives during the post-1967 construction boom. In this atmosphere of development, the project was unique in that it exposed the establishment to the ultimate Jewish Other – the ultraorthodox that had been excluded from Israeliness – but also persistently distanced itself from the secular Zionist pioneering spirit. The vision weaved by the Ministry of Housing of an architectural product that evolves through a direct dialogue between the architect and future residents, and represents values of locality and cultural authenticity, was realized precisely by a community whose separateness had been the starting point of the project. In other words, local planning was inspired by a community whose character was distinctly a-local and executed in close collaboration with Israeli authorities, from which the community distanced itself.

The above quote indicates that in the architectural character of the neighbourhood, the black exterior, achieved by the use of basalt-stone terraces, reflected the transformation of an individual marker of a bodily boundary to a collective marker of a community boundary, representing 'voluntary ghettoization' – which isolates those within it from the outside world and 'folds' the structural envelope inwards.[66]

Reznik described the community in black, united in ideology and lifestyle, as a 'body for which I had to tailor a suit'.[67] Paradoxically, it was this interaction with the non-Zionist community that provided Reznik with the opportunity to create a modernist space combined with the vision of 'blue and white' (Israeli) architecture, and thus realize the ideal of locality with the mediation of the post-1967 settlement authorities.[68]

This successful collaboration was the outcome of a shared vision of combining tradition and progress with the expression of locality, precisely out of an a-local position, making for an intriguing mixture of closeness and distance, belonging and alienation. The community's search for local roots and the architectural search for an authentic, cohesive community, touched upon one another. Each party provided a little of what the other party lacked: the community became reattached to the physical place and through it, perhaps, also to the national narrative that marginalized spiritual sacredness, whereas Reznik returned to the Jewish cultural place.

The move to Hatzor HaGlilit represents relocation from the overcrowded city to the open landscape of the green Galilee. To a certain extent, this move runs counter to the way that Israeli ultraorthodox communities are usually perceived by mainstream society and to the manner of their inclusion in the Israeli search for *place*. In terms of the Gur ideology, this move may be recast as an act of expanding the 'opening to holiness' that is the spatial status of the Land of Israel; as suggested by Avraham Farber, '[t]he mountains are graced by the feet of Hasidic Jews who have come here to expand the boundaries of holiness' [Figure 10].[69]

Practically speaking, the project was perceived and cast as a pioneering act of settlement. But unlike the community's feeling that moving to the Galilee ran against the Israeli grain, it could be seen – just like the choice of Reznik for the architect – as a cautious and exploratory identification with national trends inspired by the renewed pioneering ethos, rather than a rejection of this ethos by creating a 'Diaspora' in Israel's periphery.[70] This was articulated in the neighbourhood inauguration ceremony in the summer of 1974, when Rabbi Pinchas Menachem Alter, the future leader of the Gur sect, declared that the Jewish commandment of settling the Land of Israel was made by this Hasidic community in the Galilee, 'in a territory that is not controversial' – unlike the occupied territories settled by the Zionist-religious movement.[71] On that same occasion, Housing Minister

Figure 10: Visits of Hasidim and planners to the new neighbourhood erection site in Hatzor HaGlilit, c. 1975. Courtesy of Rabbi Asher Neuhaus, private archive.

Ofer voiced a similar sentiment: 'You are the real settlers'– a statement often quoted by my interviewees.[72]

The Hasidic community's negotiations with state and local authorities, as well as with the planner, repositioned theirs as a proactive, productive, and pioneering community.[73] It seems that once the community utilized government bureaucracy and its agents, which subordinate the individual to the state ideology, the act of settlement was reciprocally appropriated by the establishment, becoming part and parcel of the national settlement narrative. The project thus embodies the power of the community, but also the power of the state, whose values and resources stimulated the community's desire to resemble, participate, and cooperate, heralding the beginning of a much broader trend of ultraorthodox settlement outside its traditional centres.[74] This led to a unique situation where, despite the insistence on keeping the community body separate from its non-Hasidic environment, the black suit of the Hasidic Community somehow did intertwine with the Israeli white and blue.

Today, the Gur neighbourhood in Hatzor HaGlilit is home to some 200 families. As noted above, it has been expanded in various ways that are incompatible with the original plan and development process hoped for by Reznik. Nevertheless, even forty years later we can still discern in Hatzor the outlines dictated by Reznik's plan and its basic principles, which laid the groundwork for future planning.

The collaboration between the architect and the Hasidic community was irreparably cut short due to the latter's fervent opposition to the building of the Brigham Young Mormon University of Jerusalem (1980–87), planned by Reznik, who sincerely believed in opening Jerusalem to a diversity of cultures and religions. Thus, the ideological discussion surrounding the concept of place turned into a stumbling block in the relations between them.[75]

I would like to end on a personal note. A week before his death in 2012, David Reznik sent me a short, handwritten letter, expressing his joy at the completion of my study as well as his sorrow at not having completed the neighbourhood plan. He concluded his letter with the words 'More cultured days are yet to come'. The logo at the bottom of the page depicted Jerusalem with its multiple and diverse structural icons, a drawing symbolic of Reznik's pluralistic approach to architectural culture that ultimately ended his cooperation with the Gur sect. Reznik's final words can therefore be read as wishing for a time when open discussion would be not only the hallmark of architectural research, but also the cornerstone of architectural practice.

Bibliography

Hed HaKirya: Organ of the Hasidic Neighborhood in Hatzor HaGlilit, Hatzor Haglilit, April–May 1978, 2 (In Hebrew).

Alfasi, Yitzhak. *Glory of Glories: The History of the Gur Dynasty*. Tel Aviv: Sinai, 1993 (In Hebrew).

Banham, Reyner. *The New Brutalism: Ethic or Aesthetic?* London: Architectural Press, 1966.

'Ceremony for Establishing a Hasidic Community in Hatzor HaGlilit'. In *Hasidic Community in Hatzor HaGlilit*, n.p. (In Hebrew).

Chalfi, Raquel. 'Airplane, Three Birds'. *Helicon: Anthological Journal of Contemporary Poetry* 73 (2006): 93 (In Hebrew).

Churchman, Arza and Amnon Frenkel. *Guidelines for Residential Buildings for the Ultraorthodox Population*. Haifa: Technion – Israel Institute of Technology, 1992 (In Hebrew).

Chermayeff, Serge and Alexander Christopher. *Community and Privacy: Toward a New Architecture of Humanism*. Garden City, NY: Anchor Books Doubleday & Co., 1963.

Dekel-Caspi, Sophia. *David Reznik: Retrospective*. Tel Aviv: Genia Schreiber University Art Gallery and Yolanda and David Katz Faculty of the Arts, Tel Aviv University, 2005 (In Hebrew).

Efrat, Elisha. *Development Towns in Israel: Past or Future?* Tel Aviv: Ahiasaf, 1987 (In Hebrew).

Efrat, Zvi. *The Israeli Project: Building and Architecture, 1948–1973*. Tel Aviv: Tel Aviv Museum of Art, 2004 (In Hebrew).

Eisenstadt, Shlomo Noah. *Transformations in Israeli Society*. Tel Aviv: Ministry of Defense, 2004 (In Hebrew).

Eldar, Akiva and Idith Zertal. *Lords of the Land: The War over Israel's Settlements in the Occupied Territories, 1967–2004*. Or Yehuda, Israel: Kinneret, Zmora-Bitan, Dvir, 2004 (In Hebrew).

Elhanani, Aba. *The Struggle for Independence: Israeli Architecture in the 20th Century*. Tel Aviv: Ministry of Defense, 1998 (In Hebrew).

Erlik, Abraham. *On Architecture and City Building*. Haifa: Technion – Israel Institute of Technology, 1983 (In Hebrew).

Farber, Avraham. 'The Hasidic Neighborhood in Hatzor: The Jewel in the Upper Galilee's Crown', *Diglenu* (1978), 8–9 (In Hebrew).

Hameiri, Yehezkel. 'A Volcano Called Hatzor'. *Yediot Ahronot*, December 24, 1971, 15 (In Hebrew).

Gorny, Yosef. 'The "Melting Pot" in Zionist Thought'. *Israel Studies* 6.3 (2001): 54–70.

Gurevitch, Zali and Gideon Aran. 'On Place (Israeli Anthropology)'. In *On Israeli and Jewish Place*, edited by Zali Gurevitch, 9–44. Tel Aviv: Am Oved, 2007 (In Hebrew).

Hanani, Hadas. *The Residential and Housing Culture in Ashkenazi Ultraorthodox Society in Israel*. Ph.D. diss., Haifa University, 2008 (In Hebrew).

Holston, James. *The Modernist City: An Anthropological Critique of Brasilia*. Chicago: University of Chicago Press, 1989.

Jacobson, Yoram. 'Diaspora and Redemption in the Gur Hasidic Sect'. *Daat* 2–3 (1978–79): 175–215 (In Hebrew).

Kallus, Rachel and Hubert Law-Yon. 'National Home/Personal Home: The Role of Public Housing in the Shaping of Space'. *Theory and Criticism* 16 (2000): 153–80 (In Hebrew).

Karmi, Ram. 'Encounter between Tel Aviv and Jerusalem'. *Tvay* 21 (1982): 3–4 (In Hebrew).

——— 'Human Values in Urban Architecture'. In *Israel is Building 1977*, edited by Amiram Harlap, 320–28. Tel Aviv: Meir Tadmor, 1977 (In Hebrew).

——— 'A Shadowy Architecture'. *Kav* 3 (1965): 50–63 (In Hebrew).

Kimmerling, Baruch. *Immigrants, Settlers, Natives*. Tel Aviv: Alma/Am-Oved, 2004 (In Hebrew).

——— *The Invention and Decline of Israeliness: State, Society and the Military*. Berkeley: University of California Press, 2001.

Maguire, Penny. 'An Eye on Israel: Reznik at Kirya'. *Architectural Review* (June 1979), 359–60.

Malkin, Yaakov. *Quality of Life and Renascence of Community*. Givatayim-Ramat Gan: Masada, 1976 (In Hebrew).

Mumford, Eric P. *The CIAM Discourse on Urbanism, 1928–1960*. Cambridge: MIT Press, 2000.

Mumford, Lewis. *The Culture of Cities*, London: Secker & Warburg, 1938.

——— 'The Neighborhood and the Neighborhood Unit'. *Town Planning Review* 24.1 (1954): 256–70.

Neuhaus, Asher. Phone interview with Oryan Shachar. February 16, 2006.

Nitzan-Shiftan, Alona. 'Contested Zionism-Alternative Modernism: Erich Mendelsohn and the Tel Aviv Chug in Mandate Palestine'. *Architectural History* 39 (1996): 147–80.

——— 'Nationalize and Eradicate: The Sense of Place in Jerusalem'. *Alpayim* 30 (2006): 139–55 (In Hebrew).

——— *Seizing Jerusalem: The Architecture of Unilateral Unification*. Minneapolis: University of Minnesota Press, 2017.

——— 'Seizing Locality in Jerusalem'. In *The End of Tradition?*, edited by Nezar Alsayyad, 231–55. London and New York: Rutledge, 2004.

——— 'Whitened Houses'. *Theory and Criticism* 16 (2000): 227–32 (In Hebrew).

Ockman, Joan and Edward Eigen, eds. *Architecture Culture, 1943–1968: A Documentary Anthology*. Rizzoli, NY: Columbia Books of Architecture, 1993.

Picard, Avi. 'Populating the Development Towns'. In *The Development Towns*, edited by Zvi Zameret, Aviva Halamish, and Esther Meir-Glitzenstein, 195–216. Jerusalem: Yad Ben Tzvi, 2009 (In Hebrew).

Ravitzky, Aviezer. *Messianism, Zionism and Jewish Religious Radicalism.* Tel Aviv: Am Oved, 1997 (In Hebrew).

Reznik, David. Interview with Oryan Shachar. Jerusalem, February 14, 2005.

——— Interview with Oryan Shachar. Jerusalem March 1, 2006.

Risselada, Max and Dirk van den Heuvel, eds. *TEAM 10, 1953–1981: In Search of a Utopia of the Present*. Rotterdam: NAi, 2005.

Shachar, Oryan. '"Round World, Right-Angled World": Modern Architectures and Urban Communities in Hatzor HaGlilit, 1950–1976'. Ph.D. diss., Technion – Israel Institute of Technology, 2012 (In Hebrew).

Shapira, Anita. 'A Generation in Israel'. In *New Jews, Old Jews*, edited by Anita Shapira, 122–53. Tel Aviv: Am Oved, 1997 (In Hebrew).

Sharon, Arieh. *Physical Planning in Israel.* Jerusalem: Government Printer, 1951 (In Hebrew).

Sheleg, Yair. *The New Religious Jews: Recent Developments among Observant Jews in Israel.* Jerusalem: Keter, 2000 (In Hebrew).

Shilhav, Yosef. *Small Jewish Town within a City: Geography of Separation and Integration.* Jerusalem: Institute for Israel Studies, 1991 (In Hebrew).

Smithson, Alison and Peter. 'The New Brutalism: An Editorial'. *Architectural Design* (January 1955), 1, see also in Reyner Banham, *The New Brutalism: Ethic or Aesthetic?* (London: Architectural Press, 1966), 45–46.

Smithson, Alison and Team X. *Team 10 Primer*. Cambridge: MIT Press, 1968.

Skolasky, David. 'Hasidic Community in Hatzor HaGlilit: "The Torah Searches for a Home of Its Own"'. *Gilion Beit Yaakov* 198 (n.d.) (In Hebrew), 20–21.

Notes

1 A Hebrew version of this chapter was published in Tula Amir and Shelly Cohen, eds, *Housing Forms in Israel* (Tel Aviv: Xargol, 2007) (In Hebrew). The chapter is based on my dissertation, '"Round World, Right-Angled World": Modern Architectures and Urban Communities in Hatzor HaGlilit, 1950–1976', (Haifa, Israel: Technion IIT, 2012). (In Hebrew). Supervised by Prof. Alona Nitzan- Shiftan and Prof. Rachel Sebba.

2 Raquel Chalfi, 'Airplane, Three Birds', trans. Ami Asher, *Helicon: Anthological Journal of Contemporary Poetry* 73 (2006): 93 (In Hebrew).

3 Avraham Farber, 'The Hasidic Neighborhood in Hatzor: The Jewel in the Upper Galilee's Crown, *Diglenu* (1978): 8–9 (In Hebrew).

4 Yaakov Malkin, *Quality of Life and Renascence of Community* (Givatayim-Ramat Gan: Masada, 1976), 168 (In Hebrew). This issue was also raised in an interview with Rabbi Asher Neuhaus, Head of the Yeshiva and of the Hasidic community in Hatzor HaGlilit. Rabbi Asher Neuhaus, interview with Oryan Shachar, February 8, 2006. See also David Skolasky, 'Hasidic Community in Hatzor HaGlilit: "The Torah Searches for a Home of Its Own"', *Gilion Beit Yaakov* 198 (n.d.): 20–21 (In Hebrew).

5 Malkin, *Quality of Life*, 166–67.

6 Farber, 'The Hasidic Neighborhood in Hatzor', 8–9; David Skolasky, 'Hasidic Community in Hatzor HaGlilit', 20–21; Moshe Yosefun, *Hed HaKirya: Organ of the Hasidic Neighborhood in Hatzor HaGlilit* (April–May 1978): 10–11 (In Hebrew).

7 The Gur community is unique in its profound theosophical thought. Many members of the Gur sect immigrated to Palestine in the 1920s following their rebbe's call to settle the Land of Israel. As a result of the Holocaust, it became the largest Polish-Jewish Hasidic sect in Israel. See also Yitzhak Alfasi, *Glory of Glories: The History of the Gur Dynasty* (Tel Aviv: Sinai, 1993) (In Hebrew); Aviezer Ravitzky, *Messianism, Zionism and Jewish Religious Radicalism* (Tel Aviv: Am Oved, 1997) (In Hebrew).

8 See Yoram Jacobson, 'Diaspora and Redemption in the Gur Hasidic Sect', *Daat* 2–3 (1978–79): 175–215 (In Hebrew).

9 On architectural modernism as a Zionist tool, see Alona Nitzan-Shiftan, 'Whitened Houses', *Theory and Criticism* 16 (2000): 227–32 (In Hebrew); Alona Nitzan-Shiftan, 'Contested Zionism – Alternative Modernism: Erich Mendelsohn and the Tel Aviv Chug in Mandate Palestine', *Architectural History* 39 (1996): 147–80.

10 On locality and its significance, see Zali Gurevich and Gideon Aran, 'On Place (Israeli Anthropology)', in *On Israeli and Jewish Place*, ed. Zali Gurevitch (Tel Aviv: Am Oved, 2007): 9–44 (In Hebrew).

11 Neuhaus, interview, February 8, 2006.

12 The main document identified with this approach is the master plan for the State of Israel. See: Arieh Sharon, *Physical Planning in Israel* (Jerusalem: Government Printer, 1951) (In Hebrew). See also: Elisha Efrat, *Development Towns in Israel: Past or Future?* (Tel Aviv: Ahiasaf, 1987) (In Hebrew); Rachel Kallus and Hubert Law-Yon, 'National Home/Personal Home: The Role of Public Housing in the Shaping of Space', *Theory and Criticism* 16 (2000): 153–80 (In Hebrew).

13 On the architectural expressions of the triple negation of the Jewish Diaspora, the bourgeoisie, and the Arab Orient, see Nitzan-Shiftan, 'Whitened Houses', 227–28, and 'Contested Zionism – Alternative Modernism', 154–58.

14 Yosef Gorny, 'The "Melting Pot" in Zionist Thought', *Israel Studies* 6.3 (2001): 54–70; Baruch Kimmerling, *The Invention and Decline of Israeliness: State, Society and the Military* (Berkeley: University of California Press, 2001), 96–106.

15 See Oryan Shachar, '"Round World, Right-Angled World": Modern Architectures and Urban Communities in Hatzor HaGlilit, 1950–1976' (Ph.D. diss., Technion – Israel Institute of Technology, 2012) (In Hebrew).

16 See, for example, Yehezkel Hameiri, 'A Volcano Called Hatzor', *Yediot Ahronot*, December 24, 1971: 15 (In Hebrew).

17 Zvi Efrat, *The Israeli Project: Building and Architecture, 1948–1973* (Tel Aviv: Tel Aviv Museum of Art, 2004), 329 (In Hebrew).

18 On the architectural criticism of the qualities of institutional planning in Israel's early years, see for example Ram Karmi, 'An Architecture of Shadow', *Kav* 3 (1965): 50–63 (In Hebrew).

19 Malkin, *Quality of Life*, 168. The importance of the vicinity to Safed is mentioned in interviews with Reznik by the author. David Reznik, interview with Oryan Shachar, Jerusalem, February 14th 2005; David Reznik, interview with Oryan Shachar, Jerusalem, March 1, 2006; Neuhaus, interview, February 8, 2006.

20 Avi Picard, 'Populating the Development Towns', in *The Development Towns*, eds Zvi Zameret, Aviva Halamish, and Esther Meir-Glitzenstein (Jerusalem: Yad Ben Tzvi, 2009), 195–216 (In Hebrew); Efrat, *Development Towns in Israel*; Alexander Breller, 'On the Problems of Populating and Developing the Galilee – Memorandum', July 18, 1974, Israel State Archive, Ministry of Construction and Housing File, 8353/1-גל (In Hebrew).

21 Alison Smithson and Team X, *Team 10 Primer* (Cambridge: MIT Press, 1968); Reyner Banham, *The New Brutalism: Ethic or Aesthetic?* (London: Architectural Press, 1966); Eric P. Mumford, *The CIAM Discourse on Urbanism, 1928–1960* (Cambridge: MIT Press, 2000); Max Risselada and Dirk van den Heuvel, eds, *TEAM 10, 1953–1981: In Search of a Utopia of the Present* (Rotterdam: NAi, 2005); Joan Ockman and Edward Eigen, eds, *Architecture Culture, 1943–1968: A Documentary Anthology* (Rizzoli, NY: Columbia Books of Architecture, 1993).

22 Alison and Peter Smithson, 'The New Brutalism: An Editorial', *Architectural Design* (January 1955), 1; reprinted in: Reyner Banham, *The New Brutalism: Ethic or Aesthetic?* (London: Architectural Press, 1966), 45–46.

23 Alona Nitzan-Shiftan, *Seizing Jerusalem: The Architecture of Unilateral Unification* (Minneapolis: University of Minnesota Press, 2017), 45–61.

24 For the generational divide in Israeli society, see Anita Shapira, 'A Generation in Israel', in *New Jews, Old Jews*, ed. Anita Shapira (Tel Aviv: Am Oved, 1997), 122–53 (In Hebrew).

25 On this architectural generation, see Alona Nitzan-Shiftan, 'Nationalize and Eradicate: The Sense of Place in Jerusalem', *Alpaim* 30 (2006): 139–55 (In Hebrew); Alona Nitzan-Shiftan, 'Seizing Locality in Jerusalem', in *The End of Tradition?*, ed. Nezar Alsayyad (London and New York: Routledge, 2004), 231–55, 237; Nitzan-Shiftan, *Seizing Jerusalem*, 45–78.

26 Ram Karmi, 'Human Values in Urban Architecture', in *Israel Builds*, ed. Amiram Harlap (Tel Aviv: Meir Tadmor, 1977), 320–28, 326 (In Hebrew).

27 Ibid., 326.

28 Gurevich and Aran, 'On Place', 42. On the political changes involved, see Shlomo Noah Eisenstadt, *Transformations in Israeli Society* (Tel Aviv: Ministry of Defense, 2004) (In Hebrew); Baruch Kimmerling, *Immigrants, Settlers, Natives* (Tel Aviv: Alma/Am Oved, 2004) (In Hebrew).

29 Karmi, 'Human Values', 326.

30 For a biography of Reznik and his architectural approach, see Sophia Dekel-Caspi, *David Reznik: Retrospective* (Tel Aviv: Genia Schreiber University Art Gallery and Yolanda and David Katz Faculty of the Arts, Tel Aviv University, 2005), 8–34 (In Hebrew).

31 James Holston, *The Modernist City: An Anthropological Critique of Brasilia* (Chicago: University of Chicago Press, 1989).
32 Dekel-Caspi, *David Reznik*, 27.
33 Reznik cited in Malkin, *Quality of Life*, 170.
34 Ibid., 173.
35 Ibid., 168–69.
36 Ibid., 170.
37 Reznik, interview, March 2006.
38 See Ram Karmi, 'Encounter between Tel Aviv and Jerusalem', *Tvay* 21 (1982): 3–4 (In Hebrew); Aba Elhanani, *The Struggle for Independence: Israeli Architecture in the 20th Century* (Tel Aviv: Ministry of Defense, 1998), 160–69, 174–83 (In Hebrew).
39 Nitzan-Shiftan, 'Seizing Locality in Jerusalem'.
40 Malkin, *Quality of Life*, 173.
41 Ibid., 176; Dekel-Caspi, *David Reznik*, 21.
42 Lewis Mumford, *The Culture of Cities* (London: Secker & Warburg, 1938); Lewis Mumford, 'The Neighborhood and the Neighborhood Unit', *Town Planning Review* 24.1 (1954): 256–70.
43 Efrat, *The Israeli Project*, 807–24; Abraham Erlik, *On Architecture and City Building* (Haifa: Technion – Israel Institute of Technology, 1983), 86 (In Hebrew).
44 Serge Chermayeff and Christopher Alexander, *Community and Privacy: Toward a New Architecture of Humanism* (Garden City, NY: Anchor Books Doubleday & Co., 1963). On the inspiration for the idea to separate vehicles from pedestrians in housing complexes, see Dekel-Caspi, *David Reznik*, 22.
45 Malkin, *Quality of Life*, 174.
46 On the planning patterns for ultraorthodox populations in Jerusalem and Bnei Brak, see Arza Churchman and Amnon Frenkel, *Guidelines for Residential Buildings for the Ultraorthodox Population* (Haifa: Technion – Israel Institute of Technology, 1992) (In Hebrew).
47 For a discussion of this separation in the local context, see Karmi, 'Human Values', 325–27; for the international context, see Chermayeff and Alexander, *Community and Privacy*, 84–89.
48 Malkin, *Quality of Life*, 175; Reznik, interview, March 2006.
49 Rabbi Neuhaus emphasized the importance of a separate education system for a community interested in maintaining the age-old continuity of Hasidic education. Neuhaus, interview.
50 Translated from the invitation to the inauguration ceremony, Hatzor HaGlilit, August 11th 1976.
51 Malkin, *Quality of Life*, 176–78.
52 Reznik, interview, February 2005; Reznik, interview, March 2006.
53 Ibid. See also Dekel-Caspi, *David Reznik*, 128.
54 Karmi, 'Encounter', 3–4; Reznik, interview, February 2005; Reznik, interview, March 2006.
55 Malkin, *Quality of Life*, 179.
56 According to Dekel-Caspi, this configuration is reminiscent of the planning principles of the De Stijl movement, such as the irregular positioning of apartments in a single complex in asymmetrical geometric patterns, and playing on privacy, exposure, and formal diversity. Dekel-Caspi, *David Reznik*, 131.

57 On the trend of planning the communal space as a substitute for the stairwell, see Aba Elhanani, *The Struggle for Independence*, 161.
58 Reznik, interview, March 2006.
59 Avraham Ofer, 74th Knesset Hearing, Agenda Proposals, July 17, 1974, Israel State Archive, Ministry of Construction and Housing File, 8353/1-גל (In Hebrew).
60 Neuhaus, interview; and tour with his wife, Pesia Neuhaus (May 2006).
61 Reznik, interview, February 2005.
62 Reznik, interview, March 2006. When touring the neighbourhood with Ms Neuhaus on May 2006, I found out that two small apartments were often merged for family use.
63 Reznik, interview, February 2005; tour with Pesia Neuhaus (May 2006).
64 *Hed HaKirya: Organ of the Hasidic Neighborhood in Hatzor HaGlilit* (Hatzor Haglilit, April–May 1978), 2 (In Hebrew); Elhanani, *The Struggle for Independence*, 179.
65 Reznik, interview, February 2005.
66 Yosef Shilhav, *A "Shtetel" (Small Town) within a Modern City: A Geography of Segregation and Acceptance,* (Jerusalem, The Jerusalem Institute for Israel Studies, 1991), 11 (In Hebrew).
67 Malkin, *Quality of Life*, 173.
68 Reznik, interview, February 2005; Reznik, interview, March 2006.
69 Farber, 'Hasidic Neighborhood', 9.
70 On ultraorthodox identification with Israeli nationalism, see Yair Sheleg, *The New Religious Jews: Recent Developments among Observant Jews in Israel* (Jerusalem: Keter, 2000), 136–69 (In Hebrew).
71 'Ceremony for Establishing a Hasidic Neigborhood in Hatzor HaGlilit' Hatzor HaGlilit, August 19th, 1974 , in *Hasidic Community in Hatzor HaGlilit*, n.p. (In Hebrew) – a brochure distributed by the the committee for establishing a Hassidic Qirya at Hatzor HaGlilit, courtesy of Neuhaus. Ultraorthodox Jews began settling in the occupied territories only in the early 1980s, mainly for economic rather than for ideological reasons. See Kimmerling, *Immigrants, Settlers, Natives*; Sheleg, *The New Religious Jews.*
72 Conversation with inhabitants (Hatzor HaGlilit, December 2005); phone call with Rabbi Neuhaus (February 2006).
73 The Hasidic settlement was described as an invaluable pioneering endeavour and an 'act of inner truth'. Personal letter from Israel Shaham, Deputy Director General of the Ministry of Housing, to Rabbi Asher Neuhaus, Summer 1976, courtesy of Neuhaus.
74 On this trend, see Hadas Hanani, 'The Residential and Housing Culture in Ashkenazi Ultraorthodox Society in Israel' (Ph.D. diss., Haifa University, 2008) (In Hebrew); on ultraorthodox settlements in the occupied territories, see Akiva Eldar and Idith Zertal, *Lords of the Land: The War over Israel's Settlements in the Occupied Territories, 1967–2004* (Or Yehuda, Israel: Kinneret, Zmora-Bitan, Dvir, 2004), 91, 158 (In Hebrew).
75 For the ultraorthodox opposition to the project, see Dekel-Caspi, *David Reznik*, 176–91. The architect's ideological commitment is reflected in his response to his Hasidic detractors: 'You are judging me in Earthly Jerusalem – things will be different in Heavenly Jerusalem' (Reznik, interview, March 2006).

Both City and Village: The West Bank 'Communal Settlement' as an Architecture and Planning Lab

Yael Allweil

Introduction[1]

In 2013, Netanyahu's government approved the construction of 673 housing units in the West Bank settlement of Itamar, legalizing Itamar's 137 housing units, accumulated illegally since 1984, and declaring the addition of 538 more units within a proper plan.[2] Itamar is not the exception to the rule of West Bank settlements, rather the rule itself, in that based on a seed settlement, it can be easily expanded to take in an undetermined number of additional settler families. What makes West Bank settlements, known as 'communal settlements' to distinguish them from other settlement types, so easily expandable, based on the house unit, to the extent that they can multiply seven-fold while maintaining their integrity? As a settlement type, what makes the communal settlement a distinct planning typology?

The communal settlement is a surprisingly flexible spatial model when positioned vis-à-vis Zionism's two leading – and opposing – housing and settlement types: the communal agricultural kibbutz framework, duplicated to produce a network of settlements across the country while remaining small in scale and size; and the capitalist Hebrew city framework, which produced dense population clusters and expanded concentrically.[3] In-between typologies – most significantly the 'new town' typology of post-independence immigrant 'development towns' – were explicitly planned to mitigate urban size with 'agricultural' layout, but are unanimously considered as failures on both counts.[4] This study traces the early history of West Bank housing and settlement in order to trace the development of its specific communal settlement typology (1967–77), and points to the ingenuity of this typology as a unique settlement model capable of producing tiny, isolated outposts as well as large, urban, populous settlements based on the single-family home as a building block [Figures 1–3].

This chapter thus examines Israel as a modern laboratory of planning and architecture by inquiring into a phenomenon that unsettles established narratives regarding the nature, agents, and time frame of experimentation: the West Bank settlement project of 1967–96. In general, the historiography of Israeli architecture and planning is confounded primarily by the conception of the state mechanism as a key actor in planning, design, and construction, conceiving planning and architecture as tools for nation building. The dominance of the Ministry of Housing – the central government's arm for direct and consistent intervention in housing and settlement – as a building patron has cemented the period of socialist central government as one of state-sponsored experimentation (1948–77). Discussion of the 1977 regime change to the political right, still in effect, has largely conceptualized an all-encompassing transformation of the built environment due to the receding state and

Figure 1: Aerial photograph of Mizpe Dani, 2014. Photograph by Dvir Raz. Accessed January 21, 2019.

Figure 2: Aerial photograph of Leshem and Pduel, 2017. Photograph by Elad Raviv. Accessed January 21, 2019.

Figure 3: Aerial photograph of Ma'ale Edumim, 2014. Source: Leitersdorf Ben-Dayan Architects. Accessed January 21, 2019.

the relegation of design and construction to the open market, producing a profit-driven landscape replacing the experimental period of Zionist nation-building.[5]

Pointing to the experimental attributes of the West Bank settlement project, initiated and executed by citizens rather than the government, this chapter questions the limits of experimentation. As the settlement project commenced in 1967 and operated both before and after the 1977 regime change, initiated and enacted by citizens *in manipulation of state mechanisms*, the project transcends our scholarly focus on the state apparatus and challenges a historiography distinguishing the period of state planning (1948–77) from the period of market-driven planning (1977–present), proposing that experimentation and design laboratories are not limited to the 1948–77 period but are ongoing.

Historical accounts of Israel's settlement project in the West Bank and its communal settlement character can be placed on two distinct strands. The first, focusing on early settlement (1967–77), studies the ideological evolvement of 'religious Zionism' as a political theology and its capacity to penetrate and effect state actions.[6] The second, focusing on the architecture and planning of settlements by the state and the military, identifies the period of settlement consolidation (1977–present) and its use as a tool for political negotiations over the future of the West Bank.[7] Nonetheless, the communal settlement type was not developed by professional planners but was produced as a result of a long process of settlement experimentations by settlers in search of a model that would prove viable vis-à-vis state authorities (left and right) as well as the general public in view of its explicit illegality. This chapter will focus on the communal settlement typology as an unlikely mesh between 'the village' and 'the city', bridging the long-debated divide between the rural and the urban in Zionist architecture, planning, and historiography. While the kibbutz has been declared 'neither town nor village', this chapter will claim that the communal settlement is both *city* and *village*, a quality that renders it flexible, independent from scale, and adaptable to change.

'Both City and Village': The Flexible Typology of Communal Settlement

Much of the scholarly inquiry into the planning of Zionist settlements is devoted to study of the urban–rural divide in Zionist ideology and practice. Troen, Kahana, Azaryahu, Cohen, Katz, Chyutin, and others have discussed the deep divide between socialist and capitalist Zionism as a deep divide between these ideologies' built environments, namely the communal framework of agricultural kibbutz and moshav settlements versus the capitalist Hebrew city of Tel Aviv.[8] Yet, while the 'rejection of the city' as degenerate indeed reflected some of the discourse in socialist-Zionist circles, the fact remains that the leadership of socialist Zionism pre-statehood operated from Tel Aviv, whose 'old north' neighbourhoods of the Geddes plan were developed by urban workers as part of their struggle with capitalists over the city.[9] Moreover, Zionist rejection of both the city and the traditional village should be viewed beyond the geographical context of Palestine, in the

Figure 4: View of Kfar-Eztion, 1968. Photograph by David Hirshfeld. Source: Jewish National Fund.

context of the social reform movements of the late nineteenth century that are the backdrop to the consolidation of the discipline of modern city planning, which is facing the industrial 'city of dreadful night' and the socio-economic deterioration of the traditional village. The Garden City movement in Britain, Germany, the Low Countries, and even America, proposed numerous planned models that reject the traditional village as well as the unplanned city, reflected in Richard Kauffmann's vast body of work for the Palestine Land Development Company.[10]

The West Bank and Gaza settlement project has quite explicitly been a laboratory for expanding the boundaries of the Israeli State by making a home for Israeli citizens beyond state borders. These experiments in dwelling and settlement forms were citizenry initiatives backed by segments of the general public, the military, and the political sphere, rather than acts of planning. After a long series of experiments, discussed here in detail, the West Bank and Gaza settlement form was consolidated as what is known in Israeli discourse as the communal settlement typology. The communal settlement typology is the product of numerous clashes over the legality, location, resources, conditions, and compositions of settlements, in an ongoing process of negotiation between settlers and state. This chapter identifies three periods in the history of the Israeli settlement project: 1967–77, 1977–91, and 1991–present. In the scope of this chapter and in the context of this collection of essays, I focus on the first two periods and examine the West Bank as a laboratory for the formation of the communal settlement as a significant housing and settlement type capable of mitigating the urban–rural divide germane to Zionist settlement, by producing an expandable typology whose main rationale is dwelling.[11]

Early Experiments in West Bank Settlement, 1967–77

Much has been written about the experimental period of settlement in the West Bank (1967–77) that need not be repeated here, focusing primarily on political manoeuvring of the state and on the settlement movement's political theology of 'Kookism', which introduced Rabbi Abraham Isaak Kook's theology to mainstream Zionism.[12] Surprisingly little study investigates the experimental period's built environment – namely the 'design' of experimental settlement and housing – to examine how was settlement articulated and exercised by early settlers and ideologues in order to sustain and hold as viable. What form, layout, and materiality have served the settlement project and why?

Sources available for study of this question are primarily pamphlets, historical photographs and videos, news reports, and oral testimonies, since settlement attempts were conducted via temporary structures and were all quickly removed. Planning documents prepared by professional architects and planners can be found only for the later stages of the consolidation of settlement and the construction of permanent structures for dwellings, public institutions, and infrastructure, starting in 1978.[13]

Between 1967 and 1974, Jewish settlement in the West Bank was limited to two specific sites where Jews had previously resided, and which had played a significant role in the formation of the State-of-Israel-in-the-making and the collective memory of Israelis: the Jewish Quarter of Hebron, which was deserted after the 1929 massacre, and Gush-Etzion Religious Kibbutz settlements, traumatically lost on the last day of the 1948 War.[14] Citizens, rather than the state, initiated the resettlement of Hebron and Gush-Etzion. The Israeli government permitted 'return' to these limited sites, which was justified by the idea of a personal return home and seemingly not disturbing to the status quo, yet it resisted the formation of any new settlements on occupied land as determined by international law.

The 'children of Gush-Etzion' were evacuated before the fall of their kibbutzim during the 1948 War. Immediately after participating in the triumph of the 1967 War, now as young adults, they demanded to 'return home' in unison. As the West Bank was held by the Israel Defense Forces (IDF) as an occupied military area according to international law, Israeli civilians were explicitly barred from settling there. Gush-Etzion returnees therefore argued among themselves whether they should seek a state permit for resettlement or settle disregarding the state, eventually choosing the more established option. Yohanan Ben-Yaacov, one of the leaders of the group, said

> I claimed that in the case of Kfar-Etzion our parents fell here in defense of the State of Israel, and in their honor the state should rebuild this home. If we had done this as thieves in hiding it would be harming [our parents'] deep connection to this area and to the state.[15]

The 'children of Gush-Etzion' met with Prime Minister Levi Eshkol, who famously said, 'Well kids, if you want to – ascend.'[16] Insisting on a specific date for resettlement rather than vague permission, returnees demanded the opportunity to hold the New Year prayer in the resettled kibbutz, a request that was granted by Eshkol. Kfar-Etzion civilian resettlement was celebrated on September 27, 1967, four months after its 1967 conquest by the IDF.

Kfar-Etzion's status as a kibbutz settlement was significant for this process, as part and parcel of the 'Kibbutz Movement, which carried Israel's first rebirth struggles on its back and set [Israel's] borders', and therefore enjoyed the support of the kibbutz leadership of the time, who held significant positions of power in politics and intellectual life.[17] Kfar-Etzion was part of the Religious Kibbutz network, a faction of the Kibbutz Movement whose members mitigated socialist Zionism with Jewish piety, though it was far less influential during these 'first rebirth struggles'. The fall of Kfar-Etzion on the last day of the 1948 War and its rebuilding and resettlement, asserted the Religious Kibbutz as the new leader of kibbutz ideology by adding religious ideology to kibbutz socialism. Ben-Yaacov discusses the fascinating intersection between two ideological axes of the Religious Kibbutz:

> one axis [stretches] between man and Place [one of the acronyms for God], extending from the world to the earth and the second axis extending among men [...] Religious Kibbutz [ideology] stated that social values hold an integral part of the struggle to hold onto land.[18]

Despite this, a key debate among the 'children of Kfar-Etzion' concerned whether to rebuild as a kibbutz or as a 'regular' settlement. Some argued that 'our parents built a Kibbutz based on social-ethical conception, therefore if we are to follow them we should build a Kibbutz', while others argued for a regular (non-communal) settlement advancing the goal of settling as many Jews in Judea and Samaria.[19] In practice, maintaining the kibbutz framework restricted early ideas of mass settlement to the tight social and physical communal structure of the kibbutz form. This structure involved a tight commune sharing most of life's functions in such shared institutions as the communal kitchen, showers, children's house, and so forth. This framework accepted the entire kibbutz as one's home, with the dwelling being one's sole private space.[20] Kfar-Etzion returnees established civilian dwellings on military-held land, setting an important precedent for the settlement movement; yet, by re-establishing their settlement in the kibbutz framework they did not produce a new housing or settlement form [Figure 4].

Following the rebuilding of Kfar-Etzion, citizens made demands for re-establishing the Jewish Quarter of the city of Hebron, which was populated till the massacre of Hebron Jews in 1929, which escalated ethno-national violence in British-held Palestine. After 1967, the Israeli military governor holding Jewish property in Hebron did not make this property available to Jewish settlers; rabbis' appeals to re-establish the Hebron Yeshiva were turned down as well by Defense Minister Moshe Dayan. Resettlement activists failed to purchase any houses in Hebron in order to establish a civilian Jewish settlement in the city. Therefore, in April 1968, activists rented Hotel Park in the city where they conducted the Passover Seder as a declarative event. As Hebron was included

Figure 5: Kiryat-Arba–Hebron, 1972. Photograph by Moshe Milner. Source: National Photo Collection.

in the Israeli government's Allon Plan as part of Israel proper, key leaders, such as former Prime Minister David Ben-Gurion, supported resettlement. Yet the Israeli parliament approved Jewish settlement only outside of the Old City, in the framework of a Jewish neighbourhood named Kiryat-Arba, or 'city of the four forefathers'. Hotel Park settlers were allowed to stay in the Hebron Governor House for two years, until the construction of their permanent homes in Kiryat-Arba in 1971 [Figure 5]. Kiryat-Arba was designed and constructed as an urban neighbourhood of 250 housing units on the hill overlooking the Old City, following the urban model for housing that proliferated after statehood the 'opposite' settlement model of the communal, agricultural Kfar-Etzion.[21]

Sebastia: Experimenting with Civilian Settlement Forms

The idea of forming *new* settlements in the West Bank was first articulated in 1974, seven years after the 1967 occupation and resettlement of Kfar-Etzion and three years after the population of Kiryat-Arba as a proxy for the Old City of Hebron. Students of Rabbi Zvi Yehuda Kook founded the political-messianic activist movement of Gush-Emunim, demanding civilian settlement in the occupied biblical lands of Judea and Samaria as part and parcel of the national home. The movement enacted a settlement arm called Elon-More, which was to execute its ideology via settlement.[22] Judea and Samaria were held since 1967 by the IDF as a military zone whose only civilian population was Palestinian, administered by the military rather than by civilian state mechanisms. Elon-More demanded inclusion of the West Bank in the civilian homeland, by allowing Israeli citizens to make it their home by settlement. The state, on the other hand, conceived of the West Bank as occupied territory, restricted from civilian settlement by international law.

One of the leading figures in proposing new (rather than returning) settlements and articulating settlement beyond the limited kibbutz format was Hanan Porat, one of the 'children of Kfar-Etzion' and the elected secretary of the resettled Kfar-Etzion. Porat, closely affiliated with Rabbi Kook as a student of Mercaz-Harav Yeshiva in Jerusalem, possessed a vision of Judea and Samaria that extended well beyond Kfar-Etzion. On February 5, 1974, Porat hosted the initial meeting of activists that formed Gush-Emunim, intended to brainstorm ways to resist the Israeli government's Allon Plan, which proposed withdrawal from most of Judea and Samaria, wherein it proposed Palestinian – rather than Israeli – civil autonomy.[23] Unlike the government-approved resettlement of Kfar-Etzion and the state-provided housing in Kiryat-Arba, Gush-Emunim's attempts to form *new* settlements to accommodate a significant Jewish population were carried out in defiance of state policy and IDF military governors. Elon-More aspired to form cities and attract thousands of Israelis to the West Bank, so as to transform its status from military area to civilian homeland.

Elon-More activists enacted eight performative events of full settlement in Samaria, echoing the concept of 'ascent' in Jewish immigration to Zion since the 1880s, as well as the concept of ascent to holy sites, primarily Jerusalem's Temple Mount. As Elon-More civilians had no permit to settle in land held under martial law, they were repeatedly evacuated by the IDF.

Elon-More's first settlement attempt took place on June 5, 1974, in Horon, south of Nablus, amassing 100 settlers, including spiritual leader Rabbi Kook. They hauled equipment required to form a settlement, including a generator, kitchen facilities, furniture, and religious artefacts. They fenced an area of two hectares and set up ten tents for a synagogue, dwellings, a kitchen, a kindergarten, and a flagpole, all elements of a 'proper' settlement. The army and government refused to allow settlers to stay. As settlers refused to leave, they were surrounded by soldiers and military police, who carried them one by one to evacuation buses.[24]

Following the failure of this first attempt, well-documented by the press, Elon-More published a pamphlet addressing the public, stating: '[W]e set today to found *a city* in the heart of Eretz Israel near Nablus.'[25] In addressing the public, Elon-More aspired to convey that settlement in Judea and Samaria was an issue of civil rather than military concern. In appealing to public participation, Elon-More wished to demonstrate wide support of their cause in order to circumvent government resistance to settlement. The chosen site for the second attempt was the old Ottoman train station by the Palestinian village of Sebastia, associated with biblical Samaria, including some 200 adults and children with equipment to serve them for two weeks. Settlers were joined by a group of right-wing members of

Figure 6: Elon-More settlement in Sebastia, 1974. Photograph by Moshe Milner. Source: National Photo Collection.

Figure 7: The Samaria March, March 1975. Photograph by Israel Sun.

parliament; a number of writers and intellectuals; and numerous reporters, who documented 'Elon-More – renewal of Jewish settlement in Samaria.' Settlers cleaned the old train station and used it for toilets, a dining room, an infirmary, a youth movement room, and a teaching room, where teach-ins on Gemara and Jewish history were held. The settlement remained through the weekend, held by about 300 people, making this a settlement attempt no one could ignore.[26]

Despite declaring the goal to be 'a city' and involving a large number of settlers, this settlement attempt relied on the kibbutz model, especially in its Tower and Stockade iteration of the 1930s, which had produced instant settlements intended to circumvent British restrictions on the establishment of new Jewish settlements.[27] Namely, Elon-More produced the performance of a settlement by including all aspects of a 'proper' settlement – from kindergarten to flagpole – to convey pioneer civilian settlement in defiance of the State of Israel as foreign/other. The Elon-More justification for conducting 'illegal settlement' relied on kibbutz settlements as precedent, rather than on the city framework proclaimed in the pamphlet. As settlers refused to leave, again military personnel carried them one by one to evacuation buses.

Elon-More's ambitious third attempt aimed again at the city model, drawing 10,000 people in twenty convoys towards Jericho and Nebi-Salach on October 8, 1974 [Figure 6]. This attempt failed to materialize in a settlement, as all convoys were stopped en route by the military. Small-scale attempts to settle where all stopped, which discouraged Elon-More activists. The fourth attempt (March 5, 1975) returned to the Tower and Stockade strategy, namely another attempt to found an instant settlement, this time by carrying parts for two modular permanent structures and bricks for constructing a public synagogue, kitchen, and dining room [Figure 7]. Settlers entrenched themselves in their permanent structures and on the roof of the train station, making their evacuation the hardest thus far. Yet another attempt took place March 18, 1975, and involved expanding the stone structure erected two weeks earlier and settlers entrenching themselves in the train station, which was again evacuated in a few hours.[28]

The sixth and seventh attempts were again two test-trials of the two key strategies of mass mobilization of the general public, and of small-scale barricading in Sebastia. The Elon-More conclusion of both attempts marked them as strategies insufficient for sustaining lasting rather than declarative civil settlement. Moreover, activists discovered that the military had removed the stone roof of Sebastia station to prevent entrenchment; they further observed that the general public was willing to express support for their cause in the framework of a festive picnic-like march, yet not in violent clashes with military police over permanent settlement.

Kibbutz and City

Elon-More's successful eighth attempt of November 30, 1975, meshed the two strategies described above: mass mobilization of the public and the performance of permanent settlement in Sebastia. Activists organized thousands of citizens on a march from Netanya to Sebastia during Hanukah, as a festive march of families with young children, demonstrating broad public support for civilian hold of the West Bank as a national home, rather than military occupation of enemy territory. In addition, activists organized transportation of equipment and building materials to form an instant settlement that housed these families.

The marching civilians encountered harsh weather conditions on their way across unpaved roads to Sebastia, which particularly affected young children. As they reached Sebastia, they found a military post occupying the area to prevent settlement attempts. The soldiers allowed the children into their tents and supplied them with food and blankets. In the face of the crisis, the military also allowed provisions with the condition that they did not include construction materials. Again, settlers produced an instant settlement, including all abovementioned communal institutions as well as a public space named 'Zionism square' and even a post office, the semblance of official settlement. Despite the restriction, contractor Avner Elich from Tel Aviv managed to transfer a truck full of precast elements for concrete structures, smuggled them into the site, and assembled them to form a structure of six rooms to house a girls' residence, religious school, and synagogue. The tent town formed by settlers remained through the weekend and attracted large crowds of additional supporters.[29]

Figure 8: Studying the Talmud inside a tent in Sebastia, 1975. Photograph by Moshe Milner. Source: National Photo Collection (NPC).

Elon-More leaders used the large crowd of civilians to argue for mass civil support of their demand for civilian instant settlement, threatening violence in the form of civil war should they be forced to evacuate Sebastia.[30] Negotiations between settlers, the government, and the army ended in a compromise: in exchange for voluntary evacuation of Sebastia, the Minister of Defense in charge of martial law in the West Bank would allow a group of 30 civilian families to remain in Samaria within the nearby Kedum army camp.[31] The performance of full settlement in the form of a mesh of kibbutz and town thus proved successful in arguing for civilian settlement in Samaria. The performance of a kibbutz 'full settlement' type, declared as the nucleus of a 'city' for the general public, was the first iteration of the communal settlement's successful mesh of these two Zionist settlement types.

Experimenting with the Communal Settlement Typology

The compromise reached at Sebastia involved accepting the residency of 30 settler families of Elon-More activists in Samaria within an army base, similar to the Hotel Park settlers' residency at the Governor House until their state-built Kiryat-Arba houses were complete. Yet, while Kiryat-Arba was accepted by the Israeli government as a 'return', Sebastia was clearly a new settlement. As far as the state and army were concerned, housing civilians at the Kedum camp was to reflect that Samaria was maintained as a military rather than civilian area, and no alterations were made to the Kedum camp layout or its facilities in order to take in the families. Settlers were housed in the camp's military-police prison and not allowed to use camp facilities serving the soldiers, such as the kitchen and washrooms. Settlers therefore had to care for their own housing and communal facilities within the camp, employing the design of a civilian-built environment as a major tool for transforming the camp into a civilian settlement. As the army did not provide them with supplies, Kedum settlers successfully argued for the introduction of supplies from outside the camp. Provisions included trailers and construction materials donated by civilian groups with varied interests – from kibbutzim who viewed settlers as the ideological continuation of pioneer settlement, to contractors interested in the business opportunity proposed by settlement. In addition, settlers argued for and succeeded in obtaining civilian services such as postal deliveries and public bus transportation from Tel Aviv and Jerusalem to Kedum. Other services, like medical care, were provided pro bono by supporters who had arrived especially for that reason. Befriending the camp commander and Nablus governor, settlers gained access to more and more camp facilities and areas, arguing for an industrial area and other civilian functions, and for a civilian entrance to the camp. Elon-More's demand for permanent dwellings in winter time was met with 45 mobile homes supplied by the Jewish Agency, a compromise between durability and temporality.[32] The state, settlers, and army thereby negotiated the terms of civilian presence in the military-held West Bank upon the everyday built environment of settler housing. As recounted by Gush-Emunim secretary Zvika Slonim in January 1980, five years later,

> seven families were housed in improvised structures on the camp, in wooden shacks and at the prison. Single men were housed in tents [...] in 'basement' conditions yet 'roof-apartment' morale [...] the settlement gradually constructed itself as a separate entity [...] old shacks donated by supporting Kibbutzim were brought in to intake more families [...] smuggled into camp and [...] constructed by members [...] The first days resembled Kibbutz [old days]: do you remember [...] the communal kitchen, rotation duties, singing at Shabbat dinners – and on the other hand the showers and chemical toilets? [...] The peculiar status of unrecognized settlement provoked residents' wish for actions and symbols. The tiny streets were named after verses from Moses' blessing of Josef, on whose [Biblical] estate we settled [...] The settlement appealed to the nation [...] Supporters who came here saw the making of a new form of pioneer life, a united society with shared interest and challenges. Those thousands were sparked with the seed that fruited with more and more Elon-More [settlements] in Judea and Samaria.[33]

Upon rising to power in 1977, Menachem Begin's right-wing administration realized its protracted promise of support of Gush-Emunim by granting Kedum settlers a permit to settle permanently, declaring 'we stand on the land of liberated Israel', and providing incentives such as land allocation, loans for housing, and physical and social infrastructure.[34] The permanent settlement of Elon-More, Kedumim, was founded south of Kedum camp in several prefabricated concrete cubical housing units and later split into two settlements: Elon-More by Mount Kebir and Kedumim, literally 'ancients', reflecting the idea of reconnecting to biblical space–time. Kedumim, the permanent allocation of site and resources for a civil settlement, materialized the temporary performance of settlement in Sebastia into concrete achievement. As they could determine their own settlement layout, Kedumim settlers produced the first permanent iteration of the communal settlement typology, first experimented on in Sebastia.

Relying on state support of the settlement movement, Elon-More took the opportunity to employ the state mechanism's strongest tool – planning. In 1978, Elon-More published their vision for regional planning for the West Bank, including cities, towns, 'garden cities', communal settlements, and rural settlements across Judea and Samaria [Figure 8]. The Jewish Agency took up this civilian initiative and produced the 'Gush-Emunim master plan' of 1978, which outlined a five-year plan for settling 27,000 families in 46 new settlements, as well as additions to 38 existing ones. The plan's 'map of proposed and existing settlements in Judea and Samaria' does not distinguish between Jewish and Palestinian settlements (which would have reflected an image of 'conflict'). Further, no distinction is made between settlements in Israel proper versus the occupied West Bank, reflecting the conception of both as civilian homeland [Figure 9].

Moreover, the settlement budget was calculated 'based on the addition of families who would occupy Judea and Samaria according to the plan', namely based on the family as the civil unit.[35] The budget was calculated per family unit at 2 million lira, broken down into items including infrastructure; temporary housing; permanent housing, including public institutions; water; means of production; and 'other'. Readers familiar with the literature on the settlement movement might take note that this plan dedicates no funds to security or military purposes, unlike what has been commonly accepted as a military-motivated plan using civil settlements as a proxy for battle posts, as suggested by Weizman and others.[36]

Yet the 1977 regime change, which brought political supporters of Elon-More to power, soon proved a disappointment to the movement. The new Prime Minister, Begin, indeed celebrated his victory in Kedum, declaring, 'there will be many more Elon-More', and supported the movement with resources and political backing.[37] However, his tenure included returning the Sinai to Egypt in the 1978 peace treaty, accepting occupied land as foreign land held temporarily, and demanding that settlements be defined as military posts in order to meet international law dictum that only military purposes are valid in occupied territories. State support for the settlement project under the conception of military purpose was, for Elon-More ideologues, a double-edged sword they feared would undermine their entire enterprise. Such state initiatives as Arieh Sharon's twelve-point plan for settlement strongholds on strategic West Bank hilltops were discussed at the time as explicitly countering settlement purpose and ideology, which was explicitly posited on being civilian rather than military.[38]

Gush-Emunim soon resisted the Begin regime as well, protesting the 1978 peace accord by forming instant settlements and launching a public campaign against the 'militarization' of settlement.[39] Disillusion with planning and the state mechanism led the way to a typology of flexibility independent of scale, as it was based on the single family as a unit of population accumulation. The foundation of communal settlements on this housing unit made it possible for the settlement to vary from a five-family outpost, to a 500-family settlement like Efrat, and to a town of 5000 families, such as Ariel. This study proposes that the settlers' struggle of the 1970s to transform the West Bank from military zone to civil homeland has largely been won via the communal settlement: by 1993, civilian settlements already housed 116,000 settlers in permanent and temporary structures served by publicly funded infrastructure, civil services, and defence.[40] Planning documents for Elon-More and Kedumim – made as early as 1982 and as late as 2007 – demonstrate formal planning for suburban layout and infrastructure that render Kedumim and Kiryat-Arba – whose formative story differs significantly as seen above – as essentially the same built environment.

The pivotal case I identify as demonstrative of the centrality of housing is again in Kedumim, which used as a pretext the commemoration of one of its residents, killed in combat in Lebanon, to establish a residential outpost named after him, founded in 1996. Mizpe-Yishai – literally 'Yishai Overlook' – was erected at a strategic location, facing Kedumim on the opposite side of road 55 to Nablus. Now a formal neighbourhood of Kedumim, Mizpe-Yishai was initially a makeshift housing environment of mobile homes and haphazard houses built without plan or permit, later consolidated by parliament. In a video, produced by Etrog Studios, of Kedumim on the occasion of Mizpe-Yishay's tenth anniversary, historical images and footage of the early days are embedded within the

Figure 9: Kedumim first trailer homes, Kedum, 1978. Photograph by Moshe Milner. Source: National Photo Collection.

Figure 10: First trailer home of Mizpe-Yishai. Source: Amazia Haeitan, *Mizpe-Yishay History* (Kedumim: Etrog Films, 2003), 12 minutes.

official historiography of the stronghold neighbourhood [Figure 10]. The twelve-minute documentary includes interviews with leaders and activists who recount the strategies they had employed, as well as pictures of the makeshift structures taken at the time, collected from the individual settlers involved. This video clearly expresses the role assigned by Kedumim settlers to the housing units marking the new settlement stronghold in their struggle over the homeland. Kedumim chairperson Daniella Weiss is interviewed and states, 'this neighbourhood, Mizpe-Yishai, is not only the houses – 30 houses, 50 houses, or 100 houses – it is part of a plan for 500 housing units that would extend with God's help to 5000, reaching Havat-Gilad not far from us', reflecting the housing unit as the building block of a scale-less built environment.[41]

Conclusion: Communal Settlement as a Housing-Based 'Both City and Village' Typology

The kibbutz was famously described by leader Yizhak Tabenkin as 'neither a city nor a village', reflecting Zionist ideology regarding these two settlement types, against which the kibbutz was to serve as a radically new built environment for the radically new Zionist society.[42] This chapter identifies the West Bank communal settlement typology as *both city and village*, aspiring to transform the biblical homeland of the West Bank into an everyday home for masses of Israeli citizens, by using the family home as the building block of any scale of settlement.

The Sebastia experiments mitigated performances of instant settlement and large social mobilization, engendering a new settlement typology that mediated between two key models in the history of Zionist settlement: the communal kibbutz settlements of the 1920s and 1930s, and the mass accumulation of Jewish settlement of the Hebrew city. Aspiring for the social leadership of the Kibbutz Movement, as seen above, communal settlements included all the shared social institutions characterizing kibbutz society, except for dwelling. Rather than basing society on the individual as its basic social unit, the communal settlement is based on the family unit and family home. Rather than the closed typology of early pioneer kibbutz and moshav settlements, communal settlements were intended for expansion and could not be limited by dependence on shared institutions. The Gush-Emunim goal of mass Jewish settlement in Samaria identified the family housing unit as its building block, relegating the communal institutions of the settlement to such functions as the synagogue, kindergarten, and clinic.

Much discussion has been devoted to communal settlements' suburban political economy, based on commuting to the Tel Aviv and Jerusalem metropolises.[43] Yet the communal settlement typology is distinct from a regular suburb for its independence from scale restrictions, equally capable of sustaining both a small 100-family settlement like Itamar and a town of thousands like Efrat. In fact, the very strategy of communal settlement formation involves, as seen above, the gradual accumulation of more and more single-family dwelling units around a nucleus outpost, gradually developing into a formal settlement. Examining what makes this typology so flexible and adaptable, extending from tiny to large scale, I point to the single-family housing unit as the basic communal unit, whose accumulation is the main purpose of the West Bank settlement project, aiming to attract as many Israeli families to the West Bank and render it forever part of the national homeland. The settlement project in the West Bank spans from small-scale 'outposts' of ten families on isolated hilltops, to the towns of Ariel and Efrat amounting to 20,000 and 8000 people, respectively. While seemingly dramatically different – as discussed above regarding Itamar – small-scale settlements and towns are on a continuous spectrum of development that transcends this rural–urban divide and renders it largely irrelevant. The West Bank communal settlement type studied here is based on the single-family dwelling unit as its expandable unit of flexibility, developed as such by concrete experimentations in housing and settlement forms, applied not by professional architects and planners, but by future dwellers for the purpose of seeking dwelling forms that would one day be viable and permanent.

As this edited volume argues, and as I show elsewhere, the Israeli nation-building enterprise produced a laboratory of dwelling and settlement planning involving form, programme, habitation, construction, finance, and policy.[44] This housing-based lab for nation building extended both the time period associated with Israeli nationhood and the agents involved. Namely, Zionist nation-building is based on housing as its main strategy for sovereignty. Housing enabled the gradual accumulation of future citizens starting in the 1860s, in the name of whom the Israeli nation-state would be founded. After statehood, housing was the strategy for state grounding and consolidation by naturalizing immigrants as citizens via individual stakes in the national home. Further, housing serves for extending state borders via citizen dwellings outside those delineated borders.[45] Housing served Zionism as the key strategy for sovereignty, surpassing other much-discussed strategies as obtaining military superiority or providing a space for Hebrew culture.[46] Producing dwellings in the effort to (re)connect Zionists with Zion involved experimenting with viable housing and settlement forms. The 'laboratory workers' of this lab have included not only leaders, settling agencies, and governing institutions but – most significantly – the future citizens themselves as leading figures in initiating and defining terms and conditions for experimentation.[47]

The Israeli focus on housing as the generator of built environments and political societies is exceptional (yet not unique), setting it apart from well-known examples, where overarching national and urban planning were the key instruments for state building, as discussed by Scott.[48] Other nation-states whose nation-building enterprise involves a highly meaningful use of housing include the United States, where homeownership has repeatedly defined the American Dream; Singapore, where ethno-religious tensions are mitigated by unifying housing estates; and China, where provisional and political citizenship is determined by one's place of residence.[49] Arguably, the Israeli lab is not characterized by state planning. Rather, Israel's much-discussed 1951 master plan for population dispersal by Arieh Sharon was, and still is, the exception to the norm, whereby the majority of planning efforts both before and after statehood took part at the regional and settlement levels.[50] Much of the political discussion of the settler milieu hijacking the Israeli State, lamenting the lack of state-rule over settlers neglects the fact that the 160-year-long history of Zionist settlement has largely been the history of small-scale housing experiments led by the dwellers themselves, including Zionism's two leading settlement forms, the kibbutz and the Hebrew city.[51]

Bibliography

Allweil, Yael. 'Anarchist City? Sir Patrick Geddes' Housing-Based Plan for Tel Aviv, and the Housing Protests of 2011'. In *The Practice of Freedom: Anarchism, Geography, and the Spirit of Revolt*, edited by Richard J. White, Simon Springer, and Marcelo Lopes de Souza, 43–63. Lanham, MD: Rowman & Littlefield, 2016.

——— *Homeland: Zionism as Housing Regime, 1860–2011*. London: Routledge, 2017.

——— 'West Bank Settlement and the Transformation of Zionist Housing Ethos from Shelter to Act of Violence'. *Footprint* 19.2 (2016): 13–36.

Aran, Gideon. *Kookism: The Roots of Gush-Emunim, Jewish Settlers' Sub-Culture, Zionist Theology, Contemporary Messianism*. Jerusalem: Carmel Publishing, 2013.

Archer, John. *Architecture and Suburbia: From English Villa to American Dream House, 1690–2000*. Minneapolis, MN: University of Minnesota Press, 2005.

Azaryahu, Maoz. *Tel Aviv: Mythography of a City*. New York: Syracuse University Press, 2007.

Chyutin, Michael and Bracha Chyutin. *Architecture and Utopia: The Israeli Experiment*. Farnham, UK: Ashgate Publishing Company, 2007.

Cohen, Avner. *Israel and the Bomb*. New York: Columbia University Press, 1998.

Cohen, Erik. 'The City in the Zionist Ideology'. *Jerusalem Quarterly* 4 (1977): 126–44.

Drobles, Matityahu. *Masterplan for Developing Settlement in Judea and Samaria for the Years 1979–1983*. Jerusalem: WZO Settlement Department, 1978.

Efrat, Elisha. *The West Bank and Gaza Strip: A Geography of Occupation and Disengagement*. London: Routledge, 2006.

Efrat, Zvi. *The Israeli Project: Building and Architecture 1948–1973*. Tel Aviv: Tel Aviv Museum of Art, 2004.

ElonMore. *Elon More: Renewal of Jewish Yishuv in Samaria Chronicles*. Elon-More, n.d.

Feige, Michael. *Settling in the Hearts: Jewish Fundamentalism in the Occupied Territories*. Detroit: Wayne State University Press, 2009.

Fleishman, Itamar and Atila Shumalpbi. 'Itamar Hugely Growing: 675 Housing Units Addition'. *Yedioth Aharonot*, June 12, 2013.

Gal, Shilo, Pinhas Walerstein, Reuben Rozenblatt, Meir Har Noy, Zeev Friedman and Eliezer Zelko. *Why Do We Hunger Strike?* Elon-More, 1979, 1–4.

Gerson, Allan. *Israel, the West Bank, and International Law*. New York: Frank Cass and Company, Ltd., 1978.

Goh, R. B. H. 'Ideologies of Upgrading in Singapore Public Housing: Post-Modern Style, Globalization, and Class Construction in the Built Environment'. *Urban Studies* 38.9 (2001): 1589–604.

Gorenberg, Gershom. *The Accidental Empire: Israel and the Birth of the Settlements, 1967–1977.* New York: Macmillan, 2006.

Haeitan, Amazia. *Mizpe-Yishay History*. Kedumim: Etrog Films, 2003. 12 minutes.

Hall, Peter. *Cities of Tomorrow*. Berkeley: University of California Press, 1988.

Hall, Peter and Colin Ward. *Sociable Cities: The Legacy of Ebenezer Howard*. London: Wiley, 1998.

Helman, Anat. '"Even the Dogs in the Street Bark in Hebrew": National Ideology and Everyday Culture in Tel-Aviv'. *Jewish Quarterly Review* 92 no. 3–4 (2002): 359–82.

——— *Young Tel Aviv: A Tale of Two Cities*. Hanover, NH: University Press of New England, 2010.

Kahana, Freddi. Kahana, Freddy. *Neither Town nor Village – The Architecture of the Kibbutz 1910–1990*. Tel Aviv: Yad Tabenkin, 2011 (In Hebrew).

Kampinski, Yonni. 'Netanyahu: They Kill, We Build'. *Israel Hayom*, March 13, 2011.

Karmon, Naomi and Dan Chemanski. *Housing in Israel, from Planned Economy to Semi-Free Market Management*. Haifa: Center for Urban and Regional Studies, Technion, 1990.

Klain, Yossi. *The Americanization of Tel Aviv*. Tel Aviv: Carmel, 2010.

Levin, Michael, Marina Epstein-Pliousch and Tzafrir Feinholtz, eds. *Richard Kauffmann and the Zionist Project*. Tel Aviv: HaKibutz HaMeuchad, 2016.

Lieblich, Amia. *The Children of Kfar Etzion*. Haifa: University of Haifa Press, 2007 (In Hebrew).

Marom, Nathan. *City of Concept*. Tel Aviv: Babel, 2009.

Misselwitz, Philip, ed. *City of Collision: Jerusalem and the Principles of Conflict Urbanism*. Basel: Birkhäuser Architecture, 2006.

Newman, David. 'Colonization as Suburbanization'. In *City of Collision*, edited by Philip Misselwitz. Basel: Birkhäuser Architecture, 2006, 113–120.

Ohana, David. 'Kfar Etzion: The Community of Memory and the Myth of Return'. *Israel Studies* 7.2 (2002): 145–74.

Porat, Yosef Rabbi. *Renewal of Jewish Settlement in Shomron (Samaria): Eight Ascends that Mark the Begining of the Road*. Elon-More: Elon More Sechem, n.d.

Raanan, Tsvi. *Gush Emunim*. Tel Aviv: Sifriat Poalim, 1980.

Reichner, Elyashiv. '"Hanan Was the Dynamo of Return to Kfar-Ezion": Three "Kfar-Ezion Children" Talk About Its Resettlement 45 Years After'. *Makor Rishon Yoman*, September 21, 2012.

Rotbard, Sharon. 'Tower and Stockade: The Mold for Israeli Planning'. *Sedek* 2 (2008): 36–49.

Ruttenburg, Ariyeh and Sandy Amichai. *The Etzion Bloc in the Hills of Judea*. Kfar Etzion: Kfar Etzion Field School, 1997.

Scott, James. *Seeing Like a State: How Well-Intentioned Efforts to Improve the Human Condition Have Failed*. New Haven: Yale University Press, 1998.

Shadar, Hadas. 'Between East and West: Immigrants, Critical Regionalism, and Public Housing'. *Journal of Architecture* 9.1 (2004): 23–48.

Shafat, Gershon. *Gush-Emunim: The Story Behind the Scenes*. Beit El: Sifryat Beit El, 1995.

Sharon, Arieh. *Physical Planning in Israel 1948–1953*. Jerusalem: Government Printer, 1951.
Shoshan, Malkit. *Atlas of the Conflict: Israel-Palestine*. Rotterdam, the Netherlands: 010 Publishers, 2010.
Slonim, Zvika. 'Kedum Settlement'. In *Daf Lamityashev*. Kedumim: Gush Emunim, 1980, 1–2.
Troen, S. Ilan. *Imagining Zion: Dreams, Designs, and Realities in a Century of Jewish Settlement*. New Haven: Yale University Press, 2008.
Tsur, Zeev. *From the Partition Dispute to the Allon Plan*. Ramat Epha: Tabenkin Institute, 1982.
Tzfadia, Erez. 'Public Housing as Control: Spatial Policy of Settling Immigrants in Israeli Development Towns'. *Housing Studies* 21.4 (2006): 523–37.
Weiss, Daniella. 'This Was My Home: Daniela Weiss Remembers Sebastia Settlement'. *Ma'ariv*, October 12, 2009.
Weizman, Eyal. 'The Architecture of Ariel Sharon'. *Al Jazeera English*, January 11, 2014, http://www.aljazeera.com/indepth/opinion/2014/01/architecture-ariel-sharon-201411114171030885 5.html.
——— *Hollow Land: Israel's Architecture of Occupation*. New York: Verso Books, 2007.
Yacobi, Haim. 'Architecture, Orientalism, and Identity: The Politics of Israeli Built Environment'. *Israel Studies* 13.1 (2008): 94–118.
Zhang, Li. *Strangers in the City: Reconfigurations of Space, Power, and Social Networks within China's Floating Population*. Palo Alto, CA: Stanford University Press, 2001.

Notes

1 All translations from Hebrew to English are the author's own, unless otherwise specified.

2 Yonni Kampinski, 'Netanyahu: They Kill, We Build', *Israel Hayom*, March 13, 2011; Itamar Fleishman and Atila Shumalpbi, 'Itamar Hugely Growing: 675 Housing Units Addition', *Yedioth Aharonot*, June 12, 2013. See discussion of the interchange of violence and construction in the West Bank in Yael Allweil, 'West Bank Settlement and the Transformation of Zionist Housing Ethos from Shelter to Act of Violence', *Footprint* 19 (2016): 13–36.

3 Ilan Troen, *Imagining Zion: Dreams, Designs, and Realities in a Century of Jewish Settlement* (New Haven: Yale University Press, 2008); Maoz Azaryahu, *Tel Aviv: Mythography of a City* (Syracuse, NY: Syracuse University Press, 2007); Nathan Marom, *City of Concept* (Tel Aviv: Babel, 2009); Freddi Kahana, *Neither Town nor Village – Kibbutz Architecture 1910–1990* (Jerusalem: Yad Tabenkin, 2011); Michael Chyutin and Bracha Chyutin, *Architecture and Utopia: The Israeli Experiment* (Farnham, UK: Ashgate Pub Co, 2007); Yael Allweil, *Homeland: Zionism as Housing Regime, 1860–2011* (London: Routledge, 2017).

4 Erez Tzfadia, 'Public Housing as Control: Spatial Policy of Settling Immigrants in Israeli Development Towns', *Housing Studies* 21.4 (2006): 523–37; Zvi Efrat, *The Israeli Project: Building and Architecture 1948–1973* (Tel Aviv: Tel Aviv Museum of Art, 2004); Hadas Shadar, 'Between East and West: Immigrants, Critical Regionalism and Public Housing', *Journal of Architecture* 9.1 (2004): 23–48; Haim Yacobi, 'Architecture, Orientalism, and Identity: The Politics of Israeli Built Environment', *Israel Studies* 13.1 (2008): 94–118.

5 Yossi Klain, *The Americanization of Tel Aviv* (Tel Aviv: Carmel, 2010); Naomi Karmon and Dan Chemanski, *Housing in Israel, from Planned Economy to Semi-Free Market Management* (Haifa: Center for Urban and Regional Studies, Technion, 1990).
6 Gershon Shafat, *Gush-Emunim: The Story Behind the Scenes* (Beit El: Sifryat Beit El, 1995).
7 Eyal Weizman, *Hollow Land: Israel's Architecture of Occupation* (New York: Verso Books, 2007).
8 Troen, *Imagining Zion*; Kahana, *Neither Town nor Village*; Erik Cohen, 'The City in the Zionist Ideology', *Jerusalem Quarterly* 4 (1977): 126–44; Chyutin and Chyutin, *Architecture and Utopia*; Azaryahu, *Tel Aviv*; Anat Helman, *Young Tel Aviv: A Tale of Two Cities* (Hanover, NH: University Press of New England, 2010).
9 Yael Allweil, 'Anarchist City? Sir Patrick Geddes' Housing-Based Plan for Tel Aviv, and the Housing Protests of 2011', in *The Practice of Freedom: Anarchism, Geography, and the Spirit of Revolt*, ed. Richard J. White, Simon Springer, and Marcelo Lopes de Souza (Lanham, MD: Rowman & Littlefield, 2016).
10 Peter Hall, *Cities of Tomorrow* (Berkeley: University of California Press, 1988); Peter Hall and Colin Ward, *Sociable Cities: The Legacy of Ebenezer Howard* (London: Wiley, 1998); Michael Levin, Marina Epstein-Pliousch, and Tzafrir Feinholtz, eds, *Richard Kauffmann and the Zionist Project* (Tel Aviv: HaKibutz HaMeuchad, 2016).
11 For discussion on the 1991–present period, see Allweil, 'West Bank Settlement', 13–36.
12 Shafat, *Gush-Emunim*.
13 Studies of early settlement by leading scholars like Raffi Segal, Eyal Weizman, and David Newman focus on the period of state involvement and support of the settlement movement starting in 1977. They discuss formal planning by means of master plans and detailed planning, housing and settlement bureaucracy, and the politics involved in administration.
14 David Ohana, 'Kfar Etzion: The Community of Memory and the Myth of Return', *Israel Studies* 7.2 (2002): 145–74.
15 Ben-Yaacov cited in Elyashiv Reichner, '"Hanan Was the Dynamo of Return to Kfar-Ezion": Three "Kfar-Ezion Children" Talk About Its Resettlement 45 Years After', *Makor Rishon Yoman*, September 21, 2012, 22; Amia Lieblich, *The Children of Kfar Etzion* (Haifa: University of Haifa Press, 2007).
16 A slightly different transcript of this quote, appearing in Kfar-Etzion's formal history, reads 'children. You may return home'. Ariyeh Ruttenburg and Sandy Amichai, *The Etzion Bloc in the Hills of Judea* (Kfar Etzion: Kfar Etzion Field School, 1997).
17 Ben-Yaacov cited in Reichner, '"Hanan Was the Dynamo"', 22; Lieblich, *Children*; Ohana, 'Kfar Etzion'.
18 Ibid.
19 Lieblich, *Children*, 24.
20 Kahana, *Neither Town*.
21 Michael Feige, *Settling in the Hearts: Jewish Fundamentalism in the Occupied Territories* (Detroit: Wayne State University Press, 2009); Gershom Gorenberg, *The Accidental Empire: Israel and the Birth of the Settlements, 1967–1977* (New York: Macmillan, 2006).
22 Gideon Aran, *Kookism: The Roots of Gush-Emunim, Jewish Settlers' Sub-Culture, Zionist Theology, Contemporary Messianism* (Jerusalem: Carmel Publishing, 2013).

23 Shafat, *Gush-Emunim*; Zeev Tsur, *From the Partition Dispute to the Allon Plan* (Ramat Ephal: Tabenkin Institute, 1982); Malkit Shoshan, *Atlas of the Conflict: Israel-Palestine* (Rotterdam: 010 Publishers, 2010).
24 ElonMore, *Elon More: Renewal of Jewish Yishuv in Samaria Chronicles* (Elon-More: ElonMore, n.d.).
25 Shafat, *Gush-Emunim*, 77 (original emphasis).
26 Yosef Rabbi Porat, *Renewal of Jewish Settlement in Shomron (Samaria): Eight Ascends that Mark the Begining of the Road* (Elon-More: Elon More Sechem, n.d.).
27 Sharon Rotbard, 'Tower and Stockade: The Mold for Israeli Planning', *Sedek* 2 (2008).
28 ElonMore, *Elon More*.
29 Daniella Weiss, 'This Was My Home: Daniela Weiss Remembers Sebastia Settlement', *Ma'ariv*, October 12, 2009.
30 Shafat, *Gush-Emunim*, 202–03.
31 Ibid.
32 Tsvi Raanan, *Gush Emunim* (Tel Aviv: Sifriat Poalim, 1980); Porat, *Renewal of Jewish Settlement in Shomron (Samaria)*; Shafat, *Gush-Emunim*.
33 Zvika Slonim, 'Kedum Settlement', in *Daf Lamityashev* (Kedumim: Gush Emunim, 1980), 1–2.
34 Allan Gerson, *Israel, the West Bank and International Law* (New York: Frank Cass and Company, Ltd., 1978).
35 Matityahu Drobles, *Masterplan for Developing Settlement in Judea and Samaria for the Years 1979–1983* (Jerusalem: WZO Settlement Department, 1978), 12.
36 Weizman, *Hollow Land*; Philip Misselwitz, *City of Collision: Jerusalem and the Principles of Conflict Urbanism* (Basel: Birkhauser, 2006).
37 Avi Shilon, 'Begin, 1913–1992' (Tel Aviv: Am Oved, 2007), 273.
38 Eyal Weizman, 'The Architecture of Ariel Sharon', *Al Jazeera English*, January 11, 2014, last accessed December 20, 2018. http://www.aljazeera.com/indepth/opinion/2014/01/architecture-ariel-sharon-20141111417103088 55.html; Shilo Gal, Pinhas Walerstein, Reuben Rozenblatt, Meir Har Noy, Zeev Friedman, and Eliezer Zelko, *Why Do We Hunger Strike?* (Elon-More, 1979), 1–4.
39 ElonMore, *Elon More*; Raanan, *Gush Emunim*.
40 Elisha Efrat, *The West Bank and Gaza Strip: A Geography of Occupation and Disengagement* (London: Routledge, 2006).
41 Amazia Haeitan, *Mizpe-Yishay History* (Kedumim: Etrog Films, 2003), 12 minutes.
42 Kahana, *Neither Town*.
43 See, for example, David Newman, 'Colonization as Suburbanization', in *City of Collision*, ed. Philip Misselwitz (Basel: Birkhäuser Architecture, 2006).
44 Allweil, *Homeland*.
45 Ibid.
46 Anat Helman, '"Even the Dogs in the Street Bark in Hebrew": National Ideology and Everyday Culture in Tel-Aviv', *Jewish Quarterly Review* 92.3–4 (2002): 359–82; Avner Cohen, *Israel and the Bomb* (New York: Columbia University Press, 1998).
47 Allweil, *Homeland*.

48 James Scott, *Seeing Like a State: How Well-Intentioned Efforts to Improve the Human Condition Have Failed* (New Haven: Yale University Press, 1998).
49 See, for example, John Archer, *Architecture and Suburbia: From English Villa to American Dream House, 1690–2000* (Minneapolis, MN: University of Minnesota Press, 2005); Li Zhang, *Strangers in the City: Reconfigurations of Space, Power, and Social Networks within China's Floating Population* (Palo Alto, CA: Stanford University Press, 2001); R. B. H. Goh, 'Ideologies of Upgrading in Singapore Public Housing: Post-Modern Style, Globalization, and Class Construction in the Built Environment', *Urban Studies* 38.9 (2001): 1589–604.
50 Arieh Sharon, *Physical Planning in Israel 1948–1953* (Jerusalem: Government printer, 1951); Allweil, *Homeland*, 167–193.
51 Feige, *Settling in the Hearts*.viii.

Landscape Modernism and the Kibbutz: The Work of Shmuel Bickels (1909–1975)[1]

Elissa Rosenberg

In 1960, Shmuel Bickels, architect of the United Kibbutz Movement, contributed an article to a special issue of the gardening journal *Hasadeh Le-Gan Ve-Lanof* dedicated to the subject of the kibbutz landscape. Landscape, he argued, was central to the design of the kibbutz:

> The kibbutz is neither a city nor a village, and the gardenscape (*noi*) within it is not that of a village or of a city suburb. Nor is it a park in the traditional sense of a place of recreation. With the urbanistic development of the kibbutz settlement, the concept of the gardenscape has developed as a value of increasing importance. [...] The kibbutz settlement as a complete creation finds its full expression in the specific kibbutz gardenscape.[2]

His text, along with his sketches and diagrams, presented a new expanded vision of landscape that united aesthetic concerns with a social and ethical agenda. According to Bickels, the kibbutz landscape provided a spatial framework for everyday collective living and was inseparable from its architecture.[3] This vision suggests the need for an analytic framework that transcends the stylistic questions that preoccupied most historians of the kibbutz landscape, as well as its practitioners.[4] The issue of style has only obscured its fundamental innovation. Rather than describe the evolution of kibbutz planning in terms of 'geometric' or 'naturalistic' styles or compare 'formal' to 'informal' styles, this chapter proposes to situate the principles of kibbutz planning within the wider European discourse of post-war landscape modernism. Curiously, while kibbutz architecture has been clearly associated with the development of Israeli modernism, its landscape has not been studied through the same lens. Yet, just as the kibbutz served as an arena of experimentation for many of the pre-eminent modernist architects of the time, it was also a laboratory for an emerging local modernist landscape.[5] The kibbutz would have a significant impact on the development of an Israeli landscape architectural idiom.[6] This chapter examines Shmuel Bickels's concept of the kibbutz landscape in relation to the principles of landscape modernism and evaluates his unique contributions to this discourse. Though his focus was the kibbutz, Bickels's ideas resonate far beyond. His writings, together with his expressive sketches and drawings, present a remarkably rich and unique conception of landscape design as both a social and spatial idea.

Landscape Modernism

Landscape modernism is a term that remains open to interpretation.[7] The paucity of manifestos in landscape architecture accounts for the elasticity of the concept. Its principles have evolved since its origins in the beginning of the twentieth century, and frequently had distinct regional expressions.[8] In general, landscape modernism rejected the adherence to historical styles. It was based instead on a rational approach to the conditions created by industrial society, using contemporary materials and technologies, and social needs as a basis for form.[9] The landscape was viewed as a medium for social reform.[10] This development took place alongside a shift away from private garden commissions to larger-scale, more ambitious public work, especially in the areas of public housing and recreation. While private garden design had been associated with stylistic formulas, public design demanded a rational approach that emphasized functional considerations and social benefit. An early proponent of this new view was German Werkbund member, Leberecht Migge, a landscape architect who authored several manifestos in 1918 and 1919 on the modern role of the garden to improve urban life.[11] He viewed the rationalized garden as a natural extension to rationalized housing, based on the efficient use of new technology and a functional aesthetic based on simple geometric forms.[12] Migge was known for the utilitarian productive gardens he introduced in the new *siedlung*, or housing estates, to provide food and economic self-sufficiency for its residents as well as physical and mental benefits.[13]

By the late 1930s, the landscape architect Christopher Tunnard popularized these ideas in a series of articles published in the influential British journal *The Architectural Review*, urging landscape architects to engage with the new spirit of modern architecture: 'Our gardens desperately need new ideas. The first of these ideas must be the understanding that *modern landscape design is inseparable from the spirit, technique, and development of modern architecture*.'[14] There was a growing desire among landscape architects to break down disciplinary boundaries between architecture and landscape architecture, based on what they perceived to be a shared agenda that drew on a common set of social and aesthetic imperatives.[15]

However, the aesthetic of the modern landscape remained a vexing question. What form would the modern landscape take? What were its defining principles? And how were these unique to landscape, as distinct from architecture? Such a framework was notably absent from avant-garde architectural theory. For many modern architects, landscape remained generic and abstract. For Le Corbusier, for example, the landscape was a 'timeless' representation of nature, ideally viewed as a neutral foil for the building, an architectural object.[16] In their influential analysis of the 'International Style', Hitchcock and Johnson echoed this view, deeming 'untouched nature' as the ideal setting for modern buildings.[17] Even as landscape architects sought to align the discipline with architecture, critics such as Elizabeth Kassler pointed out the differences between the disciplines, stressing the singularity of landscape.[18] Landscape, she claimed, is not an 'architectural appendage' but must be interpreted in its own right and requires its own theoretical framework.[19] There was a general agreement that the new landscape aesthetic must be freed from the constraints of style and based instead on function – yet function was not enough.[20] The manifesto of the International Association of Modernist Garden Architects, an organization founded in 1938 by Tunnard and Belgian landscape architect Jean Canneel-Claes, reinforced this conviction: 'We consider that that the design of rational gardens must follow the principle of "function determines form." However, relying on function to create beauty does not preclude aesthetic concerns.'[21] A new spatial sensibility emerged in landscape architecture influenced by modernist architecture and the plastic arts, based on an idea of space that was continuous and flowing.[22] Abstract art and cubism influenced ideas of space, replacing symmetry and axial planning with spatial strategies of omnidirectionality, transparency, and overlapping planes.[23] These qualities were reinforced by an aesthetic of economy and simplicity which eschewed ornamentation and decorative forms, stressing 'the pleasure that can be gained from the contemplation of simple forms and flowing lines'.[24] One of the key effects of this spatial conception was the integration of indoors and outdoors as a single spatial unit.[25]

These ideas were expressed in planting design, which stressed the spatial qualities of vegetation over its horticultural, or decorative characteristics.[26] The sculptural use of a single plant reflected the structural, architectonic, and textural interest in plants, and stressed their functional benefits, such as providing shade and cooling. The modernist embrace of technology and social purpose led to a different understanding of nature.[27] Tunnard claimed that landscape design could no longer be based on a romantic desire for wilderness, which he dismissed as sentimental and misguided.[28] Instead, the modern landscape was to be a 'humanized landscape'. Tunnard wrote:

> Gardening is not a fine art: it is an art of the people. Do not go to the fashionable gardens for design inspiration. Go out and study the design of orchards, of truck gardens and experimental grounds where plants are grown scientifically.[29]

Christopher Tunnard's 1938 book, *Gardens in the Modern Landscape*, was a seminal text whose key concepts would find their way to Palestine in 1944 in Hebrew translation. Tunnard had argued for a new appreciation of landscape as an integral element of the planning repertoire, founded on a belief in its ability to provide social and environmental solutions that could respond to the conditions of modern life.[30] He argued that landscape must be released from the boundaries of the garden: 'The eighteenth century brought the landscape into garden planning; the twentieth century must bring the garden into the landscape. Through such a progress can arise the humanized landscape, the social conception of the countryside, and the garden of tomorrow'.[31] In 1944, landscape architect Jakob Schwarzmane (Shur) published an outline of Tunnard's approach in Hebrew translation, emphasizing the social conception of the landscape:

> Tomorrow's garden will no longer be a private garden plot bounded by a fence, but a complete unit forming part of the landscape, cultivated for the common good [...] gardens and nature are the foundations on which the growth and progress of the individual and society rests.[32]

Landscape architects and planners practicing in Palestine in this period would have also been familiar with German landscape modernism through the works and writings of Migge, Lange, Wagner, Koenig, and Barth,[33] some of whom were published in the professional journals in Hebrew translation.[34] Although Bickels did not reference Tunnard or other sources in his writing, these ideas appeared to be assimilated in his conception of the kibbutz landscape.

The Development of the Kibbutz Landscape

The kibbutz offers a critical lens on the emerging discourse of landscape in Mandatory Palestine, and in many ways served as a laboratory for the development of an Israeli landscape design culture as a whole. The kibbutz developed in the early twentieth century as a collective settlement based on an ideology of equality, shared property, and land and mutual aid.[35] It was not a traditional settlement that evolved organically, but rather one whose form was extensively debated, theorized, and planned.[36] The utopian social ideology of the kibbutz inspired new typologies of both buildings and landscapes. Architecture, planning, and landscape were deployed to create a new integrated spatial model developed within a relatively short and intense period by the independent kibbutz planning and engineering departments, the architects and landscape architects they worked with, and the active participation of the kibbutz members themselves.[37]

The realignment of public and private life on the kibbutz was a critical issue for its spatial planning. In contrast to the traditional enclosed German agrarian courtyard model of the *kvutzah*, the forerunner of the kibbutz,[38] or the monolithic mega-building that had been imagined by many utopian movements,[39] the expanding kibbutz was based on a low-density dispersed model based on modular growth and clear zoning of public and private functions.[40] The central core was given over to the public life of dining and cultural and leisure activities. New building types emerged to house new social institutions: the dining hall, which was the social centre of the settlement, various cultural buildings and the children's houses where children were reared communally. Adult members lived in apartments with a typical area of only 25 square metres, arranged in blocks.[41] In kibbutz terminology, this was not a 'house' or 'home' but was referred to as 'the room'. Only a small part of daily domestic life took place here; the communal realm of the kibbutz was effectively the expanded collective 'home', where eating, childrearing, and most leisure activities took place. Vehicular traffic was limited to the periphery and the kibbutz was organized on a hierarchical system of footpaths. In this way, open space became the connective tissue of the various functions of daily life that were now disaggregated from the domestic realm. In the absence of private property and the demarcations of individual lots, the collective open space formed a single flowing system that redefined the relationship between the public and private realms.[42]

Early modernist principles of rational planning and functionalism characterized the kibbutz landscape from the beginning. Landscape was approached as essential infrastructure, and planting was introduced to provide necessary shade from the harsh sun and to stabilize erosive soils.[43] In some cases, extensive tree planting took place before the permanent buildings were erected.[44] In the early period, landscape work was referred to as an 'improvement', underscoring its functionalist, instrumental character.[45] Only in the 1930s did gardening become valued in its own right, although, because it was viewed as an unproductive branch of the kibbutz economy, it remained a low priority in terms of budgetary and manpower allocations.[46] Simplicity, another key principle of modern design, was a constant theme in the local gardening literature, consistent with the kibbutz ethos of austerity.[47] Many of the landscape architects writing in the journals, particularly Schwarzmane (Shur), stressed the anti-bourgeois emphasis of the kibbutz garden, decrying ornament and any expression of ostentation.[48] In his 1944 article entitled 'The Garden and the Society', Schwartzmane (Shur) called for the development of new aesthetic principles suited to the social reality of the kibbutz.[49] Most gardening traditions, he noted, had served the ruling class, creating spaces that were inaccessible to working people. Only if these concepts are adapted to the social reality, he wrote, would the concepts of the garden cease to be an abstract concept and instead become an organic component of the new kibbutz society, 'in which the tree, the garden and nature will become the basis for the development and the advancement of the individual and of society'.[50]

A Garden for the Whole Day

Shmuel Bickels served as the chief architect of the Technical Bureau of the United Kibbutz Movement from 1951 until his death in 1975. After studying engineering and architecture at Lvov (Lemberg) Polytechnic Institute, which was then in Poland, Bickels emigrated to Palestine in 1933 and settled in Kibbutz Tel Yosef.[51] He was one of the few kibbutz architects of that period who was also a kibbutz member. He joined the Technical Bureau in 1937, one year after its founding. Bickels designed the master plans of over sixty kibbutzim, and over 25 cultural institutions including his masterpiece, the Museum of Art at Ein Harod, where his archive is located today.[52] Despite his prolific contribution to kibbutz architecture and master planning over the course of his long career, Bickels's work hardly figures in the mainstream histories of kibbutz and to this day has received little scholarly attention.[53]

In his writings, Bickels echoed Schwartzmane (Shur) and others in calling for a new definition of the garden to suit kibbutz society.[54] He rejected the nostalgic imagery of the traditional rural village, as well as urban and suburban landscape models, which he considered to be spatial expressions of a capitalist economy. The kibbutz, a new classless society, demanded a new form of landscape:

> The value of the kibbutz landscape is equal to all of its buildings; it is an organic part of the overall planning. The garden expresses the society that created it; not a 'display garden' and not a public park or cultivated landscape at the edge of the city, this is a

garden in which a person lives, works and rests. This is a garden for the whole day. I think that perhaps this is the best definition.[55]

The phrase 'garden for the whole day' captured the unique role of the landscape as the setting for everyday life. Bickels developed this concept most fully in his 1960 article 'On Some Problems of Gardening in Kibbutz Settlement Planning'.[56] Expanding upon the narrowly defined functionalism of the early kibbutz garden, Bickels stressed its aesthetic qualities: 'Its function is not solely utilitarian – although this is "a garden for the whole day", not a garden for recreation – but at the same time it has to serve as a distinctive formal frame visually and experientially.'[57]

The 'garden for the whole day' was characterized by the organic unity of architecture and landscape, which for Bickels was a cornerstone of kibbutz planning. This new unity signalled a radical shift in kibbutz planning. This shift has been commonly discussed by landscape historians in stylistic terms, who stressed the transition from geometric to naturalistic forms.[58] Style was also the defining framework for the practitioners of the time, who framed the debate in the gardening journals in terms of 'formal' and 'informal' styles. Bickels, however, evaded this stylistic debate, and instead explained the change in spatial terms [Figures 1–3].[59] His main focus was on the relationship of architecture to landscape. Whereas the earlier planning model was hierarchical, characterized by a

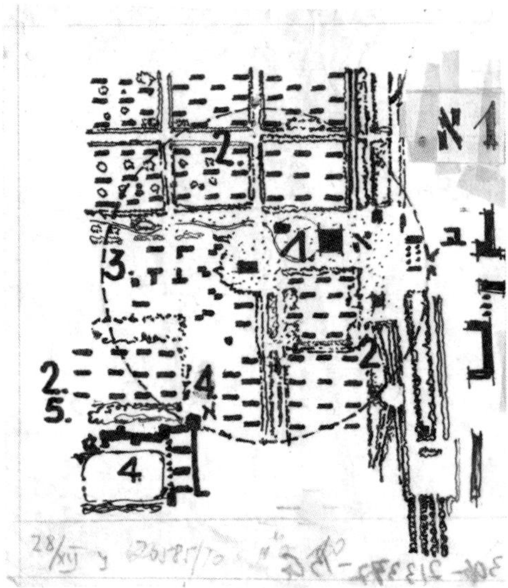

Figure 1: The first of three diagrams that were included in the 1960 article to illustrate the evolution of the open space of the kibbutz. In this diagram, the main open space is located in the central zone of the kibbutz, separate from the residential buildings. Shmuel Bickels, original ink sketch. Yad Tabenkin Archives, Ramat Gan.

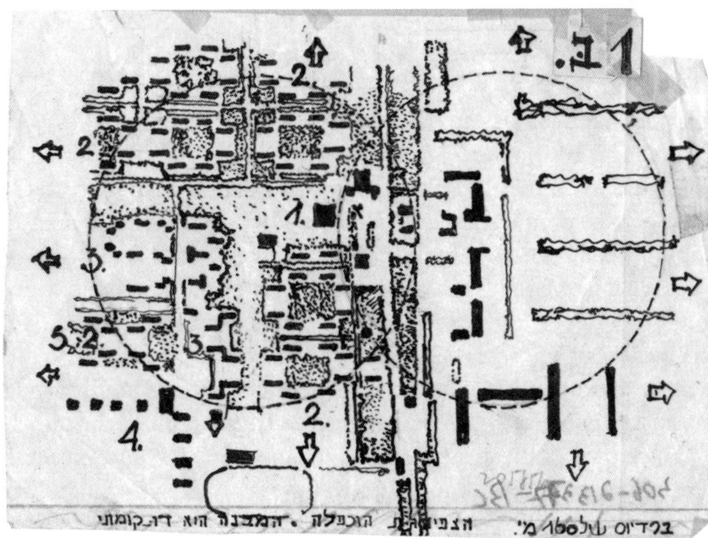

Figure 2: The second diagram represents a more integrated plan in which the residential gardens are integrated with the central open space. Shmuel Bickels, original ink sketch. Yad Tabenkin Archives, Ramat Gan.

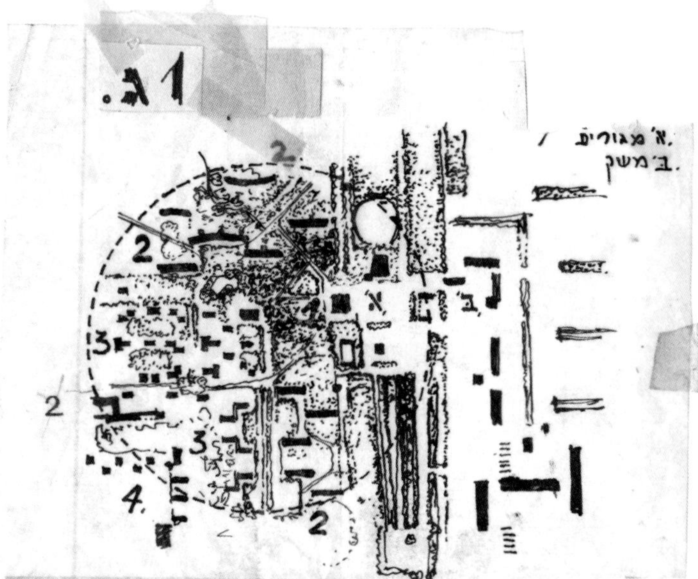

Figure 3: The third diagram shows the 'autonomous gardenscape' in which the residential zone is dispersed and set into the garden. Shmuel Bickels, original ink sketch. Yad Tabenkin Archives, Ramat Gan.

central open space flanked by secondary open spaces that surrounded the houses, the later model was non-hierarchical. Buildings and landscape had become fully integrated within a single unified, continuous landscape.[60] This model was not defined by its style but rather by an innovative spatial vision.[61] The morphology of the neighbourhood was no longer shaped by the logic of the parcel or the property line. Instead it was redefined by the new relationship between the public and private realms of the collective society, which emphasized the role of common space. Thus, landscape became the settlement's overarching, organizing idea, which, according to Bickels, also had a significant relationship to its regional context: 'Here the space of the garden opens on to the landscape, the region. The integration of the spaces here is complete, so that they are no longer defined by the buildings.'[62]

The question of how to design an 'organic synthesis' of buildings and landscape seems to have been a lifelong preoccupation for Bickels, as evidenced by the prolific sketches found in his estate [Figure 4].[63] His drawings add a deeper understanding to the 1960 text. Bickels's use of two drawing types – the analytical diagram and the eye-level perspective – reflect his holistic

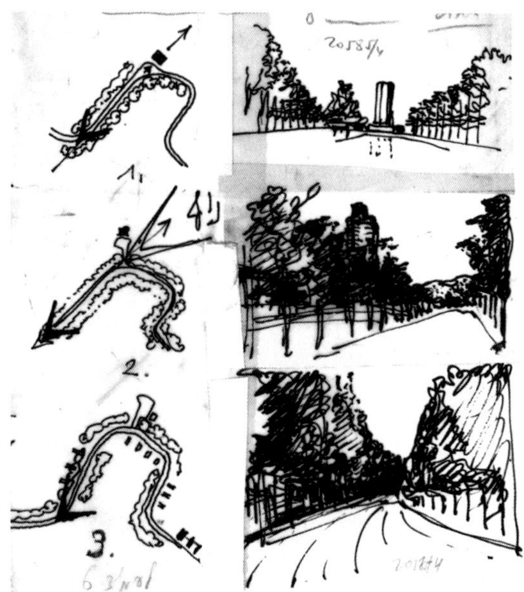

Figure 4: Bickels's concept of harmony between architecture and landscape is illustrated in the pair of sketches in the centre. This balanced condition is contrasted with the condition where the landscape is dominant, shown in the sketch above, and where the structures are dominant, shown in the sketch below. Shmuel Bickels, original ink sketch. Yad Tabenkin Archives, Ramat Gan.

understanding of landscape. He viewed landscape as a functional and conceptual framework for built form, and as a lived space. He used the diagram abstractly to represent new spatial models and to explore morphological questions, such as the siting of houses in relation to roads, topography, open space, and, significantly, in relation to views of the surrounding landscape [Figure 5]. The perspective sketches, on the other hand, stressed the visual and experiential dimension of landscape. In these simple, fluid drawings, he conveyed the visual impact of the kibbutz garden, alluding to its immersive quality. He noted that the long perspectival view of the landscape was at the core of its 'emotional experience'.[64] These illustrative eye-level-perspective sketches incorporated the active, moving viewer into the composition and approached the landscape as a source of visual pleasure and emotional power.[65]

One example of Bickels's affective use of landscape centred on the kibbutz entrance, which was the subject of considerable design study.[66] The entrance represented a 'significant problem, which [was] sometimes critical [...] to the first (emotional)

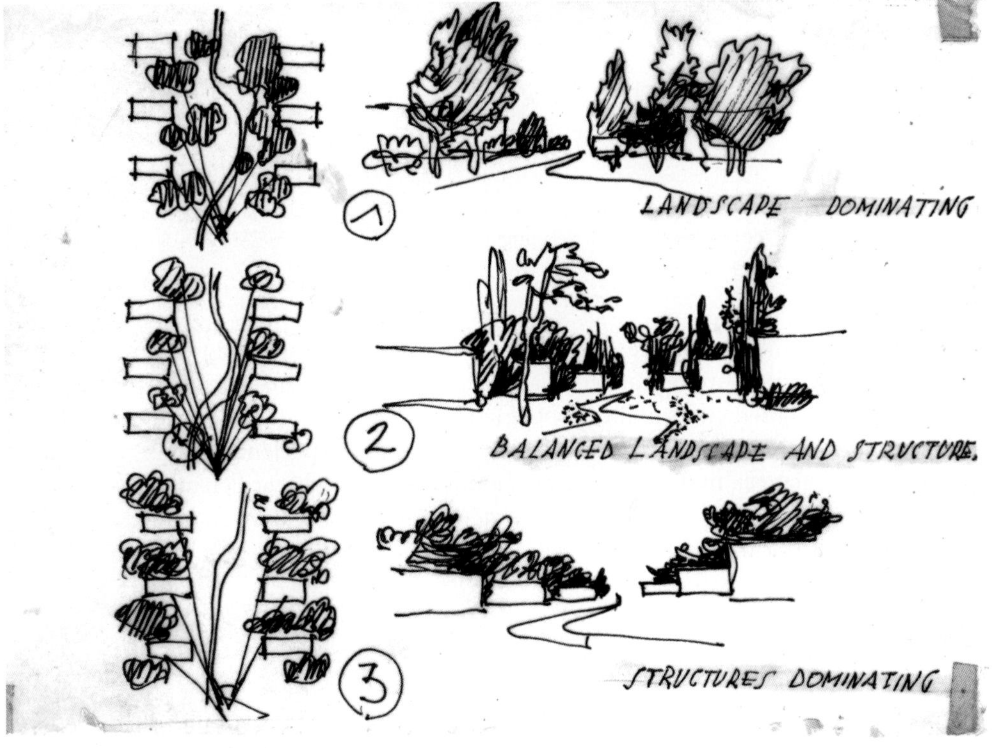

Figure 5: Plan and perspective sketches of three types of avenues of trees illustrating the effect of the view on the experience of space and movement. The first is an axial view terminated by an architectonic focal point; the second provides a vista to the distant landscape; and the third is open to lateral views. Shmuel Bickels, original ink sketch. Yad Tabenkin Archives, Ramat Gan.

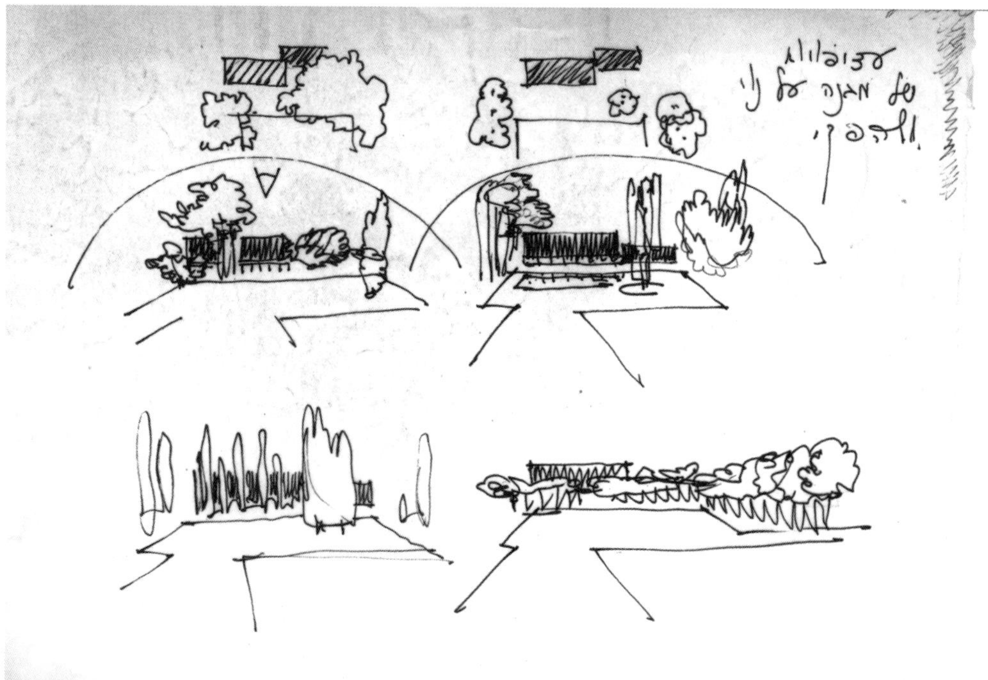

Figure 6: Four planting strategies illustrating different hierarchies of building and landscape: 'preference of building over the gardenscape, and the reverse'. Shmuel Bickels, original ink sketch. Yad Tabenkin Archives, Ramat Gan.

experiential encounter from the outside with the formal kibbutz way of life'.[67] Here he proposed the design of an entrance square to provide transition from outside to inside with carefully designed views of the kibbutz landscape [Figure 6]. This instance highlights Bickels's experimentation with form as a way of shaping experience, rather than out of any stylistic allegiance: 'In my opinion we should not totally discard elements of a formal garden just as we should not make the garden formless. We have to remember that a formalism of "no form" also exists.'[68]

The Kibbutz and the Region

The green landscape of the kibbutz stood in sharp contrast to its semi-arid Mediterranean context. It reflected and reinforced the prevailing ethos of 'something from nothing' that defined the modernist project of Zionism, a project of national renewal and rebuilding.[69] Few regional differences existed among the kibbutzim, despite their geographic diversity. Almost all were designed according to an Arcadian image, a landscape composed of spacious lawns and lush subtropical gardens.[70] This was clearly a 'constructed' not a 'natural' landscape; the work of the designer was aptly referred to as the 'creation of the landscape'.[71] The garden was a social artefact, constructed *ex nihilo* for human use. A small group of landscape gardeners and naturalists opposed the erasure of local identity that resulted from the indiscriminate and repetitive use of a limited selection of acclimatized plants.[72] Among these was the landscape architect Alfred Weiss, who lamented the disconnection of the kibbutz from the region and from the local culture.[73] In 1953, he described the kibbutz in this way: 'What has been created is a jumble of plants, a new green landscape with a strange and foreign look. A landscape without a past, without a cultural tradition and without restraint.'[74]

Bickels's concept of the region represented a minority view. His emphasis on the relationship between the kibbutz garden and its surrounding landscape was the basis of an idea of locality that ran counter to the dominant Israeli ethos of designing from a *tabula rasa*. He viewed the relationship of the kibbutz to the region as part of a spatial continuum, which he famously represented as a radial diagram of concentric rings overlaid on a textured, three-dimensional bird's-eye perspective of the landscape [Figure 7].[75]

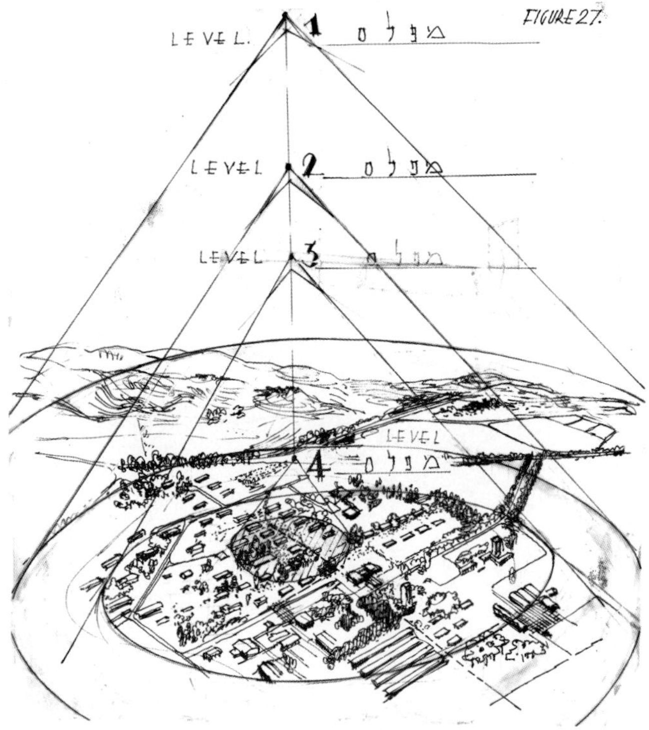

Figure 7: Radial diagram of a kibbutz, showing five levels of spatial organization: the region, the 'settlement zone', the 'settlement level', the 'sub-zone', and the underground level. Shmuel Bickels, original ink drawing. Yad Tabenkin Archives, Ramat Gan.

These rings, or 'levels', presented a series of nested spatial scales from the basic unit of the house and garden, to the larger scale of the settlement and on to the region beyond. The final ring represents the underground infrastructure that remains invisible, but nonetheless significantly shapes the kibbutz plan. Only by recognizing all of these levels, according to Bickels, can we get a full picture of the kibbutz gardenscape.[76] The concentric organization stressed the nested, interlocking relationship of each unit, presenting an idea of space that is flowing and continuous across scales: 'It is imperative to integrate the dominant of the external landscape into the planning of the central gardenscape.'[77] The diagram presents a comprehensive vision that stresses the interdependence of all scales and aspects, from the technical subsurface systems to the ineffable, experiential qualities of the surrounding environment. Whereas the gardenscape is described as an architectonic space, defined by 'depth, breadth and height', the region 'has an additional dimension-time'.[78]

In the master plans that Bickels designed, the relationship of the kibbutz plan to its regional context was often a significant feature.

> The topographic structure, soil and climate conditions all together (as well as each of them separately) pose a particularly serious problem in the settlement's planning. A settlement either in the maritime plain or in the valley will be planned quite differently from that

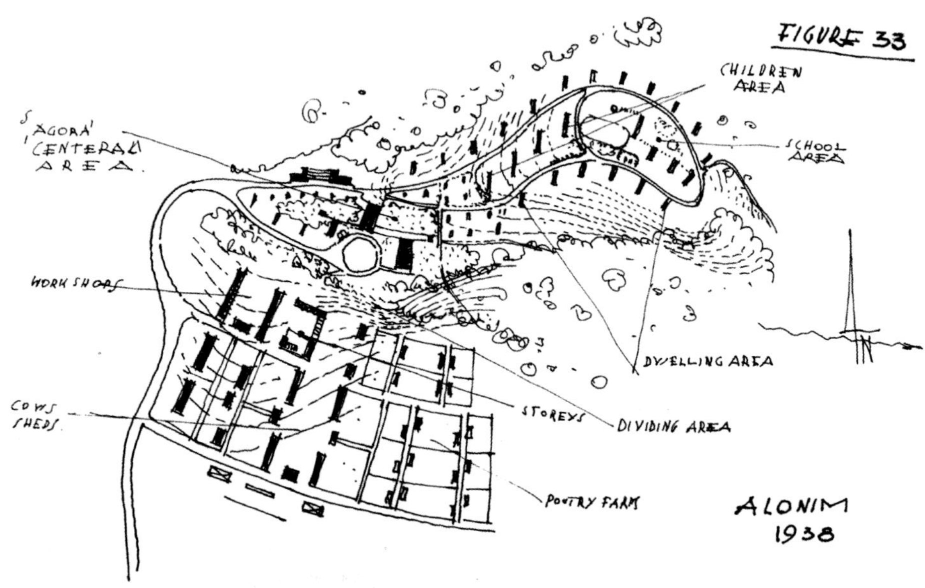

Figure 8: Plan of Kibbutz Alonim, 1938. Shmuel Bickels, original ink sketch. Yad Tabenkin Archives, Ramat Gan.

situated in a mountainous region [...] Climatic conditions in the different regions call for specific planning, adapted to the prevailing conditions.[79]

He broke down the kibbutz settlement into three regionally defined typologies: hillside, coastal (including on the Sea of Galilee), and desert.[80] Each of these geographic locations suggest a distinct morphology, with different site-planning strategies and building orientations. For example, in the kibbutz settlements of Manara, Beit Oren, and Misgav-Am, which Bickels planned in the 1940s, he developed various hillside typologies in which 'ribbon' housing formed linear terraces along the topographic contours. Alonim is another example in which the kibbutz plan was determined by the topography as well as the existing vegetation [Figure 8]. There the public buildings were located on the ridge and the houses were set into the slope and integrated into the native woodland of Mount Tabor oak (*Quercus ithaburensis*). The kibbutz was conceived as a wild natural garden in which the local maquis vegetation was preserved.[81] In the case of waterfront sites, Bickels describes the importance of creating open views of the water, such as at Kibbutz Ginosar (planned in the 1940s), where the open space is located near the shore and provided panoramic views of the Sea of Galilee [Figure 9].

Figure 9: Aerial view of Kibbutz Ginosar, 1939. Kibbutz Ginosar Archive.

Figure 10: Plan and perspective sketch diagrams illustrating the relationship of foreground planting to the views of the distant landscape. Shmuel Bickels, original ink sketch. Yad Tabenkin Archives, Ramat Gan.

The view was carefully used to connect the kibbutz to the surrounding landscape [Figure 10]. Through a series of sketches pairing plan and perspective views, Bickels illustrated the potential of the kibbutz garden to act as a framing device that situated the kibbutz within the regional landscape. This new reach of the designed landscape echoed Tunnard's claim that landscape must be released from the boundaries of the garden, and that the 'garden must be brought into the landscape'.[82]

Conclusion

Bickels explicitly associated the kibbutz with modern architecture: 'The kibbutz is an autonomous architectural creation, based on socialism, and whose form follows its functions, a creation of modern architecture.'[83] Although he did not discuss landscape specifically in these terms, his search for a new landscape model reprises many of the themes that were debated within the European and American search for the principles of modern landscape design. His definition of the kibbutz garden as an organic unity of built and open space reflects a modernist conception of space, based on the continuity of inside and outside and the integration of building and landscape as a single unit. The flowing space of the public realm, unfettered by the demarcation of property lines, recalls Tunnard's landscape version of the "'free plan" where "an attempt is made to let space flow by breaking down divisions between usable areas"'.[84] This open fluid quality of space provided a solution to the realignment of the public and private realms in the kibbutz. Like Tunnard, Bickels valued the 'humanized landscape', which was the defining feature of the gardenscape. This was not a pastoral, nostalgic garden, but space organized around human needs for everyday living such as comfort, shade, and rest. Functionality was a key consideration. According to Bickels, the configuration of open spaces is related to the design of efficient and comfortable walking routes, microclimates, irrigation, drainage, and sewage.[85]

Bickels expanded the modernist framework to include an emphasis on the regional landscape, and thus introduced the overlooked discourse of locality to kibbutz planning [Figure 10]. His text and drawings are remarkable for their nuanced blend of pragmatic, functional concerns with the emotive and experiential aspects of the landscape. The 'humanized' kibbutz garden, designed for everyday use, operated in dialogue with the larger landscape, or as Bickels described it, 'the experiential value' of the region.[86] His understanding of the regional landscape as a source of place identity, bound up with history, distinguished him from many of his architectural contemporaries designing the kibbutz.

The kibbutz landscape was an important arena for the development of landscape modernism in Israel. The vision of a 'garden for a whole day' provided the visual and experiential framework for the creation of a new collective society and affirmed the power of the landscape to enrich everyday life.

Acknowledgements

A version of this chapter appeared in Hebrew in *Cathedra* 162 (2016), 1–16.

Bibliography

Bar Or, Galia. 'The Initial Phases: A Test Case'. In *Kibbutz: Architecture without Precedents*, edited by Galia Bar Or and Yuval Yasky, 17–50. Ein Harod: Museum of Art, 2010 (In Hebrew).

——— *Our Life Requires Art*. Sde Boqer: Ben Gurion University, 2010 (In Hebrew).

Ben Arav, Yosef. 'On the Image of the Kibbutz Garden'. *Hasadeh Le-Gan Ve-lanof* 10–11.8 (1953): 131–33 (In Hebrew).

Benvenisti, Meron. *Sacred Landscape: The Buried History of the Holy Land Since 1948*. Berkeley: University of California Press, 2000.

Bickels, Shmuel. *Halacha Le'Ma'aseh*. Tel Aviv: Kibbutz Meuchad Planning Division, 1976 (In Hebrew).

——— 'On Some Problems of Gardening in Kibbutz Settlement Planning'. *Hasadeh Le-Gan Ve-lanof* 5–6.15 (1960): 229–39 (In Hebrew).

——— 'Theory and Practice in Planning of the Kibbutz Settlements'. *International Seminar in Rural Planning*. Jerusalem: Ministry of Foreign Affairs, 1961. Yad Tabenkin Archives, Ramat Gan, Israel.

Burmil, Shmuel and Ruth Enis. *The Changing Landscape of a Utopia*. Worms: Wernersche Verlagsgesellschaft, 2011.

Burns, Carol. 'On Site'. In *Drawing Building Text: Essays in Architectural Theory*, edited by Andrea Kahn, 146–67. Princeton, NJ: Princeton Architectural Press, 1991.

Chyutin, Michael and Bracha Chyutin. *Architecture and Utopia: The Israeli Experiment*. London: Ashgate, 2007.

Constant, Caroline. *The Modern Architectural Landscape*. Minneapolis: University of Minnesota Press, 2012.

Eckbo, Garrett, Dan Kiley and James Rose. 'Landscape Design in the Urban Environment'. In *Modern Landscape Architecture: A Critical Review*, edited by Marc Treib, 76–82. Cambridge: MIT Press, 1939, repr. 1993.

Enis, Ruth. 'The Impact of the "Israelitische Gartenbauschule Ahlem" on Israeli Landscape Architects'. *Die Gartenkunst* 2 (1998): 311–30.

——— 'On the Pioneering Work of Landscape Architects in Israel: An Historical Review'. *Landscape Journal* 11.1 (1992): 22–34.

Enis, Ruth and Yosef Ben Arav. *60 Years of Gardens and Landscape in the Kibbutz (1910–1970)*. Jerusalem: Ministry of Defence, 1994 (In Hebrew).

Forty, Adrian. *Words and Buildings: A Vocabulary of Modern Architecture*. London: Thames and Hudson, 2000.

Haney, David. 'No House Building without Garden Building!' ('Kein Hausbau ohne Landbau!'): The Modern Landscapes of Leberecht Migge'. *Journal of Architectural Education* 54 (2001): 149–57.

Har Gil, Gil. 'An Historical Analysis of the Landscape of the Kibbutz Garden'. Ph.D. diss., Technion – Israel Institute of Technology, 1992 (In Hebrew).

Helphand, Kenneth. *Dreaming Gardens*. Santa Fe, NM: Center for American Places, 2002.

Hitchcock Jr, Henry-Russell and Philip Johnson. *The International Style: Architecture since 1922*. New York: W.W. Norton, 1932.

Imbert, Dorothée. *Between Garden and City: Jean Canneel-Claes and Landscape Modernism*. Pittsburgh: University of Pittsburgh, 2009.

——— *The Modernist Garden in France*. New Haven: Yale University Press, 1993.

Kahana, Freddy. *Neither Town nor Village: The Architecture of the Kibbutz 1910–1990*. Tel Aviv: Yad Tabenkin, 2011 (In Hebrew).

Kassler, Elizabeth. *Gardens in the Modern Landscape*. New York: Museum of Modern Art, 1964.

Lange, Willy. 'The Natural Garden' (trans. Shlomo Oren Weinberg), *Alon Le'ganan* 7 (1944): 2–3 (In Hebrew).

Marx, Leo. 'The American Ideology of Space'. In *Denatured Visions: Landscape and Culture in the Twentieth Century*, edited by Stuart Wrede and William Howard Adams, 62–78. New York: Museum of Modern Art, 1991.

Mitchell, W. J. T. 'Holy Landscape: Israel, Palestine and the American Wilderness'. *Critical Inquiry* 26.1 (2000): 193–223.

Neckar, Lance. 'Strident Modernism/Ambivalent Reconsiderations: Christopher Tunnard's Gardens in the Modern Landscape'. *Journal of Garden History* 10.4 (1990): 237–46.

O'Malley, Therese and Joachim Wolschke-Bulmahn. *Modernism and Landscape Architecture, 1890–1940*. New Haven: Yale University Press, 2015.

Oren Weinberg, Shlomo. 'Planning the Kibbutz Garden'. *Hasadeh Le-Gan Ve-lanof* 1.1 (1945): 3–4 (In Hebrew).

Rose, James. 'Freedom in the Garden'. *Modern Landscape Architecture: A Critical Review*, edited by Marc Treib, 68–67. Cambridge: MIT Press, 1938, repr. 1993.

Rosenberg, Elissa. 'Landscape and Commemoration: The Kibbutz Cemetery'. *Studies in the History of Gardens and Designed Landscapes* 35.1 (2015): 25–42.

——— '"Something from Nothing": Constructing Israeli Rurality'. *Landscape Research* (July 2018 www.tandfonline.com/doi/abs/10.1080/01426397.2018.1472752).

Schwarzmane (Shur), Jakob. 'The Garden and the Society'. *Alon Le'ganan* 10 (1944): 1–2 (In Hebrew).

——— 'Towards a New Technique in the Garden – an Adaptation of Tunnard's *Gardens in the Modern Landscape*'. *Alon Le'ganan* 13–14 (1944), 4–5 (In Hebrew).

Shur, Yaakov. 'The Kibbutz Gardenscape'. *Hasadeh Le-Gan Ve-lanof* 4.2 (1949): 19–20 (In Hebrew).

Sluyter, Andrew. *Colonialism and Landscape: Postcolonial Theory and Applications*. Lanham, MD: Rowman and Littlefield, 2002.

Tal, Emanuel. 'The Structural Image of the Early Kibbutz'. Ph.D. diss., Tel Aviv University, 1991 (In Hebrew).

Treib, Marc. *The Architecture of Landscape, 1940–1960*. Philadelphia: University of Pennsylvania Press, 2002.

——— 'Axioms for a Modern Landscape'. In *Modern Landscape Architecture: A Critical Review*, edited by Marc Treib, 36–67. Cambridge: MIT Press, 1993.

Treib, Marc and Dorothée Imbert. *Garrett Eckbo: Modern Landscapes for Living*. Berkeley: University of California Press, 2005.

Tunnard, Christopher. *Gardens in the Modern Landscape*. London: Architectural Press, 1938.

——— 'Modern Gardens for Modern Houses: Reflections on Current Trends in Landscape Design'. *Landscape Architecture Magazine* 32 (1942): 57–64.

Walker, Peter and Melanie Simo. *Invisible Gardens: The Search for Modernism in the American Landscape*. Boston: MIT Press, 1996.

Yasky, Yuval. 'Landscape Urbanism: Landscape Design in the Kibbutz'. In *Arcadia: The Gardens of Lipa Yahalom and Dan Zur*, edited by Nurit Lissovsky and Diana Dolev, 231–58. Tel Aviv: Babel, 2012 (In Hebrew).

——— 'Neither City, nor Village – A Kibbutz'. In *Kibbutz: Architecture without Precedents*, edited by Galia Bar Or and Yuval Yasky, 17–50. Ein Harod: Museum of Art, 2010.

Zakim, Eric. *To Build and Be Built: Landscape, Literature, and the Construction of Zionist Identity*. Philadelphia: University of Pennsylvania Press, 2006.

Notes

1 All translations from Hebrew to English are the author's own, unless otherwise specified.
2 Shmuel Bickels, 'On Some Problems of Gardening in Kibbutz Settlement Planning', *Hasadeh Le-Gan Ve-lanof* 5–6.1 (1960): 229 (In Hebrew). The term 'gardenscape' is translated from the Hebrew 'noi' – a word that was coined in the context of the kibbutz and referred to the kibbutz landscape.
3 Ibid.
4 Ruth Enis and Yosef Ben Arav, *60 Years of Gardens and Landscape in the Kibbutz (1910–1970)* (Jerusalem: Ministry of Defence, 1994) (In Hebrew); Gil Har Gil, 'An Historical Analysis of the Landscape of the Kibbutz Garden' (Ph.D. diss., Technion – Israel Institute of Technology, 1992) (In Hebrew).
5 Prominent kibbutz architects included Bauhaus-trained Munio Gitai Weinrib, Arieh Sharon, and Shmuel Mestechkin, as well as other modernist architects such as Lotte Cohen and Leon Krakauer.
6 Yuval Yasky cites the influence of Bickels on the work of Israeli landscape architects Lipa Yahalom and Dan Zur, especially in their design of numerous kibbutz landscapes. He notes the 'paradigm shift' that Bickels brought to kibbutz design. Yuval Yasky, 'Landscape Urbanism: Landscape Design in the Kibbutz', in *Arcadia: The Gardens of Lipa Yahalom and Dan Zur*, eds Nurit Lissovsky and Diana Dolev (Tel Aviv: Babel, 2012) (In Hebrew).
7 Lance Neckar, 'Strident Modernism/Ambivalent Reconsiderations: Christopher Tunnard's Gardens in the Modern Landscape', *Journal of Garden History* 10.4 (1990): 237; Marc Treib, 'Axioms for a Modern Landscape', in *Modern Landscape Architecture: A Critical Review*, ed. Marc Treib (Cambridge: MIT Press, 1993), 36–67; Marc Treib, *The Architecture of Landscape, 1940–1960* (Philadelphia: University of Pennsylvania Press, 2002); Caroline Constant, *The Modern Architectural Landscape* (Minneapolis: University of Minnesota Press, 2012); Dorothée Imbert, *Between Garden and City: Jean Canneel-Claes and Landscape Modernism* (Pittsburgh: University of Pittsburgh Press, 2009).
8 Treib, *The Architecture of Landscape*.
9 Christopher Tunnard, *Gardens in the Modern Landscape* (London: Architectural Press, 1938); Treib, 'Axioms'.
10 Treib, 'Axioms'.
11 David Haney, 'No House Building without Garden Building!' ('Kein Hausbau ohne Landbau!'): The Modern Landscapes of Leberecht Migge'. *Journal of Architectural Education* 54 (2001): 149–57.
12 Ibid., 150.
13 Ibid.; Imbert, *Between Garden and City*.
14 Christopher Tunnard, 'Modern Gardens for Modern Houses: Reflections on Current Trends in Landscape Design', *Landscape Architecture Magazine* 32 (January 1942): 58.

15 The 1938 manifesto of the International Association of Modernist Garden Architects (AIAJM) stated: 'We consider that garden architecture is not a decorative art but a branch of architecture, inextricably linked to the problems of housing and urbanism and needed to fulfill the physical and moral needs of individuals and groups.' Imbert, *Between Garden and City,* 116.
16 Dorothée Imbert, *The Modernist Garden in France* (New Haven: Yale University Press, 1993); Constant, *The Modern Architectural Landscape.*
17 Henry-Russell Hitchcock, Jr. and Philip Johnson, *The International Style: Architecture Since 1922* (New York: W.W. Norton, 1932), 77.
18 Kassler wrote: 'Landscape art has a possibility that lies beyond architecture. It can offer an experience of architecture. It can also offer, with or without the assistance of architecture, an experience of universal nature.' Kassler cited in Constant, *The Modern Architectural Landscape*, 4.
19 Ibid., 5.
20 The Danish landscape architect Gudmundt Brandt argued that functionalism was limited and there was also a need to recognize the intangible, spiritual aspects of the garden. Imbert, *Between Garden and City*, 9.
21 Ibid., 116.
22 Tunnard, 'Modern Gardens', 60.
23 Treib, 'Axioms', 47
24 Tunnard, 'Modern Gardens', 63.
25 Ibid., 58. Garrett Eckbo, Dan Kiley and James Rose, 'Landscape Design in the Urban Environment', *Modern Landscape Architecture: A Critical Review,* ed. Marc Treib (Cambridge: MIT Press, 1939, repr. 1993); Treib, 'Axioms', 59; Tunnard, *Gardens.*
26 Treib, 'Axioms', 55–56; Tunnard, *Gardens*, 117.
27 Tunnard, 'Modern Gardens', 58–60
28 Tunnard, *Gardens*, 80.
29 Tunnard, 'Modern Gardens', 64.
30 Tunnard, *Gardens*, 81.
31 Ibid.
32 Jakob Schwarzmane (Shur), 'Towards a New Technique in the Garden – an Adaptation of Tunnard's *Gardens in the Modern Landscape*', *Alon Le'ganan* 13–14 (1944), 5 (In Hebrew).
33 Ruth Enis, 'On the Pioneering Work of Landscape Architects in Israel: An Historical Review', *Landscape Journal* 11.1 (1992), 32–33.
34 Willy Lange, 'The Natural Garden', trans. Shlomo Oren Weinberg, *Alon Le'ganan* 7 (1944): 2–3 (In Hebrew).
35 Galia Bar Or, 'The Initial Phases: A Test Case', in *Kibbutz: Architecture without Precedents*, eds. Galia Bar Or and Yuval Yasky (Ein Harod: Museum of Art, 2010), 17 (In Hebrew).
36 Emanuel Tal, 'The Structural Image of the Early Kibbutz' (Ph.D. diss., Tel Aviv University, 1991) (In Hebrew).
37 Before the kibbutz planning departments were established in the early 1930s, planning was undertaken by the Palestine Land Development Company, which was founded by the Zionist Organization. Bar Or, 'Initial Phases'.

38 Tal, 'Structural Image'.

39 Many utopian communities were based on a single collective building type, such as Fourier's Phalanstère. Tal, 'Structural Image', viii. Michael Chyutin and Bracha Chyutin, *Architecture and Utopia: The Israeli Experiment* (London: Ashgate, 2007); Freddy Kahana, *The Architecture of the Kibbutz 1910–1990* (Tel Aviv: Yad Tabenkin, 2011) (In Hebrew).

40 Bar Or, 'Initial Phases'.

41 Tal, 'Structural Image'.

42 Yuval Yasky, 'Neither City, nor Village – A Kibbutz', in *Kibbutz: Architecture without Precedents*, eds Galia Bar Or and Yuval Yasky (Ein Harod: Museum of Art, 2010).

43 Joseph Ben Arav, 'On the Image of the Kibbutz Garden', *Hasadeh Le-Gan Ve-lanof* 10–11.8 (1953): 131–33 (In Hebrew).

44 Enis and Ben Arav, *60 Years*.

45 Ibid.

46 Ben Arav, 'On the Image', 132.

47 Ibid.

48 Shur, Yaakov. 'The Kibbutz Gardenscape'. *Hasadeh Le-Gan Ve-lanof* 4.2 (1949): 19 (In Hebrew).

49 Jakob Schwarzmane (Shur), 'The Garden and the Society', *Alon Le'ganan* 10 (1944): 1–2 (In Hebrew).

50 Ibid., 2.

51 Galia Bar Or, *Our Life Requires Art* (Sde Boqer: Ben Gurion University, 2010), 255–56 (In Hebrew).

52 Ibid., 255.

53 Ibid., 256.

54 Shmuel Bickels, *Halacha Le'Ma'aseh* (Tel Aviv: Kibbutz Meuchad Planning Division, 1976) (In Hebrew).

55 Ibid., 17.

56 Shmuel Bickels, 'On Some Problems of Gardening in Kibbutz Settlement Planning', *Hasadeh Le-Gan Ve-lanof* 5–6.15 (1960) (In Hebrew).

57 Ibid., 231.

58 Enis and Arav, *60 Years*; Har Gil, 'Historical Analysis'.

59 Bickels, 'On Some Problems'.

60 The terms he used for these two models of open space are 'divided' and 'autonomous'. Bickels, 'On Some Problems'.

61 Ibid.

62 Ibid., 233.

63 Yad Tabenkin Archives, Ramat Gan, Israel (In Hebrew).

64 Bickels, undated handwritten notes and sketches. Yad Tabenkin Archives Ramat Gan, Israel (In Hebrew).

65 In his handwritten lecture notes (1957), Bickels wrote the following: 'Planned space has great influence on the psyche of the person who lives it [...] it creates experiences.' Yad Tabenkin Archives, Ramat Gan, Israel (In Hebrew).

66 Bickels, undated handwritten notes and sketches. Yad Tabenkin Archives, Ramat Gan, Israel (In Hebrew).
67 Shmuel Bickels, 'Theory and Practice in Planning of the Kibbutz Settlements', *International Seminar in Rural Planning* (Jerusalem: Ministry of Foreign Affairs, 1961), Yad Tabenkin Archives, Ramat Gan, Israel, 2. The word 'emotional' was crossed out and replaced with 'experiential'.
68 Bickels, 'On Some Problems', 238.
69 Elissa Rosenberg, '"Something from Nothing": Constructing Israeli Rurality', *Landscape Research* (2018).
70 Enis and Ben Arav, *60 Years*.
71 Ben Arav, 'On the Image', 132.
72 This group included European-trained landscape architects such as Alfred Weiss and Hanke Huppert-Kurz, as well as naturalist Azaria Alon, who published extensively in gardening journals in the 1950s and 1960s on the subject of native plants. Rosenberg, '"Something from Nothing"'.
73 Alfred Weiss, cited in Enis and Ben Arav, *60 Years*, 51.
74 Ibid.
75 Bickels, 'On Some Problems'.
76 Ibid.
77 Ibid., 239.
78 Bickels, 'On Some Problems', 230.
79 Bickels, 'Theory and Practice', 7.
80 Bickels, handwritten lecture notes (1957). Examples cited of hillside kibbutzim include Manara and Misgav Am; waterfront kibbutzim include Nachsholim, Ein Gev, and Ginosar (the latter on the shores of the Sea of Galilee); and Sde Boqer in the desert.
81 Shmuel Burmil and Ruth Enis. *The Changing Landscape of a Utopia* (Worms: Wernersche Verlagsgesellschaft, 2011), 136.
82 Tunnard, *Gardens*, 81.
83 Bickels cited in Bar Or, *Our Life Requires Art*, 259.
84 Tunnard, 'Modern Gardens', 60.
85 Bickels, 'On Some Problems', 235.
86 Bickels, undated handwritten notes and sketches. Yad Tabenkin Archives, Ramat Gan, Israel (In Hebrew).

Section II

Public Architecture as a Testing Ground

A Museum in Between: The Israel Museum, Jerusalem, 1965[1]

Eliyahu Keller

Ever since its establishment in 1965, the Israel Museum in Jerusalem has been considered one of the most important architectural works in the nation's history [Figure 1].[2] Studies have explored both its modernist roots and vernacular inspiration and pointed out its political implications and meaning.[3] Different views of the museum's design have swung from formal, historical, and ideological analyses, all of which have examined it through an isolating lens. Whether as a standalone architectural object, or within the political complexities that characterize Israeli architecture, the museum's place within a larger architectural discourse has been somewhat overlooked. This chapter will situate the museum as a representative of conceptual shifts, and as an expression of concepts that exceed the physical boundaries of its site.

Building upon recent historical research carried out by the architect and architectural historian Eran Neuman,[4] this chapter adds an additional layer to the museum's tale. It analyses its role within a wider cultural and historical context beyond Israeli borders. The analysis includes a comparison of the museum with another modernist icon: the Amsterdam Orphanage, designed by the Dutch architect Aldo van Eyck [Figure 2]. Several reasons call for this comparison: their historical contemporaneity, their designers' critique of modernism, their formal similarities, and their related conceptual and historical roots and inspirations. Through this lens – and following Van Eyck's 'twinphenomena' theory, which focused on a wholeness that is sustained by the differences in between the distinct parts – the Israel Museum and Amsterdam Orphanage become discrete, yet comparable expressions of post-war modernism.[5] The chapter focuses first on the museum's history and the people involved in its design, and then compares it to the orphanage.

The Background of the Museum, Its Architect and Interior Designer

Seventeen years after Israel's independence and only two years before the Six-Day War reshaped the country's future, Theodore Kollek took to the stage to inaugurate the Israel Museum [Figure 3].[6] The event was decorated with a row of banners, donors, and public figures, and framed by a view of the recently completed parliament building and the National Library. In his speech, Kollek, the future Mayor of Jerusalem, drew a clear connection between the establishment of the nation and its newest national institution:

Figure 1: The Israel Museum, view from east, Jerusalem, 1965 © Israel Museum.

Figure 2: Amsterdam Orphanage, Amsterdam, aerial view, *c.* 1960 © Aldo van Eyck. Courtesy of the Aldo van Eyck Archive.

Figure 3: Standing during the national anthem at the inauguration of the Israel Museum in Jerusalem from left to right: US Ambassador Walworth Barbour, Minister of Education Zalman Arran, Kadish Luz, Teddy Kollek, President Zalman Shazar, and Prime Minister Levy Eshkol, 1965. Photograph by Moshe Pridan © National Photo Collection.

> I cannot avoid the conclusion that it is Jerusalem and the Land of the Bible that impelled forty-three museums and famous collectors [...] to lend us some of their greatest treasures [...] They knew that their works of art would be on display only a mile from a frontier. They also knew that we are engaged in a great task of nation building. They were happy to take part in sharing our perils and our high purpose.[7]

As Kollek's words expose, the Israel Museum was viewed as an emblem of the link between architecture and politics, a connection allegedly shaping the entire history of Israeli architecture.[8] Designed by the architect Alfred (Al) Mansfeld and the designer Dora Gad, the museum is an example of the nexus of ideology, architecture, and the making of a sense of place.[9] Kollek, speaking of the museum's erection within Israel's process of nation building, makes the motivation for its constitution clear. The national institution was created to serve as a cultural symbol of the Jewish State and the fate of its gathered people, rather than simply a building to contain art. The history of this institution and the biographies of its designers reveal a complex story.

Thirty years after the establishment of Israel, the architectural historian Gilbert Herbert stated that 'perhaps the most significant architecture of a new country is that of its institutions [...] [T]heir importance is more symbolic than pragmatic'.[10] Indeed, the Israel Museum falls within this category. The conceptual cornerstone for its construction lies, however, in a historical process that precedes the establishment of the state. Martin Weyl, one of the museum's former directors, provides a glance into this process in an article celebrating the building's 30th anniversary.[11] His depiction, however biased, provides the historical framework that triggered the museum's establishment. He quotes Israel's first prime minister, David Ben-Gurion:

> Despite the daily preoccupations with defense and security, economic and social development, and housing the newcomers, it has been resolved to spend part of our resources, energy and talent in what is destined to become the most impressive cultural center in the country.[12]

This speech, given at the Israeli parliament in 1960, represents both the importance and challenges that characterized the project. As the German architect, Philipp Misselwitz, notes, the museum was indeed 'one of the most significant national institutions in Israel', but also one 'which, at the time, had neither funds nor content to match its ambition'.[13]

Ben-Gurion's words mark the final steps towards the fulfilment of an endeavour initiated by several Jewish European artists, the most prominent of whom was Boris Schatz, the founder of the Bezal'el School of Arts and Crafts in Jerusalem. Schatz had presented his plans for an academy and a museum to Theodor Herzl, the spiritual father of Zionism, and to the Seventh Zionist Congress.[14] Despite his crowd's limited concern 'with the issue of national culture, and even less with the question of art', his plan was carried out and the school was formed in 1925.[15] Schatz later secured support for the establishment of the Bezal'el Museum, an inseparable part of the adjacent school.

Weyl mentions Schatz's 'search for a new national style', which 'made it essential to collect local flora and fauna, archaeology, [and] folk art', and with which the ground for the museum was laid.[16] The site chosen was a complex of Ottoman villas in today's city centre of Jerusalem. For Schatz, Weyl notes, the act of bringing Jewish art into his museum was one of 'pure Zionism'; it was an ideological and political museology.[17] As the collection grew, the building too needed expansion, as well as a new name: the National Museum of Eretz Israel. As the number of Jewish immigrants from Europe grew, the collection kept expanding; its interests spanned from Judaica to modern art. The museum began to serve its cultural and Zionist purpose in full capacity, becoming the architectural and institutional analogue to the Israeli State. Whereas Israel was conceived as a haven for Jewish people, its National Museum became a sanctuary for the cultural and artistic collections belonging to and created by Jews from around the world. The National Museum was to art what the nation was to its people.

Kollek, serving as a delegate at the Israeli Embassy in Washington, DC in the 1950s, was first to realize the need for the establishment of an iconic structure as a national museum. His mission ended a decade later after funds were allocated from both the Israeli and American governments.[18] Towards the end of the decade a site adjacent to the Israeli parliament and the Hebrew University – the Hill of Tranquility – was chosen. After much bureaucratic preparation a limited architectural competition was announced, to which Al Mansfeld and Dora Gad had applied and won.[19]

Mansfeld's story also begins with a movement from Europe towards Mandatory Palestine. Growing up in Russia, and moving to Germany as a child, his life in 1920s Germany was greatly affected by the changing surroundings. In his personal account, Mansfeld describes the images of German castles and churches colliding with those of an evolving metropolis. Like many others surrounded by these contemporary changes,[20] Mansfeld and his brother 'listened patiently while watching the cars driving by', which were 'still novelty to us'.[21] Still, Mansfeld claims to have been even more fascinated by 'drawing and painting equipment'.[22]

After a brief and relatively unsuccessful career in graphic design, Mansfeld followed the advice of his teacher – the Russian painter Vadim Falileyev – and applied to architecture school.[23] As a student at the Technische Hochschule in Berlin, he was introduced to the idea of 'designing a building as an organic whole', which seemed to him to be a 'good didactic principle'.[24] In a recent study, Eran Neuman notes Mansfeld's exposure to 'notions of organic architecture espoused in contemporary German Expressionist circles'.[25] The guidance of architects Hans Poelzig and Heinrich Tessenow gave him the first taste of a modern avant-garde that was far from the rigid International Style.[26] Neuman claims that the expressionist ideas espoused by his teachers were a substantial influence and a formal and methodological inspiration for the design of the museum.[27]

His time in Berlin ended abruptly, following an expulsion from the school by SS (Schutzstaffel) officers. In 1933, Mansfeld moved to Paris to study under Auguste Perret. Berlin's organic expressionism gave way to the 'order and discipline' that dominated the halls of the École Speciale d'Architecture.[28] Mansfeld struggled with the modernist rationality espoused by his teacher. Mentioning an argument with his teacher, Mansfeld quotes Perret's statement that '[a]rchitecture is that which makes beautiful ruins'.[29] For Mansfeld, the concrete and steel modernist buildings were less likely to leave behind such beauty. Nevertheless, his writings stress that the lessons he had learned from Perret – such as 'the ability to develop clean ground plans and design logical structures' – found expression in his later work.[30]

After Paris, and partly due to financial difficulties, Mansfeld moved to Palestine in 1935, where his parents had already settled.[31] Like other young Jewish European-educated architects, he too immigrated to the Jewish 'Land of the Fathers' to pursue both professional and national ambitions.[32] For Mansfeld, not an active Zionist, the idea of a Jewish return to Land of Israel was exciting. He reached Palestine and was present during the 1947 declaration of UN Resolution 181, otherwise known as the 'Partition Plan for Palestine,' that effectively established the State of Israel in 1948. For Mansfeld the declaration of the foundation of the State of Israel was 'liberation from great peril, almost like a redemption'.[33]

In Palestine, Mansfeld would gain his most substantial professional experience while working with Munio Weinraub, a Bauhaus graduate and student of Hannes Meyer. Weinraub, Mansfeld writes, was a former employee of Ludwig Mies van der Rohe, and one of 'the few Jewish ex-students of the Bauhaus who consistently represented the school's spirit and minimalistic aesthetic'.[34] This was 'not a problem' for young Mansfeld, who began gaining recognition and commercial success.[35] Like many buildings designed by German-educated architects in Palestine, those created by Weinraub and Mansfeld demonstrated exemplary modernist architecture. A quarter-century later, and after Mandatory Palestine transformed into the State of Israel, Mansfeld earned a unique opportunity to design a project that would not only demonstrate his talent but would also become symbolic of the path taken by him and many other Jews.

The museum's interior designer, Dora Gad, collaborated with Mansfeld on the Zim ships project for almost a decade before working on the design proposal for the museum.[36] Awarding Gad the Israel Prize for Architecture in 1966 made her the first of two female designers to have ever won the prize since its establishment.[37] Gad, albeit somewhat overlooked by Israeli architects, is considered one of the most significant interior designers in the country's history, 'the main designer of the new Israeli establishment'.[38] Her projects included, among several others, the interior design of the official ships of the Israeli fleet, as well as that of the Israeli parliament.

The collaboration started during the museum's competition stage, to which the two designers, Gad and Mansfeld, were invited as a team.[39] After the project was awarded to the two, their separate offices worked together towards the execution of the winning proposal. Architect Ran Shechori notes in his review of Gad's career that the division of labour was clear. While Mansfeld's office focused on 'the constructional aspects of the work', Gad's contribution 'dealt with the building's finishes'.[40] Still, Shechori mentions that both Gad and Mansfeld articulated the museum's unique design strategy.

In the museum, Gad would express the unique combination of traditional and local motives and techniques within a contemporary and modern style, which was particularly characteristic of her work, 'creating an up-to-date mixture of tradition and contemporary art'.[41] The blend of styles, methods, materials, and approaches, combined with the overall structural logic of the museum's design, became a fitting symbol of the unique amalgam of cultures, histories, techniques, and inspirations.

The Museum: An Open Scaffold

Mansfeld and Gad's project employed a 'strategy of using a modular structure which could grew in stages'.[42] This architectural concept of 'an open-ended, evolving building process that has no historical equivalent' was, in fact, one of the first of its kind,[43] and still 'one of the most important yet little known examples of field architecture in the world'.[44] The budget constraints, Mansfeld testifies, were the catalyst for the use of an innovative design system.[45] Instead of designing what Mansfeld referred to as an 'empty monument', the designers created a 'museum that would grow slowly', taking after the organicism that he was exposed to in Berlin.[46] The motto for the project was 'Growth, Change and Uncertainty', values that were juxtaposed against the limitations of a rational three-dimensional grid system [Figure 4].[47]

The 'Luda model' system, based on a playful instrument, was comprised of balsa wood modules of defined proportions that 'could be shifted, pushed up or down, so that eventually the Luda model would reflect the spatial arrangements of a building'.[48] These defined the locations and sizes of all the building elements and allowed organic growth while preserving the boundaries of the site and the inner proportions of the building [Figure 5]. As Neuman notes, 'the Luda model – as its reference to homo ludens suggests – was about playfulness and the freedom to explore various possibilities within the system', while maintaining a systematic view of the entire project, 'its grammar and its cumulative potential'.[49]

The structuralist approach, which embodied a learning process, was a reaction to modernist determinism. In cybernetic fashion this model allowed Mansfeld and Gad to clarify the museum's concept but moreover to 'control the building process'.[50] For Mansfeld, it was a tool not only of conceiving architecture but also for communicating with the outside. It had the capacity to expound for the designers and clients the many ways and variations in which the museum could develop through 'time and space aesthetically, functionally and economically'.[51] The actual modules were built using contemporary, cutting-edge construction methods. A mushroom-shaped column, holding a hyperbolic parabolic concrete roof, at times only 10 cm thick, centred every module of space [Figure 6]. These were based on cubic units of 12×12 metres, and were designed in a way that would allow expansion without the need to demolish any of the exterior walls, as was requested in the project's brief.[52] The cubes could either be divided or joined by other modules, maintaining the relative spatial ratio. In between the cubes, intermediate links were inserted, connecting the modules to one another and providing the possibility of 'opening an entire wall to the view'.[53]

The mushroom column contains all infrastructural systems and provides for the roof's drainage, leaving the exterior concrete walls at minimal thickness.[54] Above, clerestory windows encircle the gap between the walls and roof, gracefully permitting light into the exhibition halls [Figure 6]. The volumes were exteriorly clad with traditional Jerusalem limestone, as required by the city's master plan and ordinance ever since British rule.[55] Thus, the stone cladding creates a contrast between the concrete dominating the interior spaces and the exterior façade of the building. Still, none of the traditional Arab masonry methods were used, and the cladding was sawed and polished, giving it the appearance of white stucco. Disassociating and dematerializing the stone from both its local practice and appearance had pushed the visual scales towards a contemporary look [Figure 7].

Figure 4: Growth diagram for the Israel Museum, 1959. © Al Mansfeld Archive.

Figure 5: Luda Model, 1975. © Al Mansfeld Archive.

Figure 6: The Israel Museum exhibition hall interior with the signature mushroom column, hyperbolic-parabolic roof, and clearstory window. Photograph from the exhibition *Social Construction: Modern Architecture in British Mandate Palestine*. Curated by Oren Sagiv. Photograph by Elie Posner, Jerusalem, 2016 © Israel Museum.

Figure 7: The Israel Museum under construction, Jerusalem, *c.*1965 © National Photo Collection.

From afar, the image of the Arabic village is evoked by Mansfeld and Gad. 'Mansfeld and Gad,' writes Yael Allweil, 'explicitly presented the Arab village typology as an illustration for their theory of cumulative spatial growth, on which they based the museum's design scheme'.[56] This is made clear by Mansfeld's sketch of an Arab village presented on one of the competition panels, and labelled 'village near Jerusalem'.[57] The white volumes, gently placed on the hill, faintly mimic the silhouette of local villages in various places in Israel and elsewhere. This, however, was an abstracted image, manipulated and processed through a modern and grid-based system. The mix of a modern methodology with vernacular motifs was not unique to Israeli architecture or the museum itself. It seems that this amalgam of cultures and styles was used as inspiration in other parts of the world.[58] For example, in Amsterdam, where no vernacular Arab settlements existed, similar images were being used to shift modern architecture towards a new path.

Negotiating Two Stages of Modernism

Providing Mansfeld with a 'strong but by no means exclusive guiding principle of the museum growth', the design system of the museum demanded something else.[59] It was, as architect and historian Zvi Efrat claims, Mansfeld's 'intuitive mediation'; a mediation, one could say, between modernist systematic logic and the absolute freedom of play.[60] Although Neuman suggests that this aspect is usually attributed to the typology of a traditional Arab village, or to the origins of expressionism, the Luda model's Latin name points to the writings of the Dutch philosopher Johan Huizinga and his investigation of play's cultural importance.[61] This nominal connection paves the way to a comparison between the Israel Museum and the Amsterdam Orphanage designed by the Dutch architect Aldo van Eyck between the years 1955 and 1960 [Figure 2]. Mansfeld, a self-declared structuralist like van Eyck, was undoubtedly aware of the latter's work. While the possibility of direct quotation is unlikely due to the overlapping years of both projects, the morphological resemblance, the relationship of both architects to the notion of play, and their attraction to vernacular architecture, call for further examination.

Van Eyck's professional history is full of spaces of literal play. As an employee of Amsterdam's planning department, he designed hundreds of playgrounds in the city beginning in 1948. Throughout his career – and the orphanage is no exception – van Eyck provided spaces for formative play.[62] Still, his ideas of playfulness permeated deeper levels of architectural understanding.

This profound insight stems from van Eyck's theoretical work and his critique of modernism,[63] a critique related to his investigations of vernacular settlements. As noted, Mansfeld drew inspiration from the local typology and image of scattered Arab villages. Gad, albeit in less of a structuralist fashion, also combined local motives and traditional techniques with her contemporary and modern style. Van Eyck too, and as part of his collaboration on the architectural journal *Forum*, was fascinated with the concept of collective form that resulted in critiquing CIAM's (Congrès Internationaux d'Architecture Moderne) modernism and its failed urban conceptions, while looking to the model of the kasbah.[64] It is my observation that the kasbah concept inspired by both Middle Eastern and South American settlements mobilized density and compact spatial organization towards a physical denunciation of the urban sprawl that modernism espoused. Offering a different past to be learned from, it rejected the modernist tabula rasa in favour of a local understanding, contextual local materials, and a new relationship with and appreciation of practical know-how.[65]

For van Eyck, the kasbah was a critique of individualist society; it offered alternative social structures and aimed to draw and learn from the 'image of collective form'.[66] The *Forum* members were attracted to this collectivity, which allowed 'the tight integration of built and open space characterizing these settlements'.[67] The Amsterdam Orphanage, the design of which coincided with *Forum*'s first publication, was a manifestation of these values.

To elaborate on these ideas, van Eyck coined the term 'twinphenomena', which would become his 'poetic interpretation of relativity'.[68] Applicable both to architecture and culture, it did not attempt to provide a single truth. Rather, van Eyck aimed to let two opposites, whatever those may be, remain in opposition, and with the 'correct level of tension […] achieve equilibrium'.[69]

For van Eyck, coherence lay not in the things themselves but in the way they related to one another.[70] Accordingly, the orphanage's design was not governed by a specific centre but rather by the relations between the different volumes, thus making the 'relations as important as the things themselves'.[71] The design created a spatial experience governed by the multiplicity of experiences between spaces, people, and ideas; an architecture that aimed to engage its users in a different manner than what its function traditionally demanded.[72]

Describing the orphanage through such means, Francis Strauven marks it as exemplifying 'unity and diversity', reading it as an architecture existing between two things.[73] In van Eyck's publication of the orphanage in *Forum*, he states that 'diversity is only attainable through unity, unity only through diversity; that unity and diversity are each other's mirror image'.[74]

The twinphenomena is expressed in the orphanage on several levels. The project, Strauven notes, is 'rooted as much in the classical as in the modern tradition'.[75] The plan, reminiscent of 'Fatehpur Sikri, Topkapi, Katsura, Alhambra', is composed of a repetitive spatial module, which establishes its framework and structure.[76] At 3.6 metres (11.8 feet) on each side, the squared modules are significantly smaller than those of the Israel Museum. Intended for the use of children, naturally, they provide a much more domestic scale than that of the museum's halls. This is further manifested in the geometrical organization of the modules, the Renaissance inspired courtyards, and the design of the façades of the modules themselves: 'a latter day version of the Classical Orders, with "architraves" resting upon columns and solid walls, covered with continuous eaves and crowned with domes'.[77] The domes – 328 small units and eight large modules, equivalent in their size to nine small modules – give the entire structure its visual identity; an identity that resembles, not unlike the Israel Museum, the image of an agglomerated kasbah [Figure 8].[78] The building's diversity and interpretative symbolism suggests that architecture is a cultural structure upon which various symbols and representations can latch. Situated within a paradox similar to that of Israeli architecture, the orphanage can be seen as symbolic of Israel's analogous problem, albeit on a different conceptual scale; for what is the Jewish State if not a type of national orphanage for those whose homes and ancestors have been taken away?

The design of the Israel Museum seems to be concerned with similar ideas, although the approach to the concept of play is used as part of the design process, rather than as a programmatic characteristic of the space designed. Rather than being a space for play, the museum is a result of the play embedded in its design process. Much like the orphanage, the museum too has no defined centre. Its central axis is neither dominant nor compulsory, and with the adjacent Billy Rose Art Garden (designed by Isamu Noguchi), it allows an array of circulation schemes. The dialogue is intensified by the rigidity of each space, and the subtlety created by the vertical positioning of volumes, which recalls 'the timeless wisdom and beauty of old oriental terraced town housing'.[79] The content of the museum provides the final note to this dialogue. Between styles, periods, and various geographies, the museum gathers and holds in tension a universe of oppositions and ideas.

As noted, the orphanage alludes through abstraction to classical orders.[80] The walls, columns, and architrave bear the load of its vernacular looking domes, visualizing a meeting of two traditions. The museum, on the other hand, takes another step away from this. Its traditions are subsumed under the logic of the white modernistic cubes and contemporary technologies. Similarly, the difference in material strategies in the two buildings is significant

Figure 8: Amsterdam Orphanage, courtyard with columns, architrave, and dome. Amsterdam, *c.* 1960 © Aldo van Eyck. Courtesy of the Aldo van Eyck Archive.

and inverted. In the museum, there is a stark contrast between the exterior white cladding and the dominant concrete of the interior space. In the orphanage, conversely, the industrial concrete appears in its exterior façades and its exposed interior ceiling. The exterior brick walls, circulating around the lower level of the building, permeate the interior space and remain unpainted. Combined with large curtain walls, they seem to blur the boundary between inside and out.

The structural system differs as well. The orphanage latches different visual content – that of the kasbah – on a classical tectonic structure in the form of columns, an architrave, and a dome. The classical scheme, however, is complicated visually by the utterly foreign image of the kasbah. The museum, on the other hand, uses an innovative structural technology, which enables more than the flexibility of function required by its program and use. The mushroom columns help free the walls from any structural or infrastructural responsibility, allowing a design strategy that makes the museum's infinite growth possible.

Still, and despite an abundance of differences, the museum demonstrates one of van Eyck's most noted statements on architecture and its relation to urban form: 'A house must

Figure 9: The Israel Museum, aerial view, Jerusalem, 2011 © Israel Museum.

be like a small city if it's to be a real house; a city like a large house if it's to be a real city.'[81] Indeed, the Israel Museum was designed to evoke the image of a small city, an image that would extend into its spatial organization as well. Yet, domesticity exists here too, within every intimate exhibition hall lit by the delicate light underneath its hyperboloid roof. It is, after van Eyck, both a home for art, and a city of art [Figure 9].

Between Nationalism and Internationalism

Architectural historian Alona Nitzan-Shiftan notes that it was modernism's 'lack of identity with forms associated with European nations' that gave Zionists the opportunity to claim modernist architecture and ideology as their own.[82] Furthermore, the notion of a tabula rasa provided a perfect tool for Zionism to claim an 'empty' land and endow it with a style and ideology in order to create a new sense of place. Although the cultural link of the Jewish people with the land had been cultivated for centuries, the physical surroundings did not demonstrate such a connection in an unequivocal way.. Alexander Keith, a minister for the Church of Scotland writing in the nineteenth century, had already described the Jews as 'a people without a country; [and] even [...] their own land, as subsequently to be shown, is in a great measure a country without a people'.[83] This phrase then became one of Zionism's most famous mottos, describing Mandatory Palestine as 'a land without people for a people without land', perpetuating the connection between Israel and the Jews while also questioning the very same connection.

This political engine driving the building enterprises in Mandatory Palestine and Israel was not only a matter of style, but also of twentieth-century, Zionist architectural scholarship, which focused on 'architects who shaped the built landscape of the Jewish population in Mandatory Palestine'.[84] Such studies presented 'a perfect fit between modern architecture and Zionism. Both Le Corbusier and the leaders of the Zionist Movement, the argument goes, were simultaneously creating "something out of nothing"'.[85]

The intentional connection between Zionist ideology and modernistic architecture is the reason that 'perhaps more than any other architectural tradition', as architect Sharon Rotbard writes, 'Israeli architecture has a tendency to reveal its own politics'.[86] He points to the import of the European International Style to the new city of Tel Aviv in the 1930s as a vehicle to connect modernism's ideas of progress with the pure forms and whiteness of modern architecture.[87] For Rotbard, the International Style is a manifestation of a modernistic fantasy, which problematically and paradoxically projects 'an image of the world as European, international and universal, all at the same time'.[88] This projection, he notes, had no place in Europe, and could only 'realize itself in the distant, heterotopic provinces of the continent'.[89] Israeli modernism, and the Israel Museum in particular, are a case in point.

Modernistic architecture became instrumental in this cultural and architectural construction. This unification of a non-place style with a one-place-only ideology has created two main streams within Zionism that were expressed in the architecture created in Palestine. The first was that of political Zionism, which aspired to make the future State of Israel a 'nation like any other, within a community of nations'.[90] This idea was represented by a group of Tel Aviv-based architects referred to as 'the Chug'.[91] The members of the Chug were European-educated architects who had brought the ideas and style of the modern movement to Palestine in an 'uncritical' manner.[92] It should be noted that Munio Weinraub, Mansfeld's first collaborator, was one of them. Their white and formally clean designs were perhaps adjusted to the climatic conditions of the non-European sites,[93] yet still demonstrated the ideals and ideological motivation of modernist architecture.

Yet this was not the only manifestation of modernist architecture in Mandatory Palestine. Nitzan-Shiftan also mentions the Jewish architect Erich Mendelsohn, who arrived in Palestine in 1934 and whom she aligns with the stream of cultural Zionism.[94] Mendelsohn's thoughts, intertwined with that of Jewish thinker Martin Buber, were not 'anti-nationalist'; rather, they negated internationalism in favour of 'super-nationalism', which 'maintains national borders, yet frees humanity'.[95] This view suggested a different relation between nations, rather the dissolution of national differences; a perception that is reminiscent of van Eyck's concept of the twinphenomena.[96]

The Israel Museum stands in between these national, international, and super-national worldviews. On the one hand, it continues the modernistic lineage stemming from Mansfeld's partnership with a Chug architect, demonstrating, with its white cubes, the uncritical modernism of which Rotbard speaks. Conversely, given its contextual inspiration, it could be viewed as critical of the Chug's modernism. Much like the views and architecture of Mendelsohn or even van Eyck, Mansfeld and Gad's proposal saw modernism's universality in a critical manner, and questioned its break from history and context. As such, the Israel Museum is an expression of a multiplicity of personal histories, national concepts, and architectural ideas.

Indeed, the museum strives to be not only a representative of Israeli architecture, but also an original object in its continuous formation, which demarcates a path towards what could be deemed today a national style, as it evolves through time and space. If we consider, however, a structuralist approach and a contemporary discourse at the time of its creation, the museum is one among many others, challenging the ubiquity of the International Style. Yet, perhaps there is a third way, another in-between. The Israel Museum, given its specific location, gives form to the universal investigations of local forms of knowledge in a specific place and time. As a testing ground, it comes forth as an original laboratory in which western ideas were given a supposedly pristine test tube in a local context.

Symbolizing the nation whose name it bears, the museum represents both an original entity with a clear yet problematic origin myth, and one that is an agglomeration of immigrants, traditions, and nations, stripped from their origins and brought into an existing and populated landscape. Between the modernist idea of tabula rasa, and the contextual, historical reality, the Israel Museum becomes a symbol, not only of Israeli architecture, but also of the inherent contradictions within the State of Israel.

Summary and Conclusion

Linking together personal, communal, and national histories, as well as local traditions, the Israel Museum is a unique piece of Israeli architecture. However, its uniqueness exceeds its aesthetic and formal expression, or the innovative design methodology it established. Rather, and as seen through the comparison to van Eyck's work, the museum comes forth as a manifestation of a never-ending negotiation between reciprocal parts and ideas. Fluctuating between the old and new, the local and the universal, the rational and the emotional, the innovative and the traditional, and the national and the international, the museum is both a representation of Jewish and Israeli culture and an example of the growing criticism of modernist ideals.

The multiplicities existing in a permanent tension within the museum offer an insight not only into its past, but also into its present and future, like those of the state. The use of an Arab vernacular indeed appropriates the local images and practices of the land, but also suggests, through collective form, a place for the creation of a community, albeit one that is still looking to define itself. Employing the style of its time to define itself as both new and eternal, the museum was and still is a tool in the formation of the national society.

Through the lens offered by van Eyck's twinphenomena, the Israel Museum becomes both a member in an architectural community of creations that sought to rearticulate modernist architecture in the decades following World War II, and a unique expression of the negotiations and conflicts between modernism's universal ideals and the specific realities in which modernist architecture made its physical marks. Lastly, the museum is also a personal work, embodying the particular experiences of its designers who were looking to articulate a public and national symbol: its past, present, and future.

The museum in between expresses the new twinphenomena in that it resides between the constructed image of the Promised Land and the artificial image of a desolated hill; between rigid concrete walls and the winding topography; between the politically ideological and the personally emotional; between the logic of an innovative model and the intuition of a free hand. The political and national history behind the establishment of the museum is now almost lost under the building's iconic stature. Indeed, it was the challenging conflux of specific conditions, histories, and contexts that gave birth to the amalgam of innovation and tradition offered by Al Mansfeld and Dora Gad. To this day, the Israel Museum is an icon of Israeli architecture not only as a built symbol, but also as a testimony of its own history and that of the Israeli State. So is the face of Israeli modernism and perhaps of the Zionist project as a whole: a troubled, yet almost miraculous birth; a confused, contested, and always politicized present; and above all, an unknown future. As Al Mansfeld would say: change, growth and uncertainty. Whatever histories the future holds, it seems that the Israel Museum will be there to record and represent them.

Bibliography

Allweil, Yael. *Homeland – Zionism as Housing Regime 1860–2011*. London: Routledge, 2017.

Ashbee, Charles Robert, ed. *Jerusalem, 1918–1920: Being the Records of the Pro-Jerusalem Council during the Period of the British Military Administration*. London: J. Murray [for the Council of the Pro-Jerusalem Society], 1921.

Barsky, Vivianne. 'Mobile Truth: The Israel Museum, Jerusalem, 1965/2010'. *Third Text* 27.4 (2013): 485–501.

Davidi, Sigal. 'Dora Gad | Jewish Women's Archive'. Accessed January 5, 2019. https://jwa.org/encyclopedia/article/gad-dorah.

Efrat, Zvi. *The Israeli Project: Building and Architecture 1948–1973*. Tel Aviv: Tel Aviv Museum of Art Publication, 2004 (In Hebrew).

——— 'Vernacular'. In *The Israeli Project: Building and Architecture 1948–1973*, 436–437. Tel Aviv: Tel Aviv Museum of Art Publications, 2004 (In Hebrew).

Eyck, Aldo van. *The Child, the City and the Artist: An Essay on Architecture: The In-Between Realm*. Writings, vol. 1. Amsterdam: SUN, 2008.

——— *Collected Articles and Other Writings, 1947–1998*. Amsterdam: SUN, 2008.

——— 'The Medicine of Reciprocity'. In *Collected Articles and Other Writings, 1947–1998*, 312–323. Amsterdam: SUN, 2008.

Frampton, Kenneth. 'Prospects for a Critical Regionalism'. *Perspecta* 20 (1983): 147–62.

Gad, Dora, Ran Shechori, Boaz Ben Menease, Richard Flantz, and Avraham Ḥai. *Dora Gad, the Israeli Presence in Interior Design*. Tel Aviv: Architecture of Israel, 1997.

Geva, Anat. 'Rediscovering Sustainable Design through Preservation: Bauhaus Apartments in Tel Aviv'. *APT Bulletin* 39.1 (2008): 43–49. Accessed January 5, 2019. https://doi.org/10.2307/25433937.

Herbert, Gilbert. 'Unity and Diversity: The Paradox of Israeli Architecture'. *Architectural Science Review* 21 (1978): 93–98. Accessed January 5, 2019 http://doi.org/10.1080/00038628.1978.9697241.

Huizinga, Johan. *Homo Ludens: A Study of the Play-Element in Culture*. Mansfeld, CT: Martino, 1994.

Isaacs, Reginald R. *Gropius: An Illustrated Biography of the Creator of the Bauhaus*. Boston: Little, Brown and Co., 1991.

Jaschke, Karin. 'City Is House and House Is City: Aldo van Eyck, Piet Blom and the Architecture of Homecoming'. In *Intimate Metropolis: Urban Subjects in the Modern City*, edited by Vittoria Di Palma, Diana Periton, and Marina Lathouri. London: Routledge, 2009.

Keith, Alexander. *The Land of Israel According to the Covenant with Abraham, with Isaac, and with Jacob*. Edinburgh: William Whyte and Co., 1843.

Levin, Michael D. *White City: International Style Architecture in Israel, a Portrait of an Era*. Tel Aviv: Tel Aviv Museum, 1984.

Lewitt, Irène and Muze'on Yiśra'el. *The Israel Museum, Jerusalem*. New York: Vendome, 1995.

Mansfeld, Alfred. *Al Mansfeld: Architekt in Israel = An Architect in Israel*, edited by Anna Teut. Berlin: Ernst & Sohn, 1999.

Misselwitz, Philipp. 'Landscape of Change, Growth and Uncertainty: Reworking the Israel Museum'. *Quader's d'arquitectura* 243.3 (2005): 18–31.

Neuman, Eran. 'Al Mansfeld and the Interpretation of the Israel Museum'. *Journal of Architecture* 20.3 (2015): 803–30. Accessed January 5, 2019 http://doi.org.10.1080/13602365.2015.1092166.

Nitzan-Shiftan, Alona. 'Contested Zionsm – Alternative Modernism: Erich Mendelsohn and the Tel Aviv Chug'. In *Constructing a Sense of Place: Architecture and the Zionist Discourse*, edited by Haim Yacobi. Aldershot: Ashgate, 2004, 17–51.

Oxman, Robert, Hadas Shadar, and Ehud Belferman. 'Casbah: A Brief History of a Design Concept'. *Architectural Research Quarterly* 6.4 (2002): 321–36. Accessed January 5, 2019 http://doi.org.10.1017/S1359135503001854.

Rotbard, Sharon. *White City Black City: Architecture and War in Tel Aviv and Jaffa*. Cambridge, MA: MIT Press, 2015.

Shechori, Ran. 'Projects for the State'. *Dora Gad, the Israeli Presence in Interior Design*, edited by Dora Gad, Ran Shechori, Boaz Ben Menease, Richard Flantz, and Avraham Ḥai. Tel Aviv: Architecture of Israel, 1997, 95–130.

Simmel, Georg. 'The Metropolis and Mental Life'. In *On Individuality and Social Forms; Selected Writings*. Chicago: University of Chicago Press, 1971, 324–329.

Strauven, Francis. *Aldo van Eyck's Orphanage: A Modern Monument*. Rotterdam: NAi Publishers, 1996.

——— 'Aldo van Eyck – Shaping the New Reality from the In-Between to the Aesthetics of Number' (Paper presented at *CCA Mellon Lectures*, Montreal, May 24, 2007). Accessed January 5, 2019 http://taak.me/wp-content/uploads/2013/05/in-betweenness_Aldo-van-Eyck.pdf.

Weyl, Martin. 'The Creation of the Israel Museum'. In *The Israel Museum, Jerusalem*, edited by Irene Lewitt. New York: Vendome Press, 1995, 8–21.

Yacobi, Haim, ed. *Constructing a Sense of Place: Architecture and the Zionist Discourse*. Aldershot: Ashgate, 2004.

——— 'Introduction: Whose Order, Whose Planning'. In *Constructing a Sense of Place: Architecture and the Zionist Discourse*, edited by Haim Yacobi, 3–16. Aldershot: Ashgate, 2004.

Notes

1 All translations from Hebrew to English are the author's own, unless otherwise specified.

2 Architects Alfred Mansfeld and Dora Gad received the 1966 Israel Prize in Architecture for the design of the museum. This prize had only been given thirteen times prior to 2013.

3 Zvi Efrat, 'Vernacular', in *The Israeli Project: Building and Architecture 1948–1973* (Tel Aviv: Tel Aviv Museum of Art Publications, 2004) (In Hebrew).

4 Eran Neuman, 'Al Mansfeld and the Interpretation of the Israel Museum', *Journal of Architecture* 20.3 (2015): 803–30. Accessed January 5, 2019. http://doi.org.10.1080/13602365.2015.1092166.

5 The 'twinphenomena' was a guiding concept for van Eyck. It suggested a worldview that draws from ideas of relativity, dissolution of established hierarchies, and a reciprocal relationship between parts. Francis Strauven, 'Aldo van Eyck – Shaping the New Reality from the In-Between to the Aesthetics of Number' (Paper presented at *CCA Mellon Lectures*, Montreal, May 24, 2007). Accessed January 5, 2019. http://taak.me/wp-content/uploads/2013/05/in-betweenness_Aldo-van-Eyck.pdf.

6 Theodore 'Teddy' Kollek served for six terms as Jerusalem's mayor, starting in 1965 and ending in 1993. Prior to his role as Mayor of Jerusalem, Kollek served as an Israeli delegate in Washington, DC as well as the Director of the Prime Minister's Office under David Ben-Gurion from 1952 to 1964.

7 Theodore Kollek cited in Viviane Barksy, 'Mobile Truth: The Israel Museum, Jerusalem, 1965/2010', *Third Text* 27.4 (2013): 485–501.

8 Neuman mentions Meron Benvenisti, an Israel political scientist and former Deputy Mayor of Jerusalem under Teddy Kollek, and states that 'several scholars linked the evolution of the museum's design to a tendency that underwent a considerable change during the period between the beginning of Jewish immigration to the Middle East and the establishment of the State of Israel. Initially, the immigrants treated the area as a tabula rasa, as a non-occupied land'. Neuman, 'Al Mansfeld', 806.

9 Though architecture can be linked to political aspirations and regimes before the periods to which Haim Yacobi points, the emphasis is on the formation of modern states and European nationalism that architecture wielded as a state tool. Haim Yacobi, 'Introduction:

Whose Order, Whose Planning', in *Constructing a Sense of Place: Architecture and the Zionist Discourse*, ed. Haim Yacobi (Aldershot: Ashgate, 2004).

10 Gilbert Herbert, 'Unity and Diversity: The Paradox of Israeli Architecture', *Architectural Science Review* 21 (1978): 95. Accessed January 5, 2019. http://doi.org/10.1080/00038628.1978.9697241. The title will be elaborated on in relation to Francis Strauven's reading of Aldo van Eyck's architecture in the section 'Negotiating Two Stages of Modernism'.

11 Martin Weyl, 'The Creation of the Israel Museum', in *The Israel Museum, Jerusalem*, ed. Irene Lewitt (New York: Vendome Press, 1995).

12 David Ben-Gurion cited in Weyl, 'Creation', 8.

13 Philipp Misselwitz, 'Landscape of Change, Growth and Uncertainty: Reworking the Israel Museum', *Quader's d'arquitectura* 243.3 (2005): 20.

14 Weyl, 'Creation', 9.

15 Ibid.

16 Ibid.

17 Ibid., 10.

18 Ibid., 13.

19 Ran Shechori, 'Projects for the State', *Dora Gad, the Israeli Presence in Interior Design*, eds Dora Gad, Ran Shechori, Boaz Ben Menease, Richard Flantz, and Avraham Ḥai (Tel Aviv: Architecture of Israel, 1997), 109.

20 For instance, in his seminal 1903 essay, 'The Metropolis and Mental Life', Georg Simmel offers an incisive look into the paradoxes brought up by the industrialization and modernization of city life and experience. Georg Simmel, 'The Metropolis and Mental Life', in *On Individuality and Social Forms; Selected Writings* (Chicago: University of Chicago Press, 1971), 324–329.

21 Alfred Mansfeld, *Al Mansfeld: Architekt in Israel = An Architect in Israel*, edited by Anna Teut (Ernst & Sohn, Berlin, 1999), 14.

22 Mansfeld, *Al Mansfeld*, 14.

23 Ibid.

24 Ibid., 24.

25 Neuman, 'Al Mansfeld', 808.

26 Ibid.

27 Neuman points specifically to Hans Poelzig's Soldier Memorial in Bad Berka from 1932, and its formal resemblance to the Israel Museum. Ibid., 816–24.

28 Mansfeld, *Al Mansfeld*, 24.

29 Ibid., 30.

30 Ibid., 30.

31 Ibid., 31.

32 Mansfeld mentions in his memoirs his motivation in moving to Palestine, as well as the move of several other architects educated in Europe around the same time. One of these was Munio Weinraub, with whom Mansfeld collaborated during his first years in Palestine. Ibid., 33–34.

33 Mansfeld, *Al Mansfeld*, 34.

34 Ibid.

35 Ibid.

36 Shechori, 'Projects', 109.
37 Ada Karmi-Melamed received the prize in 2007, 41 years after Gad.
38 Sigal Davidi, 'Dora Gad | Jewish Women's Archive'. Accessed January 5, 2019. https://jwa.org/encyclopedia/article/gad-dorah.
39 Shechori, 'Projects', 109.
40 Ibid., 111.
41 Davidi, 'Dora Gad'.
42 Shechori, 'Projects', 111.
43 The Israel Museum could be considered a predecessor to the mat-building typology of the 1970s, such as Free University in Berlin. Another example inspired by the kasbah concept and manifested in a mat typology is also from Israel. 'Shikon Le'Dugma' (meaning 'model settlement' in Hebrew) was a desert town project built between 1958 and 1966 in Be'er Sheva, the largest city in the Negev desert in the south of Israel. Often referred to in Hebrew as 'The Carpet Settlement', the project was designed by Israeli architects Dan Havkin and Nahum Zolotov (it was part of a larger planning scheme created with architects Avraham Yaski, Amnon Alexandroni, and Ram Karmi). This neighbourhood's aim was to 'provide an appropriate local form for a neighborhood in a desert climate'. Robert Oxman, Hadas Shadar, and Ehud Belferman. 'Casbah: A Brief History of a Design Concept'. *Architectural Research Quarterly* 6.4 (2002): 321–36. Accessed January 5, 2019 http://doi.org.10.1017/S1359135503001854.
44 Misselwitz, 'Landscape', 20.
45 Mansfeld, *Al Mansfeld*, 62.
46 Ibid., 20.
47 Ibid., 62.
48 Neuman, 'Al Mansfeld', 818.
49 Ibid.
50 Mansfeld, *Al Mansfeld*, 62.
51 Ibid., 62.
52 Shechori, 'Projects', 111.
53 Ibid.
54 Misselwitz, 'Landscape', 22.
55 Charles Robert Ashbee, ed. *Jerusalem, 1918–1920: Being the Records of the Pro-Jerusalem Council during the Period of the British Military Administration* (London: J. Murray [for the Council of the Pro-Jerusalem Society], 1921).
56 Yael Allweil, *Homeland – Zionism as Housing Regime 1860–2011* (London: Routledge, 2017), 213.
57 Ibid.
58 The architectural historian Kenneth Frampton points to such tendencies in his seminal article 'Prospects for a Critical Regionalism'. Separating the 'simplistic evocation of a sentimental or ironic vernacular', Frampton notes a tendency in architectural production in the 1960s, 1970s, and 1980s, in which the appearance of vernacular motifs in modern architecture is a conscious attempt to 'deconstruct universal modernism in terms of values and images which are locally cultivated'. Such an approach, Frampton suggests, acknowledges that

'no living tradition remains available to modern man other than the subtle procedures of synthetic contradiction'. Kenneth Frampton, 'Prospects for a Critical Regionalism', *Perspecta* 20 (1983): 147–62.

59 Misselwitz, 'Landscape', 27.

60 Ibid.

61 As mentioned, Neuman states that 'the Luda model – as its reference to homo ludens suggests – was about playfulness and the freedom to explore various possibilities within the system'. Neuman, 'Al Mansfeld', 818.

62 Huizinga points to the interwoven nature of the concepts of play and culture. Play, for Huizinga, is in part a preparation; a formative action that readies 'the young creature for the serious work that life will demand later on'. Johan Huizinga, *Homo Ludens: A Study of the Play-Element in Culture* (Mansfeld, CT: Martino, 1994), 2.

63 Karin Jaschke mentions the critique of modernist architecture made by various architects such as Team X and in particular Aldo van Eyck. This critique stemmed from the post-war need of these architects to 'respond to society rather than to reinvent it' as modernism aspired to do. Karin Jaschke, 'City Is House and House Is City: Aldo van Eyck, Piet Blom and the Architecture of Homecoming', in *Intimate Metropolis: Urban Subjects in the Modern City*, eds Vittoria Di Palma, Diana Periton, and Marina Lathouri (London: Routledge, 2009), 180–01.

64 Oxman et al., 'Casbah', 323.

65 Ibid., 326.

66 Ibid., 323.

67 Ibid., 324.

68 Ibid., 11.

69 Ibid.

70 Strauven, 'Aldo van Eyck'.

71 Francis Strauven, *Aldo van Eyck's Orphanage: A Modern Monument* (Rotterdam: NAi Publishers, 1996), 10.

72 The director of the orphanage, Francis van Meurs, created a brief for the project that was significantly different from the common brief for such an institution. Van Meurs 'did not want a boarding school or any other type of oppressive institution, but a house'. Strauven, *Aldo van Eyck's Orphanage*, 5.

73 Ibid., 10. Interesting to note, Gilbert Herbert used the exact same terms – Unity and Diversity – in his generalization of Israeli architecture. Herbert, 'Unity and Diversity'.

74 Aldo van Eyck, 'The Medicine of Reciprocity', in *Collected Articles and Other Writings, 1947–1998* (Amsterdam: SUN, 2008), 315.

75 Strauven, *Aldo van Eyck's Orphanage*, 12.

76 In his short text introducing Francis Strauven's book, Herman Hertzberger seems to deliberately refer to four examples – a sixteenth-century Indian city; a thirteenth-century Moorish fortress; a fifteenth-century Ottoman palace; and a seventeenth-century Japanese imperial residence – and their resemblance to van Eyck's orphanage, both in terms of their grandeur and non-western inspiration and appearance. Strauven, *Aldo van Eyck's Orphanage*, 3.

77 Ibid., 12–13.
78 Ibid., 31.
79 Ibid., 59.
80 Strauven, 'Aldo van Eyck'.
81 Aldo van Eyck, cited in Strauven, *Aldo van Eyck's Orphanage,* 11.
82 Alona Nitzan-Shiftan, 'Contested Zionsm – Alternative Modernism: Erich Mendelsohn and the Tel Aviv Chug', in *Constructing a Sense of Place: Architecture and the Zionist Discourse,* ed. Haim Yacobi (Aldershot: Ashgate, 2004), 21.
83 Alexander Keith, *The Land of Israel According to the Covenant with Abraham, with Isaac, and with Jacob* (Edinburgh: William Whyte and Co., 1843), 43.
84 Nitzan-Shiftan, 'Contested Zionism', Ibid., 17.
85 Ibid.
86 Sharon Rotbard, *White City Black City: Architecture and War in Tel Aviv and Jaffa* (Cambridge, MA: MIT Press, 2015), 161.
87 Ibid., 161–81.
88 Ibid., 162.
89 Ibid.
90 Ibid., 22.
91 Ibid., 17.
92 Ibid., 21.
93 Michael Levin points to the 'National Aspects of the International Style', by which he means the regional and national elements embedded in modernist architecture around the world. He specifically notes the 'attempts to adapt European International Style architecture to the climate of the Middle East'. Michael D. Levin, *White City: International Style Architecture in Israel, a Portrait of an Era* (Tel Aviv: Tel Aviv Museum, 1984), 71; Anat Geva, 'Rediscovering Sustainable Design through Preservation: Bauhaus Apartments in Tel Aviv', *APT Bulletin* 39.1 (2008): 43–49. Accessed January 5, 2019. https://doi.org/10.2307/25433937.
94 Nitzan-Shiftan, 'Contested Zionism', 30–33.
95 Erich Mendelsohn, cited in Nitzan-Shiftan, 'Contested Zionism', 33.
96 Not coincidentally, van Eyck himself refers to Buber's philosophy in the formulation of the concept. Karin Jaschke, who looks at van Eyck's critique of modernism's failure to address the issue of the domesticity of space, mentions that in addition to his interest in structural anthropology, van Eyck's twinphenomena stemmed from 'contemporary philosophical and anthropological writings, in particular Martin Buber's theory of the "in-between" and studies in anthropology that conceived of society and culture as structural entities, or systems of psycho-social and material relations'. Jaschke, 'City Is House', 185.

Genia Averbuch: Modernism Meets the Vernacular – Youth Villages for New Immigrants, 1948–1955

Sigal Davidi

Genia Averbuch (1909–1977) was a prolific architect, who launched her career in Tel Aviv in 1930[1]. In fact, she is often described as the unchallenged queen of modernist architecture in Tel Aviv.[2] She was one of the first practicing women architects in Palestine under the British Mandate (Mandatory Palestine, 1920–48), and among the first modernist architects in the country. Modern architecture, especially the International Style, became dominant in Tel Aviv in the early 1930s. The buildings designed in this style typically featured prisms, rectilinear geometry, long balconies with built-in shading elements, horizontal openings, and flat roofs. It was architecture devoid of decoration, and its exterior finish was usually non-textured white plaster. In pre-state Israel, Averbuch was a prominent and highly influential adherent of the International Style. She designed with creativity and with sensitivity to the local climate and left a substantial mark on the urban landscape of Tel Aviv, where she grew up, lived, and worked throughout her life.

In 1911, aged 2, Averbuch left Smila (now in Ukraine) with her parents, and settled in Tel Aviv. She studied architecture in the Regia Scuola di Architettura in Rome, and then in Belgium, first in Ghent and later in Brussels. In 1930, aged 21, she received her architecture diploma from the Royal Academy of Arts in Brussels. On her return to Tel Aviv, she pursued a professional career. At that time, women architects were rare in Mandatory Palestine as around the world. In fact, only three women architects were active in the country in 1930.[3] Tel Aviv, the first Hebrew city, a modern urban centre and the heart of the Jewish community in Mandatory Palestine, attracted many new immigrants. The large immigration wave of middle-class German Jews in the early 1930s was followed by intensive construction in the city, in which Averbuch played an important role. In 1932, Averbuch founded in Tel Aviv an independent firm with architect Shlomo Ginsburg (Sha'ag). Over the course of the 1930s, she designed numerous apartment buildings and urban villas, first with Sha'ag (until 1934) and later with engineer I. Greynetz. In 1934, at the young age of 25, she gained widespread publicity having won the prestigious competition for designing the Zina Dizengoff Square, which became the city's focal public space and a symbol of its modernity. The Zina Dizengoff Square, as well as many of Averbuch's apartment buildings, are located in the White City area, designated by UNESCO a World Cultural Heritage Site.[4] Many of her works were selected for preservation by the Tel Aviv Municipality. Of Averbuch's total output, her Tel Aviv works have featured prominently in academic research and in the media, gaining acclaim and broad recognition of her contribution to the development of modernist architecture in the Jewish Yishuv, and subsequently to Israeli architecture.[5]

After World War II, Zionist women's organizations, which were active in pre-state Israel, undertook to provide care and education for immigrant children and adolescents in Israel, many of whom were Holocaust survivors who had lost their families. They came forward to assist young refugees in rebuilding their lives in their new homeland. With this purpose in mind, they built youth villages with dormitories and schools, and converted existing

Figure 1: Genia Averbuch, Hadassim Children and Youth Village, near Even Yehuda, model, 1940s. WIZO Collection, WIZO Headquarters, Tel Aviv, Israel.

women's agricultural boarding schools into accommodations for both girls and boys. This social enterprise catered to one of the most urgent and central needs of the young state. From the mid-1940s through the mid-1950s, these women's organizations entrusted the planning of their youth villages to Averbuch, offering her an opportunity to mould the image of these new social establishments.

Unlike her Tel Aviv projects, where she strictly adhered to the modernist language, Averbuch now had to plan social establishments in rural environments. At first sight, her architectural approach and the style she developed for these projects are surprising. In planning these villages, Averbuch departed from the pure International Style of her earlier modernist work and used forms and materials that seemed to stand in contrast to modernism. She designed pitched red-tiled roofs on top of modern white buildings, arcades, and smooth and rough stone-clad walls. These were all extraordinary, even unlikely choices for Averbuch the modernist.

This chapter discusses Averbuch's architecture as manifested in three youth villages: the Hadassim Children and Youth Village near Even Yehuda (inaugurated in 1948, commissioned by the Women's International Zionist Organization [WIZO]) [Figure 1]; the

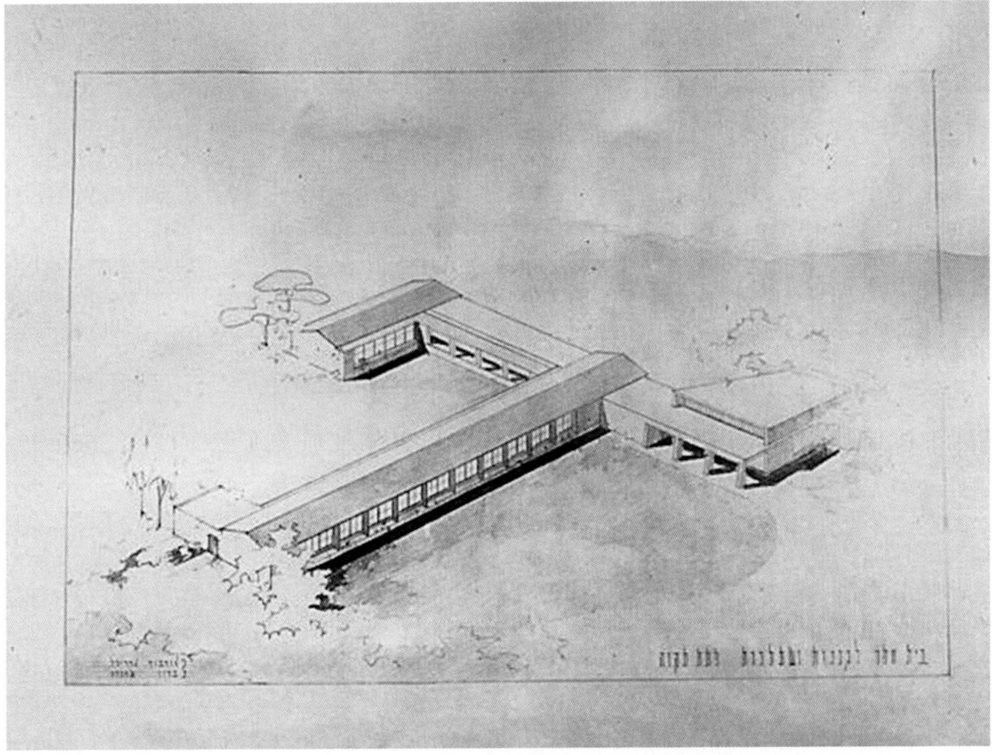

Figure 2: Genia Averbuch, Horticulture and Planting School building, Petah Tikva, 1954. WIZO Collection, WIZO Headquarters, Tel Aviv, Israel.

Figure 3: Genia Averbuch, Ba'it Va'Gan Children's Home campus, Jerusalem, 1955. Jerusalem Hills Children's Home Collection.

Horticulture and Planting School in Petah Tikva (1954, commissioned by WIZO and the General Council of Women Workers in Eretz Israel) [Figure 2]; and Ba'it Va'Gan Children's Home in Jerusalem (1955, commissioned by B'nai B'rith Women of America [BBW]) [Figure 3]. These villages, commissioned all by women's organizations, were built in the early years of Israel's statehood, and shed new light on Averbuch's work. All three represent her varied modernist work, manifesting her interpretation of local modern architecture and her way of formulating an individual architectural language under the influence of vernacular architecture (*genius loci*) and natural landscapes.[6]

Women Join Forces to Assist Young Refugees

Once the World Zionist Organization (WZO) acknowledged the urgent need to establish villages for Youth Aliyah children, the Zionist women's organizations immediately proceeded to promote their construction. The Youth Aliyah Organization was a WZO body set up to facilitate the immigration of Jewish children to Mandatory Palestine. The children, whose parents remained in Europe, arrived on their own, first from Germany and later from other countries as well.[7] From 1932 on, the Youth Aliyah worked to bring youth groups (and later younger children) to Mandatory Palestine, and place them in educational frameworks that could train them for life in agricultural villages. The youngsters were put up in kibbutzim and in youth villages that were in fact agricultural boarding schools.

The need to integrate the youngsters who were brought in by the Youth Aliyah led to revolutionary changes in the agricultural institutions established earlier for women by WIZO and the Women Workers' Council . Over the 1940s and 1950s, the women workers' farms (*mishkei po'alot*), established in the 1920s and 1930s to provide agricultural training to women, were gradually converted into agricultural boarding schools for youth groups of both genders.

Placing children in agricultural boarding schools was regarded as normative in pre-state Israel. It was viewed as an integral part of the Zionist revolutionary and pioneering ethos, even if statistically it only involved a small percentage of the total number of the community's youth. Under the British Mandate, youth villages groomed their students for significant sociopolitical tasks, eventually also caring for young Holocaust survivors and at-risk teenagers. From the 1920s through to the mid-1960s, the youth villages were perceived as prestigious schools for the would-be social elite.[8] Although the new youth villages were primarily built to provide a home for the thousands of children and teenagers whose previous lives had been shattered by World War II, the pioneering ethos made those agricultural boarding schools an accepted, even preferred educational alternative. The youth villages offered a unique combination of education, work, and group activity; they fostered a sense of connection to agriculture and nature, focused on body culture, and offered an opportunity to become part of a youth community. From the 1930s through the 1950s, these and other features of boarding school education turned the youth villages into powerful implements of social change.[9] Israeli sociologist Oz Almog claims that youth villages and agricultural boarding schools were unique 'sabra' (native Israeli) frameworks. The villages shaped the sabra personality and cultural imprint through Zionist-Hebrew education inspired by the myth of the pioneer.[10] The intensive lifestyle of these closely knit groups substituted the nuclear family in many ways.[11]

This model, which combined childcare with agricultural training, perfectly matched the philosophy of the Zionist women's organizations. Providing quality education and caring for children, 'developing Israel's most precious asset', was a top priority of both women's organizations and of the Zionist community in general.[12] The Zionist national goal of moulding a 'New Jew' leaned on agricultural-socialist ideals.[13] Youth villages were the arena where Zionist women's organizations were free to implement their ideology by training Israel's future generations for a life of rural, pioneering workers. Beba Idelson, leader of the Women Workers' Council, states: 'In other countries, agricultural schools provide education, nothing more. But here, we must tend and nurture these young plants to bear the fruits of agricultural and pioneering life'.[14]

'The Woman in Her'[15]

Zionist women's organizations and women architects formed a professional bond during the British Mandate, when women's organizations often invited women architects to participate in architectural competitions for designing projects for women. Winning such competitions meant further invitations to plan other establishments for those organizations.[16] In their projects for children and adolescents, these women's organizations upheld their policy of working with women architects, thereby demonstrating their wish to promote collaboration between women and advance women architects.

Averbuch participated in numerous architectural competitions, and won several prizes and citations.[17] In 1939, she won the competition for designing the Women Pioneers' House (lodgings for single urban women) in Jerusalem, together with engineer Zalman Baron, later her associate for 35 years. Winning this competition marked the beginning of Averbuch's professional collaboration with five Zionist women's organizations throughout the 1940s and 1950s.

By the 1940s, Averbuch was already held in high esteem by the architectural community and the Yishuv. Her work was widely acknowledged in local and international professional publications of the time, such as *Building in the Near East* – journal of the Eretz Israel architects' circle; in the daily press; and in women's magazines, such as the socialist *Dvar HaPo'elet* (the Women Workers' Council monthly magazine), as well as the bourgeois *Olam HaIshah* (*Woman's World*).[18] The female reporters of women's magazines took much pride in the work of women architects, underscoring their gender. Averbuch's first youth village (Kfar Batya, Ra'anana, 1947), received abundant accolades for its modern design:[19]

> One cannot remain indifferent to Genia Averbuch's work (*Woman's World* takes pride in this beautiful work by a woman [...]), who has managed to overcome all the difficulties and resolved all the problems involved in building a youth village that is both rural and modern in character.[20]

An article in *Dvar HaPo'elet*, celebrating the opening of the Horticulture and Planting School building in Petah Tikva, designed by Averbuch, also mentioned that the planner was a woman. In this case, the woman reporter also pointed out the ongoing collaboration between the women's organizations, the headmistress of the village, and the architect, throughout the process of construction, proudly stating, 'Women are building!'[21]

The protocols of pre-planning meetings of WIZO and Women Workers' Council representatives with the Ministry of Agriculture clearly indicate that the women's organizations gave preference to Averbuch in planning their villages.[22] Having collaborated with Averbuch in earlier projects, they were already familiar with her work, and even suggested including her in the decision-making process. As WIZO's Hadassah Goldgert said:

> I suggest contacting the engineer Genia Averuch, who has experience, having planned several institutions of similar character. She has solid opinions and the ability to thoroughly explore and understand any problem. Her suggestions could serve as a basis for future discussions.[23]

Youth villages were large and complex construction projects that involved planning the village master plan as well as designing individual buildings. That both WIZO and later the B'nai B'rith Women chose to entrust the villages' planning to Averbuch was proof of the confidence the women's organizations had in her professional abilities.

As already mentioned, Averbuch was involved in diverse projects. However, none of them defined her professional identity and underscored her gender more than her plans and designs for women's and children's establishments. Although her career covered all the professional aspects of architectural planning, her successful cooperation with women's organizations defined her publicly as a planner *for* women and children. Women's magazines that wished to promote women architects and advertise their success, inadvertently added conservative gender connotations to Averbuch's success. An article dedicated to Averbuch in the popular women's magazine *LaIshah* chose to emphasize the link between Averbuch's gender and her professional preferences: 'The woman in her drew her towards architectural endeavors related to women and children'.[24] In his 1956 *Encyclopedia of the Founders and Builders of Israel*, David Tidhar quoted this statement, thus perpetuating the idea in public awareness.[25] This clearly shows that Averbuch's gender and her portrayal as a planner for women and children significantly overshadowed her professional success in this distinctly masculine profession. Moreover, descriptions such as this one preserved the divide between 'feminine' and 'masculine' works even within the same profession. Labelling a certain style or field as 'feminine' immediately puts it at risk of being undervalued, and it has been shown to tacitly increase workplace inequality.[26]

In spite of expressions linking gender and profession, Averbuch pursued a successful career spanning five decades. She was a groundbreaker in many ways: developing a successful career in a predominantly masculine field; practising all aspects of architectural planning and urban development; and significantly contributing to the formulation of planning models for new social establishments.

Averbuch Builds Youth Villages for Women's Organizations

In its early years as an independent state, Israel took in hundreds of thousands of immigrants from Europe and the Arab world, among them many children who had lost their families or could not be supported by their parents. An urgent need emerged to look after these young people's welfare and education, and the women's organizations undertook to address it. The assistance of women's organizations in funding, planning, building, and managing the youth villages was invaluable.

The idea of setting up children's villages was first brought up by the women's organizations while war was still raging in Europe. As early as 1944, WIZO, whose activities were mainly dedicated to women's welfare and education, outlined necessary organizational changes, and emphatically expressed its desire to join the WZO in supporting immigrant children. A 1951 review of the villages' history, quotes the following pre-state message:

> Our idea is to establish a colony for immigrant children in the name of our Organization to help meet not only an immediate need but also to fit in with post-war building plans, to help take care of the large influx of refugees that we feel confident will be coming into Palestine.[27]

The first village WIZO planned especially for children was Hadassim. Construction, which began in November 1946, was carried out in stages, and lasted over a decade. Hadassim was designed as a boarding school for 500 children aged 8–18, both Holocaust refugees and Israeli-born, to create a heterogeneous community.[28] The village offered extensive agricultural training whose purpose was defined by WIZO as follows:

> to instill in the children and youth, entrusted to its [WIZO's] care, a love for the homeland and its soil; to give them a home, a sense of security, an all-round secondary education and to imbue them with the values that will make them good citizens of a democratic society.[29]

WIZO appointed Averbuch to design Hadassim, its largest project yet, even though it was their first joint project. Averbuch drafted the master plan and designed the buildings themselves. The construction was funded by WIZO's Canadian Federation (Canadian Hadassah-WIZO, CHW), which also paid for its maintenance.[30] It was built on a 1.1 km^2 plot located near the agricultural village of Even Yehuda (now a small town) in Israel's central coastal plain (*haSharon*), leased from the Jewish National Fund (JNF, HaKeren Hakayemet). Next to a school building and dormitories, a farm was built, complete with a herd of sheep and goats, a chicken coop, an orange grove and an orchard, a vegetable plot, crop fields, and a plant nursery. Averbuch planned ten children's dormitories, staff quarters, a kitchen and a dining room, two schools (elementary and secondary), as well as carpentry and weaving workshops [Figure 1]. Architect Alexander Klein, the supervising consultant for structures built on JNF lands, a world-renowned town planning expert, and a Technion professor, gave his approval to Averbuch's plans.

The success of the Hadassim project prompted WIZO to commission Averbuch to devise the master plan for the Horticulture and Planting School in Petah Tikva as well. The school, inaugurated in 1954, was one of a kind in Israel. Like many agricultural youth villages of the state's early years, it had originally been founded as a women workers' farm (*meshek po'alot*), an independent agricultural training farm for women. Its founders were women of the Second and Third Aliyah. After 1930, it came into the joint ownership of the Women

Workers' Council and WIZO, which also provided funding. In the years that followed World War II, the farm accepted orphaned young survivors who were brought to Israel by the Youth Aliyah. By 1952, mixed groups of immigrant and Israeli-born youth had graduated from the school and joined agricultural villages and kibbutzim.

In pre-state Israel, horticulture was perceived as a secondary agricultural category, even a luxury, compared with other agricultural crops that were more conducive to the advancement of the rural Jewish community. The idea of dedicating the school to horticulture was put forth by Rivka Braizman, the school's founder and first director, who saw it as a cultural, educational, and economic lever that would significantly advance the young state. Together with the Women Workers' Council and WIZO, and with the support of the Israeli Department of Agricultural Education, Braizman initiated and promoted the establishment of the school.[31] Many new cooperative agricultural communities (moshavim) built at that time, were in need of horticulture experts and instructors, to plan their landscaping and plant their gardens. Agricultural high schools and other educational institutions also required agricultural instructors and teachers. The new Horticulture and Planting School was designed as a two-year boarding school for 120 students. The curriculum included theoretical horticulture studies and practical work, as well as growing flowers and other houseplants in greenhouses and nurseries. The school's ultimate goal was to advance the young state by developing horticulture as a future agricultural export.[32]

The original 0.068 km^2 of the women workers' farm, with the buildings built in the 1920s and 1930s by Ya'akov Pinkerfeld, were used as an academic campus and living quarters. They featured three dormitories for students and staff, a dining room, and a laundry room. Averbuch designed the master plan of the new campus, an additional classroom building, and the greenhouses. The renowned landscape architect, Lippa Yahalom, was entrusted with planning the campus's arboretum. The school was inaugurated in September 1952, but the central classroom building [Figure 2] was not completed until 1954, with the graduation of its first class.

Another milestone in Averbuch's career as a youth village planner was when in 1952, the B'nai B'rith Women of America commissioned her to plan their new campus in Jerusalem – Ba'it Va'Gan Children's Home, opened in 1955.[33] B'nai B'rith had begun running a "Children's Home, Home for Maladjusted Children," in central Jerusalem in 1943 at the request of Henrietta Szold, after the arrival of the 'Teheran Children'.[34] At the time of its establishment, this home was the first of its kind in the country, and sheltered 35 children aged 7–14. Half of them were Teheran Children, and the others were locally born children who were referred to the home by the social welfare division of the Jewish National Council (Ha'Va'ad Ha'Leumi). The children were placed in the home for rehabilitation that was to prepare them for a normal life and regular schooling.

Initially, the home was funded and operated by B'nai B'rith, the Youth Aliyah, and the welfare department of the Jewish National Council. By 1949, the Ministry of Social Welfare and the Youth Aliyah were no longer able to meet their financial commitments to the children's home, and B'nai B'rith had to bear most of the financial burden of running costs.

By then, the home's capacity no longer met the growing needs, and many children had to be rejected.[35] To prevent shutting down the home, the B'nai B'rith Women Supreme Council (WSC, also known as B'nai B'rith Women of America) undertook to support it, as well as fund the establishment of a new campus at a cost of US $250,000.[36] In late 1951, the organization purchased 0.02 km^2 in Ba'it Va'Gan, a garden neighbourhood at the western-most edge of Jerusalem. Averbuch was commissioned to outline the campus layout, which was to eventually accommodate 100 children. First, she planned three buildings: two children's dormitories, to house 40 children; and a main building with the village priority facilities: classrooms, a club, offices, director and matron quarters, a clinic, and a sickbay [Figure 3]. The cornerstone (October 8, 1952) and inauguration (October 11, 1955) ceremonies were attended by prominent personalities: the mayor of Jerusalem, senior officials of the Jewish Agency and of the Israeli government, the Chief Rabbi of Israel, and a representative of the American Embassy.[37]

Vernacular Modernism in Averbuch's Youth Villages

While the architectural representation of urban Zionism was generally modernist in nature, another architectural style was used to represent the rather utopian Zionist ideology, dominated by the vision of cultivating and living off the land. The iconic image of the rural house was a white cube, with a pitched red-tiled roof. This was a common attribute of the Jewish rural landscape, which often featured in posters and publications of Zionist institutions, both in the pre-state era and in the early days of statehood. Women establishments followed this twofold approach. While urban women's establishments typically featured a modernist architectural style, the design of their rural counterparts displayed an effort to combine the modernist language with the symbolic rural one. The first Agricultural School for Women in Nahalal, planned by Lotte Cohen for WIZO in 1925, as well as most of the women workers' farms set up by the Women Workers' Council, adhered to that image.[38]

In the research literature, modernism is usually contrasted with local architecture and vernacular revival. In reality, however, from the mid-1930s onwards, many modernist architects endeavoured to capture the intimacy and natural quality of traditional vernacular construction, retaining at the same time a modern approach to materials, and showing great respect for nature. Leading modernist architects, such as Le Corbusier, Eileen Gray, and Charlotte Perriand, rediscovered vernacular architecture and the appeal of being close to nature and the simple life[39]. In pre-state Israel and in the early years of statehood, modernist architects made scattered experiments in introducing the vernacular into modernist architecture.

Architects such as Leopold Krakauer, Moshe Gerstel, and Arieh Sharon synthesized western and oriental elements, incorporating arches into their designs. Erich Mendelsohn even added three domes to the Hadassah hospital building shortly before its completion.[40]

Architectural historian Gilbert Herbert named this local modernist architecture, whose ideas and shapes derived from both international modernism and *genius loci*: the 'Bauhaus vernacular'.[41]

In the 1950s, as modern architecture and later Brutalist architecture became overwhelmingly dominant in Israel, Israeli architects experimented with borrowed traditional Arab materials and shapes, using rough local stone, vaults, and even adopting the traditional construction methods of unskilled labourers.[42] These sparse and tentative experiments did not become common and widespread until 1967, when adopted local materials and forms began representing the new Jewish neighbourhoods built around Jerusalem.[43]

In planning the youth villages in the late 1940s, Averbuch, a pioneer of 'pure' modernism in the 1930s, first experimented with the idea of combining the vernacular with modernist architecture. Her work sprang from distinctive circumstances: building in a rural landscape and meeting the specific programme of these unique youth villages. To this end, she chose a planning approach that gave preference to typical local characteristics over a system of universal principles. It was an approach that corresponded well with the ideology of the women's organizations, who wished the youth villages to convey an image of modernity and progress without changing or undermining the Zionist rural context.

Averbuch did not replicate any existing style in her work. Rather, she created a new vocabulary inspired by existing local architectural solutions. She used those solutions to create a personal lexicon of forms adjusted to the varied settings of the modernist style, without imitating the local oriental architecture. She incorporated local elements in her modernist language, using plastered walls that she integrated with stone-clad ones; and pitched red-tiled roofs next to flat roofs, arcades, and even arch-decorated façades. These were not meant to merely express rurality within modernity, but to produce a variety of complex forms that created a homelike rather than an institutional atmosphere.

In each of the youth villages, Averbuch designed covered walkways to facilitate movement between or through the buildings. The Hadassim dormitories, for example, had an adjacent staff apartment with a separate private entrance that was connected to them by an external arcade-like, flat-arched walkway. This allowed the children access to an adult supervisor without having to exit the building. These open passages were inspired by the local Middle Eastern arcades, providing much needed shading and ventilation in the almost year-round glaring sunlight and torrid heat of the local climate [Figure 4]. Notably, arches were not common in Israeli architecture of that time, highlighting Averbuch's unique interpretation of local modernism. In the Horticulture and Planting School, the classrooms were connected by a wide shaded and airy corridor-like passageway that provided additional space for student activity [Figure 5]. Similarly, in the Ba'it Va'Gan campus, Averbuch planned a walkway that connected the main building and the children's dormitories, but here she gave it a very modernist look – round steel columns supporting a thin concrete ceiling [Figure 6].

To avoid oversized buildings in youth village campuses, Averbuch designed interconnected geometrical masses that differed in height, materials, and roof shapes. In planning the Hadassim

Figure 4: Arcade-like flat-arched walkway in Hadassim dormitories, 1948. WIZO Collection, WIZO Headquarters, Tel Aviv, Israel.

dormitories, she evaded designing one massive structure by planning the ten dormitories as two visibly distinct units. By creating height differences between the ground levels and the roofs of the two parts of the building, and giving them different façades, she created the visual impression of two adjacent buildings, closer in proportion to a family home than to an institutional building. The two units were differently styled: the taller, more dominant, children's dormitory had an iconic rural design – a smoothly plastered white box with a red pitched roof, albeit with an arcade-like passageway. Adjacent to it stood the staff quarters – a partially stone-clad structure [Figure 7]. Averbuch designed in stone the garden stairs and retaining walls around the buildings, a landscaping feature that became popular in the 1950s, giving stone a material dominance. Her modernistic-vernacular design of the children's dormitories won great appreciation in WIZO circles. Over four decades later, Zvi Levi, the village manager between 1976 and 1993, continued hailing the design.[45]

Levi analyses the physical layout of Hadassim, and praises the children's dormitories, which were designed to create a homelike environment. Due to the great attention given to aesthetic and symbolic values, the dormitories were not perceived merely as a protected environment. According to Levi, the dormitories' compound was the most outstanding and attractive area of the entire village. Although all the dormitory buildings were similarly

Figure 5: Shaded passageway in Horticulture and Planting School, Petah Tikva, 1954. WIZO Collection, WIZO Headquarters, Tel Aviv, Israel.

Figure 6: Walkway connecting the main building with the children's dormitories, Ba'it Va'Gan Children's Home, Jerusalem, 1955. Jerusalem Hills Children's Home Collection.

designed, Averbuch managed to incorporate unique features in each of them. All the buildings had three levels, with up to four bedrooms per level. All the buildings had the same number of rooms, and similar adjoining units such as a recreation room, bathrooms, and a storeroom. Yet no residential building was identical to another; each building had differently designed outdoor stairs and varying surrounding greenery [Figures 7–8]. Levi mentions that the village design, particularly that of the children's dormitories, was perfectly adjusted to the establishment's educational goals. By positioning the dormitories and the staff apartments on the two sides of the village main street, the children actually walked along a traditional 'rural main street' that had all the characteristics of everyday family life: pets, bicycles, clothes hanging to dry, and so on. Levi notes that the village design distinctly reflected the founders' intentions: the children's dormitories were positioned in the centre, as children were considered the heart and core of village life. The dormitories stood next to the facilities that were at the children's disposal and away from loud noise, pollution, and the village edges, thereby giving the children a strong

Figure 7: Children's dormitory (right) and staff quarters (left), Hadassim, 1949. WIZO Collection, WIZO Headquarters, Tel Aviv, Israel.

Figure 8: Staff apartment (left) adjacent to children's dormitory building, Hadassim, 1950s. WIZO Collection, WIZO Headquarters, Tel Aviv, Israel.

sense of security. The design perfectly met the goals set by WIZO: 'to create a place that nurtures the child's spirit and mind based on freedom, within a community of peers, in a rural atmosphere'.[46]

The idea of creating a non-institutional appearance is clearly apparent in Averbuch's design of the Ba'it Va'Gan Children's Home campus. The main administration building, including the campus main entrance, was composed of several interconnected structures of different sizes and heights [Figure 9]. Together, they created a built-up façade overlooking the street that marked the campus boundary, concealed the children's dormitories that stood behind it, and hid the inner campus area from the street. According to Jerusalem building regulations, all building façades had to be stone-clad. Averbuch chose to use a reddish-brown *Wild Bau* – a random rubble masonry pattern, of the kind that was most commonly used in retaining walls and fences or as pavement material in pathways and yards. In the early 1950s, the *Wild Bau* cladding style was

Figure 9: Entrance of the Ba'it Va'Gan Children's Home campus. The main building, Jerusalem, 1955. Jerusalem Hills Children's Home Collection.

often used in Jerusalem's public housing projects, particularly in the Gonen (Katamon) neighbourhood, due to its low cost.[47] Averbuch's modernist architectural language is noticed in the walls' details. She did not choose using machine-cut rectangular stone claddings, which were popular among many modernist architects in Jerusalem. Her cladding stones, while following the random masonry pattern, were arranged in a way that created a smooth, even surface and did not accentuate the joints (as was often the case in other housing projects). Into this stone pattern, she introduced elements built in bare concrete [Figure 6]. Similar to other Jerusalem buildings of the British Mandate era, the windows had narrow cast concrete frames (and not the stone beams and sills of traditional Arab construction). Averbuch also created shading using thin concrete beams protruding from the dormitory walls, and, as mentioned, a shaded passageway made of thin steel columns with a cast concrete covering. The daily press praised the way her architecture blended into the natural landscape: 'The three buildings are built with pink cyclopean stone, and merge well with the mountainous scenery.'[48]

Figure 10: Genia Averbuch, Horticulture and Planting School building, Petah Tikva, 1954. WIZO Collection, WIZO Headquarters, Tel Aviv, Israel.

In planning the Horticulture and Planting School, specific attention was given to the issue of its architectural appearance. This is clearly manifest in the protocols of meetings held between representatives of the women's organizations and Ministry of Agriculture officials, during which the school's layout was discussed together with its pedagogical purposes and curriculum: 'Whoever comes here must feel that this is a horticulture school – not just a regular school of agriculture. It must be emphasized by the particular style in which its open spaces and buildings will be designed.'[49]

Averbuch designed a typical rural building, a kind of farmhouse, with a combination of flat and pitched roofs, open corridors, and closed spaces. Of the three planned wings, only the central one was finally built [Figures 2 and 10]. The entrance featured a wooden pergola that was shaded and decorated by vines. A press report published at the opening of the school's third year, noted with approval the school's rural appearance:

> Walking down Ehad Ha'Am Street near the center of town, one spots from afar, out of the trees and greenery that surround it, the big, spacious, white building, with a red-tiled roof in the rural style, and one immediately knows – the Horticulture and Planting School is here.[50]

The overall design of this building indicates the important role that the local climate played in choosing specific building principles. The classrooms' deep-set windows, the entrance pergola covered with vines, the open shaded corridor – all these elements served the building well on hot sunny days throughout the year, especially in summertime.

Genia Averbuch: Creator of a Unique Modernist Architectural Language

The youth villages built during Israel's early statehood years were modern socio-educational establishments, initiated by women to attain social and national goals deemed to be of utmost importance. They were funded, managed, and planned by women. Women's organizations viewed the architectural projects as visual manifestations of their public work, therefore putting much thought into the planning and design of their projects. The significance they ascribed to this architectural representation is also revealed in the contrasting architecture of their urban and rural establishments. In the city, WIZO and the Women Workers' Council preferred to express the collective presence of women in the urban sphere through 'white architecture' with a straightforward modernist look.[51] In the countryside, however, they aspired to uphold the Zionist rural image alongside modernist values of progress and innovation. Both the urban and rural buildings of the women's organizations stood out for their design, which challenged the boundaries and visions of contemporary architecture.

Even though Averbuch was acknowledged as quintessentially modernistic throughout her career, in designing the youth villages she introduced a unique style and her own personal interpretation of a modern rural building approach. The projects she designed for women's organizations allowed Averbuch to experiment with and develop an original architectural language. Unlike the urban projects she planned for Tel Aviv's middle class, the rural orientation of her youth village projects enabled her to convey a regional identity and create an original architectural language. Through rich use of materials and forms, she created a personal modernist language that was inspired by nature and local traditions. She perceived regionalism as one facet of modernism, rather than its antithesis.

In the 1950s, Averbuch continued planning apartment buildings in Tel Aviv in a distinctively modernist style. However, the lasting effect that the youth village projects had on her is evident in the way that she planned her own private residence in 1957. Although the house stands in central Tel Aviv, she designed it in the vein of vernacular modernism.

Bibliography

Almog, Oz. *The Sabra – The Creation of a New Jew*. Tel Aviv: Am Oved, 1997. (In Hebrew).

Alper, Rivka. 'How Have We Reached Graduation Parties!' *Dvar HaPo'elet* 9 (September 1954): 196–98 (In Hebrew).

Barkai, Sam and Julius Posener. 'Habitations Individuelles. Architects: Averbough et Ginzburg'. *L'Architecture d'Aujourd'hui* 9, no. 9 (September 1937): 23.

Benton, Tim. 'Modernism and Nature'. In *Modernism: Designing a New World 1924–1939*, edited by Christopher Wilk, 311–39. London: V&A Publications, 2006.

'The Children's Village Grows Up'. *Wizo in Israel* IV.29 (1951): 10.

David Zaidenberg, Mikve Yisrael agriculture school representative, meeting minutes, April 1952. IV-104-1200-14. Rivka Braizman personal archive, Pinchas Lavon Institute for Labour Movement Research, Tel Aviv (Lavon Institute) (In Hebrew).

Davidi, Sigal. 'The Women Architects of Mandatory Palestine and the Creation of Social Modernism'. Ph.D. diss., Tel Aviv University, 2015 (In Hebrew).

——— 'By Women for Women: Modernism, Architecture and Gender in Building the New Jewish Society in Mandatory Palestine'. *Architectural Research Quarterly* 20, no. 3 (2016): 217–30.

——— 'From the Margins to the Center: Urban housing for single Jewish women in pre-state Israel'. *Women's History Review* 28, no. 1 (2019): 85–110.

——— 'German and Austrian Women Architects in Mandatory Palestine, 1920–1948'. In *Frau Architekt: Over 100 Years of Women in Architecture*, edited by Mary Pepchinski, Christina Budde, Wolfgang Voigt, and Peter Cachola Schmal, Frankfurt-am-Main: Wasmuth & Deutsches Architekturmuseum, 2017, 49–57.

Efrat, Zvi. *The Israeli Project: Building and Architecture, 1948–1973*. Tel Aviv: Tel Aviv Museum of Art, 2004 (In Hebrew).

'An Exemplary Youth Village'. *Olam HaIsha*, September 30, 1947 : 6 (In Hebrew).

'First Prize Awarded to Woman Architect'. *Palestine Post*, August 6, 1944 : 3.

Gelber, Yoav. *New Homeland: The Immigration and Absorption of Central European Jews 1933–1948*. Jerusalem: Yad Izhak Ben-Zvi, 1990 (In Hebrew).

——— 'The Shaping of the "New Jew" in Eretz Yisrael'. In *Major Changes Within the Jewish People in the Wake of the Holocaust*, edited by Yisrael Gutman, 443–61. Jerusalem: Yad Vashem, 1996.

'Genia Averbuch, the Tel Aviv Bauhaus Queen'. Accessed June 30, 2017. http://www.mytelaviv.co.il/GeniaAberboch (In Hebrew).

'Genia Averbuch: A Groundbreaking Woman Architect in Tel Aviv'. *Globes*, January 9, 2011. Accessed December 18, 2018. https://www.globes.co.il/news/article.aspx?did=1000614096 (In Hebrew).

Grundig, Lea. 'The Woman Architect of Eretz Yisrael'. *Dvar HaPo'elet* 2–3 (March 16, 1948): 25–26 (In Hebrew).

Herbert, Gilbert and Silvina Sosnovsky. *Bauhaus on the Carmel and the Crossroads of Empire*. Jerusalem: Yad Izhak Ben-Zvi, 1993.

Herbert, Gilbert. 'Bauhaus Architecture in the Land of Israel: Is the Concept of Modern, Architect-Designed Vernacular a Contradiction in Terms?' In *The Search for Synthesis: Selected Writings on Architecture and Planning*, edited by Gilbert Herbert, 334–39. Haifa: Jubilee Edition, Technion, 1997.

'Home for Disturbed Children to Open in Jerusalem'. *Herut*, October 11, 1955 (In Hebrew).

Horticulture and Planting School in Petah-Tikva. IV-104-1200-15. Rivka Braizman personal archive, Pinchas Lavon Institute for Labour Movement Research, Tel Aviv (Lavon Institute) (In Hebrew).

Idelson, Beba. 'Women Workers' Council and Its Activities'. *Davar*, December 12, 1948 (In Hebrew).

'An Institution for Disturbed Children in Ba'it Va'Gan'. *Ha'aretz*, December 12, 1955 (In Hebrew).

Israeli, Dafna. 'Gendering in the Workplace'. In *Sex, Gender, Politics*, edited by Dafna Israeli, Ariella Friedman, Henriette Dahan-Kalev, Sylvie Fogiel-Bijaoui, Hanna Herzog, Manar Hasan, Hannah Naveh , 167–215. Tel Aviv: Kav Adom, 1999 (In Hebrew).

Kroyanker, David. *Architecture in Jerusalem: Arab Construction Outside the Walls*. Jerusalem: Keter Publishing House & Institute for Israel Research, 1985 (In Hebrew).

Lefaivre, Liane. 'Critical Regionalism, a Facet of Modern Architecture Since 1945'. In *Critical Regionalism, Architecture and Identity in a Globalized World*, edited by Liane Lefaivre and Alexander Tzonis, 22–55. New York and London: Prestel Publishing, 2003.

Levin, Michael. *The White City*. Tel Aviv: Tel Aviv Museum of Art, 1984 (In Hebrew).

Levy, Zvi. 'Negotiating Positive Identity in a Group Care Community: Reclaiming Uprooted Youth: Hadassim Youth Village – A Project of Canadian WIZO in Israel'. *Child and Youth Services* 16, no. 2 (1993): 73–85.

Meeting minutes, March 18, 1952. IV-104-1200-14. Rivka Braizman personal archive, Pinchas Lavon Institute for Labour Movement Research, Tel Aviv (Lavon Institute) (In Hebrew).

Meeting protocol, April 1952. IV-104-1200-14. Rivka Braizman personal archive, Pinchas Lavon Institute for Labour Movement Research, Tel Aviv (Lavon Institute) (In Hebrew).

Metrany, Keren and Irit Amit-Cohen. 'The Heritage of Modern Movement in Tel Aviv'. *Docomomo* (Special issue: 'Tel Aviv: A Century of Modern Buildings', edited by Jérémie Hoffmann)40 (March 2009): 83–88.

Metzger-Szmuk, Nitza. 'Genia Averbuch'. *Studio* 66 (November-December 1995): 72–76 (In Hebrew).

Meyer-Maril, Edina. 'Women Architects in Building the Country'. In *Women Artists in Israel 1920–1970*, edited by Ruth Markus, 143–48. Tel Aviv: Hakibbutz Hameuchad, 2008 (In Hebrew).

Minutes, B'nai B'rith meeting on Children's Home, October 30, 1949. J97/934. B'nai B'rith in Eretz Israel collection, Central Zionist Archives (CZA), Jerusalem.

Nitzan-Shiftan, Alona. *Seizing Jerusalem: The Architectures of Unilateral Unification*. Minneapolis and London: University of Minnesota Press, 2017.

'Personality of the Week: Architect Genia Averbuch'. *La'Isha*, October 20, 1947 (In Hebrew).

Proposal for Horticulture and Planting School, 1952. IV-104-1200-14. Rivka Braizman personal archive, Pinchas Lavon Institute for Labour Movement Research, Tel Aviv (Lavon Institute) (In Hebrew).

Protocol of the B'nai B'rith Children's House Managing Board, July 16, 1950. J97/934. B'nai B'rith in Eretz Israel collection, Central Zionist Archives (CZA), Jerusalem.

Schiffman, Ya'acov. 'The New Palestine'. *Architectural Review* LXXXIV, no. 503 (October 1938): 142–54.

Shamir, Gadith. *The 'Teheran Children': Since the Eruption of Second World-War*. Public Commission to Commemorate the 'Teheran Children'. Tel Aviv: Yaron Golan Publishing, 1989 (In Hebrew).

Shalom P. Doron (treasurer) to Ms. Arthur G. Laufman, March 29, 1951. J97/934. B'nai B'rith in Eretz Israel collection, Central Zionist Archives, Jerusalem.

Shalom Kassan to Frank Goldmann, October 16, 1952. J97/934. B'nai B'rith in Eretz Israel collection, Central Zionist Archives (CZA), Jerusalem.

Shapira, Anita. 'The Fashioning of the "New Jew" in the Yishuv Society'. In *Major Changes within the Jewish People in the Wake of the Holocaust*, edited by Yisrael Gutman, 427–41. Jerusalem: Yad Vashem, 1996.

Tidhar, David. 'Genia Averbuch-Elperin'. In *Encyclopedia of the Founders and Builders of Israel*, edited by David Tidhar, 2857. Tel Aviv: Sifriyat Rishonim, 1956 (In Hebrew).

'Today, Inauguration of the B'nai Brith Children's Home in Jerusalem'. *HaTzofe*, October 11, 1955 (In Hebrew).

Women's International Zionist Organization (WIZO) leaflet, 1951. F49\1230-31. WIZO collection, Central Zionist Archives (CZA), Jerusalem.

——— F49\1230-32. WIZO collection, Central Zionist Archives (CZA), Jerusalem (CZA).

Notes

1 All translations from Hebrew to English are the author's own, unless otherwise specified.

2 Nitza Metzger-Szmuk, 'Genia Averbuch', *Studio* 66 (November-December 1995): 72–76 (In Hebrew); 'Genia Averbuch: A Groundbreaking Woman Architect in Tel Aviv', *Globes*, January 9, 2011, accessed December 18, 2018, https://www.globes.co.il/news/article.aspx?did=1000614096 (In Hebrew); 'Genia Averbuch, the Tel Aviv Bauhaus Queen', accessed December 18, 2018, http://www.mytelaviv.co.il/GeniaAberboch (InHebrew).

3 'German and Austrian Women Architects in Mandatory Palestine, 1920–1948', in *Frau Architekt: Over 100 Years of Women in Architecture*, eds Mary Pepchinski, Christina Budde, Wolfgang Voigt, and Peter Cachola Schmal (Frankfurt-am-Main: Wasmuth & Deutsches Architekturmuseum, 2017), 49–57.

4 Keren Metrany and Irit Amit-Cohen, 'The Heritage of Modern Movement in Tel Aviv', *Docomomo* (Special issue: 'Tel Aviv: A Century of Modern Buildings', ed. Jérémie Hoffmann) 40 (March 2009): 83–88.

5 Sigal Davidi, 'The Women Architects of Mandatory Palestine and the Creation of Social Modernism' (Ph.D. diss., Tel Aviv University, 2015) (In Hebrew); Edina Meyer-Maril, 'Women Architects in Building the Country', in *Women Artists in Israel 1920–1970*, ed. Ruth Markus (Tel Aviv: Hakibbutz Hameuchad, 2008), 143–48 (In Hebrew).

6 Vernacular architecture stands for folk construction that does not involve professional architects, based on local needs and materials and using traditional construction methods. It develops gradually over generations, and reflects the cultural, historical, technological, and environmental contexts of its various locations. Gilbert Herbert,

'Bauhaus Architecture in the Land of Israel: Is the Concept of Modern, Architect-Designed Vernacular a Contradiction in Terms?' in *The Search for Synthesis: Selected Writings on Architecture and Planning*, ed. Gilbert Herbert (Haifa: Jubilee Edition, Technion, 1997), 334–39.

7 Yoav Gelber, *New Homeland: The Immigration and Absorption of Central European Jews 1933–1948* (Jerusalem: Yad Izhak Ben-Zvi, 1990), 185–221 (In Hebrew).

8 The most prominent among them were Mikve Israel (1870), Meir Shfeya (1891), Ben Shemen (1927) and Kaduri (1933).

9 Zvi Levy, 'Negotiating Positive Identity in a Group Care Community: Reclaiming Uprooted Youth: Hadassim Youth Village – A Project of Canadian WIZO in Israel.' *Child and Youth Services* 16, no2 (1993): 73–85.

10 Oz Almog, *The Sabra – The Creation of a New Jew* (Tel Aviv: Am Oved, 1997), 13, 245.

11 According to sociologist Oz Almog, the youth villages and agricultural schools were unique youth centres, where Hebrew-Zionist education moulded the sabra character of its students with a view to fulfil the pioneering ethos. Almog, *The Sabra*, 13, 245).

12 Women's International Zionist Organization (WIZO) leaflet, 1951, F49\1230-31, WIZO collection, Central Zionist Archives, Jerusalem (CZA).

13 Anita Shapira, 'The Fashioning of the "New Jew" in the Yishuv Society', in *Major Changes within the Jewish People in the Wake of the Holocaust*, ed. Yisrael Gutman (Jerusalem: Yad Vashem, 1996), 427–41 (In Hebrew); Yoav Gelber, 'The Shaping of the "New Jew" in Eretz Yisrael', in *Major Changes Within the Jewish People in the Wake of the Holocaust*, ed. Yisrael Gutman (Jerusalem: Yad Vashem, 1996), 443–61 (In Hebrew).

14 Beba Idelson, 'Women Workers' Council and Its Activities', *Davar*, December 12, 1948, 5 (In Hebrew).

15 David Tidhar, 'Genia Averbuch-Elperin', in *Encyclopedia of the Founders and Builders of Israel*, ed. David Tidhar (Tel Aviv: Sifriyat Rishonim, 1956), 2857 (In Hebrew).

16 Sigal Davidi, 'By Women for Women: Modernism, Architecture and Gender in Building the New Jewish Society in Mandatory Palestine', *Architectural Research Quarterly* 20, no. 3 (2016): 217–30.

17 Including Zina Dizengoff Square, Tel Aviv, 1934 (first prize); Water Tower, Tel Aviv, 1935 (second prize, with engineer I. Greynetz); Women Pioneers' House, Jerusalem, 1939 (first prize); Yad Hama'avir neighbourhood, Tel Aviv, 1944 (fourth prize); Shevah trade school, Tel Aviv, 1944 (first prize); Wauchope Square, Netanya, 1946 (honourable citation); Malchei Yisrael Square, Tel Aviv, 1947 (fifth prize).

18 Sam Barkai & Julius Posener, 'Habitations Individuelles. Architects: Averbough et Ginzburg', *L'Architecture d'Aujourd'hui* 9, no. 9 (September 1937): 23; Ya'acov Schiffman, 'The New Palestine.' *Architectural Review* LXXXIV, no. 503 (October 1938): 142–54; 'First Prize Awarded to Woman Architect', *Palestine Post*, August 6, 1944, 3; Lea Grundig, 'The Woman Architect of Eretz Yisrael', *Dvar HaPo'elet* 2–3 (March 16, 1948): 25–26 (In Hebrew).

19 The Kfar Batya youth village for holocaust survivor children was founded in 1945 by the Mizrachi Women of America (MWOA), the women's organization of the Mizrachi religious

Zionists. Although it was designed by Averbuch, it is not included in this chapter as it precedes the works designed in Israel's early years of statehood.

20 'An Exemplary Youth Village', *Olam HaIsha*, September 30, 1947, 6 (In Hebrew).

21 Rivka Alper, 'How Have We Reached Graduation Parties!', *Dvar HaPo'elet* 9 (1954): 198 (In Hebrew).

22 Meeting minutes, March 18, 1952, IV-104-1200-14, Rivka Braizman personal archive, Pinchas Lavon Institute for Labour Movement Research, Tel Aviv (Lavon Institute) (In Hebrew).

23 Hadassah Goldgert, representative of WIZO's Division of Agricultural Education. Meeting protocol, April 1952, IV-104-1200-14, Rivka Braizman personal archive, Pinchas Lavon Institute for Labour Movement Research, Tel Aviv (Lavon Institute) (In Hebrew).

24 'Personality of the Week: Architect Genia Averbuch', *La'Isha*, October 20, 1947, 1, 4 (In Hebrew).

25 Tidhar, 'Genia Averbuch-Elperin,' 2857.

26 Dafna Israeli, 'Gendering in the Workplace', in *Sex, Gender, Politics*, eds Dafna Israeli, Ariella Friedman, Henriette Dahan-Kalev, Sylvie Fogiel-Bijaoui, Hanna Herzog, Manar Hasan, Hannah Naveh (Tel Aviv: Kav Adom, 1999), 167–215 (In Hebrew).

27 'The Children's Village Grows Up', *Wizo in Israel* IV.29 (1951): 10.

28 Women's International Zionist Organization (WIZO) leaflet, 1951, F49\1230-32, WIZO collection, Central Zionist Archives (CZA), Jerusalem.

29 Women's International Zionist Organization (WIZO) leaflet, 1951, F49\1230-31.

30 In 1921, WIZO expanded to include the Canadian federations of the Hadassah Women's Organization. Hadassah Canada funded the agricultural school for women in Nahalal (1925) and the Hadassim youth village (1948).

31 Proposal for Horticulture and Planting School, 1952, IV-104-1200-14, Rivka Braizman personal archive, Pinchas Lavon Institute for Labour Movement Research, Tel Aviv (Lavon Institute) (In Hebrew).

32 Horticulture and Planting School in Petah-Tikva, IV-104-1200-15, Rivka Braizman personal archive, Pinchas Lavon Institute for Labour Movement Research, Tel Aviv (Lavon Institute) (In Hebrew).

33 The B'nai B'rith Women Supreme Council (WSC), today the Jewish Women International (JWI).

34 The 'Teheran Children' were a group of holocaust refugee children, who arrived in Teheran from Poland after an arduous journey, and were finally brought to Mandatory Palestine in 1943 by the Youth Aliyah. Gadith Shamir, *The 'Teheran Children': Since the Eruption of Second World-War*. Public Commission to Commemorate the 'Teheran Children'(Tel Aviv: Yaron Golan Publishing, 1989) (In Hebrew).

35 Shalom P. Doron (treasurer) to Ms. Arthur G. Laufman, March 29, 1951, J97/934, B'nai B'rith in Eretz Israel collection, Central Zionist Archives (CZA), Jerusalem; Protocol of the B'nai B'rith Children's House Managing Board, July 16, 1950, J97/934, B'nai B'rith in Eretz Israel collection, Central Zionist Archives, Jerusalem (CZA).

36 Minutes, B'nai B'rith meeting on Children's Home, October 30, 1949, J97/934, B'nai B'rith in Eretz Israel collection, Central Zionist Archives (CZA), Jerusalem; 'Today,

Inauguration of the B'nai B'rith Children's Home in Jerusalem', *Ha Tzofe*, October 11, 1955, 4 (In Hebrew).

37 Shalom Kassan to Frank Goldmann, October 16, 1952, J97/934, B'nai B'rith in Eretz Israel collection, Central Zionist Archives (CZA), Jerusalem; 'Home for Disturbed Children to Open in Jerusalem', *Herut*, October 11, 1955, 4.

38 Davidi, 'Women Architects', 162, 227.

39 Tim Benton, 'Modernism and Nature', in *Modernism: Designing a New World 1924–1939*, ed. Christopher Wilk (London: V&A Publications, 2006), 311–39; Liane Lefaivre, 'Critical Regionalism, a Facet of Modern Architecture Since 1945', in *Critical Regionalism, Architecture and Identity in a Globalized World*, eds Liane Lefaivre and Alexander Tzonis (New York and London: Prestel Publishing, 2003), 22–55.

40 Gilbert Herbert and Silvina Sosnovsky, *Bauhaus on the Carmel and the Crossroads of Empire* (Jerusalem: Yad Izhak Ben-Zvi, 1993), 248–63 (In Hebrew); Michael Levin, *The White City* (Tel Aviv: Tel Aviv Museum of Art, 1984), 18–21 (In Hebrew).

41 Herbert referred to Nikolaus Pevsner's term –'modern vernacular' – which he used to describe the modern architecture of Johannesburg in the 1950s. Gilbert Herbert, 'Bauhaus Architecture'.

42 Zvi Efrat, *The Israeli Project: Building and Architecture, 1948–1973* (Tel Aviv: Tel Aviv Museum of Art, 2004), 437–51 (In Hebrew).

43 Alona Nitzan-Shiftan, *Seizing Jerusalem: The Architectures of Unilateral Unification* (Minneapolis and London: University of Minnesota Press, 2017) 45–78.

44 Anat Helman, *Urban Culture in 1920s and 1930s Tel Aviv* (Haifa: Haifa University Press, 2007), 136 (In Hebrew).

45 Levy, 'Negotiating Positive Identity'.

46 Women's International Zionist Organization (WIZO) leaflet, 1951, F49\1230–31.

47 David Kroyanker, *Architecture in Jerusalem: Arab Construction Outside the Walls* (Jerusalem: Keter Publishing House & Institute for Israel Research, 1985), 388, 393 (In Hebrew).

48 'An Institution for Disturbed Children in Ba'it Va'Gan', *Ha'aretz*, December 12, 1955; 'Home for Disturbed Children to Open in Jerusalem', *Herut*, October 11, 1955, 4.

49 David Zaidenberg, Mikve Yisrael agriculture school representative, meeting minutes, April 1952, IV-104-1200-14, Rivka Braizman personal archive, Pinchas Lavon Institute for Labour Movement Research, Tel Aviv (Lavon Institute) (In Hebrew).

50 Horticulture and Planting School in Petah-Tikva, IV-104-1200-15, Rivka Braizman personal archive, Pinchas Lavon Institute for Labour Movement Research, Tel Aviv (Lavon Institute) (In Hebrew).

51 Sigal Davidi, 'From the Margins to the Center: Urban housing for single Jewish women in pre-state Israel', *Women's History Review* 28, no. 1 (2019): 85–110.

The Modern Israeli Synagogue as an Experiment in Jewish Tradition

Naomi Simhony

The present chapter analyses the exceptional designs of three synagogues built during Israel's first three decades of statehood. In the reviewed period, Israeli architecture was devoted to the building of a nation and the forging of a new Jewish and Israeli identity. The construction of synagogues was part of the pursuit of a design policy that would highlight this tendency. With this in mind, the Israeli Ministry of Religious Affairs formulated guidelines for the design and construction of new synagogues.[1] The works of several local architects, such as Meir Ben Uri, Israel Komet, and Yosef Shenberger, reflect an effort to determine the architectural identity of Israeli synagogues.[2] In spite of this attempt the architecture of several synagogues built in that period is characterized by exceptional expressive features. Such are the synagogues reviewed in this chapter: the Central Synagogue in Nazareth Illit, designed by architect Nahum Zolotov (1960–1968); the Military Officers' School Synagogue in Mitzpe Ramon, designed by architects Alfred Neumann and Zvi Hecker (1967–1969); and the Heichal Yehuda Synagogue in Tel Aviv, designed by architect Yitzhak Toledano and structural engineer Aharon Rousso (1972–1980).

Architectural historian Amiram Harlap describes these synagogues in his book, where he portrays them as expressing Jewish symbols and ideas.[3] I maintain that Harlap's interpretation contributed to these buildings' later reception as canonical Israeli synagogues. The present research investigates the tension between the synagogues' designs and their interpretations. My argument is that this tension represents the consolidation process of Jewish national identity in Israel's formative years.

Synagogues in Israel as an Experimental Laboratory

> In the synagogues of our time the link with the past is rarely felt [...] The Jewish symbols glued here and there and the Torah scrolls in the Holy Ark are the only indications that this is indeed a synagogue.[4]

The design of synagogues during Israel's first three decades could be defined as experimental for several reasons. First, the fast-growing number of new settlements (cities, towns, and collective settlements) increased the demand for synagogues. According to Halakhic sources, every Jewish settlement must have a house of worship.[5] Consequently, an unprecedented number of new synagogues were built in Israel at that time.

Second, the architectural style of Israel's modern synagogues differed from that of ancient synagogues built in the Holy Land, and from that of the early modern European and American synagogues.[6] Halakhic sources include strict instructions for the interior design of a synagogue, such as the position of the *bimah* (central platform) relative to the ark, and the worshippers' seating arrangement. However, no architectural guidelines are given for the exterior, except for orienting the building to face Jerusalem.[7] In his article, architect Meir Ben Uri, advisor to the Ministry of Religious Affairs , discusses the Halakhic restrictions related to imitating the design of Christian or Muslim architecture and of Diaspora synagogues.[8] He states that the establishment of the State of Israel changed the circumstances of synagogue construction.[9] Therefore, during Israel's first three decades architects made experiments towards devising a style that would be appropriate for Israeli synagogues as part of the quest for a new Jewish and national identity.

Third, many synagogue designers in Israel were young secuar architects. In a critical essay published following the architecture competition for the design of the Central Synagogue in Nazareth Illit, architectural critic Aba Elhanani noted that 'most of the projects reflect an immense ideological embarrassment that is very characteristic of our generation [...] which handles sacred buildings with secular hands'.[10]Furthermore, in Israel's early decades, local architecture underwent a generational revolution. In her 2004 article, 'Seizing Locality in Jerusalem', architectural historian Alona Nitzan-Shiftan argues that in the 1930s and 1940s, the architects of the 'founding generation', who had been educated in Europe, adopted the International Style to symbolize the revival of the nation and the image of the 'New Jew', rejecting Diaspora traditions.[11] They were followed by the 'Generation of the State', native-born Israeli architects, who flourished after the establishment of the state, and acquired their professional education in Israel. Those architects 'built the country' during their early professional careers.[12] They spoke against their predecessors, contending that the universality of the International Style was inherently antagonistic to and inconsistent with the Zionist ideal of a 'national home'.[13] In the 1960s and 1970s, they worked to bestow a local identity on Israeli architecture. Nonetheless, their work, as demonstrated in the synagogues under discussion, was heavily influenced by modern European architectural movements, mainly Brutalism, Structuralism, and Expressionism.[14]Under the influence of these global trends, Israeli architects remodeled the synagogue design tradition. The diverse architectural influences evident in these projects clearly indicate that in creating an Israeli synagogue style they were experimenting with modernism.

Case Studies: Three Exceptional Synagogues

Each case study begins with an architectural analysis, which introduces the synagogues' location, the circumstances of their construction, the designers' intentions, and reviews of contemporary architectural trends that influenced the design process. This is followed by an analysis of the synagogues' retroactive interpretations, which aims to explore the tension between the architectural design and the connotations associated with the synagogues.

The Central Synagogue in Nazareth Illit, Architect Nahum Zolotov (1960–68)

Nazareth Illit was established in 1957 as a Jewish development town, next to the City of Nazareth, as part of a state policy of settling Jews in the Galilee.[15] On the same year, a design process began for a central synagogue.[16] Architect Meir Ben Uri, a consultant to the Ministry of Religious Affairs, affirmed that the primary purpose of the project was to strengthen the Jewish presence in Nazareth Illit by making the synagogue stand prominently against Nazareth's churches and mosques.[17] The building is rectangular, topped with an inverted dome. Its impressive dimensions and architectural composition, which contrasts the synagogue with the hills around it, suggest a symbolic function [Figure 1].[18]

The synagogue was specified for a capacity of 650 worshippers in the main prayer hall and 30 in a smaller hall.[19] Both prayer halls include women sections located in galleries overlooking the main sanctuaries.[20] The design was intended for two types of worshippers: the first is the local religious community, whose members gather for prayers in the small

Figure 1: The Central Synagogue, Nazareth Illit, ca.1968. Architect Nahum Zolotov. Courtesy of the Azrieli Architecture Archive, Tel Aviv Museum of Art, Tel Aviv, Nahum Zolotov Collection. Photographs: Nahum Zolotov, Ran Erde and Ya'acov Agor.

hall on weekdays and Shabbat.[21] The second comprises a crowd of various worshippers, who gather for prayer in large numbers during the high holidays and other Jewish festivals. On those occasions, the worshippers use the main hall and the lower courtyard situated next to the main prayer hall [Figure 2].[22]

Nahum Zolotov's proposal won an architecture competition for the design of a central synagogue in Nazareth Illit in 1960, and was commissioned for the project.[23] In accordance with the competition's specifications, simple building materials were used. The walls are made of reddish earth-coloured local stone; the inverted dome and the bearing wall are made of exposed concrete; and the courtyard floors are made of concrete bonded gravel.[24]

The most dominant feature of the building is the inverted concrete dome that covers the main prayer hall and contrasts the synagogue with the convex contour of the hill on

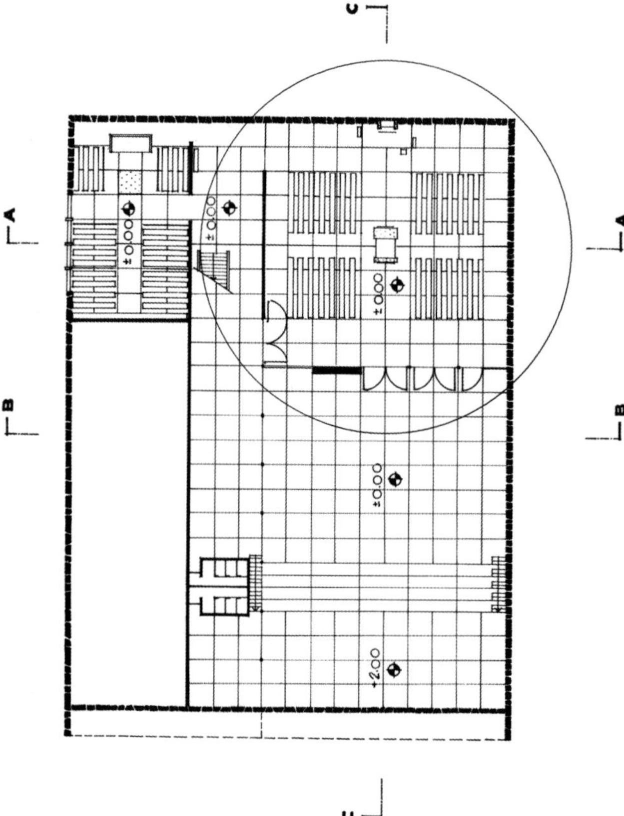

Figure 2: Plan, The Central Synagogue, Nazareth Illit, ca.1968. Courtesy of the Azrieli Architecture Archive, Tel Aviv Museum of Art, Tel Aviv, Israel, Nahum Zolotov Collection.

which it was built, giving it considerable prominence [Figure 3].[25] Zolotov revealed he had worked out the design scheme after having visited the site for the first time.[26] From an aerial view, the building seems to be planted deeply into the hill. The only feature that rises above the hill is the inverted dome: 'I chose [...] to reveal only the inverse dome, which is antithetic to the domed shape of the naked hill. Above the convex hill, the synagogue's dome would have disappeared.'[27]

Alongside the environmental aspect, the inverted dome design reflects Zolotov's concern with the prayer hall acoustics. The inverted concrete dome in Nazareth Illit meets the acoustic requirements, and dominates both the interior and exterior views of the synagogue.[28]

Supported by a slender steel frame, the massive concrete dome hangs above the main hall [Figure 3]. A long ribbon window that runs around the dome circumference and separates it from the bearing walls creates the illusion of a floating dome. Structural engineer Michael Horowitz notes that the dome is made of two units: a wide concave dome that defines the shape of the building's roof and a smaller convex dome that nestles within the larger dome and reinforces it.[29] Together, the two domes form a triangular beam that transfers the concrete dome's weight onto steel pillars placed along the building's square envelope and onto a massive concrete bearing wall.[30]

Architect Nahum Zolotov (1926–2014) was a non-religious man. His works include public and residential buildings, which represent his functional approach, in addition to four non-conventional synagogues.[31] His synagogues' unusual spatial outlines reflect his intention to create an atmosphere of holiness. When I asked him if he believed in God, he laughed and shook his head, but a few minutes later said: 'I do have faith, and I believe God enters each one of my synagogues.'[32]

The design of the Nazareth Illit synagogue corresponds to the tradition of dome construction in religious architecture and was inspired by major international architectural trends of the period. Among the precedents for domed religious edifices in Palestine and later in the State of Israel are the Hurva Synagogue in Jerusalem (nineteenth century);[33] the Goldstein Synagogue on the Edmond J. Safra campus of the Hebrew University of Jerusalem (1957);[34] and Giovanni Muzio's Basilica of the Annunciation in Nazareth (1958–69).[35] The modern interpretation of dome structures lies in its inverted shape and use of raw concrete. The most striking inspiration for the Nazareth Illit synagogue's design seems to have been

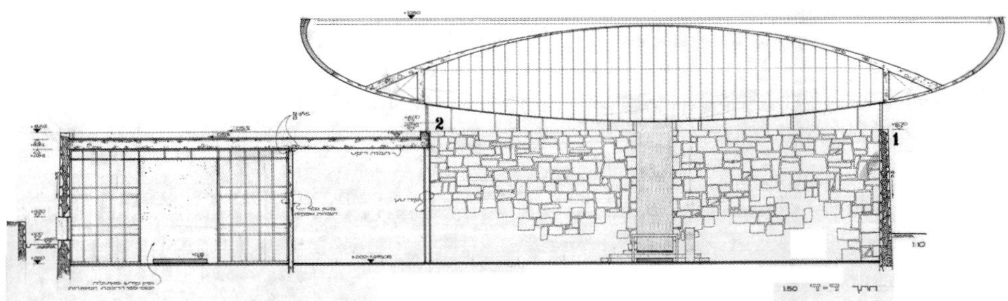

Figure 3: Section, The Central Synagogue, Nazareth Illit. Courtesy of the Azrieli Architecture Archive, Tel Aviv Museum of Art, Tel Aviv, Israel, Nahum Zolotov Collection.

Le Corbusier's Notre Dame du Haut Chapel in Ronchamp, France (1955).[36] Both buildings are situated on hilltops and are characterized by an expressive upturned concrete roof and by the separation between the roof and the building's envelope. Yet, the synagogue's design appears conservative compared to the expressive design of the chapel. The use of exposed concrete and local stone indicates that Zolotov was influenced by European Brutalist architecture, which was popular among Israeli architects of the period.[37] The emphasis placed boldly on the historical and symbolic aspects of the monumental dome has transformed the natural topography of the hill into a national landscape.

A concrete staircase that descends from the upper plaza to the sanctuaries' entrance hall characterizes the synagogue's unique circulation scheme [Figure 3, section c-c]. This architectural feature was later said to have been inspired by a biblical text. At the synagogue's inauguration ceremony, the Minister of Religious Affairs stated that the synagogue building, being embedded in the ground, echoes the vere 'Out of the depths have I cried unto thee, O LORD' (Ps. 130:1).[38] Harlap interprets the inverted dome as influenced by biblical ideas.[39] He sees it as a reference to the heavens and the earth, which are central to the Genesis creation narrative; in his view, the dome implies the existence of a divine world that exceeds human perception.[40] This interpretation intends to point out the existence of a direct link between modern Israel and Jewish biblical history. It represents an institutional intention to convert the synagogue's abstract shape into a national and religious symbol. One of numerous indications of the later reception of the building as a canonical Israeli synagogue can be found in the words of artist, curator, and designer Siona Shimshi, who described it as 'one of the synagogues that determined standards for Israeli synagogues design'.[41]

The design of the Nazareth Illit synagogue is an experiment in Jewish symbolism. First, by transforming the dome element prevalent in sacred architecture, and later by attributing religious significance to the 'secularized' inverted dome. The project thus symbolizes the consolidation process of the new Jewish identity during Israel's formative years.

The Military Officers' School Synagogue in Mitzpe Ramon, Architects Alfred eumann and Zvi Hecker, in Collaboration with Naomi Neumann (1967–69)

The synagogue was built in the Israel Defense Forces (IDF) officers' school for a capacity of 120 cadets and staff. It is situated at the edge of the base central parade ground. Zvi Hecker was involved in the preliminary design of the base during his military service in the Israeli Combat Engineering Corps. In the early 1960s, architects Hecker and his partner Eldar Sharon won a limited architecture competition for the design of the base and were commissioned for the project, which was inaugurated in 1967.[42] The synagogue's crystalline structure was designed to stand out against the surrounding desert landscape and the military base architecture [Figure 4].

A synagogue in a military base is a national institution, built and maintained by the state. Former Chief Military Rabbi Mordechai Piron defines military synagogues as educational

Figure 4: Military Officers' School Synagogue, Mitzpe Ramon, ca.1969. Architects Alfred Neuman and Zvi Hecker. Photograph: Zvi Hecker, Courtesy of Zvi Hecker, Architect.

and spiritual centres for every religious soldier.[43] He maintains that they represent the spirit and values of the Torah, and symbolize the ideals that the Jewish People have struggled for throughout history.[44] Neumann and Hecker's building is currently not in use. In 2009, a new synagogue, designed by architect Eli Armon, was inaugurated at this military base. The old synagogue and the barracks have been assigned as protected cultural heritage assets.[45]

The collaborative works of Alfred Neumann (1900-1968) and Zvi Hecker (b. 1931) belong with an experimental trend that flourished in Israeli architecture during the 1960s and 1970s. It was influenced by the European Structuralism that conceived of a building as a complex of recurring basic units.[46] Hecker believes, however, that the military synagogue structure reflects Alfred Neumann's original architectural language rather than a particular European trend.[47] The architects' joint body of work consists mainly of public and residential buildings, as well as schools. This synagogue is the most striking example of religious architecture within their works.[48]

The building is an exploration of polyhedral spatial bodies, namely, geometrical bodies composed of several identical polyhedrons whose faces are made of hexagons [Figure 4].[49] By this complex geometry, Neumann and Hecker meant to foster social, political, and cultural change.[50] By utilizing this complex morphology, which recalls Muslim abstract ornaments, the architects proposed an alternative model to the political and social denial of the Middle Eastern landscape.[51] Neumann and Hecker used geometry as a vehicle in an architectural experience that aimed to encourage a dialogue between diverse sectors within Israeli society.[52]

The synagogue's multifarious geometry reflects the architects' radical approach. Three types of polyhedral units form the synagogue structure: The basic building units are hexagonal planes. The triangular areas formed between them are used as semi-transparent yellow glass windows. These windows are located in the middle of the structure's height, admitting soft, filtered daylight. Ventilation windows built into sub-octahedrons project from the building [Figure 5].[53] Finally, the acute angles between the different surfaces create sharp light–shadow contrasts that emphasize the structure's morphology.[54]

Over the years, the radical structure has attracted considerable public attention, but the contribution of this unusual building to the development of a national synagogue style has not been investigated to date. The interior design demonstrates how the unconventional architecture functions in a house of worship. The hexagonal plan is symmetrical [Figure 6], with a main axis leading from the entrance to the *bimah* (platform) and the ark. The ark is set in a raised projecting alcove on the eastern wall, facing the direction of Jerusalem.[55] The hexagonal platform stands in the centre, and the benches are positioned on both sides of the main axis, fixing the worshippers' attention on the Torah Ark (*Heichal*) [Figure 7].[56]

The building's design is exceptional compared with the prevalent styles of earlier synagogues. According to Hecker, the unique design did not follow any particular trend, since the Jewish material culture is characterized by a multiplicity of styles rather than by one typical architectural heritage.[57] Neumann and Hecker were inspired by prominent modern European architects such as Adolf Loos and Auguste Perret, and by the traditional construction of wooden Polish synagogues.[58] The architecture and writings of Loos and Perret set the stage for Neumann and Hecker's structural and morphological explorations with concrete.[59] Their influence prompted further experimentation in complex forms based on the qualities of concrete, with fewer ornamentations, which is unusual in synagogue design. Inspired by the cross-section of Polish wooden synagogues, they designed the synagogue's space upward with indirect daylight penetration [Figure 5].[60] By this, the design of the military synagogue integrated the principles of the modern architecture movement and innovative building technology (e.g., structuralism and exposed concrete, respectively) within the architects' original use of polyhedral architecture.

Precedents for the exploration of a crystalline motif appear in German expressionism of the early twentieth century, especially in Bruno Taut's Glass Pavilion (1914) and in sketches of expressionist artists and architects such as Peter Behrens, Hans Sharoun, and Lyonel Feininger.[61] The crystalline motif was associated with material transparency but was also seen as a metaphor for spiritual metamorphosis.[62] Moreover, some Israeli architects of the time were influenced by D'Arcy Thompson's 1917 book *On Growth and Form*,[63] and explored in their work natural forms such as crystals, shells, and bones.[64]

Figure 5: The *bimah* (platform), Military Officers' School Synagogue, Mitzpe Ramon, ca. 1969. Photograph: Henry Hutter. Courtesy of Zvi Hecker, Architect.

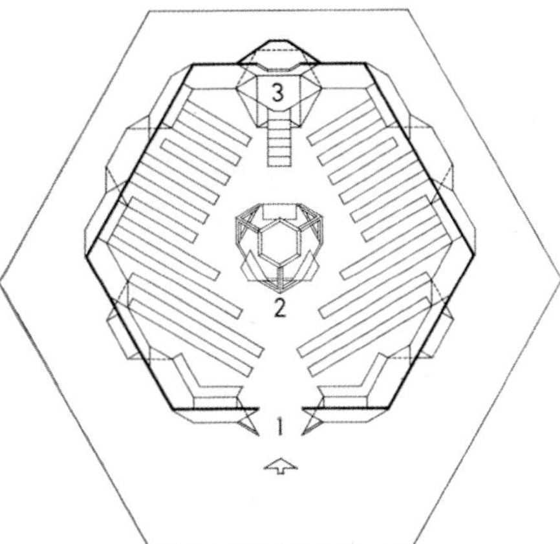

Figure 6: Ground plan, the Military Officers' School Synagogue, Mitzpe Ramon, ca. 1969. Legend: (1) entrance; (2) *bimah*; (3) Torah Ark. Courtesy of Zvi Hecker, Architect.

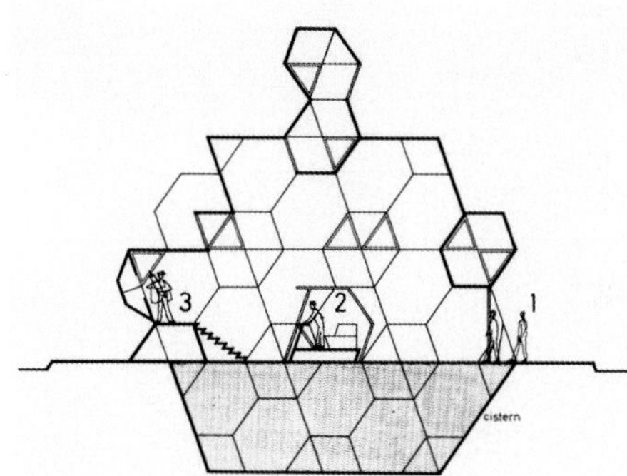

Figure 7: Section, Military Officers' School Synagogue, Mitzpe Ramon, ca. 1969. Legend: (1) entrance; (2) *bimah*; (3) Torah Ark . Courtesy of Zvi Hecker, Architect.

Over the years, architectural critics such as Robin Middleton have spoken against the morphological experiments of the architects.[65] Middleton states that while Neumann and Hecker's early works had intellectual integrity, later, geometry dictated their designs.[66] In other words, while their early works reflected an attempt to foster social and cultural shifts, the later ones, which were designed in the late 1960s, surrendered to the aesthetics of complex geometry, and as such caused functional problems and lost their social justification.

At first glance, the synagogue's structure may be interpreted as an architectural memento of the Star of David, which is implied in all the building's elements and is plainly visible on the Torah Ark.[67] However, Hecker testified that religious symbolism did not impact the design process.[68] It would appear that the architects' morphological explorations enabled them to use this shape and recall the symbol from new cultural perspectives. According to Hecker, 'the symbol constitutes an integral part of the architectural language and is not a separate added element.'[69] Thus, in this case, the symbol has connotations that exceed its traditional function as an ornament or an icon in synagogues.

Meira Yagid-Haimovici notices the visual affinity between Jewish and Islamic ornaments as manifested in Neumann and Hecker's polyhedral structures.[70] In the 1960s and 1970s, the incorporation of local vernacular elements became a trend in Israeli architecture. Its proponents tried to express an emotional attachment and a sense of belonging to the Land of Israel, formulating an architecture of place.[71] Ram Karmi, then a prominent architect and Head Architect of the Ministry of Housing, articulated an idea of 'place' that was imbued with traditional values.[72] He attempted to realize his vision by applying a set of local elements that he noticed in Arab villages to Israeli architecture.[73] In her article, Alona Nitzan-Shiftan argues that the integration of Palestinian vernacular elements into the Israeli architecture of the period reflected an attempt to evoke the Jewish biblical past and use it as a modern resource in Israel's nation-building project.[74] Architectural historian Zvi Efrat later criticized the 'vernacular' trend in Israeli architecture, claiming that it reflected an aggressive territorial and cultural appropriation of local architectural layers.[75] In contrast to their contemporary Israeli colleagues, the architectural language of Neumann and Hecker suggests a spatial dialogue, where Jewish and Islamic cultures intermingle.

The experimental facet of the synagogue is found in its complex morphology's potential ability to launch an inter-religious and multicultural dialogue. Considering the national significance of a synagogue located in a military base, this experiment and its contribution to Israeli modern architecture seem to be of utmost importance.

Heichal Yehuda Synagogue, Tel Aviv, Architect Yitzhak Toledano and Structural Engineer Aharon Rousso, in Collaboration with Architect Amiram Niv (1972–80)

Unlike the two synagogues described earlier, the Heichal Yehuda Synagogue was built for a specific group of worshippers.[76] This synagogue's community originated in Thessaloniki, Greece; its members included immigrants who arrived in Israel in the 1930s, and Holocaust survivors. The origin of the members indicates that it is a Sephardic synagogue by definition.[77] The synagogue was named after Leon Yehuda Recanati in gratitude for the generous contribution his sons made to fund the synagogue.[78] In the 1930s, the community members settled in southern Tel Aviv and worshipped in various local Sephardic synagogues.[79] Later, many members moved to the northern area of the city, where there was no Sephardic synagogue, and were forced to join various neighbourhood synagogues or gather for prayer in private homes.[80] Eventually, the community initiated and promoted the establishment of a synagogue of their own. The synagogue was designed for a capacity of 600 worshippers in the main prayer hall and a few dozen in a smaller hall. The main prayer hall was designated for use on Sabbath and during major Jewish festivals, while the smaller lower-floor hall was to be used by observant community members on weekdays.[81] Tel Aviv city allocated a plot for the synagogue in what was then the city's north.

While many of Israel's synagogues were designed by nonobservant architects, the designers of Heichal Yehuda, architect Yitzhak Toledano (1913–1973) and structural engineer Aharon Rousso (1914–2008), were both members of the Thessaloniki community, and as such were intimately familiar with its specific customs. They had immigrated to Israel together, studied at the Israel Institute of Technology, and were partners in a firm they established in Tel Aviv.[82]

From an aerial view, the building resembles a shell. Its concrete envelope is made of three adjacent barrel vaults with two smaller vaults on either side [Figure 8]. The vaults stretch from the northern façade and converge towards the southern side of the building, where they curve down towards the ground, behind the *heichal* (Torah Ark). The convergence point of the symmetrical shell-like envelope determines the *heichal* as the focal point of the prayer hall. This is also emphasized by the main circulation axis, which connects the entrance with the *tevah (bimah)* and the *heichal* (Ark). Moreover, the shell-like shape enhances the acoustics of the main prayer hall, making a Torah reading ring throughout the space.[83] The interior design of the main sanctuary follows the accepted seating arrangement of Sephardic synagogues: the seats are arranged around the *bimah*, which is located at the centre of the hall. A women's section is located in a gallery above the entrance.

The main structural challenge faced by the planners and designers were designing the span of the main hall's roof without supporting columns. The problem was resolved by installing longitudinal beams along the length of the vaults to buttress each vault on both sides. To establish the beams' construction, the designers used a computer – then a pioneering innovation in Israeli architecture. The computer determined the beams' coordinates and the casting moulds were built accordingly [Figure 9].[84]

Since the design scheme was completed before the allocation of the plot, it did not take into account the plot's shape. It later turned out that the building's shape did not fit into the plot's bounds. To adjust the structure's layout to the plot it had to be rotated, so that the ark is located at the southern end of the prayer hall rather than the eastern end facing Jerusalem, as required by the Halakhic sources.[85] According to Shimon Tzaiag, a senior community member, the synagogue founders had consulted several rabbis before construction was

Figure 8: Perspective, the Heichal Yehuda Synagogue, Tel Aviv. Architect Yitzhak Toledano and Structural Engineer Aharon Rousso. Drawing: Architect Norberto Kahan, early 1970s.

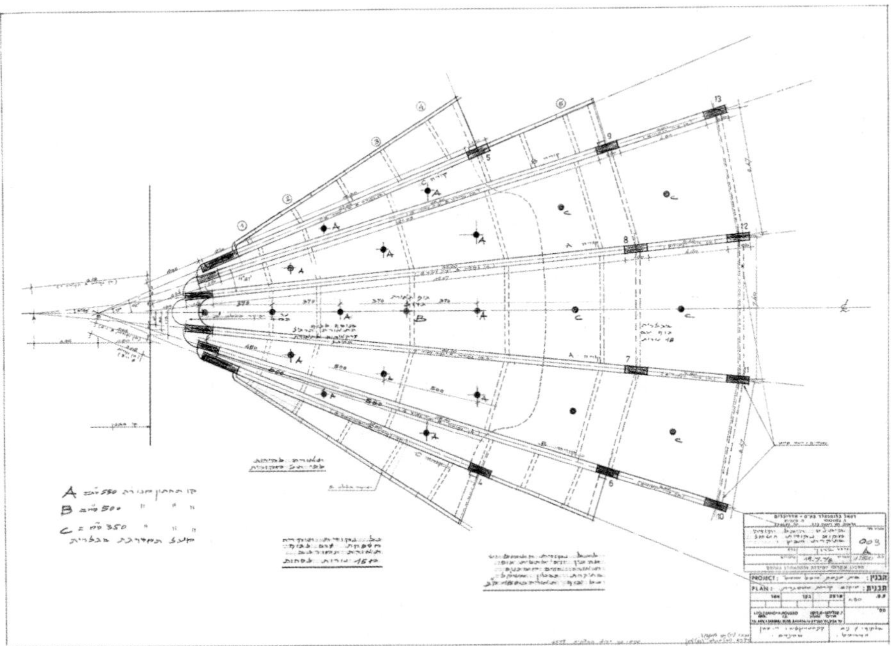

Figure 9: Structural plan, the Heichal Yehuda Synagogue, Tel Aviv, 1978. , Courtesy of Toledano – Rousso Collection.

begun.[86] The rabbis approved the final blueprints declaring that in the Land of Israel, worshippers are not obliged to face Jerusalem in prayer.[87]

The precedents for the use of concrete shells in twentieth-century religious architecture include the works of architects such as Eduardo Torroja,[88] Heinz Isler,[89] and Félix Candela.[90] One such example is the shell structure in Candela's Church of Our Lady of the Miraculous Medal in Mexico City (1955), primarily in the spatial vaults of the prayer hall.[91] The main sanctuary of Heichal Yehuda bears a striking resemblance to Alvar Aalto's Church of Holy Spirit in Wolfsburg, Germany (1962).[92] The synagogue's main hall is similar to the shell-like church interior, where wide wooden planks stretch from the ceiling at the entrance to the other end of the prayer hall and curve down towards the ground, behind the altar.

The synagogue's shell structure was associated with a number of symbolic meanings. The planners disclosed that the shell motif was designed to evoke the memory of Thessaloniki's waterfront.[93] Roni Toledano, Yitzhak Toledano's son, and Levana Eshed, Rousso's daughter, who was herself involved in the design process, maintain that the shape of the shell, whose curves converge into a single point, represents the concept of Judaism as an introverted religion that withdraws into itself [Figure 10].[94] Another interpretation identified the

Figure 10: View of the main prayer hall, the Heichal Yehuda Synagogue, Tel Aviv. Photograph by Author, 2018.

structure's shape as seven adjoining *shofars* (ritual ram horns).[95] Shimon Tzaiag attests that the Chief Rabbi of Tel Aviv, Rabbi Yedidya Frankel, was the one to discern the seven *shofars* when he attended the synagogue's inauguration ceremony.[96] According to this interpretation, the ark stands for the mouthpiece of the *shofars*, while their sound is cast forward through the windows overlooking the city.[97] David Recanati rejected this interpretation.[98]

The story of Heichal Yehuda Synagogue begins with the architects' intention to evoke the memory of Thessaloniki through the structure's seashell design. Later on, they embraced modern architectural trends to promote the community's status in the secular urban culture of Tel Aviv. A variety of symbolic meanings that were retroactively attributed to the synagogue structure defined the project as an experiment in biomorphic architecture, where modern design and symbolism intertwined, bringing together structural considerations, memory, and local identity.

Conclusion: Blending Modern Architecture and Symbolism

Over the years, the exceptional designs of the synagogues under discussion were associated with two types of symbolic interpretations: national and religious. While their modern architecture was perceived as reflecting Zionist national ideology, they were also given various religious interpretations. The blending of modern architecture and religious symbolism served different purposes in each of the synagogues. The inverted dome of the Nazareth Illit synagogue conveyed a political statement affirming the dominance of Jewish presence in that region and throughout the country, while creating a link with domed houses of worship. The crystalline structure of the military officers' school synagogue in the Negev introduced an alternative prototype into the multicultural Middle Eastern environment. Heichal Yehuda's biomorphic architecture aimed to recall the community's origins in Thessaloniki as well as portray a Jewish symbol within the secular urban context of Tel Aviv.

The extraordinary architecture of all three synagogues demonstrates how the traditional meaning of these religious institutions became imbued with modern and national ideology in the young state. The architectural metamorphosis that these synagogues underwent points to a rejection of previous Jewish architectural heritages, and an adoption of major trends in contemporary architecture around the world . The changes in form represent the ideological shift brought about by Zionism. Along with the national ideology of forging a new modern Jewish society, the synagogues' interpretations represented an institutional attempt to turn Jewish history into a modern resource. As Alona Nitzan-Shiftan argues, it helped the Israelis imagine that their biblical past was accessible and real, linking modern life in the State of Israel with Jewish history in the Land of Israel.[99] This link between the synagogues' modern architecture and their symbolic interpretations represents the search for an architectural identity in Israel's synagogues.

The development of the Israeli synagogue as a modern institution in a young state mirrors the process of identity regeneration that occurred during the State's first decades. Gershom Scholem examines the change that occurred in the meaning of the Star of David following the establishment of the State of Israel.[100] He argues that during World War II, the Star of David was etched into our collective memory as the symbol of Judaism, when the yellow star badge was worn as a mark of disgrace. Later, when it was emblazoned on Israel's national flag, it became a source of pride.[101] The national significance of the Star of David is evident in Israeli synagogues, where it is displayed on the buildings' façades, and recurs on liturgical artefacts and interior decorations.[102]

By associating the synagogues' designs with Jewish symbols and ideas, the buildings' interpretations reflect an attempt to establish the synagogue as a modern state institution recalling ancient worship traditions. Ben-Gurion's biblical doctrine followed the same philosophy.[103] According to historian Anita Shapira, Ben-Gurion viewed the rebirth of the Jewish nation in Israel as anchored in its ancient history.[104] He considered the biblical narrative as historical evidence of the Jewish right to inherit the land of their ancestors.[105] Shapira argues that Ben-Gurion's doctrine underscores the practical values of settling the land, but neglects the unique spiritual values of Judaism.[106]

From another angle, symbols could be conceived of as unrealizable content. In his book, Zali Gurevitch sketches the dual perception of 'place' in Jewish culture.[107] He argues that it is a combination of what is far and what is near, weaving together yearning and alienation.[108] The Jewish custom of facing Jerusalem in prayer demonstrates this point. It is a physical gesture that represents an intrinsic relationship with the Land of Israel, yet it defines the worshipper as situated far away from his homeland. Judaism is thus conceived of as a diasporic consciousness whose sense of place is purely symbolic.[109] Gurevitch's reading reveals a gap between physical presence and symbolic meaning.

In light of Gurevitch's investigation, I argue that the religious interpretations given to the exceptional designs of the synagogues under discussion represent an institutional attempt to bridge the gap between physical shape and various ideological stands. By attributing religious symbolism to the abstract buildings' shapes, they enhanced the synagogues' reception within the secular atmosphere of Zionism, and promoted their retrospective status as iconic Israeli synagogues. This inevitably leads to the conclusion that the architecture of the discussed synagogues was an experiment in modern architecture, but even more so in the metamorphosis that Jewish identity underwent in an age of radical transformations.

Acknowledgements

This research is supported by the Mandel-Scholion Interdisciplinary Research Center in the Humanities and Jewish Studies at the Hebrew University of Jerusalem. I would like to thank Zvi Hecker, Ella Zimmerman, and Roni Toledano; Nahum Zolotov; Tali Tzuker-Zolotov; Roni Toledano; Levana Eshed; David Recanati; Shimon Tzaiag; Shaul Lavi; Yair Ben Uri; Keren Sagi; and Daniel R. Schwartz; and Yair Ben Uri for their generous assistance. I am also grateful to Dr Roy Kozlovsky for his comments on earlier versions of this chapter. Finally, I would like to thank the editors of this volume, Anat Geva and Inbal Ben-Asher Gitler, for their contributions to this chapter.

Bibliography

'Adolf-Loos'. *Encyclopedia Britannica*. Accessed October 16, 2017. https://www.britannica.com/biography/Adolf-Loos.

Amir, Tula. *Nahum Zolotov – Architect and City Planner*. Tel Aviv: Ama, 2011 (In Hebrew).

'Auguste Perret'. *Encyclopedia Britannica*. Accessed October 16, 2017. https://www.britannica.com/biography/Auguste-Perret.

Bletter, Rosemarie Haag. 'The Interpretation of the Glass Dream-Expressionist Architecture and the History of the Crystal Metaphor'. *Journal of the Society of Architectural Historians* 40.1 (1981): 20–43.

Britton, Karla. *Auguste Perret*. London: Phaidon, 2001.

Ben Uri, Meir. 'Synagogue Design in the State of Israel'. In *The Synagogue: Articles and Essays*, edited by Mordechai HaCohen, 195–242. Jerusalem: Government Printer, 1955 (In Hebrew).

Casciato, Maristella. *Chandigarh 1956: Le Corbusier, Pierre Jeanneret, Jane B. Drew, E. Maxwell Fry*. Zürich: Scheidegger and Spiess, 2010.

'The Central Synagogue, Nazareth'. *Tvai* 8 (1970): 58–61 (In Hebrew).

Chiton, John. *Heinz Isler: The Engineer's Contribution to Contemporary Architecture*. London: Thomas Telford Publishing, 2000.

Curtis, William J. R. *Modern Architecture since 1900*. Oxford: Phaidon, 1982.

Dekel Caspi, Sophia. ed. *David Reznik: A Retrospective*. Tel Aviv: Genia Schreiber University Art Gallery, 2005. Exhibition catalogue.

Dvir, Noam. 'A Look into the Life of the Most Important, Yet Forgotten, Architects'. *Haaretz*, January 19, 2012. Accessed March 5, 2018. http://www.haaretz.com/print-edition/features/a-look-into-the-life-of-one-of-israel-s-most-important-yet-forgotten-architects-1.408087.

Efrat, Zvi. *The Israeli Project: Building and Architecture 1948–1973*. Tel Aviv: Tel Aviv Museum of Art, 2004 (In Hebrew).

Elhanani, Aba. 'Editor's Preface'. *Engineering and Architecture – Association of Engineers in Israel* 19.11 (1961): 1 (In Hebrew).

Encyclopaedia Britannica, 'Adolf-Loos', accessed October 16, 2017, https://www.britannica.com/biography/Adolf-Loos.

——— 'Auguste Perret', accessed October 16, 2017, https://www.britannica.com/biography/Auguste-Perret.

Even, Tamar. 'A Portrait of a Synagogue as a Concrete Crystal'. *BaMahane*, July 7, 1970 (In Hebrew).

Eshed, Levana. Interview with Naomi Simhony. Tel Aviv. February 20, 2017.

Fishbein, Sigalit. 'The Beautiful Synagogues of Israel'. *Ynet Judaism*. Last modified October 6, 2008. Accessed March 5, 2018. https://www.ynet.co.il/articles/0,7340,L-3601381,00.html (In Hebrew).

Gafni, Reuven, Arie Morgenstern, and David M. Cassuto, eds. *The Hurvah Synagogue: Six Centuries of Jewish Settlement in Jerusalem*. Jerusalem: Yad Ben Zvi, 2010 (In Hebrew).

Gravagnuolo, Benedetto. *Adolf Loos – Theory and Works*. New York: Rizzoli, 1982.

Gurevitch, Zali. *On Place*. Tel Aviv: Am Oved, 2007 (In Hebrew).

HaCohen, Mordechai, ed. *The Synagogue: Articles and Essays*. Jerusalem: Ministry of Religious Affairs , Government Printer, 1955 (In Hebrew).

Halevi, Masha. 'Reshaping a Sacred Landscape: Antonio Barluzzi and the Rebuilding of the Catholic Shrines in the Holy Land: Political, Geographical and Cultural Influences'. Ph.D. diss., Hebrew University of Jerusalem, 2009 (In Hebrew).

——— 'The Politics Behind the Construction of the Modern Church of the Annunciation in Nazareth'. *Catholic Historical Review* 96.1 (2010): 27–55.

Harlap, Amiram. *Synagogues in Israel from the Ancient to the Modern*. Israel: Ministry of Defense, Dvir Publishing House, 1985 (In Hebrew).

Hayon, Eliezer. 'Tour of the Month: The "Shell" Synagogue'. *Worldwide Synagogue Association Website*. Last modified May 11, 2009. Accessed March 5, 2018. http://www.hagabay.net/component/content/article.html?id=165:2009-07-16-15-55-51 (In Hebrew).

Hecker, Zvi. Interview with Naomi Simhony. Ramat Gan. December 28, 2015.

——— Interview with Naomi Simhony. Ramat Gan. December 3, 2017.

——— *Zvi Hecker: Sunflower*, Israel: Tel Aviv Museum of Art, 1996. Exhibition Catalogue.

——— 'Synagogue in the Negev Desert'. *Zvi Hecker*. Accessed March 5, 2018. http://www.zvihecker.com/projects/synagogue_in_the_negev_desert-60-1.html.

'Heichal Yehuda Synagogue, Tel Aviv'. *Tvai* 22 (1984): 70–73 (In Hebrew).

Herzel, Isaiah. Interview with Naomi Simhony. Nazareth Illit, November 20, 2017.

Ilan, Isaiah, Abraham Stahl, and Zvi Steiner. *A Little Sanctuary: Synagogues' Interior Design Anthology*. Jerusalem: Ministry of Education, 1975 (In Hebrew).

Karmi, Ram. 'Human Values in Urban Architecture'. *Israel Builds* 1977 (1977): 320–28 (In Hebrew).

Krinsky, Carol Herselle. *The Synagogues of Europe: Architecture, History, Meaning*. New York: Dover, 1985.

Levin, Michael. 'Jewish Identity in Architecture in Israel'. In *Jewish Identity in Contemporary Architecture*, edited by Angeli Sachs, 33–34. München: Prestel, 2004.

Loos, Adolf. 'Ornament and Crime (1908)'. In *Programs and Manifestoes on 20th Century Architecture*, edited by Ulrich Conrads, 19–23. Cambridge, MA: MIT Press, 1971.

Maimonides, 'Tefilah and Birkat Kohanim – Chapter 11', trans. Eliyahu Touger, accessed March 5, 2018, http://www.chabad.org/library/article_cdo/aid/920174/jewish/Tefilah-and-Birkat-Kohanim-Chapter-Eleven.htm.

'Nazareth Illit's Synagogue – Conditions of the Open-Limited Competition', 24.7.1959. Materials for the design competition and jury protocol 320.10-0. Meir Ben Uri Archive, Nazareth (In Hebrew).

Nitzan-Shiftan, Alona. 'Seizing Locality in Jerusalem'. In *The End of Tradition?*, edited by Nezar AlSayyad,. London: Routledge, 2004. 231–55.

——— 'On Concrete and Stone: Shifts and Conflicts in Israeli Architecture'. *Traditional Dwellings and Settlements Review* 21.1 (2009): 51–65.

——— '"There Are Stones with a Human Heart": On Monuments, Modernism, and Conservation at the Western Wall'. *Theory and Criticism* 38–39 (2011) (In Hebrew).

Nordenson, Guy, ed. *Seven Structural Engineers: The Felix Candela Lectures*. New York: Museum of Modern Art, 2008.

Ofrat, Gideon. 'The Shell and the Pearl'. *Haaretz*, March 28, 1980 (In Hebrew).

Pehnt, Wolfgang. 'Zvi Hecker: The Love of Geometry'. In *Zvi Hecker: Sunflower*, ed. Zvi Hecker. Israel: Tel Aviv Museum of Art, 1996. Exhibition Catalogue.

Pinkerfeld, Jacob. *The Synagogues of Eretz Yisrael from the End of the Geonim Era to the Rise of Hasidism*. Jerusalem: Central Press, 1945 (In Hebrew).

Piron, Mordechai. 'The Military Synagogue'. In *The Synagogue: Articles and Essays*, ed. Mordechai HaCohen (Jerusalem: Ministry of Religious Services, Government Printer, 1955), 69–74 (In Hebrew).

Rabinowitz, Dan. *Overlooking Nazareth: The Ethnography of Exclusion in Galilee*. Cambridge: Cambridge University Press, 1997.

Recanati, David. Interview with Naomi Simhony. Tel Aviv. March 6, 2017.

Rotbard, Sharon. *Avrahm Yasky, Concrete Architecture*. Tel Aviv: Babel, 2007 (In Hebrew).

Sachs, Angeli, ed. *Jewish Identity in Contemporary Architecture*. Munchen: Prestel, 2004.

Scholem, Gershom. 'The Curious History of the Six Pointed Star: How the "Magen David" Became the Jewish Symbol'. *Commentary* 8 (1949): 243. Accessed 23 December 2018. https://www.commentarymagazine.com/articles/the-curious-history-of-the-six-pointed-starhow-the-magen-david-became-the-jewish-symbol/.

Segal, Rafael. 'Unit, Pattern, Site: The Space Packed Architecture of Alfred Neumann, 1949–68'. Ph.D. diss., Princeton University, 2011.

Serraino, Pierluigi. *Eero Saarinen 1910–1961: A Structural Expressionist*. Köln: Taschen, 2005.

Shapira, Anita. 'Ben Gurion and the Bible: The Forging of a Historical Narrative'. *Middle Eastern Studies* 33.4 (1997): 645–74.

Shenberger, Yosef. 'The Synagogue Yard – Its Function and Design'. In *A Little Sanctuary: Synagogues' Interior Design Anthology*, edited by Isaiah Illan, Abraham Shtall, and Zvi Steiner, 63–67. Jerusalem: Ministry of Education, 1975 (In Hebrew).

Shimshi, Siona. *The Synagogue's Structure in Israel: 1948–1992*. Jerusalem: Ministry of Education and Culture and Bezal'el Academy of Arts and Design, 1992 (In Hebrew). Exhibition Catalogue.

——— 'The Synagogue's Structure in Israel: A Discussion', in *The Synagogue's Structure in Israel: 1948–1992* (Jerusalem: Ministry of Education and Culture and Bezal'el Academy of Arts and Design, 1992): 14–24 (In Hebrew). Exhibition Catalogue.

Thompson, D'Arcy. *On Growth and Form (1917)*, edited by John Tyler Bonner. Cambridge: Cambridge University Press, 1961.

Toledano, Roni. Interview with Naomi Simhony. Tel Aviv. March 8, 2017.

Torroja, Eduardo. *Philosophy of Structure*. California: University of California Press, 1958.

Tzaiag, Shimon. Interview with Naomi Simhony. Tel Aviv. January 26, 2017.

Weston, Richard. *Alvar Aalto*. London: Phaidon Press, 1995.

Yagid-Haimovici, Meira. 'Zvi Hecker: The Stance of the Other – An Alternative to Conventional Practice'. In *Zvi Hecker: Sunflower*, ed. Zvi Hecker. Israel: Tel Aviv Museum of Art, 1996. Exhibition Catalogue.

Zvielli, Alexander. 'Teddy Kollek and His Life Long Dedication'. *Jerusalem Post*. January 2, 2007. Accessed 22 December 2018. http://www.jpost.com/Features/Teddy-Kollek-and-his-life-long-dedication.

Zolotov, Nahum. Interview with Naomi Simhony. Hod HaSharon. November 9, 2009.

Notes

1 *The Synagogue: Articles and Essays*, ed. Mordechai HaCohen (Jerusalem: Government Printer, 1955) (In Hebrew).

2 Amiram Harlap, *Synagogues in Israel from the Ancient to the Modern* (Israel: Ministry of Defense, Dvir Publishing House, 1985), 114–15, 116–17, 122, 136 (In Hebrew). Most of Meir Ben Uri's projects have not been published. However, his articles introduce his concepts of synagogue design in the State of Israel; see, for example Ben Uri, 'Synagogue Design'.

3 Harlap, *Synagogues in Israel.*

4 Jacob Pinkerfeld, *The Synagogues of Eretz Yisrael from the End of the Geonim Era to the Rise of Hasidism* (Jerusalem: Central Press, 1945), 59 (In Hebrew). All translations from Hebrew to English are the author's own, unless otherwise specified.

5 As Maimonides states,'Wherever ten Jews live, it is necessary to establish a place for them to congregate for prayer at the time of each prayer service. This place is called a *Beit K'nesset*. The inhabitants of a city can compel each other to construct a synagogue'. Maimonides, 'Tefilah and Birkat Kohanim – Chapter 11', trans. Eliyahu Touger, accessed March 5, 2018, http://www.chabad.org/library/article_cdo/aid/920174/jewish/Tefilah-and-Birkat-Kohanim-Chapter-Eleven.htm. See also Zvi Efrat, *The Israeli Project: Building and Architecture 1948–1973* (Tel Aviv: Tel Aviv Museum of Art, 2004), 251, 56 (In Hebrew).

6 By 'early modern synagogues' I refer to those built between the late eighteenth century and the early 1930s.

7 Carol Herselle Krinsky, *The Synagogues of Europe: Architecture, History, Meaning* (New York: Dover, 1985), 5–35.

8 Ben Uri, 'Synagogue Design', 195–242.

9 Ibid., 197–98.

10 Aba Elhanani, 'Editor's Preface', *Engineering and Architecture – Association of Engineers in Israel* 19.11 (1961): 1 (In Hebrew).

11 Alona Nitzan-Shiftan, 'Seizing Locality in Jerusalem', in *The End of Tradition?*, ed. Nezar AlSayyad (London: Routledge, 2004), 231–37.

12 Ibid.

13 Ibid.

14 Nitzan-Shiftan, 'Seizing Locality', 231–55; Efrat, *Israeli Project*, 103–54, 187–234, 351–92.

15 For an ethnographic examination of Israeli–Palestinian relations in Nazareth Illit, see: Dan Rabinowitz, *Overlooking Nazareth: The Ethnography of Exclusion in Galilee* (Cambridge: Cambridge University Press, 1997).

16 'Nazareth Illit – plans for a central synagogue', 320.00-0. Meir Ben Uri Archive, Kiryat Shmuel, (In Hebrew).

17 Ibid.

18 The Central Synagogue in Nazareth Illit. Structural engineer: Michael Horowitz; interior and design: Yosef Mushli; contractor: Solel Boneh, Nazareth; relief: Ruth Zarfati; see 'The Central Synagogue, Nazareth Illit', *Tvai* 8 (1970): 58–61 (In Hebrew).

19 'The Central Synagogue', 58–61.

20 Ibid.

21 Tula Amir, *Nahum Zolotov – Architect and City Planner* (Tel Aviv: Ama, 2011), 30 (In Hebrew).

22 Ibid.

23 Ibid.

24 Ibid., 32.
25 Harlap, *Synagogues in Israel*, 128.
26 Nahum Zolotov, interview with Naomi Simhony, Hod HaSharon, November 9, 2009.
27 Ibid.
28 Ibid.
29 Michael Horowitz, cited in Amir, *Nahum Zolotov*, 31.
30 Ibid.
31 Other synagogues designed by Zolotov: the inter-communal synagogue in Be'er Sheva (1958) and the Babylonian community synagogue in Be'er Sheva (1980). Amir, *Nahum Zolotov*, 5.
32 Zolotov, interview.
33 Gafni, Reuven, Arie Morgenstern, and David M. Cassuto, eds, *The Hurvah Synagogue: Six Centuries of Jewish Settlement in Jerusalem* (Jerusalem: Yad Ben Zvi, 2010) (In Hebrew).
34 Dekel Caspi, Sophia. ed. *David Reznik: A Retrospective* (Tel Aviv: Genia Schreiber University Art Gallery, 2005), 37–44, Exhibition catalogue; Michael Levin, 'Jewish Identity in Architecture in Israel', in *Jewish Identity in Contemporary Architecture*, ed. Angeli Sachs (München: Prestel, 2004), 33–34.
35 Masha Halevi, 'The Politics Behind the Construction of the Modern Church of the Annunciation in Nazareth', *Catholic Historical Review* 96.1 (2010): 27–55; Masha Halevi, 'Reshaping a Sacred Landscape: Antonio Barluzzi and the Rebuilding of the Catholic Shrines in the Holy Land: Political, Geographical and Cultural Influences' (Ph.D. diss., Hebrew University of Jerusalem, 2009) (In Hebrew).
36 William J. R. Curtis, *Modern Architecture since 1900* (Oxford: Phaidon, 1982), 271–81.
37 Efrat, *Israeli Project*, 189–95.
38 Zolotov later noted that the association of the circulation scheme's design with the biblical verse did not occur to him during the design process. Nahum Zolotov, Architect's statement for a local newspaper, Nazareth Illit, undated. Architect's collection.
39 Harlap, *Synagogues in Israel*, 42–44.
40 Ibid.
41 The various reviews of the Nazareth Illit Central Synagogue's design include Siona Shimshi, *The Synagogue's Structure in Israel: 1948–1992* (Jerusalem: Ministry of Education and Culture and Bezal'el Academy of Arts and Design, 1992), 22, Exhibition catalogue (In Hebrew); Yosef Shenberger, 'The Synagogue Yard – Its Function and Design', in *A Little Sanctuary: Synagogues' Interior Design Anthology*, eds Isaiah Illan, Abraham Shtall, and Zvi Steiner (Jerusalem: Ministry of Education, 1975), 63–67 (In Hebrew). Over the years, the synagogue was mentioned in many reviews of beautiful synagogues in Israel. See, for example, Sigalit Fishbein, 'The Beautiful Synagogues of Israel', *Ynet Judaism*, last modified October 6, 2008, accessed March 5, 2018, https://www.ynet.co.il/articles/0,7340,L-3601381,00.html (In Hebrew).
42 Zvi Hecker, interview with Naomi Simhony, Ramat Gan, January 6, 2019.
43 Mordechai Piron, 'The Military Synagogue', in *The Synagogue*, 69–74 (In Hebrew).
44 Ibid.

45 See: The Military Officers' School preservation at the Ministry of Defence website, accessed 26 December 2018: http://www.mod.gov.il/building/engineering/Pages/preservation.aspx (In Hebrew)

46 Noam Dvir, 'A Look into the Life of the Most Important, Yet Forgotten, Architects', *Haaretz*, January 19, 2012, accessed March 5, 2018, http://www.haaretz.com/print-edition/features/a-look-into-the-life-of-one-of-israel-s-most-important-yet-forgotten-architects-1.408087; Zvi Hecker, *Zvi Hecker: Sunflower* (Israel: Tel Aviv Museum of Art, 1996), Exhibition catalogue.

47 Hecker, interview, December 28, 2015.

48 Other synagogues by Neumann and Hecker: Alfred Neumann and Zvi Hecker synagogue design proposal (project location unknown, unbuilt, 1966); Zvi Hecker, Ohel Dov Synagogue, Ramot Polin, Jerusalem (1975–77). See: Rafael Segal, 'Unit, Pattern, Site: The Space Packed Architecture of Alfred Neumann, 1949–68' (Ph.D. diss., Princeton University, 2011), 514–23; Zvi Hecker, *Zvi Hecker: Sunflower.*

49 Meira Yagid-Haimovici, 'Zvi Hecker: The Stance of the Other – An Alternative to Conventional Practice', in *Zvi Hecker: Sunflower*, Zvi Hecker (Israel: Tel Aviv Museum of Art, 1996), Exhibition catalogue.

50 Ibid.

51 Ibid.

52 Wolfgang Pehnt, 'Zvi Hecker: The Love of Geometry', in *Zvi Hecker: Sunflower* (Israel: Tel Aviv Museum of Art, 1996), Exhibition catalogue.

53 See Zvi Hecker's website: 'Synagogue in the Negev Desert', accessed March 5, 2018, http://www.zvihecker.com/projects/synagogue_in_the_negev_desert-60-1.html.

54 Yagid-Haimovici, 'Zvi Hecker'.

55 Harlap, *Synagogues in Israel*, 134.

56 Ibid.

57 Hecker, interview, December 28, 2015.

58 Zvi Hecker, interview with Naomi Simhony, Ramat Gan, December 3, 2017.

59 Encyclopaedia Britannica, 'Auguste Perret', accessed October 16, 2017, https://www.britannica.com/biography/Auguste-Perret; Encyclopaedia Britannica, 'Adolf-Loos', accessed October 16, 2017, https://www.britannica.com/biography/Adolf-Loos; Adolf Loos, 'Ornament and Crime (1908)', in *Programs and Manifestoes on 20th Century Architecture*, ed. Ulrich Conrads (Cambridge, MA: MIT Press, 1971), 19–23; Benedetto Gravagnuolo, *Adolf Loos – Theory and* Works (New York: Rizzoli, 1982), 34–78; Karla Britton, *Auguste Perret* (London: Phaidon, 2001), 10–44; William J R Curtis, *Modern Architecture since 1900* (Oxford: Phaidon, 1982), 34–36.

60 Hecker, interview, December 28, 2015.

61 Rosemarie Haag Bletter, 'The Interpretation of the Glass Dream-Expressionist Architecture and the History of the Crystal Metaphor', *Journal of the Society of Architectural Historians* 40.1 (1981): 20–43.

62 Ibid.

63 D'Arcy Thompson, *On Growth and Form (1917)*, ed. John Tyler Bonner (Cambridge: Cambridge University Press, 1961).

64 Alona Nitzan-Shiftan, '"There Are Stones with a Human Heart": On Monuments, Modernism, and Conservation at the Western Wall', *Theory and Criticism* 38–39 (2011): 78 (In Hebrew).
65 Robin Middleton cited in Efrat, *Israeli Project*, 388–89 (In Hebrew).
66 Ibid.
67 Tamar Even, 'A Portrait of a Synagogue as a Concrete Crystal', *BaMahane*, July 7, 1970 (In Hebrew).
68 Hecker, interview, December 28, 2015. See also: Segal, *Unit, Pattern, Site*, 514–23, 544–65.
69 Hecker, interview, December 3, 2017.
70 Yagid-Haimovici, 'Zvi Hecker'.
71 Nitzan-Shiftan, 'Seizing Locality', 231–55.
72 Ram Karmi, 'Human Values in Urban Architecture', *Israel Builds* 1977 (1977): 320–28, cited in Sharon Rotbard, *Avraham Yasky, Concrete Architecture* (Tel Aviv: Babel, 2007), 719 (In Hebrew). See also: Nitzan-Shiftan, 'Seizing Locality', 235–39.
73 Ibid.
74 Nitzan-Shiftan, 'Seizing Locality'. See also: Alona Nitzan-Shiftan, 'On Concrete and Stone: Shifts and Conflicts in Israeli Architecture', *Traditional Dwellings and Settlements Review* 21.1 (2009): 61.
75 Efrat, *Israeli Project*, 437.
76 Heichal Yehuda Synagogue in Tel Aviv. Rafael Bloomfield and M. Pintchuk; relief – Yehezkel Kimchi; stained glass windows – Yoseph Shaltiel. See: 'Heichal Yehuda Synagogue', 70–73.
77 In a Sephardic synagogue, the prayers follow the Sephardic version (*Nusach Sepharad*). The seats are arranged around the *bimah*, which is located at the centre of the sanctuary, differently from Ashkenazi synagogues, where the benches are arranged in rows, facing the Torah Ark. Shimshi, *Synagogue's Structure*, 36.
78 Leon Yehuda Recanati was the founder of the Israel Discount Bank. David Recanati, cited in Eliezer Hayon, 'Tour of the Month: The "Shell" Synagogue', *Worldwide Synagogue Association Website*, last modified May 11, 2009, accessed March 5, 2018, http://www.hagabay.net/component/content/article.html?id=165:2009-07-16-15-55-51 (In Hebrew).
79 Levana Eshed, interview with Naomi Simhony, Tel Aviv, February 20, 2017; David Recanati, interview with Naomi Simhony, March 6, 2017.
80 Eshed, interview; Recanati, interview.
81 'Heichal Yehuda Synagogue, Tel Aviv', *Tvai* 22 (1984): 70–73 (In Hebrew).
82 Eshed, interview.
83 Eshed, interview.
84 Ibid.
85 Gideon Ofrat, 'The Shell and the Pearl', *Haaretz*, March 28, 1980 (In Hebrew).
86 Shimon Tzaiag, interview with Naomi Simhony, Tel Aviv, January 26, 2017.
87 Ibid.
88 Eduardo Torroja, *Philosophy of Structure* (California: University of California Press, 1958)
89 John Chiton, *Heinz Isler: The Engineer's Contribution to Contemporary Architecture* (London: Thomas Telford Publishing, 2000).
90 Guy Nordenson, ed., *Seven Structural Engineers: The Felix Candela Lectures* (New York: Museum of Modern Art, 2008).

91 Ibid.
92 Richard Weston, *Alvar Aalto* (London: Phaidon, 1995): 198–225.
93 Roni Toledano, interview with Naomi Simhony, Tel Aviv, March 8, 2017; Eshed, interview.
94 Ibid.
95 Ibid.
96 Tzaiag, interview. Shimon Tzaiag is a senior member of the synagogue community.
97 Ibid.
98 Recanati, cited in Eliezer Hayon, 'Tour of the Month: The "Shell" Synagogue', *Worldwide Synagogue Association Website*, last modified May 11, 2009, accessed March 5, 2018, http://www.hagabay.net/component/content/article.html?id=165:2009-07-16-15-55-51 (In Hebrew).
99 Nitzan-Shiftan, 'On Concrete', 61.
100 Gershom Scholem, 'The Curious History of the Six Pointed Star: How the "Magen David" Became the Jewish Symbol', *Commentary* 8 (1949): 243, accessed 22 December 2018. https://www.commentarymagazine.com/articles/the-curious-history-of-the-six-pointed-starhow-the-magen-david-became-the-jewish-symbol/.
101 Ibid, 251.
102 It should be noted that the significance of the Star of David symbol in American modern synagogues of that period proudly represented the Jewish identity.
103 Anita Shapira, 'Ben Gurion and the Bible: The Forging of a Historical Narrative', *Middle Eastern Studies* 33.4 (1997): 645–74.
104 Ibid.
105 Ibid.
106 Ibid.
107 Zali Gurevitch, *On Place* (Tel Aviv: Am Oved, 2007) (in Hebrew).
108 Ibid.
109 Ibid.

Israeli Architecture at a Turning Point: Designs for the Israeli Center for Technological Awareness, 1978[1]

Jeremy Kargon

Introduction

In May 1978, the Israeli press announced the results of an architectural competition for the Israeli Center for Technological Awareness, to be built in Haifa on the slopes of Mount Carmel.[2] Most competition entries were clearly part of Israel's architectural mainstream, which had long embraced the principles of architectural modernism, its advocacy of visual consistency, and its use of materials such as exposed concrete. Some designs were terraced, to follow the steep topography of the site; others were composed of a geometric system that defined a new topography *sui generis*. The winning project, however, was visibly different: it was urbane, light, and assembled from apparently heterogeneous elements. Accordingly, the winning design for the 1978 competition marks a turning point in the development of Israeli architecture. The project introduced to Israel the formal and theoretical positions called elsewhere 'postmodern' and demonstrated a functionally logical application of those positions. As prominent Israeli architect (and competition juror) Dan Eytan later said privately to Hillel Schocken, one of the project's designers, Eytan could tell it was not 'Made in Israel'.[3]

This chapter discusses the institutional history of the Center for Technological Awareness (known for short as the Technodea)[4] and its self-conscious challenge to mainstream museum design in Israel. What follows presents the architectural competition that took place along with an analysis of the architectural themes explored by the designs awarded by the competition jury. A review of Schocken–Shaviv's first-place project will be accompanied by an examination of the designers' education at the Architectural Association in London, where they encountered stimulating (and conflicting) ideas promoted by Colin Rowe, Charles Jencks, Rem Koolhaas, James Stirling, and Cedric Price. Schocken and Shaviv's famous classmate, Zaha Hadid, described well the spirit of that time: '[A]rchitecture's role had yet to be fulfilled and [...] there were new territories which were yet to be explored [...] We, the authors of architecture, have to take on the task of reinvestigating Modernity'.[5] With their design for the Technodea, Schocken–Shaviv tried to do exactly that.

In the year 1978, Israeli architecture was poised for change. A new government, led by Menachem Begin, overturned years of political control by the socialist government that had founded the state.[6] Egyptian President Anwar Sadat's dramatic visit to Israel promised to open up opportunities for peaceful coexistence with surrounding Arab countries and the rest of the world.[7] The generation born with the state now looked eagerly beyond its borders for inspiration. Schocken–Shaviv's design was a reaction to Israel's legacy of local modernism yet was also a new interpretation of European intellectual trends. Although the Technodea was never built, Schocken–Shaviv's proposal anticipated a new wave of architectural experimentation in Israel, seeking new means for 'reinvestigating modernity'.

A New Kind of Museum

The Israeli Center for Technological Awareness emerged initially as means for promoting Israel's future industrial development. In 1972, Avigdor Bartel, director of Haifa Refineries, discussed with commercial entrepreneur and antiquities collector Reuven Hecht how to foster increased awareness of science and technology among Israeli youth. One solution was suggested by a recent trend in the planning of science museums abroad: the rise of the 'science and technology centre'. Science and technology centres were relatively recent innovations, having developed within the previous two decades in the United States and Europe from the more traditional science museum. Victor Danilov, former president and director of Chicago's Museum of Science and Industry, has written that science and technology centres 'are concerned with furthering public understanding and appreciation of the physical and life sciences, engineering, technology, [and] industry, [...] and seek to accomplish this goal by making museums both enlightening and entertaining'.[8] Science and technology centres sought to change the way institutions engaged their audiences. As Danilov further explained,

> Unlike many museums that are quiet and elitist, science and technology centers are lively and populist. They seek to further public understanding of science and technology in an enlightening and entertaining manner and do not require any special interest or background to be understood or appreciated by the average person.[9]

These characteristics could inspire interest in science and technology among the next generation of Israelis. Accordingly, at the first meeting of the Israel Technology Center Association, which took place in February 1972 in Haifa, participants endorsed the following objectives:

- To stimulate public awareness, especially among young people, of the values and challenges of applied science and technology, of the importance of industry to the Israeli economy, and of the satisfaction and rewards derived from work of a technical nature.
- To enable laymen, as well as specialists, to broaden their horizons and keep abreast of developments in the fields of applied science and technology.
- To emphasize the scientific and technological challenges facing mankind to-day [*sic*] in the fields of energy, resources and production.

- To demonstrate safety and health measures as protection against the dangers of pollution and dangers inherent in industrial and construction work.
- To exhibit the achievements of Israeli industry, technology, and research, both to local residents and to visitors from abroad.[10]

Underlying these objectives were the dual goals of awareness (meant to inspire youth towards careers in technology) and promotion (meant to advocate for Israeli achievement among both local and global audiences). Other, secondary objectives, included the following:

- Prepare special in-the-centre teaching programmes, in conjunction with specialists, as part of school curricula.
- Foster and house scientific and technical youth clubs and workshops.
- Provide learning experience [*sic*] for those unable to benefit from formal educational facilities.
- Sponsor regular lectures on current scientific and technological topics to the public at large.
- Incorporate a library and the Archives of Israel Industry and Technology.
- Place its exhibits and material at the disposal of special courses in new methods and processes, to update technical personnel from industry.[11]

To meet these objectives, the centre would depend on new strategies for display and visitor engagement.

> The emphasis will be on illustrative models that can be operated by the visitor. On the informal teaching level, the Center aims at inducing the visitor to show to himself [*sic*] the why and the how of industrial processes and other technologies, thereby making him an integral part of the display.[12]

The contrast with existing Israeli museums was stark. Through the period up to and including 1978, large museums in Israel typically housed cultural artefacts, primarily if not exclusively original artwork and antiquities. Their architecture reflected this fact: heavy, opaque masses deployed on columns, or else nested together over the natural landscape. The best-known example of the latter was Alfred (Al) Mansfeld's Israel Museum (opened 1965), discussed in this book by Eliyahu Keller. David Reznik's Archaeological Museum at Hatzor (opened 1965) was an example of the former, a treasure box set upon the cylindrical columns known by architects as 'pilotis'.[13] Influenced indirectly by Le Corbusier's 'pinwheel' museum projects of the 1950s, Dan Eytan and Itzhak Yashar's Tel Aviv Museum (opened 1971) demonstrated how to choreograph successfully visitors' encounters with works of art.[14] Taking a different approach, Eli Gwircman and Yashar's Museum of the Diaspora (opened 1978) placed exhibits and

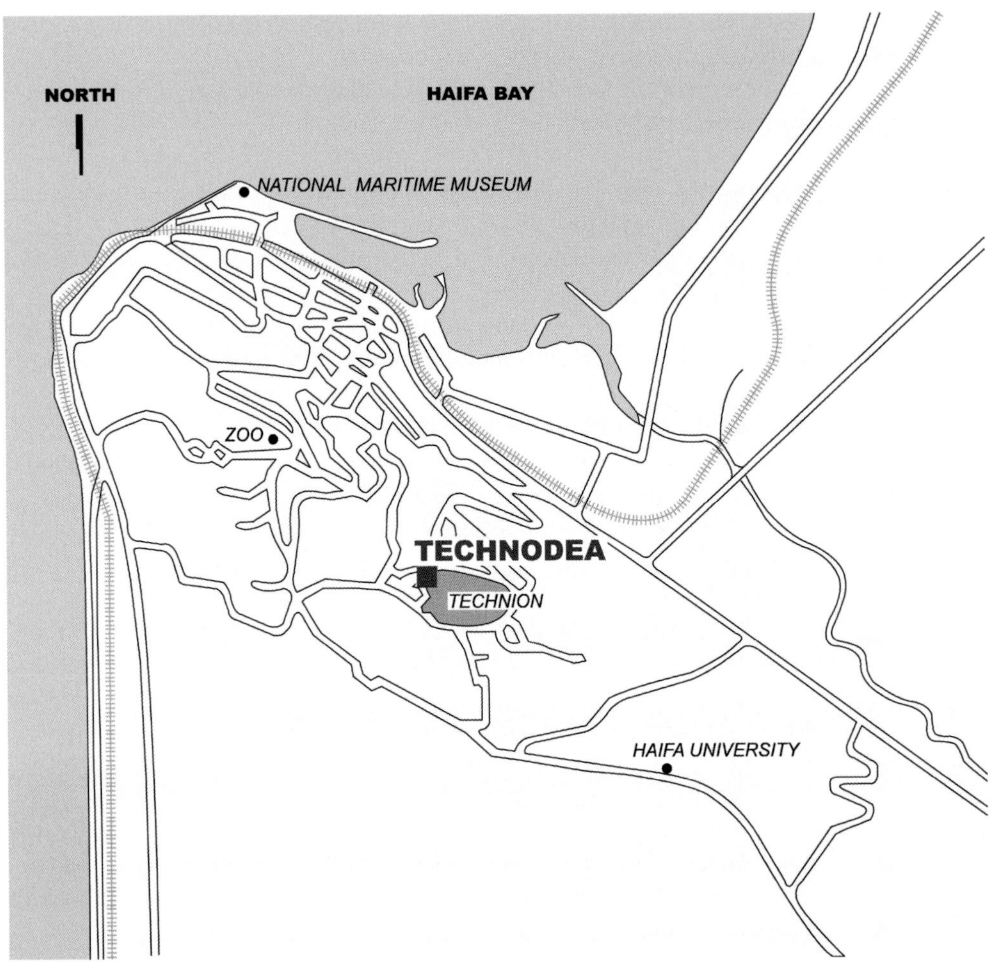

Figure 1: Jeremy Kargon, *Schematic Plan of the City of Haifa and Location of Proposed Technodea Building circa 1978*, 2018. © Jeremy Kargon.

graphics, rather than artefacts, at the core of the visitors' experience. Even so, that museum's architecture continued the trend set by earlier Israeli museums. In each of these four prominent museums, emphasis remained on visitors' *viewing*, rather than visitors' *doing*. To remain true to its founding objectives, the future home of the Israel Technology Center would have to shift that emphasis.

By 1978, Haifa Municipality had donated a prominent hillside site near the Israel Institute of Technology (Technion)'s campus [Figure 1]. Sized 12,000 m^2 in area, the site overlooked Haifa Bay and was accessible at its highest elevation by a paved road. A funicular railway from below was planned for additional access. With the endorsement of Haifa's local administration, the centre's board agreed to hold an architectural competition to determine the physical character of the Technodea's future home.

The Competition

Holding a public competition for the Technodea was a critical step towards defining the public identity of the institution. As historian Hélène Lipstadt has written, architectural competitions have 'consistently demanded an architecture that was expressive of an institution, that represented and communicated shared values, as well as functioned efficiently [...] Competitions allow these symbolic intentions and their satisfaction through design to become public issues'.[15] In the mid-1970s, competitions were an accepted method in Israel for such purposes. The Technodea competition was coordinated by the Israel Association of Engineers and Architects (IAEA), which had traditionally managed public competitions in Israel up to that time. The first phase of the competition was open to every registered Israeli architect; individuals and teams selected anonymously to proceed to the second stage were asked to develop their designs to a high degree of specificity, incorporating comments from the jury. As in other competitions coordinated by the IAEA, the jury included both client representatives and architectural professionals appointed by the IAEA; the latter would form the voting majority.[16]

Non-architect jurors included the engineer Joseph Cohen, as well as two members of the Technodea's Executive Committee: Mordecai Levy, formerly Assistant to the President of the Technion, and Jacob Porat, a high-ranking manager at Solel Boneh Ltd, the partially state-owned construction conglomerate.[17] The prominent architects appointed by the IAEA included Ram Karmi, the Committee Chair, who was one of Israel's best-known architects and later co-designer (with his sister Ada Karmi-Melamed) of the Israeli Supreme Court. The committee[18] also included Dan Eytan; Simhah Schwarz, an architect based in Haifa; and Shlomo Gilad, who had planned Haifa University's campus in the late 1960s following the preliminary design by Oscar Niemeyer.[19]

The competition called for construction in phases, so that the Technodea's exhibition space could be expanded as funds and opportunity arose. The first phase would include the core public and administrative functions, as well as the initial exhibition halls. The architects were asked to anticipate a connection to a cable-car line, which would bring visitors from lower down the hill.

The first phase was expected to reach 3500 m^2 in total area. The building programme for the first phase was to include the following:

- Exhibition areas of about 1100 m^2;
- Library and reading room, home to the Archives of Israeli Industry;
- Auditorium for 300 persons;
- Offices for administration and maintenance;
- Cafeteria;
- Workshops for technology-oriented youth clubs;
- Additional shops for exhibit preparation and building maintenance;
- Loading, receiving, and related services;
- Technical building services.[20]

Future phases were to add more than 8500 m^2 of exhibition space. It was expected also that exterior areas, including those at grade and at roof level, would contribute to the centre's exhibition space. Each competition entry had to anticipate exhibition themes for both first and future phases: basic science, energy, water resources, agriculture, mineral resources, light industry, heavy industry, architecture/construction, transportation, electronics, instrumentation/measurement, safety/ecology/health, along with technology and society.[21] The interpretation of these themes was left to the architects. In addition to meeting functional requirements, each architect was also required to address broader issues: How should a building engage such a prominent, sloped site? What is the proper architectural expression for a public institution of this kind? How might architecture shape the experience of a visitor to that institution? Most importantly, how would the Technodea differ from previous museums?

Forty-five entries in total were reviewed by the judges. At the end of their evaluation, consisting of two phases, six designs were acknowledged at an awards ceremony that took place on May 7, 1978. First prize went to Hillel Schocken, Uri Shaviv, and Tsiyona Margalit-Gerstein of Jerusalem,[22] along with engineer Yosef Edelman, of Haifa. Second prize was awarded to Meir Buchman and Bracha Chyutin, with Seffi Rodev and Ilana Behagen. Two third prizes were awarded: architects Tsvi Lissar, Yehoshua Shoshani, and Lili Grossman of Tel Aviv; and Hayim Lotner and Yitzhak Leiwand, together with the engineer, A. Ben-Aroyo of Jerusalem. Citations were given to projects by two teams: Werner Joseph Wittkower, Aryeh Adiv, and Israel Stein; and Arie Shilo and Niki Fein, in partnership with Norberto Kahan. Among all the entries, the first-prize project most clearly anticipated innovations characteristic of how Israeli architecture would change in the subsequent decade. The other projects, to varying degrees, reflected different aspects of the the Israeli mainstream, especially with respect to museum design up to that time.

Figure 2: Arie Shilo and Niki Fein, in partnership with Norberto Kahan, *Technodea Competition Entry View from the North*, 1978. © Arie Shilo Architects.

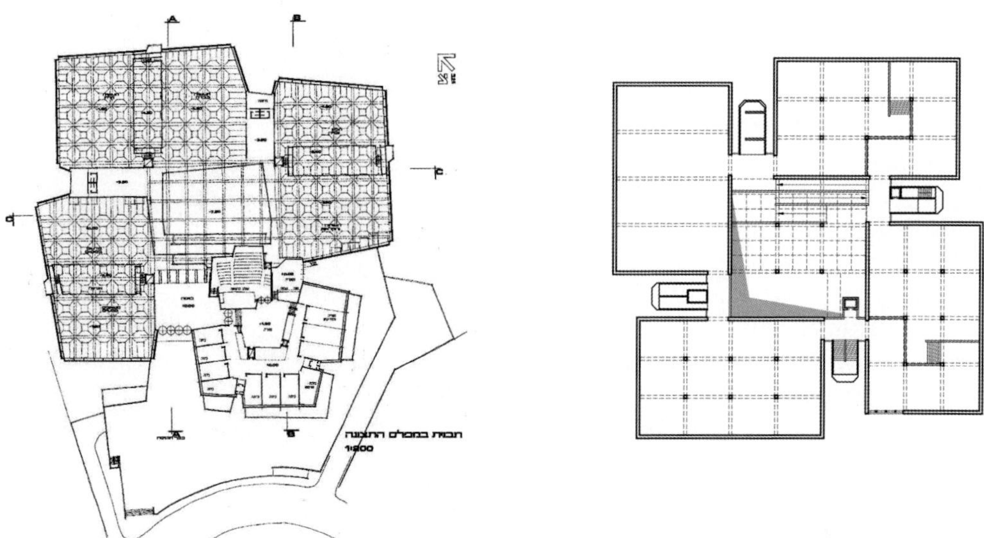

Figure 3: *Left:* Arie Shilo and Niki Fein, in partnership with Norberto Kahan, *Technodea Competition Entry Level Plan*, 1978. © Arie Shilo Architects. *Right:* Dan Eytan and Itzhak Yashar, *Tel Aviv Museum of Art Gallery-level Plan*, 1971. Drawing by the author.

An excellent example of the latter was the citation-receiving design by Shilo, Fein, and Kahan [Figure 2]. At the exterior, this design was composed of large, 'geologic' masses, as though the building might be carved out of Mount Carmel. The building's elemental atavism continued at the interior, where visitors would walk down ramps and stairs as though meandering over the site's original slope. The section drawing detailed the architects' technical means, such as concrete slabs, beams, and piers, consistent with much of Israel's recent public buildings. This design's geomorphism was reminiscent of the Jerusalem Theater, inaugurated in 1971 and designed by the firm of Shulamit Nadler, Michael Nadler, and Shmuel Bixon.[23] Shilo, Fein, and Kahan's plan drawings also recalled the Tel Aviv Museum of Art, where four gallery wings surrounded a central court, while stairs, elevators, and services were located in the spaces between the galleries [Figure 3]. At the Technodea, Shilo, Fein, and Kahan modified this approach by opening the galleries to a central court and, on the exterior, giving the gallery masses a less rigid geometry. Nevertheless, the similarity between this project and the art museum underscores the prevalent influence of art and artefact exhibition upon many designers' proposals for the Technodea.

Other designers, however, sought to base their work in the methods and patterns of science itself [Figure 4]. From today's perspective, the third-prize winning project by Tsvi Lissar and his team appears to align with Team X's structuralist lineage, including Dutch architects like Aldo van Eyck, Joop van Stigt, and Herman Hertzberger.[24] Israel's structuralism

Figure 4: Tsvi Lissar, with Y. Shoshani and H. Grossman, *Technodea Competition Entry View from the East*, 1978. © Lissar Architects & Town Planners.

was based on the relationship between spatial geometry and architectural tectonics. The structuralist approach had been promoted by several of the Technion's design faculty. The work of Alfred Neumann and Zvi Hecker demonstrated how complex geometrical forms could evoke a new kind of monumentality, ostensibly appropriate for public buildings and cultural institutions alike. The inverted ziggurat massing of their Bat Yam City Hall (1963, with Eldar Sharon)[25] anticipated the aggressive cantilevers in Lissar's design; their elemental geometry of the Technion's Laboratories for the Faculty of Mechanical Engineering (1967), also by Neumann and Hecker,[26] was in close proximity to the Technodea site. But Lissar's design was more sensitive than either with respect to the natural landscape. Indeed, Lissar's proposal suggests that structuralism could preserve unique site characteristics as well as evoke them with human-built forms.

Lissar's project also recalled the new Oceanographic Institute (1977) in Haifa, designed by David Yanai. Although not visibly 'modular' like Lissar's Technodea project, the Oceanographic Institute assumed a similar posture above an unconventional water's-edge site. Both projects had prominent towers capped with purely geometric forms. Yanai's tower supported a 26-sided polygonal form, housing radar equipment; Lissar's tower was a raised

Figure 5: Meir Buchman and Bracha Chyutin, with S. Rodev and I. Behagen, *Technodea Competition Entry Exterior View from the East*, 1978. © Meir Buchman and Bracha Chyutin.

copy of the building's basic module. Both projects demonstrated the position (common among Israeli architects educated by Neumann at the Technion) that pure geometry connoted modernity, if not 'technology', in its own right.

Meir Buchman and Bracha Chyutin's second-place project [Figure 5] shared some of the repetitive, modular character of Lissar's proposal. In this case, however, the use of repetition served the design's phased development as required by the competition brief. Furthermore, Buchman–Chyutin's design anchored their project's modularity to a whole building conceived *typologically* to reflect the technological characteristics fundamental to a science and technology centre.

> We looked for the form that would reflect in the most precise way the meaning of 'The Israeli Center for Technological Awareness' for the general public. We tried to find the architectural echo to the concept of 'technology', without doing so merely through advanced building materials and methods. We concluded that the approach lies in a design of a defined character, showing balance between a relatively composite space and structural simplicity. We assumed that a center of 'technological awareness' had to be designed as a methodical and systematic architectural system, so that visitors will be able to 'read it' clearly, externally and internally.[27]

Buchman and Chyutin borrowed a kit of parts familiar from industrial buildings in Europe and the United States, including exhaust stacks, dome-shaped skylights, curtain wall glazing, and diagonally placed roof monitors for natural light. Stylistically, one precedent was explicit: Stirling and Gowan's Engineering Building at the University of Leicester, England, completed in 1963. Chyutin has acknowledged the influence of Stirling and has explained that the British architect was 'very appreciated' in Israel at the time of the competition.[28] Yet, the buildings by Stirling that made their impact in fact dated from the early 1960s, more than a decade before the Technodea competition. The architectural works appreciated by Israeli architects were those that reflected their own interests at the time: the potential expressiveness of technology, formal plasticity, and articulation between volumes. Just as important to Buchman and Chyutin was the building's relationship to the site.

> First of all, we had the idea of how the building would engage the mountain [...]. Therefore, we came to the [solution of having] pavilions, in relation to the mountain, so that [they] would hover over it and not bother it [...]. We do not want a building that [dominates] the mountain, and so the articulation [of the building] into the pavilions gives something much more smooth on the mountain.[29]

The result of the designers' concern was a sophisticated circulation diagram that led visitors through interior and exterior spaces, extending horizontally and vertically over the existing topography [Figure 6]. The result was a design for which inside and outside activities could be especially well integrated. The apparent overall scale of the project, too, was very much reduced in comparison with most other competition entries. Moreover, the design's sequence of small spaces served effectively the complex scope of the centre's activities. The sequence was, however, extraordinarily complex. How could visitors exit the building without repeating the path by which they originally came – or without confusion?

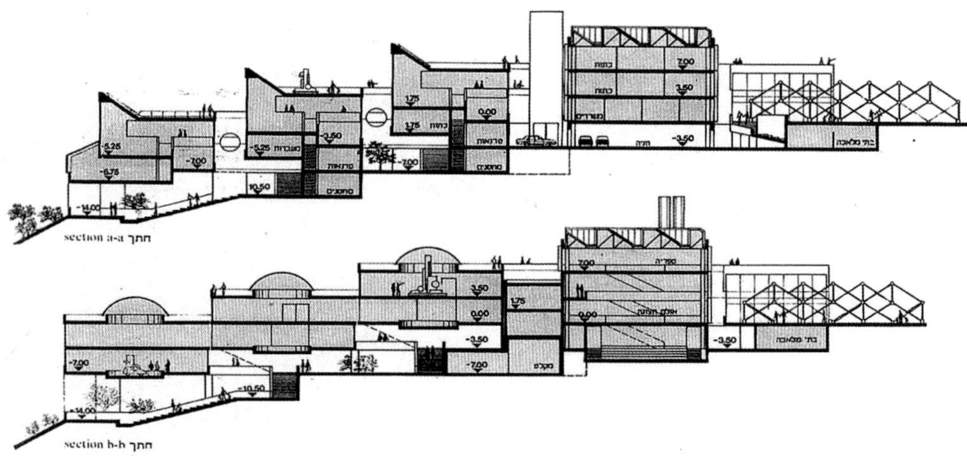

Figure 6: Meir Buchman and Bracha Chyutin, with S. Rodev and E. Berman, *Technodea Competition Entry Longitudinal Sections*. © Meir Buchman and Bracha Chyutin. Source: Meir Buchman and Bracha Hayutin, 'Israel Technology Centre, Haifa', *Architecture in Israel* 82–83 (1983): 37.

Buchman–Chyutin's second-prize-winning design for the Technodea represented, in a sense, a successful implementation of the most important concepts underlying Israeli architecture up to that time. Preoccupation with a building's vigorous sculptural form was combined with a wish to follow the contours of the landscape; attention to the visual impact of a building's structure was combined with concern for its occupants' movements throughout the building. The importance of natural light was balanced by the need to protect interior and exterior spaces from the strong Levantine sun. The building was composed of a system of repetitive architectural elements, yet these elements could be adapted easily for differing functions as needed. In contrast, however, the competition's first-prize-winning project introduced entirely new ideas and a break with Israel's architectural past.

The competition entry by Hillel Schocken and Uri Shaviv is remarkable for its heterogeneity [Figure 7]. Distinct building elements each boast a completely different architectural 'language'. Unlike the other competition entries, this project incorporates features neither completely set apart from one another nor composed within a single, consistent composition. Instead, parts of the building seem to crash into one another. A curved metal armature, marking the building's entrance and bearing energy-collecting

Figure 7: Hillel Schocken and Uri Shaviv, Architects, in partnership with Tsiona Margalit Gerstein, *Technodea Competition Entry Competition Model View from the South*, 1978. © Hillel Schocken, Uri Shaviv and Margalit Gerstein. Photograph by the author.

solar panels, intersects a solid, rectangular pavilion; a glass tube, containing an elevator and stairs, rises starkly at the point of collision. Towards the rear, metal scaffolding emerges from a rectangular base, besides which a pyramidal roof is bisected by a glass 'pergola' punctuated by a dish-shaped solar collector. A moving crane reaches out to one side, as though the mechanism of the building's fabrication is itself on display in the interest of 'Technological Awareness'.

Evident also is the typological treatment of each of the building's components. In a statement that accompanied their competition entry, Schocken and Shaviv explain that

> [t]he design for the buildings of the Israel Technology Center incorporates classical architectural considerations with a new functional and technological approach. Strategic location at the top of the hill, combination of masses and shapes, and the balance between them, large retaining walls of local stone, giant solar collectors and other technological elements all combine to create harmony which is achieved by the superimposition of the somewhat contradictory elements.[30]

What the architects meant by 'classical architectural considerations' was twofold. In contrast to the functionalist expectations of most Israeli architecture up to that date, Schocken–Shaviv's design for specific building functions was based upon 'types' derived from architectural history that, presumably, would be 'legible' also to future building visitors. The office and administration wing appears solid, bureaucratic, and conservative. The main exhibition space takes the form of an industrial shed. Between the two, the roof of another exhibition space acts as a formal terrace. Despite the obvious playfulness of their disposition on the steeply descending site, each part of the building expresses the programmatic activity within.

On the other hand, 'classical architectural considerations' meant also the project's axial organization [Figure 8]. Each part of the building was placed along a prominent spine, which served as the primary path of return circulation for building visitors. Schocken explained that 'contrary to Modernism's dogma, we looked at precedents like the Parthenon on the Acropolis and allowed ourselves to use symmetry when it was forbidden'.[31] Forbidden also (if tacitly) would have been the elements of classical and vernacular architecture: the appearance of a colonnade, punched window openings, and the unexpected relative misalignment between major building elements. Schocken and Shaviv's use of the words 'superimposition' and 'contradictory' underscore this point.[32]

Their design attested to a belief that urban (or, in this case, quasi-urban) considerations could and should be the basis of decisions about architectural form. Other competition entries were certainly interested in scale relationships. As we have seen, that interest extended also to considerations of site, including how the building would relate to the mountainside when seen from a distance. Nevertheless, those other projects were preoccupied by the building's figure as an object, distinct and separate from other buildings. Schocken–Shaviv's design approached the problem differently: as an element of a city, regardless of whether the

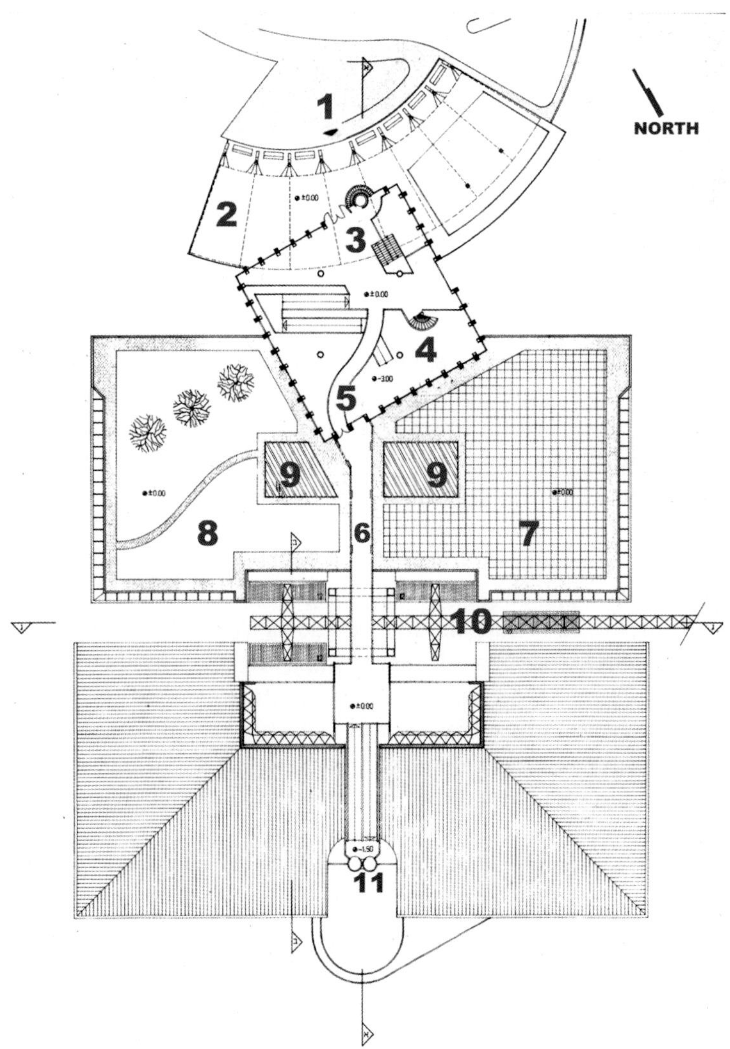

Figure 8: Hillel Schocken and Uri Shaviv, Architects, in partnership with Tsiona Margalit Gerstein, *Technodea Competition Entry Plan of the Entrance Level,* 1978. © Hillel Schocken, Uri Shaviv and Margalit Gerstein.

city – in this case, suburban Haifa – provided a coherent context. In describing their design, the architects write:

> The complex was designed as a composition of three main units, corresponding to three building phases. Each phase is a building in its own right and is independent both visually and functionally of the following phase. From the approach road, one can see only a part

> of the building so that its scale (the local scale) corresponds to that of the neighborhood development (predominantly housing). The total dimensions of the complex are revealed from long distance views (the urban scale).[33]

The first phase would include the large, curved solar collector and the tall, cube-shaped building housing the entrance hall, library, offices, classrooms, and laboratories. The rectangular, second phase would expand the Technodea's exhibition area and service functions, providing also a rooftop terrace for exterior exhibits. The third phase, designed as large sheds covered by pitched roofs, would expand the exhibition area to more than 1100 square metres.

As with all the other competition entries, visitor circulation played an important role in Schocken–Shaviv's design [Figure 9]. In this case, the choreography of visitors' movement was both a source of form-making and a method to ensure their orientation. As the architects explain, 'The visitor's route is a long succession of ramps connecting the exhibition spaces so that from any point along it and even from the entrance lobby he is aware of a large proportion of the museum's contents'.[34] The building's axial organization allowed considerable flexibility within the individual spaces without fear of confusion. 'The exhibition spaces were designed as two large halls, subdivided both vertically and horizontally by either fixed or flexible divisions so as to adapt their use to changing and unforeseen needs.'[35] The clear organization of the project's circulation set the winning project apart from the rest. One final, exuberant gesture ensured this. At the end of the building's axis, accessible from every floor, a 'paternoster' lift would convey visitors to a glass-enclosed, gantry-like bridge leading back to the building's entrance. Speaking about the competition years later, juror Dan Eytan explained its importance: 'From that perspective, the solution by [Schocken–Shaviv] was much more dramatic. You had the opportunity to finish up the procession and return in the elevator and move on the bridge

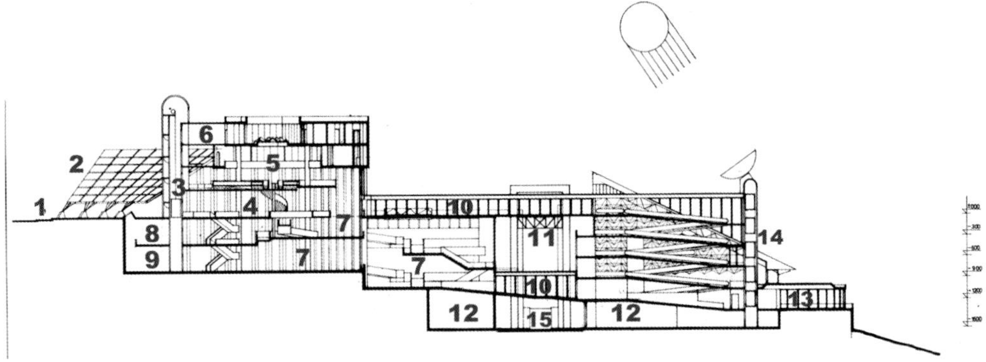

Figure 9: Hillel Schocken and Uri Shaviv, Architects, in partnership with Tsiona Margalit Gerstein, *Technodea Longitudinal Section Cut at the Main Circulation Axis,* 1978. © Hillel Schocken, Uri Shaviv and Margalit Gerstein.

above the building.'[36] The merit of this gesture was also pragmatic. As explained in the project's promotional brochure, 'Their design was selected [...] not only for its functionality and esthetic value, but also for the comparatively low cost of its construction'.[37]

The design's architectural elements also had a symbolic role. 'To emphasize the purpose of the building as a centre of technology an attempt has been made to make double use of important technical elements such as solar collectors, elevators and crane, both as functional parts of the building and as exhibits.'[38] These elements were 'signifiers' of science and technology just as much as they were practical solutions to energy consumption, transportation, and the handling of the building's exhibits. Such self-reference was unprecedented in Israeli architecture, which up to that time had displayed mostly the earnest connection between function and form, no matter how mannered or attenuated that connection might be. With this design, for the first time, appeared what had already been called internationally the 'postmodern' approach.

Hillel Schocken, Uri Shaviv: Education, Ideas, and Precedents

The designers' recent experience at London's Architectural Association (AA) was the source of this approach. Hillel Schocken and Uri Shaviv arrived separately at the AA in the early 1970s after each had left the Technion. Schocken had graduated with a degree in industrial engineering; Shaviv studied architecture but left for the AA before completing his degree. Shaviv recalled that 'the Technion was one system, very rigid [...] not interesting. And you come to the AA, and it's very open, you could talk about anything'.[39] Another difference was substantive. Schocken came to believe that '[t]he Technion was "systems architecture", mostly geometrical systems [...] based on hexagons – morphology [...] prefabrication'.[40] As students, both designers felt that the Technion's teaching of architecture remained too close to its institutional identity as a school of engineering.

Once at the AA, they found freedom, both personal and intellectual. Shaviv recalls, 'What I really liked at the AA when you joined it, every tutor had to present his program for the next year. And if he didn't get ten students, he didn't teach. [Therefore,] there were seven different attitudes towards architecture.'[41] Schocken was also impressed by the AA's openness, in contrast to the Technion at the time. 'The AA was a "marketplace" – it was a junction. Every name in architecture lectured there.'[42] Among the public lectures attended by Schocken and Shaviv during their time at the AA were those by James Stirling, Cedric Price, and Richard Rogers. Among their classes were those taught by Barbara Goldstein, Charles Jencks, and Rem Koolhaas with Elia Zenghelis. Although Schocken and Shaviv were not personally close, they did work together on at least one class project. After graduation, the two stayed in London with their families and found employment with different firms. In 1978, as Schocken recalls,

> [Uri] came to me with a proposition: 'Let's do an "ideas competition" in England. Let's do a competition so we will have something for a portfolio' [...] Friends from Israel

> were visiting, and they told us about a competition for a science museum in Haifa. A cousin of mine [...] brought the competition brief to us in London, and it looked like an interesting project.[43]

Together, Schocken and Shaviv reviewed the competition details and decided to participate. 'We did not intend to win.'[44]

The design of Schocken–Shaviv's competition submission suggests that a key theoretical influence had been the essay *Collage City*, first published in 1975 by Colin Rowe and Fred Koetter.[45] Rowe had taught at the AA in Boyarsky's London Summer Sessions at the start of the 1970s, during which his collaboration with Koetter began.[46] Rowe's fusing of historical erudition and contemporary formal analysis, as well as his long-standing connection with prominent British architects such as James Stirling, put Rowe's ideas at the centre of debates at the AA. *Collage City* proposed, as historian Grahame Shane has written,

> that cities are built in incremental fragments. Each fragment has particular characteristics and relations with other fragments [...]. Together these fragments create a conceptual framework for our experience of the city as a form of [...] collage, in our individual and collective consciousness. Each fragment was a lived world, the product of history, which could be inhabited. The differences between fragments and their inhabitants made for the diversity and vibrancy of city life.[47]

To judge from published accounts, Schocken–Shaviv's winning entry for the Technodea embodied exactly this approach. The project was designed not as one building but as several, each a unique element juxtaposed with the others. Assembled together, these elements matched those listed in *Collage City*'s prescriptive appendix, a 'list of stimulants, a-temporal and necessarily transcultural, as possible *objets trouvés* in the urbanistic collage'.[48] In a similar fashion, Schocken–Shaviv's Technodea displayed its technical infrastructure (solar collectors, elevators, and gantry cranes) to evoke the positivist effect of technology, embodied literally in the material stuff of scientific research.

Charles Jencks's arguments about semiotics and architecture had been part of Schocken and Shaviv's course curriculum at the AA. Although the scope of Jencks's theoretical writing on the topic was enormous, its lessons were distilled by his students to mean that architects must ask themselves about 'the way a building expresses itself and what it tells the guy who looks at it'.[49] Hillel Schocken had contributed drawings captioned 'Metaphors of Ronchamp' to Jencks's book *The Language of Post-Modern Architecture*, published first in 1977.[50] These pen-and-ink illustrations demonstrate the visual metaphors 'encoded' in Le Corbusier's famous chapel. Jencks writes, 'The visual codes, which here take in both elitist and popular meanings, are working mostly on an unconscious level.'[51] Jencks continues and prescribes a solution:

> Architecture is often experienced inattentively [...] One implication of this for architecture is that, among other things, the architect must over-code his buildings, using

> a redundancy of popular signs and metaphors, if his work is to communicate as intended and survive the transformation of fast-changing codes.[52]

Schocken–Shaviv's winning competition entry was certainly rich with potential metaphors, if not 'overcoded' in the sense meant by Jencks. Some of the references are obvious, and univalent: the glass-enclosed elevator and spiral stair at the building's entrance recalls an inverted test-tube, perhaps culled from the Technion's chemistry laboratories nearby; the gantry crane which extends out from the building's middle recalls similar structures located at Haifa's port. The small solar collector at the building's rear takes the form of a radar dish, then as now a signifier of technology's latest advances. Other references are more subtle and relate to architectural tradition. For instance, the large, curved metal armature at the building's entrance functions as a collector of solar energy. But, like a traditional entrance portico, it acts also as a 'collector' of building visitors. Its form recalls, too, the seating of a lecture hall, a place to impart knowledge, despite the superficial differences in material, fabrication, and even function. Throughout Schocken–Shaviv's Technodea design, many architectural elements perform a double 'semiotic' duty: they express distinctively the uniqueness of the enclosed functions *and* refer (implicitly or explicitly) to the universe of scientific instruments that might have populated the Israeli public's technological awareness. Had it been built, therefore, Schocken–Shaviv's Technodea design would have been an experiment in postmodern principles, unique in Israel at that time and among the earliest anywhere in the world.

This experiment would have tested also the practical relationships between programme and form, and between form and urban context. These relationships were among those interrogated repeatedly by two other teachers at the AA, Rem Koolhaas and Elia Zenghelis.[53] The two had founded the Office of Metropolitan Architecture (OMA) in 1975, the year before Schocken and Shaviv completed their studies. Historian and critic George Baird has characterized OMA's position at that time in terms of the following four 'polarities':

> First, an architecture which is visionary at the same time as it is implementable […].
> Second, an architecture which is surreal at the same time as it is commonsensical […].
> Third, an architecture which is puritanical at the same time as it is luxurious […].
> Last, an architecture which is revolutionary at the same times as it is evolutionist.[54]

According to Baird, therefore, incorporating antinomies in architecture could lead to 'a liberating and exhilarating potential',[55] which may be more or less successfully realized depending on the tension between apparent contradictions. In projects such as OMA's 1975 Roosevelt Island competition entry, that tension was present in the incongruity of its buildings' miniaturized Manhattan-like skyline. As students of Koolhaas and Zenghelis, Schocken and Shaviv were assigned the Roosevelt Island brief and had to consider application of the instructors' methodology. Designed three years later, the competition entry for the Technodea can be understood in part as a similar exercise in reconciling opposites.

Schocken–Shaviv's project mostly appeared 'light' and composed of elements that could be assembled quickly. Yet the office pavilion appeared 'heavy', situated in contrast to the rest. The pavilion was aligned strictly north–south, a gesture towards the port of Haifa, in contrast to the rest of the project's alignment with the site boundaries. And, at the most obvious, visual level, Schocken–Shaviv's Technodea design elevated to equal prominence elements derived from radically different sources: from contemporary science and industry, on the one hand, and from the European classical tradition, on the other. The apparent ease with which Schocken and Shaviv did so resulted from their familiarity with OMA's theoretical position no less than with Rowe's or with Jencks's.

At a more practical level, published designs by other architects provided direct examples from which young architects could learn. Both before and after Schocken and Shaviv's graduation from the AA, the work of James Stirling had made a strong impression.[56] Stirling's earlier work had been influential among many young architects in Israel. In the years leading up to 1978, however, Stirling's work had undergone a radical metamorphosis and included explicit classical compositional elements. Schocken and Shaviv were up-close witnesses to the drama surrounding Stirling's new projects. Stirling's 1975 competition entry for the North Rhine-Westphalia Museum in Düsseldorf was especially influential [Figure 10]. At a purely formal level, several elements of Stirling's project appear in Schocken–Shaviv's Technodea: the creation of a plinth; the axial organization of the main building; and, most memorably, the cube-like pavilion, set at an angle that relates to an off-site urban condition.

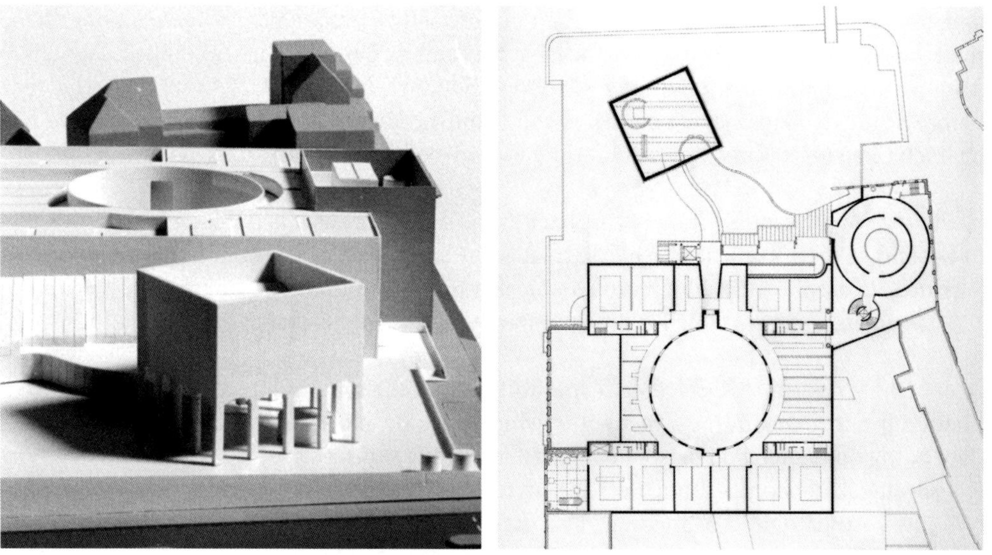

Figure 10: James Stirling and Partner, *View of Model and Typical Plan, Proposal for Nordrhein-Westfalen Museum, Düsseldorf, Germany,* 1975. Model photograph © John Donat / RIBA Collections. Plan drawing © Canadian Centre for Architecture (source: James Stirling/Michael Wilford fonds, Canadian Centre for Architecture).

In Sterling's project, the pavilion's prominence was meant 'to represent and symbolize the whole museum'.[57] In Schocken–Shaviv's project, the pavilion performs a similar role at the exterior, although it assumes a much more programmatic significance on the interior. More generally, however, Sterling's project (like his other museum projects at that time) provided for Schocken and Shaviv the earliest and best examples of Rowe's *Collage City* concepts in action.[58]

The work of Cedric Price was also familiar to students at the AA. Price's architecture, little of which was ever built, contrasted vigorously with Stirling's recent history-minded architecture and demonstrated persistent devotion to technology, flexibility, and newness. Best known among Price's paper projects was the Fun Palace, conceived in collaboration with theatrical producer Joan Littlewood between 1961 and 1963.[59] Extent drawings attest to Price's vision of an 'anti-institution', sharing little by way of planning or organization with traditional theatres or buildings of any kind. Most prominent in Price's drawings of the Fun Palace was the evidence of technology, both fixed and moveable. As historian Stanley Mathews explains,

> The explicitly 'mechanical' imagery of the Fun Palace was not an aesthetic treatment but the bare bones structural armature on which its interactive and fluid program could play. The Fun Palace was primarily there to respond to the changing needs and desires of individuals, not to house prepackaged exhibits and events for a generalized public.[60]

Potential parallels with the Technodea were obvious. Hillel Schocken, especially, saw explicit connections between the Fun Palace and the winning Technodea design.[61] As he explained, 'Cedric Price was an architect who created envelopes for events', and this proposition is easily visible in the second and third phases of Schocken–Shaviv's design: exhibit space is sheltered by large sheds, into which an array of operable gizmos facilitate exhibit display, visitor movement, and ongoing institutional growth.[62]

One other architectural precedent underscores a uniquely Israeli concern. A relic of Israel's ancient history, the Temple Mount in Jerusalem, suggested a new (and old) approach to landscape's topography. As Schocken explained,

> In Israel at the time, fitting into the landscape meant imitating the landscape [...] to imitate a mountain, the topography. The other thing was [a project that terraces] down the hill [...] And I was always impressed by the way the Temple Mount sits [...] in a way *oblivious* to the topography [...] I was feeling it was strengthening the relationship between the built environment and the topography [...] The image from [Jerusalem's] Old City was in my mind when we decided to put the square on the site.[63]

As far as site strategies are concerned, theirs was as technically feasible as any of the other competition entries. But Schocken and Shaviv's intentions had less to do with site than with a deeper strategy: a willingness to synthesize (and celebrate) architectural incongruities of style, of material, of geometry, and of epoch.

Conclusion: Architecture *after* the Turning Point

> To talk about Israel without putting it in a wider context is a big mistake. I think that what happened in Israel happened in many other places in the world [...] at the same time. It is not an 'Israeli Project' [...] it is a world project.[64]
>
> Hillel Schocken

An intellectual process that played out in Europe and in the United States played out also, in parallel, in Israel. George Baird has suggested that the late 1970s was a time when the architectural avant-garde comprised two intellectual streams that later diverged.[65] Under the label 'Rationalism' were those for whom historical erudition provided the strongest critique of 'anti-historical' architectural modernism, including late-modern architecture called Brutalist and High Tech. Given that same rubric, however, were those for whom modernism could itself be appropriated for reuse as a style. Over the course of the 1980s, the original (if tentative) consensus was abandoned.

If the prize-winning 1978 Technodea design represented a synthesis of concepts then current in London, later projects by Hillel Schocken and other, more established Israeli architects marked the disassociation of that synthesis. What that meant for Israeli architecture was openness to a broader formal palette and, in sometimes contradictory fashion, willingness to use overt historical forms in new buildings. The former might include compositions derived from conflicting geometries and surfaces bearing sophisticated materials (like stone, tile, and metal panels) formerly eschewed by modernist architects. Among early examples, landscape architect Shlomo Aronson's 1978 design for Jerusalem's Beit Shalom Park wove archaeological artefacts within new walkways, retaining walls, and stairs.[66] Dan Eytan and Chyutin Architects' design for the Genia Schreiber Art Gallery at Tel Aviv University (1984–88) demonstrated how competing geometries could resolve contextual and functional relationships.[67] Other architects found more direct inspiration from the region's complex, pre-modern architectural history and its attractive details: arches, cornices, and ornamental masonry.

The new sensibilities in Israeli architecture had received their most visible endorsement by entries for the Israeli Supreme Court competition (1985–86). Projects submitted by some Israeli architects reflected the nascent preoccupation with architectural history.[68] Hillel Schocken and Uri Shaviv collaborated again and reached the competition's final round, but their design was criticized for its mannered application of neo-classical architecture.[69] Yet the celebrated first-prize design by Ada Karmi-Melamed and Ram Karmi was also historicizing and incorporated recognizable quotations from local architectural sources. As critic Ran Shechori has written, 'It makes rich and wide-ranging references to the whole lexicon of [local] building over the centuries, starting with Herodian structures, through the Hellenistic tomb of Absalom, the Crusaders, Greek Orthodox monasteries, and up to the British Mandate period'.[70]

Like Schocken–Shaviv's earlier Technodea project, the Karmis' winning design derived its visual characteristics from the effective juxtaposition of diverse architectural elements.[71] Opened in 1992 to international acclaim, the Karmis' Israeli Supreme Court was lauded for being 'rich both in pure abstract form and in historical allusion' – an effect entirely uncharacteristic of public architecture in Israel before Schocken–Shaviv's 1978 Technodea project.[72]

In retrospect, as an opportunity to build a new kind of Israeli museum, the Technodea competition held in 1978 was inconclusive. The winning project was never built. Instead, the Technodea's board of directors found a permanent home for it in 1983 by renovating and conserving the Technion's original building (1909–24), planned by Alexander Baerwald. Nevertheless, as a 'thought experiment' among Israeli architects, the Technodea competition represents a historical watershed. An architecture of visual complexity and stylistic heterogeneity had been presented to the Israeli public and endorsed by a committee that included Israel's best-known architects. To recall Zaha Hadid's description of that historical period, the *possibility* of 'reinvestigating Modernity' had become, in architectural terms, a *necessity*.[73] Since that time, Israeli architects have inevitably had to grapple with historical movements, ideas, and precedents in their own work and in their understanding of others'.

Bibliography

Aronson, Shlomo. *Making Peace with the Land: Designing Israel's Landscape*. Washington: Spacemaker Press, 1998.

Baird, George. 'OMA, "Neo-Modern", and Modernity'. *Perspecta* 32 (2001): 28–37.

——— 'Les Extrêmes Qui se Touchent'. *Architectural Design* 47.5 (1977): 326–27.

Boyarsky, Alvin. 'Interview with Zaha Hadid'. In *Planetary Architecture Two*, by Zaha Hadid. London: Architectural Association, 1983.

Buchman, Meir and Bracha Chyutin. 'Israel Technology Centre, Haifa'. *Architecture in Israel* 82–83 (1983): 36–39 (In Hebrew and English).

Danilov, Victor. *Science and Technology Centers*. Cambridge: MIT Press, 1982.

Genia Schreiber University Art Gallery. 'About'. Tel Aviv University. https://en-arts.tau.ac.il/gallery/about. Accessed January 28, 2018.

Gilboa, Yehoshua. 'In Haifa Will Rise a Center for Technology'. *HaAretz*, May 8, 1978 (In Hebrew).

Goldberger, Paul. 'Architecture View: A Public Work that Ennobles as It Serves'. *New York Times*, August 13, 1995.

Harlap, Amiram. *New Israeli Architecture*. East Brunswick: Associated University Presses, 1982.

Heuvel, Wim J. van. *Structuralism in Dutch Architecture*. Rotterdam: 010 Publishers, 1992.

Israel Technology Center. 'Description of the Project', 1978. 'National Council for Research and Development – Scientific Foreign Relations – Israeli Center for Technological Awareness',

State Archive ID: 58.0.16.4, Physical ID: 8472/4-גל, Israel National Archives, Jerusalem (In Hebrew and English). Typewritten memorandum.

——— *The Scheme*. Haifa: Israel Technology Center, 1978.

——— *Technodea*. Haifa: Israel Technology Center, 1978.

Jencks, Charles. *The Language of Post-Modern Architecture.* New York: Rizzoli International Publications, 1977.

Levin, Michael. *The Supreme Court Building: An Architectural Competition.* Tel Aviv: Tel Aviv Museum, 1987.

Lipstadt, Hélène, ed. *The Experimental Tradition.* New York: Architectural League of New York, 1989.

Mathews, Stanley. 'The Fun Palace as Virtual Architecture: Cedric Price and the Practices of Indeterminacy'. *Journal of Architectural Education* 59.3 (2006), 40.

Perlmutter, Amos. 'Cleavage in Israel'. *Foreign Policy* 27 (Summer, 1977): 136–57.

Price, Cedric and Joan Littlewood. 'The Fun Palace'. *Drama Review* 12.3 (1968): 127–34.

Rowe, Colin and Fred Koetter. *Collage City.* Cambridge: MIT Press, 1975.

Shane, D. G. 'Colin Rowe, 1920–1999'. *Journal of Architectural Education* 53.4 (2000): 191–93.

Shechori, Ran. 'The State of the Arts: Architecture in Israel'. Israel Ministry of Foreign Affairs, July 9, 2002. http://mfa.gov.il/MFA/MFA-Archive/1998/Pages/Visual%20Arts%20in%20Israel%201995-1998.aspx. Accessed January 28, 2018.

Stirling, James. *Architectural Design Profile: James Stirling.* New York: St Martin's Press, 1982.

Tabor, Ephraim. 'The Attribution of Peaceful Intentions to the Visit by Sadat to Jerusalem and Subsequent Implications for Peace'. *Journal of Peace Research* 15.2 (1978): 193–95.

Vidler, Anthony. *James Frazier Stirling: Notes from the Archive.* New Haven: Yale University Press, 2010.

Notes

1 All translations from Hebrew to English are the author's own, unless otherwise specified.

2 Yehoshua Gilboa, 'In Haifa Will Rise a Center for Technology', *HaAretz*, May 8, 1978, 3 (In Hebrew).

3 Hillel Schocken (Architect, Tel Aviv), phone interview with the author, Baltimore, Maryland, January 22, 2016 (In English).

4 'Technodea' is a portmanteau that combines 'Techno' (from the Greek) and 'Dea' (from the Hebrew), which means 'knowing'.

5 Alvin Boyarsky, 'Interview with Zaha Hadid', in *Planetary Architecture Two,* by Zaha Hadid (London: Architectural Association, 1983), 1.

6 Amos Perlmutter, 'Cleavage in Israel', *Foreign Policy* 27 (Summer, 1977): 152.

7 Ephraim Tabor, 'The Attribution of Peaceful Intentions to the Visit by Sadat to Jerusalem and Subsequent Implications for Peace', *Journal of Peace Research* 15.2 (1978): 193.

8 Victor Danilov, *Science and Technology Centers* (Cambridge: MIT Press, 1982), viii.

9 Ibid., 2.

10 Israel Technology Center, *Technodea* (Haifa: Israel Technology Center, 1978), 5 (In Hebrew and English).

11 Ibid.
12 Ibid.
13 Amiram Harlap, *New Israeli Architecture* (East Brunswick: Associated University Presses, 1982), 247.
14 Ibid., 252–53.
15 Hélène Lipstadt, *The Experimental Tradition* (New York: Architectural League of New York, 1989), 11.
16 Dan Eytan (Architect, Tel Aviv), phone interview with the author, Baltimore, Maryland, March 13, 2016 (In Hebrew).
17 Israel Technology Center, *Technodea*, 9.
18 Gilboa, 'In Haifa', 3.
19 Harlap, *New Israeli Architecture*, 216.
20 Israel Technology Center, *Technodea*, 5.
21 Ibid.
22 Gilboa, 'In Haifa', 3. Tsiyona Gershtein-Margalit provided professional support but did not contribute to the design.
23 Harlap, *New Israeli Architecture*, 264–65.
24 J. Wim Van Heuvel, *Structuralism in Dutch Architecture* (Rotterdam: 010 Publishers, 1992), 16–21.
25 Harlap, *New Israeli Architecture*, 296–97.
26 Ibid., 212.
27 Meir Buchman and Bracha Chyutin, 'Israel Technology Centre, Haifa', *Architecture in Israel* 82–83 (1983): 36 (In Hebrew and English). Passage cited was translated from the more extensive Hebrew text.
28 Bracha Chyutin (Architect), interview with the author, Giv'atayim, June 6, 2016 (In Hebrew and English).
29 Ibid.
30 Israel Technology Center, *The Scheme* (Haifa: Israel Technology Center, 1978), 1 (In Hebrew and English).
31 Hillel Schocken, e-mail to author, December 22, 2016.
32 Israel Technology Center, *The Scheme*, 2.
33 Ibid.
34 Ibid.
35 Ibid.
36 Dan Eytan, interview.
37 Israel Technology Center, *Technodea*, 5.
38 Israel Technology Center, *The Scheme*, 2.
39 Uri Stern Shaviv (Architect, Tel Aviv), phone interview with the author, Baltimore, Maryland, January 28, 2016 (In Hebrew and English).
40 Schocken, interview.
41 Shaviv, interview.
42 Schocken, interview.
43 Ibid.
44 Ibid.

45 Colin Rowe and Fred Koetter, *Collage City* (Cambridge: MIT Press, 1975).
46 D. G. Shane, 'Colin Rowe, 1920–1999', *Journal of Architectural Education* 53.4 (2000): 193.
47 Ibid., 193.
48 Rowe and Koetter, *Collage City*, 151. The following pages include pictures of traditional urban architecture but also buildings that the authors characterize as 'scientific' and from the 'future': an offshore oil rig, the Assembly Building at Cape Canaveral, and the heterogeneous façades of an American Main Street. Ibid., 172.
49 Schocken, interview.
50 Charles Jencks, *The Language of Post-Modern Architecture* (New York: Rizzoli International Publications, 1977).
51 Ibid., 48.
52 Ibid., 50.
53 George Baird, 'OMA, "Neo-Modern", and Modernity', *Perspecta* 32 (2001): 28–37.
54 George Baird, "Les Extrêmes Qui se Touchent." *Architectural Design* 47.5 (1977): 327.
55 Ibid.
56 Schocken, interview.
57 James Stirling, *Architectural Design Profile: James Stirling* (New York: St Martin's Press, 1982), 14.
58 Anthony Vidler, *James Frazier Stirling: Notes from the Archive* (New Haven: Yale University Press, 2010), 170–85.
59 Cedric Price and Joan Littlewood, 'The Fun Palace', *Drama Review*, 12.3 (1968): 129.
60 Stanley Mathews, 'The Fun Palace as Virtual Architecture: Cedric Price and the Practices of Indeterminacy', *Journal of Architectural Education* 59.3 (2006): 40.
61 Schocken, interview.
62 Ibid.
63 Ibid.
64 Ibid.
65 Baird, 'OMA, "Neo-Modern"', 33.
66 Shlomo Aronson, *Making Peace with the Land: Designing Israel's Landscape* (Washington: Spacemaker Press, 1998), 126–27.
67 Genia Schreiber University Art Gallery, 'About', Tel Aviv University, https://en-arts.tau.ac.il/gallery/about, accessed January 28, 2018.
68 Michael Levin, *The Supreme Court Building: An Architectural Competition* (Tel Aviv: Tel Aviv Museum, 1987), 3 ('Selection Procedure').
69 Ibid., 1–2 ('Entry #1').
70 Ran Shechori, 'The State of the Arts: Architecture in Israel', Israel Ministry of Foreign Affairs, July 9, 2002, http://mfa.gov.il/MFA/MFA-Archive/1998/Pages/Visual%20Arts%20in%20Israel%201995-1998.aspx, accessed January 28, 2018.
71 Levin, *Supreme Court*, 1–2 (Entry #3).
72 Paul Goldberger, 'Architecture View: A Public Work that Ennobles as It Serves', *New York Times*, August 13, 1995.
73 Boyarsky, 'Interview with Zaha Hadid', 1.

Section III

Considering Climate

Minus 400 and Over 40 Degrees: Architecture in the Dead Sea, 1948–1971[1]

Daphne Binder and Theodore Kofman

Since ancient times, the Dead Sea region has been one of the most hostile environments known to man, infamous for biblical disasters such as the destruction of Sodom and Gomorrah and for its extreme and unique climatic conditions. During the twentieth century, multiple attempts have been made to settle the region, driven by national economic and political goals related to the formation of the State of Israel. The Sea, filled with untapped minerals valuable for commerce and industry, was the fluctuating eastern front of the newly established country.[2] The early settlements in the Dead Sea region constructed as part of the entrepreneurial and ideological efforts to secure this territory and mine its resources directly facilitated the founding of one of Israel's primary economic engines, the Dead Sea potash industry, as well as Israel's health tourism industry.[3]

The study of settlements, industrial and tourist complexes, and cultural buildings planned and built in the region during the 1960s and early 1970s reveals the ways in which ideology affected their design and construction. Did these settlements and buildings, each conceived and carried out in isolation, share common strategies or characteristics due to the region's challenging climate and topography? At the same time, were these settlements differentiated in concept, design, and construction as a result of differing interpretations of Zionist ideological fulfilment?

This chapter focuses on individual buildings and settlements in the Dead Sea as local case studies in relation to the larger state-wide initiatives that produced them. Analysis of both built and unbuilt projects, designed by some of Israel's foremost architects of the time, sheds light on the experimentation and creativity of policy makers, designers, and stakeholders in enabling the settlement of a new frontier in land previously thought uninhabitable.

The Dead Sea as Zionist Frontier

The Dead Sea, at an approximate elevation of −400 metres (1312 feet) below sea level, with recorded temperatures averaging 40 degrees Celsius (104 degrees Fahrenheit) in the summer, was an extreme frontier that Israeli settlers faced.[4] Pioneers confronted a lack of fresh water and miles of separation from other populated areas. The topography of the Judean Mountains to the west made it impossible to concentrate settlements in one place. However, the potential profit from the Sea's valuable minerals, potassium chloride and bromide, dwarfed these challenges.[5]

The Dead Sea constitutes Israel's central-eastern boundary, bordering Jordan in the southern desert region known as the Negev. During the decades immediately before and after the establishment of the State of Israel, the Negev's population was deemed critical in securing the state in perpetuity. The call by David Ben-Gurion, Israel's first prime minister, to populate Israel's south was premised on the state's limited productive land area, as well as its need to secure its borders: 'If the state doesn't liquidate the desert, the desert will liquidate the state.'[6] The Negev's 'buffering' location, separating Egypt and Jordan from the north's Jewish population, necessitated its population, Ben-Gurion explained. He asserted that, with the help of Israeli scientists and researchers, the land of the south and the Negev could 'bloom and flourish'.[7]

Ben-Gurion extolled the Dead Sea for its industrial and public health potential. The Sea's potentially harvestable minerals led him to conclude that its 'abundant health spas' should be investigated, for 'there is little doubt that the great potential for health and recuperation are stored within them'.[8] He prioritized the exploitation of the Sea's natural resources alongside other vital development projects in the Negev, including atomic and solar energy and the production of electrical power.[9] By portraying the Negev as the future site of resource extractions vital to the young country, Ben-Gurion laid out the rationale behind Israel's settlement mission.

The quest to transform desolate territories into productive agricultural lands, accommodating of human settlement, would become one of the Zionist movement's guiding principles. Ruth Kark, in her study of the Negev's settlement before 1948, found that Zionist ideology played an integral role in funnelling resources and creativity into the conquest of the desert.[10] Ideological motivation, Kark observes, is unique to Jewish settlement within the world's major settlement projects of the early twentieth century.[11] Yet Kark finds that the individual attempts to settle and harvest unsuitable land were erroneous, and hypothesizes that more emphasis should have been given instead to large-scale industrial development in the Negev.[12] While Kark criticizes the lack of broader planning within Israel's first settlement attempts in the region, she nonetheless finds 'justification in their experimentality, which contributed to the study of an unknown environment's unique conditions, [and] enabled the much broader and more established settlement in the period after the establishment of the state'.[13]

The Potash Industry and Early Settlement

The first attempts to industrialize the extraction of minerals from the Dead Sea in the 1920s led to experimentation in settlement and building design in extreme climates. Some attested that the rudimentary structures that constituted these early settlements – factories, workers' dormitories, and homes – provided significant lessons in overcoming climatic conditions that benefited Israeli architects working in Israel's arid regions in the future.[14] The Dead Sea's mineral industry was established by Moshe Novomeysky, the founder of the Palestine Potash

Company.[15] Novomeysky, a Siberian Jewish engineer and a pioneer of mineral extraction in Russia, set his eyes on the extraction of potash from the Dead Sea after reading an unpublished report on Palestine's natural resources by Otto Warburg, a German botanist and avid Zionist.[16] Novomeysky received the first of several Dead Sea franchises in 1929.[17] He commissioned the architect Richard Kauffmann to construct the company's new industrial complex on the northern shore of the Sea because of Kauffmann's novel approach to climate control.[18]

Kauffmann had been educated and worked in Germany until he was invited to Israel by Zionist leader Arthur Rupin.[19] He then worked as head planner at the Israeli Land Development Company.[20] Between 1929 and 1933, Kauffmann designed the factory, service facilities, executive home, and workers' housing in Novomeysky's complex in Kalya, a narrow beach between the company's newly constructed desalination ponds and the Sea to the west of the Jordan River Delta.[21] The location was moderately more advantageous due to the air currents that circulated between the two bodies of water.[22]

Having experimented with natural ventilation and passive cooling techniques in Kibbutz Degania in northern Israel, Kauffmann proposed a double roof system he had developed to respond to Israel's distinctive climate. He suggested an asbestos timber roof mounted 1–2 metres above the ceiling.[23] Air circulation through the roof's two layers cooled the room below, and its deep eaves provided extensive shading on ground level.[24] Kauffmann's two-storey worker's houses were made of reinforced concrete and concrete blocks, and had wide, lightweight roofs, exterior staircases, and porches.[25] Air currents ventilated the roofs and rooms through small openings, cooling interior temperatures.[26] The buildings' orientation towards the south-west allowed for unobstructed breeze, and ensured that two walls of each house would remain simultaneously in shadow during the day. Some suggested that the buildings' rotation also served to break the visual monotony of the repetitive houses.[27]

Kauffmann's buildings housed the potash industry's workers until the Israeli Declaration of Independence in 1948, at which time it was decreed that the state's new boundaries would not include Kalya or most of the Dead Sea's northern shore. The factory, settlement, and nearby Kibbutz Beit Haarava were abandoned during Israel's Independence War (1947-1949).[28] Under governmental management the potash industry eventually resumed production in 1952 on the Sea's southern basin at Sodom, until the site's abandonment in 1957 due to its harsh climate.[29]

The abandonment of Kalya, Beit Haarava, and Sodom affected the Israeli public's belief in the feasibility of settling and extracting minerals from the Dead Sea, even though the achievements there held key lessons for the future. As late as the 1960s, some feasibility studies attributed the notion that the Dead Sea could not be permanently inhabited to the failure of Sodom site.[30] People like Lieutenant General Mordechai Maklef considered the factory and settlements important evidence of the Jewish settlement's resilience in the face of hostile environments – 'a symbol of victory of man over the Malha [salt lands]' – and lamented their loss greatly.[31] Decades later, the architect-writer Michael Kuhn echoed

Maklef's sentiment in an article published in the daily newspaper *Davar.*[32] He wrote that architects like Kauffmann

> were not only the pioneers of Israeli architecture, but were also the pioneers of the best modern architecture at international standards; their experiments in architectural design, appropriate for the Israeli climate, are an achievement even by today's standards. Experiments that were done in the Dead Sea Region and in the Jordan valley, in solar protection and air circulation, have achieved important results. All of this has been forgotten.[33]

Working with the Palestine Potash Company, Kauffmann introduced a novel way of bettering the living conditions of the early Israeli pioneers who faced extraordinary challenges of climate and isolation. Future generations of architects, including Michael Kuhn, encountered similar challenges in their design of settlements, hotels, and institutions on the shores of the Dead Sea. Kauffmann's unembellished, bare-bones structures at Kalya were intended to shelter their inhabitants from the Sea's harsh climate, and to improve the worker's morale within a strict economy of means.[34] These methods and strategies were employed again by architects in the region after 1948.

Kibbutzim and New Settlements

After the establishment of the State of Israel, collective settlements, agricultural communities, and workers' neighbourhoods were planned and founded on the shores of the Dead Sea by the Jewish Agency, the Ministry of Housing, and the Kibbutzim Movement.[35] For some, the mere existence of permanent settlement on the Sea seemed impossible. The writer Ephraim Talmi reported in 1956 that the first hostel at Sodom, built in 1956, garnered national praise from the same 'sober institutions' that refused to contribute to its construction, regarding it as a 'fancifully delusional idea'.[36] While settlers were driven by shared principles of Zionist ideology, they held widely different approaches to its fulfilment in practice. Comparative analysis of the projects of two architects, Nahum Zolotov and Shmuel Mestechkin, serves to illustrate the ways in which the ideological, pedagogical, and logistical aspirations of each settlement influenced a given project's physical form and construction within the region's climate and unique landscape.

Kibbutzim, collective agricultural settlements in which all private wealth is eliminated, were integral to the Zionist movement's mission to resettle Israel.[37] Kibbutz Ein-Gedi, the first settlement founded in the Dead Sea after 1948, was significant for national security as it was the northern-most settlement on the Dead Sea after the partitioning of Palestine. The kibbutz was established near the biblical site of Ein-Gedi Spring, considered one of the most important archaeological sites in the Judaean Desert.[38] Kibbutz Ein-Gedi was recognized as an exemplar of conservation practices.[39] From the 1960s onwards, kibbutz members planted over 900 plant species within the settlement, culminating in its international recognition as the only botanical garden to reside within a community.[40] The architect Freddy Kahana states that the development of Ein-Gedi's unique landscape design was motivated by the desire to 'bloom' the desert, the Zionist principle posited by David Ben-Gurion.[41]

The establishment of the first Israeli Field School at Ein-Gedi was similarly considered as a fulfilment of Zionist principles that won the support of the Israeli leadership.[42] Established in 1959, the school served as a prototype for other institutions founded later.[43] Yossi Feldman, its first director, claimed that Ein-Gedi was the ideal place to pioneer such an 'innovative institution', since it offered a unique landscape, where 'the expanses and mystery of the desert meet the oasis dipped in greenery'.[44] The school's pedagogy was concerned with 'escorting' students as they interacted with their surroundings, rather than 'leading' them to specific spaces.[45] Feldman claimed that the 'field itself becomes a laboratory, in which the educational tools are observation, the senses, and the ability to come to conclusions from events happening in the field'.[46]

Within this pedagogical framework, architect Nahum Zolotov was commissioned to build the school's new facilities in the early 1960s. Zolotov, a Polish-born architect who trained at the Israel Institute of Technology (Technion), had already completed numerous projects, and had won several prominent awards.[47] In 1965, Zolotov said that the school's site 'only comes to a designer once in a lifetime', acknowledging the responsibility he felt 'in designing in an area with such dramatic natural beauty'.[48] Zolotov emphasized the school's integration with the surrounding landscape through massing and earthwork. In order for the school to give the impression of continuing 'the natural outlines' of the hills 'rather than obliterate them', Zolotov excavated and terraced the complex [Figure 1].[49]

The site's terracing also allowed for unobstructed views and breezes in the 250 residences.[50] One approaches the school via a service road to the east, gradually gaining elevation while moving north-west along the terraced youth hostel, student residences, and dining hall, finally reaching the faculty offices at the top of the hill [Figure 2]. To the south of the residences, a rectangular classroom building opens to a large plaza overlooking the David Stream and Sea. Here, the building's extension would have served as a base for an observatory and museum, but they were never built. A stair core would have allowed access to a prismatic exhibition space hoisted in the air, and an underground tunnel to an observation deck excavated in the hillside. Zolotov described his ambition to create a dramatic contrast between the tunnel's enclosed space and the subsequent open views.[51] Bridges, stairs, and ramps mediate the significant changes in elevation along the site. A pervasive network of pathways, lined with planters, threads through the school's different facilities and offers direct access to the surrounding summit. The expansive paving of the site also helped minimize dust.[52]

The site's terracing and retaining walls form the foundations of the two-storey residential buildings, comprised of rows of stacked modular units with outdoor spaces

Figure 1: View of Ein-Gedi Field School, Ein-Gedi, completed 1964. Architect Nahum Zolotov. Courtesy of the private archive of Nahum Zolotov.

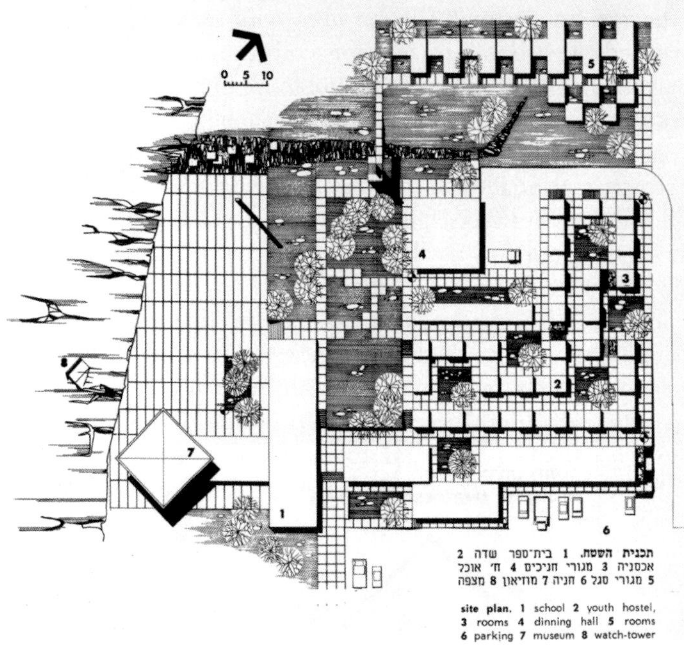

Figure 2: Plan of Ein-Gedi Field School, Ein-Gedi, completed 1964. Nahum Zolotov. Courtesy of the private archive of Nahum Zolotov.

separating each unit from the next. The second-level units provide shade for the first and are accessed from their rooftops. Zolotov used medium- to large-scale local gravel as aggregate in the concrete mixture used to construct the buildings, also known as 'no-fines concrete'. While these materials helped overcome the region's shortages and transportation challenges, they also clearly accentuate exterior walls and paths with texture and relief.[53] Gravel was also spread across rooftops for additional thermal control resulting from the stones' ability to absorb heat, thereby reducing the amount transmitted through the structure's roof.[54]

The School stood in sharp contrast to the seventeen-room housing complex of Neot Hakikar, Zolotov's other project under construction at the time. Unlike other settlements, which had governmental, financial, and ideological backing, the collective agricultural community at Neot Hakikar sought to inhabit the Dead Sea's southern extremity without the assistance of governmental agencies.[55] While Neot Hakikar did ultimately receive many subsidies from Zionist agencies, it nonetheless became the inspiration for subsequent social, agricultural, and business ventures that aimed to embrace the Sea's climate and prove the land's profitability independent of these institutions.[56]

Zolotov's housing complex is a low, horizontal *in situ* concrete building situated on a hill [Figure 3]. With minimal openings, the building is referred to as 'the fortress'.[57] The modern building is thus associated with the courtyard fortifications traditionally built in the desert. As at Ein-Gedi's, the living quarters are organized in modular units. Unlike the Field School residences, however, these do not follow the natural topography but rather are tightly arranged around three sides of an open courtyard. Individual entrance porticos line the courtyard's interior. An additional row of lower-level units on the north-east side are accessed through an internal 'street', streaked by shadows cast by the volumes above.

Zolotov's two projects in the Dead Sea, despite being constructed simultaneously, express distinctly different approaches to the fulfilment of their communities' Zionist mission in built form and design. The Field School's composition, integration of landscape

Figure 3: Neot Hakikar housing complex, Neot Hakikar, completed 1964. Architect Nahum Zolotov. Courtesy of the private archive of Nahum Zolotov.

elements, and strategic use of local materials demonstrate Zolotov's intention to promote unobstructed movement between the school and its surroundings: roofs are treated the same as floors and pathways turn into trails. The School's design directly supports its pedagogical approach, creating an innovative, outward-looking, and inquisitive environment in which to explore the surrounding landscapes. In Neot Hakikar, by contrast, the difference between inside and out is clearly defined. Even exterior spaces – the landscaped courtyard, the individual patios, and the internal 'street' – are bound under an all-encompassing roof. The design provides a sense of security, necessitated by the settlement's relative isolation, but also accentuates values of independence and privacy inherent to the community's agenda.

In 1971, only six years after the completion of Zolotov's Neot Hakikar project, the architect Shmuel Mestechkin completed the Neve Zohar housing project a few miles north. The Tamar Regional Council developed the housing primarily for tourism and potash industry service providers.[58] The project was novel in its accommodation of a group not bound by collective agreement, shared profession, or any other commitment other than intent to live by the Dead Sea. Neve Zohar was the first step in a plan to build a much larger city, Zohar-illit (Upper Zohar), where the region's service providers would live in the future.[59]

Mestechkin, born in the Ukraine, had immigrated to Israel as a young man in the 1920s and helped found Hashomer Hazair, the Zionist youth movement.[60] Despite his deep commitment to Israel, Mestechkin sought higher education at the Bauhaus in Germany from 1930 to 1933, under the tutelage of architect Ludwig Mies van der Rohe. By 1943, he was appointed the head architect for the Technical Department of the National Kibbutz in Israel, where he designed more than sixty kibbutzim and buildings.[61]

Mestechkin had already completed a youth hostel and the Beit Hayotzer museum on site when he received the Neve Zohar commission [Figure 7]. He designed twenty living units, organized in four-unit blocks, located along paved pedestrian streets with stairs, planters, and lawns that sloped towards the Sea. The two-storey units were constructed on terraces perpendicular to the slopes of the shores [Figure 4]. Distinct dividing walls separated the units, each unit slightly shifted from the adjacent one. Living rooms and front yards were located to the north, and bedrooms, kitchens, and bathrooms to the south. Exterior walls and fences were constructed of concrete set with irregular pebbles, a treatment Mestechkin had used before in the adjacent hostel and museum.

At Neve Zohar, special attention was given to privacy, amenities, and comfort. The reporter Yaakov Bar-On assured readers in 1971 that the new housing development was not 'taken from the Wild West'. Rather, it was reminiscent of 'an organized urban suburb', with units of '60 square meters organized compactly with nothing lacking'.[62] One interviewee exclaimed, 'What a wonderful finish the apartment has. I was really amazed. And there's air conditioning and a front yard and a gate!'[63]

The Neve Zohar housing project marked a new era in the Dead Sea industry: now regional and national authorities encouraged the growth of tourism as a primary economic

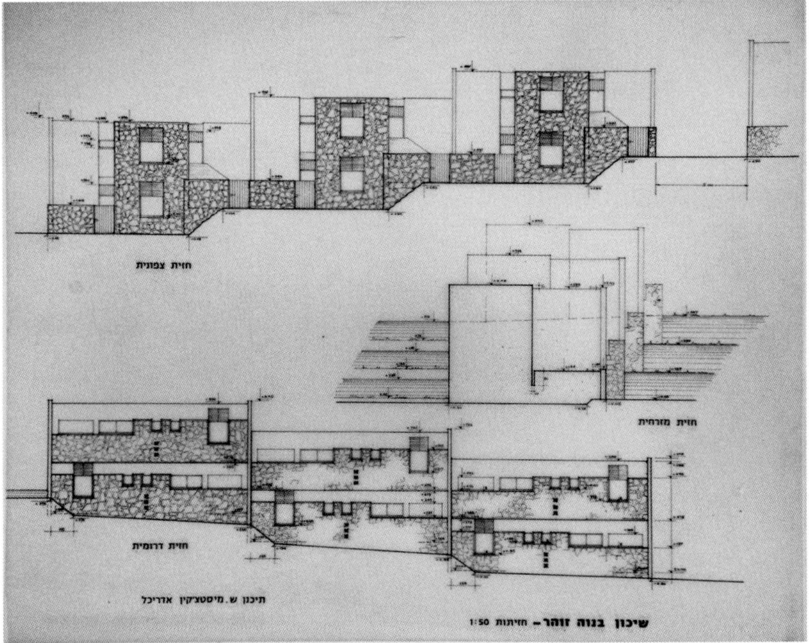

Figure 4: Elevations of Neve Zohar housing project, Neve Zohar completed 1971. Architect Shmuel Mestechkin. Courtesy of Yad Yaari Archive, Kibbutz Givat Haviva.

driver in the area.[64] Kibbutzim such as Ein-Gedi that lacked sufficient agricultural lands to expand their farming turned instead to health tourism as a basis for their future economy.[65] The dining hall in Ein-Gedi, also designed by Mestechkin and completed in 1971, was commissioned as part of the new infrastructure needed to accommodate this shift. The previous hall, built by the head of the Technical Department at the Jewish Agency, Yaakov Matrikin, had been converted to serve Ein-Gedi's newly arrived tourists instead of kibbutz residents.[66]

Since the 1930s, dining halls were the kibbutzim's central institutions, often serving multiple roles as a place of congregation.[67] In planning dining halls, Mestechkin argues that the architect should provide a 'practical solution to the kibbutz's collective functioning, that derives from ideological principles, rather than private whims'.[68] Matrikin's dining hall followed a circular open plan, surrounded by windows and covered by a domed roof. Far from this multi-directional plan, which left the hall's interior arrangement and orientation open to individual interpretation, Mestechkin's design sought to define this environment more closely [Figure 5].

Mestechkin's hall was rectangular, with each façade composed of unique elements: an inset arced entrance portico to the north, floor-to-ceiling slot windows to the south, and thick concrete protrusions framing windows and doors to the east. 'Atypical' windows and

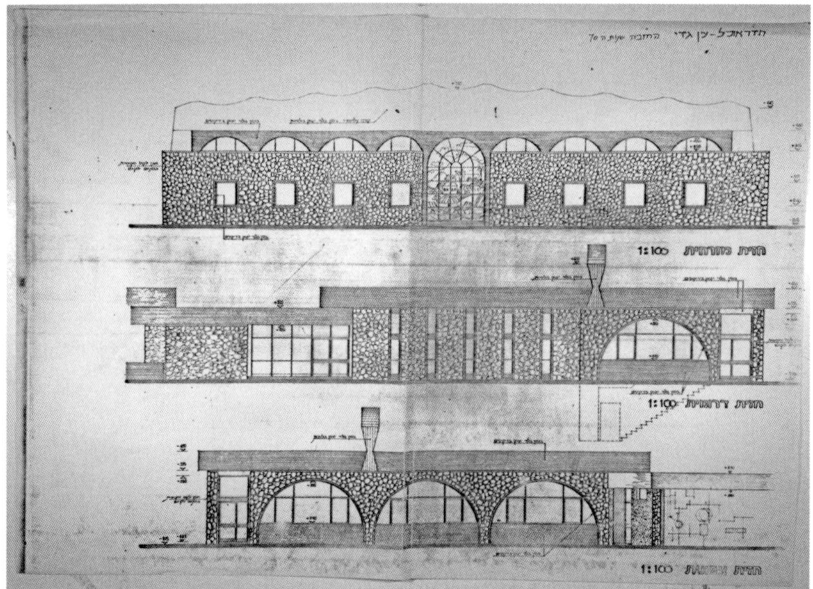

Figure 5: Elevations of Ein-Gedi dining hall, Ein Gedi, 1972. Architect Shmuel Mestechkin. Courtesy of Yad Yaari Archive, Kibbutz Givat Haviva.

shaded exterior spaces, Mestechkin noted, would serve both as important architectural expressions, and necessary protections from the elements.[69] The windows are also an organizational device for the hall's interior: 'The relationship between wall and [dining] table was defined by the window.'[70]

Despite their formal differences, architect Freddy Kahana sees similarities in Mestechkin's and Matrikin's efforts to adapt to the surroundings: 'These two dining halls symbolize, perhaps more than any other example, the uncertainty in addressing the problem of landscape integration – in Ein-Gedi's case – an extreme desert landscape.'[71] As an example, Kahana cites the dome in Matrikin's original structure, an element which Matrikin sought to integrate with the surrounding cliffs. The countered profile in the deep upturned beam of Mestechkin's roof, Kahana argues, was likely intended to do the same – it was an imitation of the landscape that served its backdrop.[72]

Kahana suggests, however, that Matrikin's and Mestechkin's attempts to 'fit in' to the regional landscape were counter-productive. The use of symbolism and imitation in the buildings, he claims, were 'methods "foreign" to architecture'.[73] Kahana, similar to Kuhn, argues for the approach taken by the architects of the 1920s and1930s, who instead 'created a simple architecture, functional and just, and were thereby successful in their integration in the landscape of the valley, in front of the Gilboa and the Carmel'.[74] For Kahana, architects like Kauffmann tried to integrate with 'climate' more than with landscape, thus creating a visual uniqueness in the site not brought about by imitation. Such methods, he notes, would have been effective in responding to both the architectural and the societal needs of the kibbutzim.[75]

Analysing an illustration of the dining hall's east façade suggests that kibbutzim now sought to promote atmospheres of recreation and leisure, a reflection of their expanding tourist economy. Here, Mestechkin integrates a central stained-glass window (not realized in the final construction) depicting a bucolic scene that resembles the kibbutz itself. The scene is reminiscent of the one depicted on the 50 Israeli lira bill at the time, in which two pioneers stand in front of a settlement similar to Ein-Gedi's. In the dining-hall scene, however, instead of the pioneers, one finds two empty beach chairs.

Ein-Gedi's tourism industry grew rapidly, propelled by its reputation as a health resort and its designation as a natural reserve.[76] Both Nahum Zolotov and Shmuel Mestechkin received commissions for the first health resorts and cultural institutions on the Sea's shores. Their achievements in the design of permanent settlements on the Dead Sea would later be tested and advanced through accommodating much larger international populations.

Health Heritage Tourism in the Dead Sea Region

Following the establishment of permanent settlements in the region, the construction of roads connecting the Sea to Israel's centre, and increased public and private investment, the Dead Sea health and heritage tourism grew rapidly. In 1964, approximately 200,000 tourists came to Ein-Gedi alone, with 15,000 visits per day during the Passover holiday.[77] The salutary effects of the Sea's environment bolstered its reputation both locally and abroad. Archaeological excavations in Masada and Qumran in the Dead Sea region, and the discovery therein of world-renowned artefacts such as the Dead Sea Scrolls, encouraged the preservation of these sites and the construction of accompanying tourist facilities.[78]

Tourist development would also serve as a mechanism of population distribution.[79] A survey of the region's development from 1965 projected that the industry could draw as many as 12,000 inhabitants to the area from Israel's populated cities.[80] On a practical level, the survey noted, the region's topography would not allow for a population of this calibre on a single site, and another city for the new workers and their families would have to be built at a higher altitude, close to Neve Zohar.[81]

The survey recognized that in addition to the Dead Sea's unique natural environment, the region was also endowed with important historical sites that served as 'the stage for our nation's chronicles'.[82]A series of cultural institutions was initiated by Yehuda Almog, a member of the third wave of immigration to Israel (the Third Aliyah). Almog envisioned a settled and lively region surrounding the Dead Sea.[83] After founding the Sea's first kibbutz, Ein Haarava (1939), which encompassed the first territories where soil desalination was successfully completed, Almog moved to the southern banks of the Sea. There he became the secretary of the newly founded Dead Sea Regional Development Company and later served as the director of the Tamar Regional Council.[84]

Almog envisioned three cultural sites on the shores of the Sea, described as 'unfathomable in regards to their national and educational content'.[85] These included a cultural pavilion at the foot of Masada, 'in which a huge epic of our nation will be depicted'; a memorial, also at the foot of Masada, commemorating the Jewish fighters of Ghetto Vilna (never realized); and Beit Hayotzer, a museum dedicated to the potash industry's achievements.[86]

An active member of the Zionist movement, Almog devoted special attention to Masada – the remains of a Herodian fortress on top of a mesa and the believed site of the Sicarii Jews' mass suicide during the Roman occupation in 73 ad. Masada's status as a Zionist pilgrimage site among Israeli youth groups was compounded by the renewed interest in exploring the site's history.[87] In the mid-1950s, Almog and volunteers reconstructed the 'Snake Trail', an arduous switchback trail that had once led to the fortress.[88] Masada's transformation into one of Israel's most important heritage sites was fuelled by the 1965 Masada expedition, Israel's largest archaeological excavation since 1948.[89] Led by renowned archaeologist and former Chief of Staff Yigal Yadin, the excavation focused on the documentation, preservation, and reconstruction of Masada's remaining structures and artefacts.[90] With Masada's public reopening, Almog organized an architectural competition for a research and education centre called the 'Pavilion for the Cultures of the Dead Sea'. Architects Freddy Kahana and Dennis Kahn won the competition, and the building was completed in 1963 [Figure 6][91]

The young architects had been trained abroad and became kibbutz members when they immigrated to Israel in the 1930s . Kahana noted that the committee was happy to learn they had won, perhaps because, as kibbutz members, they encapsulated the Zionist vision.[92] As described in their submission, their design sought to achieve 'harmony with the surrounding landscape' while providing a cool interior.[93] Based on a 'free and continuous composition', the pavilion was composed of tightly spaced curved stone walls with cast-concrete roofs, elevated on steel posts so that air could flow freely.[94] By constructing the walls of local stone, the architects envisioned the building would give the impression of being 'cut out of the hillside [...] a natural backdrop to the exhibit'.[95]

The building was also intended to serve as a 'foyer to the climb'.[96] Its orientation and programming reflect its role as the first stage of this ceremonial (and arduous) spatial sequence. A series of excavated circles delineated a large plaza by the entrance where groups could gather in the pre-dawn hours to catch the sunrise at the top. Similarly, an enclosed patio space at the rear provides a cool interior for groups returning during the hot midday hours. Circulation through the building mimics and extends the Snake Trail. Visitors moving through the exhibition are guided along the curved stone walls to an auditorium, research rooms, and library, finally emerging at the beginning of the trail's extension.

If the Masada museum chronicled the region's past, Beit Hayotzer was designed as a celebration of its present and future. The second cultural building realized under Almog's

Figure 6: Presentation model of the Masada cultural pavilion, completed 1963. Architects Freddy Kahana and Dennis Kahn. Courtesy of the private archive of Freddy Kahana.

vision was designed by Shmuel Mestechkin. It was located at the top of a hill overlooking the Sea at the future site of the Neve Zohar housing project, also designed by Mestechkin. The museum was to afford a visual overview of the potash industry's development. By the time of the museum's cornerstone ceremony in 1964, the industry was in the process of transforming the Sea's entire southern basin into evaporation pools.[97]

Mestechkin's design includes a main building with an auditorium and observation deck, a series of terraces with a switchback path leading up to it, and a youth hostel that cascades down the hill perpendicularly. The auditorium building has a square plan defined by concrete walls covered in local stone. The visitor reaches the observation deck by an exterior ramp that wraps around the building. There, a concrete roof, supported by a grid of exposed beams and tapered columns, frames a narrow view of the potash company's evaporation pools. A model of the Dead Sea, documenting its twentieth-century transformation, occupies its centre [Figure 7].

The analysis of Almog's projects illustrates that the differences between the design of his first endeavour at Masada and his second at Beit Hayotzer are striking. Kahn and Kahana's pavilion is located at the monument's foot, Masada, while Mestechkin's museum becomes the monument towards which one ascends. Both institutions were bound by Yehuda

Figure 7: Presentation model of Beit Hayutzer at Neve Zohar, completed 1964. Architect Shmuel Mestechkin. Courtesy of Yad Yaari Archive, Kibbutz Givat Haviva.

Almog's educational and cultural agenda, thus suggesting they had to portray a convincing vision of the Dead Sea's future. It can be observed that the Masada pavilion, on the one hand, expressed a future rooted in tradition, using rough materials and an organic form to reinterpret the way one approaches Israel's rediscovered heritage sites; Beit Hayotzer, on the other, seems to use exposed structure and rigid cubic forms to construct a vision of a future driven by science and industry.

During the 1960s Mestechkin also participated in the ongoing development of health tourism in the area, contributing a master plan for Ein Bokek that remains one of the Dead Sea's premier resort locations.[98] Medical studies carried out since the 1950s scientifically confirmed the salutary effects of the Sea's minerals and the sun's reduced radiation, which bolstered the Sea's reputation both locally and abroad.[99] The development of Ein Bokek and Hamei Zohar, two sites with natural sulphur springs, was sponsored by the Ministry of Development and the Dead Sea Regional Development Company.[100]

Mestechkin's plans for Ein Bokek show hotels spaced widely apart, with a large central plaza delineated by palm trees and vegetation. The plaza funnels visitors into a series of public beach facilities, including sports fields, boat launches, a man-made island, and a cafe.[101] In the *Hazofe* newspaper article, 'A Health-City in Ein Bokek', published on January 25, 1963, the reporter Arieh Arad notes that the bathhouses, eventually completed by Nahum Zolotov and Mestechkin, 'would be equipped with the best of modern technology, including air conditioning, doctor's offices, bathrooms and heating'.[102] Six- to seven-storey hotels were planned with hundreds of rooms, Arad adds, with direct access to the beach facilities.[103]

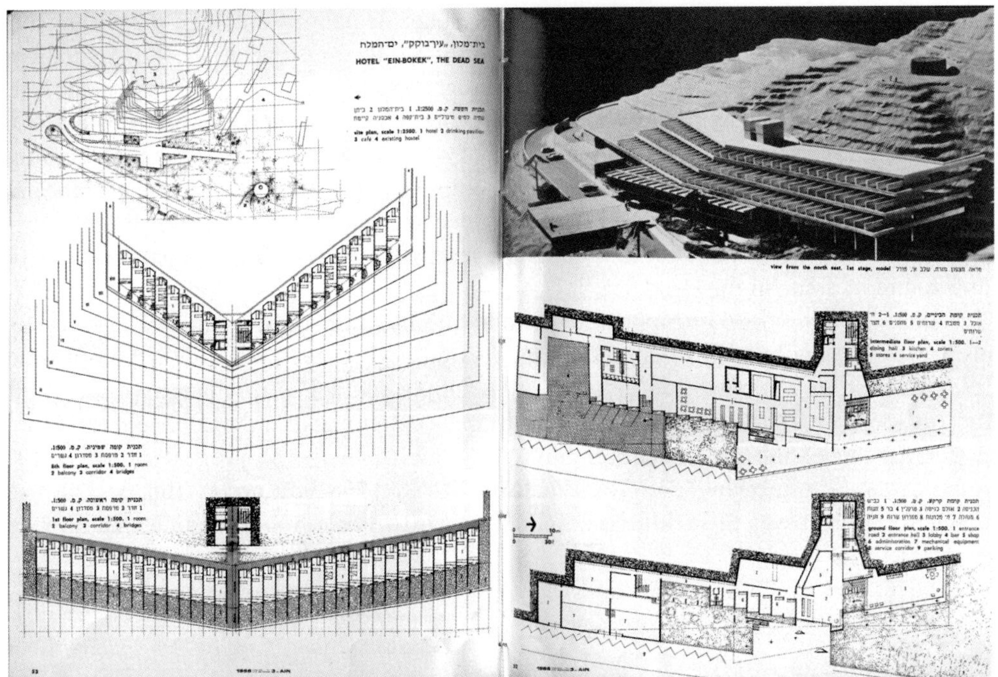

Figure 8: Plans and model photos, 'Ein Bokek' Hotel, published 1966 (not built). Architect Michael Kuhn. Source: Michael Kuhn, '"Ein Bokek" Hotel, the Dead Sea', *Arkitectura 3* (July–September 1966): 50.

Michael Kuhn saw the Ein Bokek site as an opportunity for formal experimentation, as can be inferred from his proposal for a hotel there [Figure 8]. Kuhn admired the work of Richard Kauffmann at Kalya for its adaptation of modernist principles to the Israeli climate. He built the original rudimentary structures at Ein Bokek that previously served patients from the public health services (Kupat Holim).[104] In a 1966 issue of *Arkitectura*, Kuhn revealed plans for the 250-room hotel that was intended to be used as a prototype, although it was never built.[105] In Kuhn's words, the prototype would have offered an alternative to the 'high-rise' hotels planned for the site and 'avoid obtuse deviation from the character of the landscape or a damaging of its perfection'.[106] According to Kuhn, the Regional Council approved the use of the prototype for all future buildings to be constructed on site.[107]

The 'Ein Bokek' Hotel was designed to cascade down the hillside. Parallel rows of rooms terrace the site's sloping topography, each set back from the one below. The floors take the form of concrete trays suspended on columns and walls so that the visual and physical continuity of the sloped terrain below remains uninterrupted. Kuhn writes that when the original idea of a diagonal elevator was determined to be 'impractical', a vertical elevator core was designed to be placed at the mountain's base instead, giving the floor plates a fan-like appearance.[108]

Kuhn argues in the same article that the 'Ein Bokek' Hotel was not only integrated with its environment but was also advantageous economically and structurally.[109] Essentially a series of one storey buildings, the structure was light and therefore suited for the area's soil; it could be built in stages and avoided the expensive and heavy construction process of a high-rise. Kuhn argues for the building as proof of how 'rational and economic planning does not in any way conflict with the planner's ability to give the building subjective formal characteristics, and that formal design does not need to negatively impact its functionality'.[110] Kuhn's closing statements point to an ongoing argument over form and function that had now found its arena in the Dead Sea.[111]

Nahum Zolotov's 1963 proposal for a hotel and bathhouse complex at Hamei Zohar also reveals a concern for functionality and flexibility [Figure 9]. Zolotov is said to have researched some of the world's most renowned international bathhouses in preparation for this project with the goal of providing a highly customizable and flexible operation.[112] A description of the project, never built, was published in the journal *Handasa Ve-Adrichaloot* ('Engineering and Architecture') in its 1966 edition.[113] The description notes the project was to include a hotel, an administration building, and a bathhouse complex.[114]

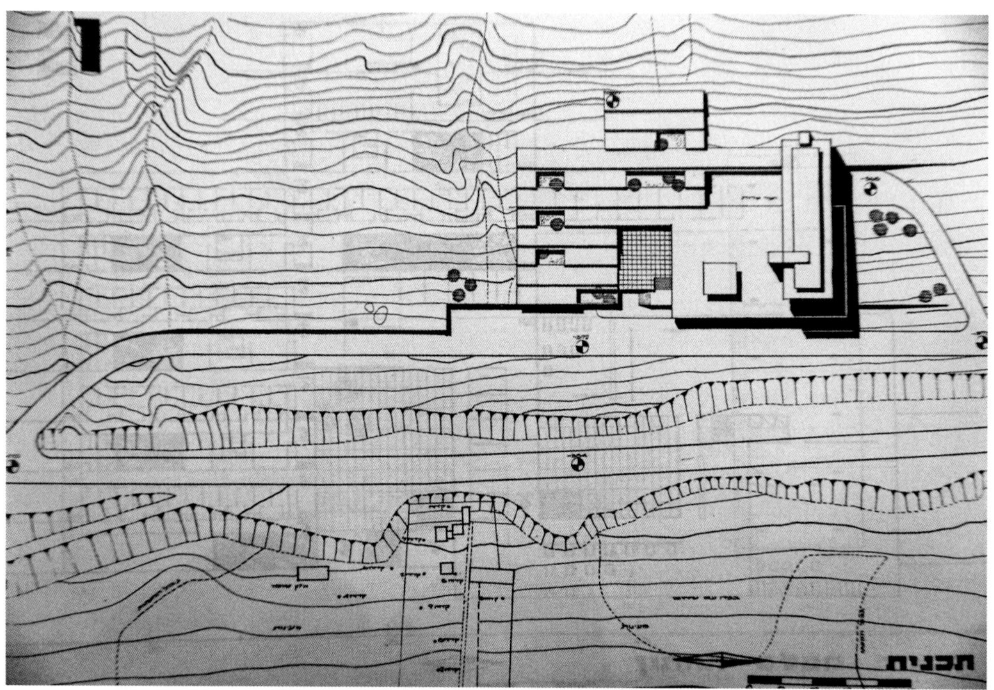

Figure 9: Sections of 'Hamei Zohar' Hotel, Hamei Zohar, published 1965 (not built). Architect Nahum Zolotov. Courtesy of the private archive of Nahum Zolotov.

The bathing facilities consisted of five parallel buildings running north–south on a sloping site, each at its own elevation. Public corridors that ran along them led to individual dressing and resting chambers. Two adjacent dressing rooms shared a bath that could be filled with customized solutions upon request, delivered via a complex plumbing system. Personnel would arrive from parallel service corridors behind the baths. The clearly defined sequence of spaces promoted circulation through the bathhouse, mirroring a patient's advancement through a treatment plan. The description also noted how the climate and topography mandated that the building be 'constructed of special building materials [...] closed to the outside, and with adjustable air conditioning throughout'.[115] Intermittent patios on every level opened the otherwise hermetic quarters to the exterior elements, allowing for sunbathing and air circulation.

The spur of tourism development in the 1970s detracted from growing evidence of the Dead Sea's shrinking footprint, among other ecological problems that the region is still facing today. Construction in Ein Bokek and Hamei Zohar disregarded the dangers that their proximity to the evaporation pools posed to the buildings' foundations.[116] While both were left unrealized, Kuhn's and Zolotov's proposals suggest that requirements for flexibility and functionality had become a priority in the design of the Dead Sea's accommodations. In the decades that followed, larger monetary investments, advancement in construction technology, and a growing reliance on mechanical ventilation meant that designing for the Dead Sea climate would become less restrictive than it had been for architectural pioneers such as Mestechkin and Zolotov, allowing larger, taller, and less opaque structures.

Isolated Commonalities: A Summary

With the Negev's settlement, the Dead Sea became an invaluable national and economic frontier. The growing potash industry drove the region's settlement in the 1920s and 1930s in a way that, in hindsight, resembles Kark's proposal for large-scale industrial development.[117] The Dead Sea Works, as the Potash Company was called after the Independence Day War (1948), continues to extract minerals from the Sea today alongside its Jordanian counterpart, the Arab Potash Company. With the construction of the western evaporation pools that constitute the southern end of the Dead Sea, the industry irreversibly altered the Sea's footprint.

The extraction of minerals from the Sea, itself an experimental venture, required a holistic vision and broad-range, long-term planning. At the same time, the region's unique topography mandated that its settlements operate separately and independently. Despite their isolation, these settlements shared common strategies and characteristics in response to the region's inhospitable environment, the lack of materials, and limited technology and accessibility. Passive cooling strategies, protection from exterior elements, and the desire to integrate within the region's landscape were paramount concerns shared across projects.

The same strategies and elements that Richard Kauffmann utilized in the construction of the early potash facilities – elevated roofs, building orientation, and minimal fenestration – are evident in the later works of Mestechkin, Zolotov, and Kahana. Building volumes were strategically designed to create a variety of microclimates, preceding the hermetic environment that mechanical air conditioners would require. Fenestrations were kept to a minimum to provide protection from dust and heat; walls and roofs, however, admitted air through slots and cavities.

Multiple architects used similar strategies to integrate with the region's landscape. While Freddy Kahana found that these strategies failed in landscape integration, they were unequivocally successful in providing thermal comfort and manifested their clients' different political and social ideologies in physical form. Zolotov's and Mestechkin's use of extensive earthwork, material selections, and formal imitation were, by the architects' own accounts, attempts to achieve an unobtrusive built environment within the Dead Sea region. But these efforts also provided essential climatic comfort that allowed the settlements to fulfil their ideological agendas. By providing acoustic and thermal comfort the architects successfully addressed issues of privacy and programmatic divisions critical to the function of collective settlements, such as kibbutzim. They also directly supported their pedagogical agendas, such as in the Ein-Gedi Field School. There, excavation, terracing, and paving provided students and visitors a seamless transition from landscape to base camp. Faced with the region's extreme challenges, designers had to strategically use the limited resources at their disposal in order to provide comfort and support the ideological message their clients wanted to convey.

The unanimous desire to integrate with the landscape and consider the climate was a means by which to fulfil the Zionist ideology that drove the settlement of the region. The design of structures both harmonious with and resilient to their surroundings expressed the Zionist ideas of overcoming the challenges that Israel's desert territories posed. Coupled with the educational and cultural programmes that pioneers such as Yehuda Almog envisioned, these structures served to frame a Zionist narrative of the past and future and make it accessible to the Israeli public.

The approaches to fulfilling the Zionist narrative are what serve to differentiate the projects from one another. The 'fortress' characteristics of the housing at Neot Hakikar not only place it within a tradition of desert archetypes, but also characterize it as an introverted, private community, adamant about fulfilling its beliefs outside of the Zionist institutions. By the same token, Neve Zohar's adaptation of suburban symbols – the gate, the front yard, the parking space – to the desert region, conveys a message that tying one's fate to the Sea should not necessarily require one to enter a collective, agrarian framework.

While function and flexibility were already sought-after goals in kibbutz and settlement design, their emergence as key considerations within tourist accommodations points to a shift in priorities. This was enabled by a confidence in the architect's accumulated knowledge and experience in construction within arid regions. The staggering differences between

Richard Kaufmann's early workers' houses and Michael Kuhn's 'Ein Bokek' prototype must be attributed to more than technological advancements in air-conditioning systems and construction practices. Having the privilege to pay attention to practicality and flexibility in one of the most rigid and impractical settings known to man results in large part from the experimentation, resourcefulness, and ingenuity of three decades of pioneering design in the Dead Sea.

Bibliography

'20 Million Lira Will Be Invested in Tourist Development in the Region'. *Davar*, December 26, 1965 (In Hebrew).

Amir, Tula. *Nahum Zolotov/Architect and Planner*. Tel Aviv: Israeli Center for Libraries, 2011 (In Hebrew).

Arad, Arieh. 'A Health-City in Ein Bokek'. *Hazofe*, January 25, 1963 (In Hebrew).

Bar-On, Yaakov. 'The Lowest Housing in the World'. *Laisha*, May 1971 (In Hebrew).

Barnes, Irston R. 'Israel Finds New Way to Help Conservation'. *Washington Post*, August 12, 1962.

'The Bathhouses at Hamei Zohar', Nahum Zolotov's private archive, 13. Pamphlet (In Hebrew).

Beilin, Yossi. 'Between Harat and Chamra'. *Davar*, April 12, 1974 (In Hebrew).

Ben Gurion, David. 'Southward'. In *Ben Gurion Looks at the Bible*, translated by Jonathen Kolatch, 173–89. New York: Jonathan David Publishers, 1972.

Biger, Gideon. 'Israel's Border at the Dead Sea'. In *The Dead Sea and the Judean Desert 1900–1967*, edited by Naor Mordechai, 56–63. Jerusalem: Yad Yitzhak Ben-Zvi, 1990 (In Hebrew).

Cohen, D. 'Soddom – a Challenge to the Youth'. *Davar*, June 10, 1964 (In Hebrew).

Doron, Asher. *Dead Sea Development Survey: For the Tamar Regional Council*. Tel Aviv: Ha-Maḥlaḳah Ha-Tekhnit Shel Kibutse Ha-Shomer Ha-Sta'ir, 1965 (In Hebrew).

Drori, Shlomo. 'From the Israeli Potash Factory to the Dead Sea Factories'. In *The Dead Sea and the Judean Desert 1900–1967*, edited by Naor Mordechai,104-109. Jerusalem: Yad Yitzhak Ben-Zvi, 1990 (In Hebrew).

'Ein Gedi Develops Health Tourism: High Demand for Sulfer Baths'. *Davar*, December 3, 1963.

Epstein-Pliouchtch, Marina and Michael Levin. *Richard Kauffmann and the Zionist Project*. Tel Aviv: Ha-Ḳibuts Ha-me'uḥad, 2016 (In Hebrew).

Feldman, Yossi. 'The Ein Gedi Field School – Israel's First'. In *The Dead Sea and the Judean Desert 1900–1967*, edited by Naor Mordechai, 157–60. Jerusalem: Yad Yitzhak Ben-Zvi, 1990 (In Hebrew).

Givon, Shlomo. 'Millions of Fish – But No Beef'. *Maariv*, April 22, 1965, 9 (In Hebrew).

Hadas, Gideon. 'Yehuda Almog, Pioneer of Developing of the Dead Sea Region'. *Negev, Dead Sea and Arava Studies* 8.3 (2016): 89–92 (In Hebrew).

'Hamei Zohar Bathouses'. *Handasa Ve-Adrichaloot* 2, no.1 (1966): 36–37 (In Hebrew).

'Hillside Centre'. *Interbuild* 12.1 (1965): 15.

Kahana, Freddy. *Neither Town nor Village: The Architecture of the Kibbutz 1910–1990*. Ramat Efal: Yad Tevenkin, 2011 (In Hebrew).

Kahana. Freddy and Dennis Kahn, *Description of the Building in English*, 1959. Freddy Kahana's personal archive.

Kark, Ruth. *The Chronicles of the Pioneering Settlement in the Negev until 1948.* Tel Aviv: Ha-Ḳibuts Ha-me'uḥad, 1973 (In Hebrew).

Kerem, Moshe. 'Kibbutz Movement'. In *Encyclopaedia Judaica*, edited by Fred Skolnik and Michael Berenbaum, 121-124. 2nd ed. Detroit: Thomson Gale, 2007.

Kreiger, Barbara. *The Dead Sea: Myth, History, and Politics*. Hanover: New Hampshire University Press of New England [for] Brandeis University Press, 1997.

Krispin, Hilla Tal. *Renaissance at Sodom: the Contribution of Palestine Potash Ltd to the development of Dead-Sea Region and Palestine , 1930-1948* Be'er Sheva: Ben Gurion University of the Negev, 2010 (In Hebrew).

Kuhn, Michael. '"Ein Bokek" Hotel, the Dead Sea'. *Arkitectura 3* (July/September, 1966), 50–53.

——— 'Architecture's Energy Scandal'. *Davar*, August 24, 1979 (In Hebrew).

Maklef, Mordechai. 'Introduction'. In *The Dead Sea and Its Israeli Shore*, edited by Ze'ev Vilnai, 5-10. Ha-Mo'atsah Ha-ezorit Tamar: 1964 (In Hebrew).

Mestechkin, Shmuel. 'How to Approach the Planning of a Point?' In *Mestechkin Builds Israel*, edited by Muki Zur and Yuval Danieli. Tel Aviv: Ha-Ḳibuts Ha-me'uḥad, 2008 (In Hebrew).

——— 'Instructions for the Planning of the Ein Hmiphraz-Mazra Dining Hall'. In *Mestechkin Builds Israel*, edited by Muki Zur and Yuval Danieli. Tel Aviv: Ha-Ḳibuts Ha-me'uḥad, 2008 (In Hebrew).

Nezer, Ehud. 'Masada – Survey, Excavation and Reconstruction'. In *The Dead Sea and the Judean Desert 1900–1967*, edited by Naor Mordechai, 185–97. Jerusalem: Yad Yitzhak Ben-Zvi, 1990).

Rau, H. and F. Schiff. 'Kauffmann Pioneered Rural Planning'. *Jerusalem Post*, March 7, 1958.

Sztankeler, Vanesa, Isaac A. Meir, and Moshe Schwartz. 'Physical Development in an Ecologically Sensitive Area: The Planning of the Dead Sea Region'. *Geography Research Forum* 32, no.1 (2006): 119–45.

Talmi, Ephraim. 'The Hostel Next to the Cave'. *Davar*, March 20, 1956 (In Hebrew).

Talmi, Menahem. 'A Health-City on the Shores of the Dead Sea'. *Maariv*, April 19, 1963 (In Hebrew).

Orni, Ephraim, Shaked Gilboa, Gideon Hadas and Benjamin Mazar. 'En-Gedi'. In *Encyclopaedia Judaica,* edited by Fred Skolnik and Michael Berenbaum, 406-408. 2nd ed. Detroit: Thomson Gale, 2007.

'The Bathhouses at Hamei Zohar' (Nahum Zolotov's private archive), 13. Pamphlet (In Hebrew).

Vilnai, Ze'ev. *The Dead Sea and Its Israeli Shore*. Ha-Mo'atsah Ha-ezorit Tamar, 1964 (In Hebrew).

Zur, Muki and Yuval Danieli, eds. *Mestechkin Builds Israel.* Tel Aviv: Ha-Ḳibuts Ha-me'uḥad, 2008 (In Hebrew).

Notes

1 All translations from Hebrew to English are the author's own, unless otherwise specified.

2 Gideon Biger, 'Israel's Border at the Dead Sea', in *The Dead Sea and the Judean Desert 1900–1967*, ed. Naor Mordechai (Jerusalem: Yad Yitzhak Ben-Zvi, 1990), 56–57 (In Hebrew).
3 Hilla Tal Krispin, *Renaissance at Sodom: The Contribution of Palestine Potash Ltd to the Development of Dead-Sea Region and Palestine, 1930–1948* (Be'er Sheva: Ben Gurion University of the Negev, 2010), 383–85 (In Hebrew).
4 Ibid., 10–12.
5 Barbara Kreiger, *The Dead Sea: Myth, History, and Politics* (Hanover: New Hampshire University Press of New England [for] Brandeis University Press, 1997), 141–46.
6 David Ben-Gurion, 'Southward', in *Ben-Gurion looks at the Bible*, trans. Jonathen Kolatch (Middle Village, NY: Jonathan David Publishers, 1972), 179–82.
7 Ibid., 181–82.
8 Ibid., 179.
9 Ibid., 188.
10 Ruth Kark, *The Chronicles of the Pioneering Settlement in the Negev until 1948* (Tel Aviv: Ha-Ḳibuts Ha-me'uḥad, 1973), 186–87 (In Hebrew).
11 Ibid.
12 Ibid., 186
13 Ibid.
14 Michael Kuhn, 'Architecture's Energy Scandal', *Davar*, August 24, 1979,17 (In Hebrew).
15 Kreiger, *Dead Sea*, 153–56.
16 Ibid., 142–43.
17 Ibid., 146–50.
18 H. Rau and F. Schiff, 'Kauffmann Pioneered Rural Planning', *Jerusalem Post*, March 7, 1958.
19 Marina Epstein-Pliouchtch and Michael Levin, *Richard Kauffmann and the Zionist Project* (Tel Aviv: Ha-Ḳibuts Ha-me'uḥad, 2016), 12–21 (In Hebrew).
20 His early achievements include notable kibbutzim and settlements such as Nahalal.
21 Krispin, *Renaissance at Sodom*, 100–04.
22 Ibid.
23 Rau and Schiff, "Kauffmann Pioneered Rural Planning," March 7, 1958 (In Hebrew).
24 Ibid.
25 Krispin, *Renaissance at Sodom*, 100–04.
26 Ibid.
27 Ibid., 102.
28 Kreiger, *Dead Sea*, 158.
29 Ibid., 162–64.
30 Asher Doron, *Dead Sea Development Survey: For the Tamar Regional Council* (Tel Aviv: Ha-Maḥlaḳah Ha-Tekhnit Shel Kibutse Ha-Shomer Ha-Sta'ir, 1965), 76 (In Hebrew).
31 Maklef was Israel's third Chief of Staff and CEO of the Dead Sea Works between 1952 and 1953. Mordechai Maklef, 'Introduction', in *The Dead Sea and Its Israeli Shore*, ed. Ze'ev Vilnai (Ha-Mo'atsah Ha-ezorit Tamar: 1964), 8 (In Hebrew).
32 Kuhn, 'Architecture's Energy,' 17.
33 Ibid.

34 Krispin, *Renaissance at Sodom*, 101.
35 Freddy Kahana, *Neither Town nor Village: The Architecture of the Kibbutz 1910–1990* (Ramat Efal: Yad Tevenkin, 2011), 8 (In Hebrew).
36 Ephraim Talmi, 'The Hostel Next to the Cave', *Davar*, March 20, 1956, 3.
37 Moshe Kerem, "Kibbutz," *Encyclopaedia Judaica*, 2nd ed. (Detroit: Thomson Gale, 2007).
38 Ephraim Orni, Shaked Gilboa, Gideon Hadas and Benjamin Mazar, 'En-Gedi', In *Encyclopaedia Judaica*, 2nd ed. (Detroit: Thomson Gale, 2007).
39 Irston R. Barnes, 'Israel Finds New Way to Help Conservation', *Washington Post*, August 12, 1962, D23.
40 Kahana, *Neither Town*, 273.
41 Ibid.
42 Yossi Feldman, 'The Ein Gedi Field School – Israel's First', in *The Dead Sea and the Judean Desert 1900–1967*, ed. Naor Mordechai (Jerusalem: Yad Yitzhak Ben-Zvi, 1990), 158 (In Hebrew).
43 Ibid.
44 Ibid.
45 Ibid, 157–59.
46 Ibid.
47 Tula Amir, *Nahum Zolotov/Architect and Planner* (Tel Aviv: Israeli Center for Libraries, 2011), 233–37 (In Hebrew).
48 'Hillside Centre', *Interbuild* 12.1 (1965): 15.
49 Ibid.
50 'Hillside Centre', 15.
51 Ibid.
52 Ibid.
53 Ibid.
54 Amir, *Nahum Zolotov*, 20.
55 Shlomo Givon, 'Millions of Fish – But No Beef', *Maariv*, April 22, 1965, 9 (In Hebrew).
56 Ibid.; Yossi Beilin, 'Between Harat and Chamra', *Davar*, April 12, 1974, 31 (In Hebrew).
57 Amir, *Nahum Zolotov*, 20.
58 Doron, *Dead Sea Development*, 84.
59 Ibid.
60 Muki Zur and Yuval Danieli, ed., *Mestechkin Builds Israel* (Tel Aviv: Ha-Ḳibuts Ha-me'uḥad, 2008), 12 (In Hebrew).
61 Ibid.
62 Yaakov Bar-On, 'The Lowest Housing in the World', *Laisha*, May 1971, 85–87 (In Hebrew).
63 Ibid.
64 '20 Million Lira Will Be Invested in Tourist Development in the Region', *Davar*, December 26, 1965, 5 (In Hebrew).
65 'Ein Gedi Develops Health Tourism: High Demand for Sulfer Baths', *Davar*, December 3, 1963, 5 (In Hebrew).
66 Kahana, *Neither Town*, 210.
67 Ibid., 146.

68 Shmuel Mestechkin, 'How to Approach the Planning of a Point?', in *Mestechkin Builds Israel*, eds Muki Zur and Yuval Danieli (Tel Aviv: Ha-K.ibuts Ha-me'uh.ad, 2008), 67 (In Hebrew).
69 Shmuel Mestechkin, 'Instructions for the Planning of the Ein Hmiphraz-Mazra Dining Hall', in *Mestechkin Builds Israel*, eds Muki Zur and Yuval Danieli (Tel Aviv: Ha-K.ibuts Ha-me'uh.ad, 2008) (In Hebrew).
70 Ibid.
71 Kahana, *Neither Town*, 10.
72 Ibid.
73 Ibid.
74 Ibid.
75 Ibid.
76 'Ein Gedi', 5.
77 Doron, *Development Survey*, 85.
78 Ibid., 64–67, 79.
79 '20 Million Israeli Lira,'5.
80 Doron, *Development Survey*, 15.
81 Ibid, 15, 84–85.
82 Ibid., 64.
83 Gideon Hadas, 'Yehuda Almog, Pioneer of Developing of the Dead Sea Region', *Negev, Dead Sea and Arava Studies* 8.3 (2016): 89–92 (In Hebrew).
84 Ibid.
85 D. Cohen, 'Soddom – a Challenge to the Youth', *Davar*, June 10, 1964, 4 (In Hebrew).
86 Ibid.
87 Ze'ev Vilnai, *The Dead Sea and Its Israeli Shore* (Ha-Mo'atsah Ha-ezorit Tamar, 1964), 136 (In Hebrew).
88 Hadas, 'Yehuda Almog', 90.
89 Ehud Nezer, 'Masada – Survey, Excavation and Reconstruction', in *The Dead Sea and the Judean Desert 1900–1967*, ed. Naor Mordechai (Jerusalem: Yad Yitzhak Ben-Zvi, 1990), 185–97 (In Hebrew).
90 Ibid.
91 Hadas, 'Yehuda Almog', 90.
92 Freddy Kahana, Interview by Teddy Kofman, January 05, 2017.
93 Freddy Kahana and Dennis Kahn, *Description of the Building in English*, 1959, Freddy Kahana's personal archive.
94 Ibid.
95 Ibid.
96 Ibid.
97 Shlomo Drori, 'From the Israeli Potash Factory to the Dead Sea Factories', in *The Dead Sea and the Judean Desert 1900–1967*, ed. Naor Mordechai (Jerusalem: Yad Yitzhak Ben-Zvi, 1990), 106 (In Hebrew).
98 Vanesa Sztankeler, Isaac A. Meir, and Moshe Schwartz, 'Physical Development in an Ecologically Sensitive Area: The Planning of the Dead Sea Region', *Geography Research Forum* 32, no.1 (2006): 119–45.

99 Menahem Talmi, 'A Health-City on the Shores of the Dead Sea', *Maariv*, April 19, 1963, 9 (In Hebrew).
100 Ibid.
101 Ibid.
102 Arieh Arad, 'A Health-City in Ein Bokek', *Hazofe*, January 25, 1963, 4 (In Hebrew).
103 Ibid.
104 'The Bathhouses at Hamei Zohar', Nahum Zolotov's private archive, 13. Pamphlet. (In Hebrew).
105 Michael Kuhn, '"Ein Bokek" Hotel, the Dead Sea', *Arkitectura 3* (July/September, 1966), 50 (In Hebrew).
106 Ibid.
107 Ibid.
108 Ibid.
109 Ibid.
110 Ibid.
111 Ibid.
112 Talmi, 'Health-City', 9.
113 'Hamei Zohar Bathouses', *Handasa Ve-Adrichaloot* 2, no.1 (1966): 36–37 (In Hebrew).
114 Ibid.
115 Ibid.
116 Sztankeler et al., 'Physical Development', 120–31.
117 Kark, *Chronicles*, 186.

Architectonic Experimentation in Early Israeli Architecture Vis-à-Vis Climatic Constraints: The Case of the Negev Desert[1]

Isaac A. Meir, Rachel Bernstein, and Keren Shalev

Israel's architecture and planning took their first steps concurrent with the country's inception as an independent state (1948). The 1949 national master plan called for a planned dispersal of the population from the country's narrow central coastal plain and lowlands to the sparsely populated extremes, primarily to the arid south – the Negev desert.[2] The Negev constitutes some 65 per cent of Israel's land, and is characterized by climatic variability, ranging from humid subtropical to hyper-arid. Most of it is continental, with hot dry summers and cold winters, low precipitation, high evapotranspiration, intense solar radiation, sparse vegetative cover, frequent dust and sand storms, and winter floods.

Until Israel's independence, the Ottoman city of Be'er Sheva was the only contemporary urban settlement in the Negev. Its plan (1900) was informed by contemporaneous European trends as it was designed by two European engineers working for the Ottoman Army. Soon after Israel's independence, brave attempts were made at creating modern clusters in this harsh environment, mixing *béton brut* (raw - exposed - concrete) and l'Unité d'Habitation-style apartment blocks, with compact patio house clusters reinterpreting oriental kasbahs (densely built traditional settlements with narrow winding streets).

Israeli architecture was from its beginning very much a modernist construct.[3] Yet, Be'er Sheva's situation following the state's foundation mixed social, technical, national, economic, environmental, as well as climatic constraints into a large architectural 'playground'.[4] The opportunity of formulating Be'er Sheva's architectural character was perceived as a *tabula rasa*, a clean slate. Often the planning and design followed 'intuitions' about the harsh environment and the appropriate ways to build within it. The budget was constrained, time was precious, and materials were simple and often inadequate in terms of their physical properties (e.g., insulation). In later years, residents and especially architects criticized the results of these attempts. However, when one closely examines the sociopolitical climate of the time; the requirements imposed by the state on planning, design, and construction; and the attempts made by the architects to create adequate, livable, functional clusters and buildings, it is difficult to discount the ingenuity, creativity, professionalism, and commitment invested in these early Israeli projects.[5]

This chapter attempts to review the process of architectural adaptations and mutations in the Negev region during the state's early years. It focuses on some of the more iconic buildings and clusters of Be'er Sheva, the capital of the Negev. The study demonstrates the evolutionary processes, from trial-and-error and empirical experimentation to the beginnings of a systematic research and its applications. This is conducted through a climatic assessment of typologies, details, and materials. Typological characteristics and details such as materials, shading devices, preferential orientation of fenestration, etc., are coupled with outdoor and indoor climate data obtained from monitoring, simulations, and infrared thermography. Heuristic trial-and-error processes produced interesting design solutions, yet lacked the rigour of building-related energy and climate systematic research.[6] Thus, they often omitted vital issues such as insulation, which was so critical in the specific environment. Much of the theoretical and historical literature and documentation is, unfortunately, only in Hebrew, yet has been cited, since it is the most authoritative and often the only source on the subject.

A Brief Note on the City's Climate

Be'er Sheva is located in a semi-arid lowlands area (270–300 m above Mean Sea Level [MSL] [885–984 ft]), bordering the desert. It is characterized by a desert climate with Mediterranean influences, with hot and dry summers and mild winters.[7] Average precipitation is 200 mm (~7.9 in.) with a high annual variability, which is typical of such climates, and is concentrated in the winter months. Snow is rare, but dust storms are very common and sand storms occur occasionally. Diurnal and seasonal temperature and humidity fluctuations are relatively wide, as can be expected in a semi-arid environment. Temperatures in summer range from 33°C (91.4°F) and above in the daytime, to less than 18°C (64°F) at night; and in winter from 15°C (59°F) in the daytime, to less than 6°C (43°F) at night. Extreme conditions often reach above 40°C (104°F) (during spring hot spells and summers) and sometimes even below 0°C (32°F) (during winter nights). Average relative humidity (RH) tends to be low during summer days (~30%), but rises at night to nearly 70% per cent. Likewise, in winter, the daily fluctuation tends to be wide (~40–70%). Extreme conditions can bring RH as high as 100% and as low as 10% and even below 5%.[8]

These conditions seem to have changed over time, as recent research has shown, with temperatures slowly increasing, especially those of the summer night minima, alongside an increase in relative humidity and a parallel drop in wind velocity during summer nights.[9] The effect of urban development on increased temperatures and humidity has been documented by comparisons between the Be'er Sheva meteorological station and a nearby agricultural one.[10] Such developments exacerbate thermal discomfort and increase air-conditioning use, as well as the dependence on cars instead of walking or biking. An additional observed climate change is the aridization expressed in a diminishing precipitation average over the years, alongside the rising average temperature.[11]

The city of Be'er Sheva is located at NL 31° 14'. This defines the following solar geometry parameters as shown in Table 1, which should inform urban planning and architectural design.

These solar altitude and azimuth angles should determine the orientation of a building and its fenestration, as well as the relative position and proportions of an open space. Solar radiation on a horizontal plane – a roof or an open space – reaches values of over

7.5 kWh/sq.m/day during summer. Northern, eastern, and western walls and fenestration will receive, in summer, more solar radiation than that reaching a southern façade (2.48 and 5.07 kWh/sq.m/day compared to 2.62 kWh/sq.m/day, respectively). In winter, the latter will receive 4.63 kWh/sq.m/day, nearly twice as much as eastern and western façades. This makes the southern orientation advantageous in winter and easy to protect in summer. Unprotected roofs and eastern and western façades can be considered as a liability in the summer.

A Brief Historical Note

Be'er Sheva has a long settlement history due to its site-specific characteristics. The site was chosen because of its proximity to the Be'er Sheva Stream and its high water table, which in the past provided wells with enough water to support permanent settlement. For a desert location, such site properties are not self-evident, especially since the settlement site is located in a basin, a fact that creates problematic microclimatic issues (e.g., pollution trapping due to inversion coupled with higher temperatures and poor ventilation). The site's rich settlement history also served as a factor in choosing the location for Be'er Sheva by the first modern planners in 1900. The Ottoman city sat on top of thousands of years of settlement spanning the Chalcolithic, Israelite, Hellenistic, Roman, Byzantine, and early Islamic eras, albeit with gaps in between the main settlement periods.[12]

Ottomans and British

The main reasons that guided the Ottomans to establish a new town in the area (known today as the Old City to distinguish it from the post-independence development), stemmed from their wish to encourage the permanent settlement of the region's Bedouin tribes, and create an administrative, commercial, and military base in the area. Thus, several public buildings and residential developments were designed and erected. The main volume of the city comprised residential quarters, which were built on a rectangular grid with 60×60 m (196×196 ft) blocks divided by 15 m-wide (49 ft-wide) streets.[13] The grid was rotated by 45° from due north, thus opening the urban space to the prevailing north-westerlies, the Mediterranean breeze. Houses opened their rooms to internal courtyards providing privacy. The plan included open public spaces. The whole urban concept was European, with no relation whatsoever to the traditional Middle Eastern kasbah layout, which usually inhibits ventilation of the built-up space, as opposed to the intentional rotation of the Old City's grid.[14] The post-World War I British interventions included mainly infill, which frequently introduced colonnades along the street façades.[15] Both the Old City of Be'er Sheva and the principles that guided its planning and development were abandoned post-independence for alternative planning concepts.[16]

First Israeli neighbourhoods and plans

The first two Israeli neighbourhoods to be established – Shikun Darom and Neve Noy (1948–1950s) – aimed to provide the basic needs for the new population by creating subsistence agricultural clusters of single family houses on plots of 1.5 dunam (0.37 acre).[17] As such, they were suburban in character and constituted a significant departure from the Ottoman city, which, though drawing from the Garden City concepts, was urban in nature.[18]

However, the most significant urban design leap came with the first plans made by Arieh Sharon.[19] They were modernist in concept, and aimed at promoting the urban growth of the city, though they seemed to be completely disconnected from their geographic and climatic context.[20] This is apparent not only in the low-density and dispersed development, which created wide, unprotected open spaces in a rather harsh climate, but also by the extensive use of the green colour so prominent in most of the drawings [Figure 1].[21] The Garden City concept, however out of context it was, remains apparent. It successfully introduced a certain level of neighbourhood self-reliance, based on local service centres, which guided the 'neighbourhood unit' concept incorporated into the city's master plan in the 1950s and 1960s.

Figure 1: Sharon Plan for a new neighbourhood (A) in Be'er Sheva, 1951. Source: Arieh Sharon, *Physical Planning in Israel* (Jerusalem: HaMadpis HaMemshalti, 1951) (in Hebrew).

Both Sharon's original plans and the 1950s neighbourhood's master plan were instigated and orchestrated by the government, like all other plans at the time. They were based on the actual influx of new immigrants and optimistic estimates for future population growth, as well as on the need to disperse the population from the country's centre to the periphery.[22] Indeed, the population of the newly born state grew at a rapid pace, from 0.87 million in 1948 to 1.3 million in 1950, to 2.48 million in 1968 and nearly 3.8 million in 1978.[23] Within this context, the dire need for basic housing became one of the main and most urgent problems of the country. Be'er Sheva's master plan aimed at a population of 250,000 by the year 2000, a target still not reached today (2018). Under such conditions, flexibility was necessary for future adaptation: land reserves were plotted within the city plan's area and roads were designed for estimated future capacity and traffic volume needs. The core of the plan was earmarked for the gradual infill of civic centre development and public facilities (among them, Ben-Gurion University's [BGU] main campus and the adjacent Soroka Medical Center). This policy – and its planning and urban implications – stand in stark contrast to the attitude of many architects of the period in discussion with the desert environment. These designers created introverted compact buildings and clusters in an attempt to differentiate the man-made environment from the natural one perceived as harsh, threatening, and inhospitable desert.

Urban Planning and Microclimate Implications

The immediate outcomes of these policies and practices created a fragmented, discontinuous urban space forcing pedestrian movement through large open, undeveloped, and untended desert leftover areas. These included the two main traffic arteries designed in the 1960s for the traffic volume they reach today, at a time when car ownership in the city was negligible. As can be identified on Google Earth, at many points, the plan reached and even exceeded 100 m (328 ft) of asphalt, hard paving, and leftover spaces between buildings on either side of the main roads [Figures 2–3].

To document and illustrate the microclimatic outcomes of such planning, we present data that were collected for a number of different projects, among them the master and detailed plans for clusters and buildings. Despite the lengthy time span of the collected data (more than 25 years), they have been carefully reassessed and verified to ensure reliability. This has also involved cross-checking the data with recent purpose-specific measurements in some cases. They were obtained with a number of different instruments, in various locations.[24] Thermal simulations for indoor spaces were performed with QUICK II simulation software.[25]

In an early pilot survey, average maximum ambient air temperatures measured in two of the traffic arteries between the months of April and August reached 35.7°C (96.2°F) (higher than the average maximum for the month of June measured at the city's meteorological

Figure 2: Car-oriented, pedestrian-hostile central urban space. *Left:* thermograph of the same spot. Note: radiative surface temperatures exceed 50ÅãC (April 19, 2017, ~13:30–14:00). *Right:* Tuviyahu Avenue, a main east–west traffic artery of Be'er Sheva today (April 2017).

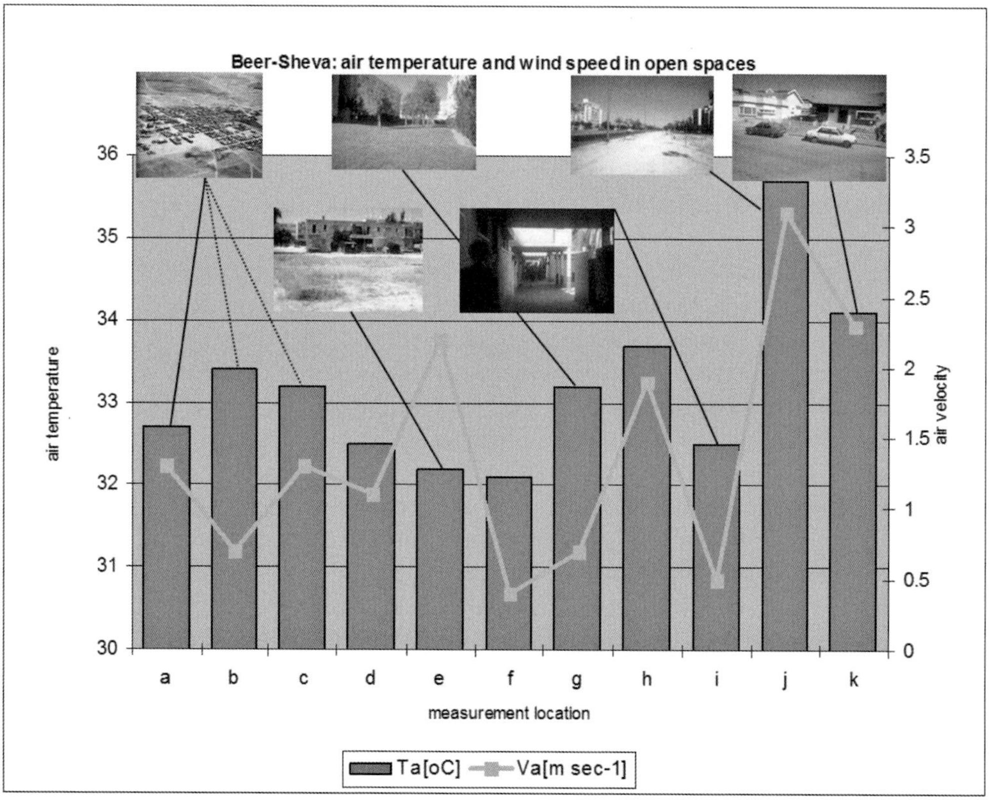

Figure 3: Microclimatic variability of urban spaces in Be'er Sheva. Average maximum temperatures (bars) and wind velocities, as measured between the months of April–August.

station at the time of the survey), while average wind velocity for the same day, time and month periods reached 3.1 m/sec (10 ft/sec) [Figure 3, measurement location j].[26] Considering the fact that most of those areas are still exposed to sun and wind despite the high-rise buildings developments of the last twenty years, one could easily reach an Index of Thermal Stress value of 700 watts and above, or thermal sensation values between 6 and 7 on a 1–7 scale, which indicate conditions of 'hot' to 'very hot'.[27]

Contrary to such expansive untreated open spaces, neighbourhoods designed within the city's new master plan tried to recreate the spatial qualities of the traditional Middle Eastern kasbah, yet under a very orderly, rectangular grid and layout. Within this grid, denser 'carpet development' low-rise/high-density clusters were designed in the late 1950s and built in the early 1960s by a team of the Israel Ministry of Construction and Housing (MOCH), headed by architects Avraham Yaski and Amnon Alexandroni. Two different prototypes of patio houses were included (designed by Daniel Havkin and Nahum Zolotov), one with alleys protected on the sides but open to the sky, the other with partly 'roofed' segments, shaded not only by the walls of the ground floors, but also by the rooms of the second floor partly hanging over the alleys and pedestrian walkways. These clusters were framed by taller apartment blocks, usually three to four storeys on open *pilotis*. One of them, known as the 'quarter-of-kilometer block',[28] is very similar to and reminiscent of Le Corbusier's l'Unité d'Habitation, in Marseille, France, both in concept and details.

The microclimate of these dense clusters stands in contrast to that of the more 'urban' development with an expansive avenue, which created a dusty, unprotected, sun-exposed, windswept no-man's-land. In the 'carpet development' clusters, the average ambient air temperature for the same time periods mentioned above ranged between 32.5-33.7°C (90.5°F-92.6°F), 2–3°C (35.6°-37.4°F) lower, and wind velocity ranged from 1.9–0.5 m/sec (6.2-1.6 ft/sec). High as these temperatures may seem, one has to consider them vis-à-vis the shaded walkways created by the dense construction [Figure 3, measurement locations h and i; Figure 4). Such results are in agreement with other urban microclimate studies in the Negev region.[29] These particular clusters have enjoyed great popularity among tenants right from the very first years of their occupancy, expressed in a significantly lower-than-average outward mobility, which was noted in a Post-Occupancy Evaluation study.[30]

It is interesting to note that air temperatures measured in the spaces in between the buildings in some of the sparsely built first clusters [Figures 3, measurement locations d and e] were the lowest (32.2–32.5°C [89.9–90.5°F]). This can be explained by the free air movement indicated by the high wind velocity measured in these areas (2.2 m/sec [7.2 ft/sec]), as well as by the fact that the ground between the buildings was covered by vegetation (mainly weeds), which shaded the soil and absorbed radiation for photosynthesis and evapotranspiration, affecting the overall energy balance. Nevertheless, a pedestrian's exposure to direct solar radiation in such areas would change the overall picture with a negative effect on thermal sensation.

Figure 4: Low rise/high density cluster. Radiative temperature differences (>15°C) between exposed and shaded pedestrian walkway segments.

The Building as the Antithesis to the Desert

As mentioned previously, the 1960s and 1970s were years that witnessed a more or less uniform attitude of architects towards the Be'er Sheva landscape and environment. Perceived as hostile and unpleasant, it was contrasted by buildings and clusters that created an enclosed, shaded, wind-protected space. Architect Ram Karmi, who designed a number of such buildings in Be'er Sheva (albeit not all of them built, or not built in their entirety), defined one of his most prominent examples, the Negev Center, as a 'building that makes a street' [Figure 5].[31] Several similar examples were built, often taking the form of a step-up/step-in ziggurat-type section, creating a shaded space into which apartment entrances and service rooms opened. Such spaces, though undoubtedly enjoying an ameliorated microclimate in summer, are noisy, tend to be unpleasantly cold in winter, and suffer from odours emitted through the service rooms ventilated into them.

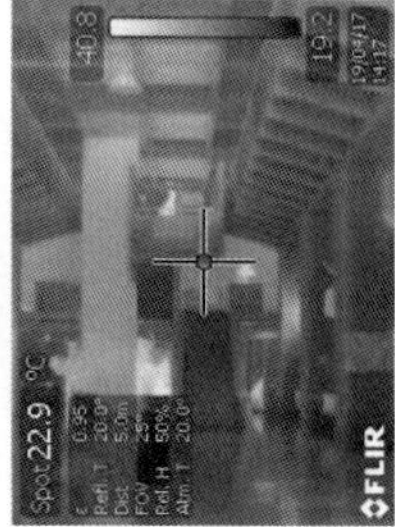

Figure 5: The multifunctional Negev Center (1963), a 'building that makes a street'. *Left:* southern façade with commerce (ground floor), offices (first floor), and apartments (second–third floors). *Centre:* internal covered street. *Right:* significantly lower radiative temperatures of the internal covered street compared to background and surfaces exposed to the outside (>15°C).

Figure 6: Ben-Gurion University of the Negev, Marcus Family Campus (1969). *Right:* Semi-enclosed courtyards flanked by four-storey blocks provide ameliorated microclimate (early afternoon, summer). *Left:* Infrared image depicts radiative surface temperatures, with white being the highest and black the lowest.

More successful concepts of internal enclosed or semi-enclosed open spaces guided the architects of the early planning of BGU main campus. An example of this building pattern is the south-central part of the campus. Avraham Yaski's Exact Sciences and Engineering four-storey buildings of classrooms, offices, and auditoria, are arranged around semi-enclosed courtyards. Being partly shaded for most of the day, though open to the sky, and ventilated through connecting passages, or through open *pilotis* ground levels, these courtyards provide an improved microclimate, and are frequented and used by students and faculty throughout most of the year. Figure 6 includes an infrared image (left) that depicts radiative surface temperatures, with white being the highest and black the lowest.

Certain similarities may be seen in Be'er Sheva's Town Hall building, designed by architects Michael and Shulamit Nadler, Shmuel Bixon, and Moshe Gil (1962), explicitly introverted, with well-protected and shaded slit windows opening to the outside [Figure 7]. The offices and halls open onto two internal courtyards, serving as the main daylight and ventilation systems of the building. The courtyards also provide green landscaped views. These are extremely important as studies have shown that a large window-view promotes faster and better performance at work. The quality of the view, such as sky and trees, has also been shown to be important.[32] Such details become all the more significant in arid environments with intense solar radiation and glare, dominated by brown and grey monochromes, which have been shown to have a negative psychological impact.[33]

Courtyards demonstrate a wide variability of microclimatic factors, both in winter and summer. Climatic monitoring (air temperature and RH), simulations, and infrared thermography show a strong relation between the treatment of the courtyard and its

Figure 7: Be'er Sheva Town Hall (1972). Well-protected and shaded recessed windows facing the street.

thermal behaviour.[34] The following factors seem to have a decisive impact on the courtyard microclimate. Orientation affects winter conditions due to the low solar altitude, relative to the proportions of the courtyard.[35] Poor design that inhibits winter solar penetration may create courtyard conditions inferior to those of the open, unprotected spaces, when the latter are exposed to the winter sun.

The same is true of the other enclosed or semi-enclosed spaces within buildings and clusters, among them the *passages* and internal streets mentioned above. On the other hand, summer shading is essential, and this has to be achieved proactively and often by dynamic means and solutions, as the mass of the building may prove insufficient, especially in smaller, lower buildings. Detailing, not least surface treatment and materials, do matter and make a difference, especially regarding paving.[36] Dark exposed surfaces will overheat and will remain hot even during night hours when air temperature drops. However, light surfaces will reflect much of the radiation reaching them (dependent on the colour and reflectivity factor) and thus may exacerbate thermal stress. Hence, movable dynamic shading over relatively light-coloured surfaces seems to be the more preferable solution. During the hot season, vegetation is much more favourable than dry, bare soil, hard surfaces, and artificial shading.[37] Enclosed courtyards have been shown to be little affected by wind, a fact that may compromise comfort conditions in these spaces due to trapped heat and settling dust (because of more stable conditions within, as opposed to the open space outside), as well as the common practice of locating heat dissipating air-conditioning units within such courtyards.[38]

The belief that internal courtyards will always provide an improved microclimate, compared to that of the open environment, has been shown to be inaccurate and often contrary to the actual measured values.[39] In the case of the internal enclosed and semi-enclosed courtyards in Be'er Sheva, both in the Old City and in contemporary buildings and clusters, such spaces have been shown to reach summer air temperatures that are significantly higher than the ambient ones.[40] They often tend to be insufficiently shaded and poorly ventilated, thus trapping radiation and heat. Likewise, in winter they may turn out to be uncomfortably cold due to shading caused by the building volume, fixed shading devices designed for the summer, and vegetation, either evergreen or deciduous.[41]

Materials and Details: Four Case Studies

Much of the architecture of the period in discussion followed the Brutalist style, its ethos and aesthetics.[42] Still, some constraints should be noted. First, as mentioned before, the need to provide adequate housing solutions, minimal as these were, at a fast-as-possible pace, for the ever-growing population, which roughly doubled every twenty years. Second, the need to achieve this at a low cost, with the most basic available materials and possible details. Third, the requirement to provide replicable solutions that would serve the growing needs in different parts of the country (branded at the time 'drawer plans'). These did not consider local factors whether social, cultural, climatic, or other. In one of his last interviews, Nahum Zolotov, the architect of part of the patio house cluster in Be'er Sheva, described the architects' task, stressing the dictate to minimize costs by not using external finish materials, and by limiting the flat concrete roof thickness to 10 cm (3.9 in.).[43] Under such constraints, with little knowledge about or availability of insulating materials and their importance in the desert climate, the quality of construction is now considered poor, at least by today's standards. Suffice to say, the building insulation standard SI 1045 became mandatory only in 1980.[44] Thus, most of the construction during the years 1948–78 was uninsulated, and very often suffered from condensation, especially in kitchens and bathrooms. In cases such as the 'carpet' patio housing, external walls were built with hollow concrete blocks without even external plaster.

In some projects, coarse whitewashed external cement plaster was used as a finish material. In other cases, especially those of standard, repetitious apartment blocks, prefabricated concrete panels and often whole units were used. Measurements and simulations have shown that most of these buildings suffer most of the day from indoor temperatures above the thermal comfort zone in the summer and below the lower thermal comfort limit in winter. These temperatures, both measured and simulated, were shown to be approximately

30–26.5°C (86–79.7°F) during a typical summer day, and 18.3–16°C (64.9–60.8°F) during a typical winter day.[45]

One of the first Be'er Sheva projects to incorporate some form of roof insulation was the Mental Health Center, designed by architects Benjamin Idelson and Gershon Tzipor, with Milo Hoffman as the building climatology consultant. Roof insulation was based primarily on 17 cm-thick (6.7 in.) Autoclaved Aerated Concrete (AAC) blocks on which a structural 6 cm (2.3 in.) concrete roof slab was poured, with the additional external roof layers topped with white pebbles, which acted as a reflective upper layer.[46] External walls were built with two layers of hollow concrete blocks with an air cavity between them, and painted white.[47] These were not standard details or practices at the time. Design considerations were included in previous reports of the relevant MOCH-funded research, which preceded the final design and construction of the complex.

Exposed concrete became the most popular material for architects at the time, especially for institutional, educational, and other public buildings. Brutalism became the predominant style, and Be'er Sheva became a fertile ground for experimentation with such buildings, their form, details, and aesthetics.[48] Though often considered appropriate for the desert climate due to its high heat capacity, concrete has been shown to be problematic when not coupled with thermal insulation, as mentioned in the previous paragraph, as well as in a number of research papers.[49] Despite the lack of insulation in these buildings, attempts were made to protect indoor spaces from what was considered the biggest climatic problem in the region – the summer sun. Thus, many of these buildings demonstrate consistent and often ingenious details to ensure sufficient indoor daylight levels, alongside protection from direct solar penetration. Some of the more prominent examples of such detailing can be seen in the Town Hall mentioned earlier, the BGU main campus, and the Soroka Medical Center.

Two BGU buildings should be mentioned in this context – the Aranne Library [Figure 8], designed by architects Michael and Shulamit Nadler, Shmuel Bixon, Moshe Gil, and Shimshon Amitai (1968); and the Social Sciences building [Figure 9], designed by architects Rafael Reifer, Amnon Niv, and Natan Magen (1968). Others are the Soroka Medical Center buildings – the outpatient clinics and the old maternity ward [Figure 10], both by Arieh Sharon's office (1959).[50] In all these cases, the overall design and orientation of the different volumes in addition to the construction materials (e.g., poured concrete on site, prefabricated concrete or other rigid elements, and brickwork) are combined in an effort to control solar radiation penetration.

The Aranne Library is a massive yet compact exposed concrete structure. It is situated explicitly facing northward with a series of beehive-like scoops allowing mostly diffuse light to penetrate deep into the library volume and spaces [Figure 8]. Other façades have only very limited recessed fenestration. Contrary to the exposed concrete vertical envelope made in a bush hammer 'corduroy' finish texture, the beehive scoops are made of smooth whitewashed concrete, thus providing reflective roof surfaces, with each scoop reflecting solar radiation onto the north-facing glazing of its neighbouring ones [Figure 8].

Figure 8: Aranne Library, Ben-Gurion University of the Negev, Marcus Family Campus, Be'er Sheva (1972). Beehive-like clerestory windows facing north, providing diffuse light in the building volume.

Figure 9: Social Sciences Faculty, Ben-Gurion University of the Negev, Marcus Family Campus, Be'er Sheva (eastern wing 1975; western wing late 1980s). *Left:* thermal image of northern façade on a summer afternoon, showing cool recessed window surfaces (in dark grey) as opposed to the rest of the building envelope. Most radiation in the summer is diffuse, and at the time the thermograph was taken (July 25, 17:00), part of the northern façade is in direct north-western radiation (see Table 1). *Right:* northern façade with concrete framed windows.

Table 1: Solar altitude (AL) and azimuth (AZ) in degrees during the longest (June 21) and shortest (Dec 21) days of the year at the latitude of Be'er Sheva (NL 31° 14').

Time	06:00/18:00		07:00/17:00		08:00/16:00		19:00/15:00		10:00/14:00		11:00/13:00		12:00	
Angle °	AL	AZ	AL	AZ	AL	AZ	AL	AZ	AL	AZ	AL	AZ	AL	AZ
Date														
June 21	12	110	24	104	37	98	50	91	62	82	75	65	83	0
Dec. 21	-	-	0	62	11	54	21	44	29	31	34	17	36	0

Facing the library, the Social Sciences Faculty building is a massive exposed concrete complex, stretching its main elongated axis from east to west [Figure 9]. It partly encloses a south facing *passage*, originally fully exposed to the low southern winter sun, though recently partially blocked by the construction of the main BGU auditorium. Both of the building's long façades, facing north and south, have windows shaded by deep concrete frames built as an integral part of the building envelope. Figure 9 (left) illustrates a thermal image of the northern façade on a summer afternoon. It shows cool recessed window surfaces (dark grey, black) as opposed to the rest of the building envelope. Most radiation in the summer is diffused, and at the time the thermograph was taken (July 25, 17:00), part of the northern façade was exposed to direct north-western radiation [see Table 1].

Similar to these two examples, the Soroka Medical Center maternity ward's western façade comprises north–north-west-facing windows on the ground floor preventing direct afternoon sun penetration, and deep prefabricated vertical elements shading the whole façade on the second and third storeys [Figure 10].

As with concrete, exposed concrete blocks are far from being an appropriate building material on their own. Their grey colour and low albedo absorb solar radiation, causing the building envelope to heat, which eventually heats the building's indoor spaces. However, when properly prepared and used on site, and appropriately maintained, exposed concrete seems to age rather well, compared to other materials that were used for external finishes at the time, mainly coarse cement plaster, which cracks, peels, and needs continuous maintenance and repainting.

In addition, when dust, so common in this arid region, is absorbed by the coarse whitewashed cement plaster used on other buildings of the period, it causes a darkening of the hue, thus increasing the finish surface's absorptivity. In contrast, in the case of exposed concrete, which begins with a dark grey hue, the process is often exactly the opposite – the deposited, comparatively light-hue dust lowers the material's absorptivity, thus actually improving its properties over time. This is not mentioned to praise climatically poor materials (e.g., exposed concrete), but rather to consider critically their performance and aging over time in the specific environmental conditions and constraints. Lack of insulation, combined with the relatively high conductivity of the building envelope materials used (concrete, concrete blocks, solid silica and burned clay bricks), causes high heat losses in winter and heat gains in the summer.[51] The resulting indoor thermal discomfort creates a growing demand for air conditioning, which is in itself one of the main and growing

Figure 10: Soroka Medical Center Maternity Ward (1959). Western façade detail photographed from north to west, showing north–north-west-facing windows on the ground floor, and deep prefabricated vertical elements shading the whole façade on the second and third storeys.

energy end users. Considering the fact that many of the buildings mentioned here are still in use, it would be more than advisable to consider their climatic retrofit. Research has shown that the addition of external thermal insulation can significantly lower the number of hours during which indoor conditions deviate (above or below) the thermal comfort limits.[52] Adding 5 cm (1.9 in.) of rigid polystyrene as external insulation to walls[53] made of prefabricated concrete or concrete blocks can raise indoor minimum temperatures in winter by 2.6°C (36.7°F), and lower indoor daily average temperatures by 1.7°C (35°F) in the summer.[54] This has in itself significant potential implications, especially when considering such indoor improvements in the context of climate changes, exacerbation of temperature extremes, and fuel poverty seen in recent years, not only in terms of inaccessibility of energy for heating, but also for cooling purposes.[55] When a building's special external architectural character must be preserved, adding internal insulation is a possible solution, even if not optimal.[56]

Conclusions and Some Practical Implications

Urban planning, building design, detailing, and materials all influence the man-made environment and have the potential to ameliorate or exacerbate climatic conditions.[57] The architect's task is to understand these environmental constraints and extremes before making decisions that can have decisive outcomes. However, in the specific case of Be'er Sheva during the period 1948 to 1978, architects seemed to have had little prior knowledge regarding appropriate design in arid environments such as the Negev desert. No time was available for on-site experimentation and analysis, and most of the projects were based on the intuition of the architects involved, who were young and professionally inexperienced in such environments.

Discrepancies between scales should be noticed. On the one hand, the large scale of the city's master plan, especially the leapfrogging development processes that occurred, created an unpleasant and uninviting urban space characterized by wide-open, untreated, and undeveloped spaces, many of them in the heart of the city. On the other hand, the smaller-scale clusters and their building design demonstrated an intuitive ingenuity expressed in the creation of protected, shaded, and often semi-enclosed open spaces within clusters, or in the development of building prototypes.[58] These attempted to turn urban spaces inside out by enclosing within them streets and public or semi-public open spaces. Inspired detailing was also used to compensate for the lack of appropriate materials (e.g., insulation). In public buildings, fixed shading solutions were developed to provide adaptability during the changing conditions of the year, including all the fixed shading devices built as part of the building envelope and the orientation of windows intended to provide daylight while avoiding glare and overheating in summer. Most residential and some institutional buildings at the time incorporated movable external shutters only post-occupancy. While a problematic practice in general, the lack of external movable shutters became a major issue in the case of east- and west-facing windows, since residential building prototypes were built in different orientations. Unfortunately, more recent architecture seems to have completely forgotten either the external fixed or the movable shading solutions, intentionally designing fully or largely glazed façades, using glass as the main material for walls. This is a poor practice, which may prove detrimental in drylands.

When considering all the above issues, one may easily become very critical of the architects who planned and designed Be'er Sheva during the first 30 years of Israel's existence and massive development. However, one should be careful not to dismiss the commendable ingenuity, creativity, sensitivity, and commitment demonstrated by the architects of the period within the broader context of social and national responsibility. The architectural heuristic trial-and-error experimentation of those early years produced architectonic precedents still relevant today. During site visits for data collection for this project, casual conversations with tenants of some of the buildings described above drew an interesting picture. Many of them, especially older residents and among them some of the original tenants, described the projects as very well designed and comfortable. Such anecdotal information supports the survey undertaken by MOCH and described earlier.[59] This can only be to the credit of the architects mentioned here and their other peers who managed to provide the 'adequate' under the constraints of the 'minimal'.

Most of the residential and multifunctional buildings of this period have, over the years, undergone ownership changes, letting and subletting, and subsequent modifications, additions, and eventual defacement. Considering their unique role in the country's sociopolitical and architectural history, it would be reasonable for the local authority to create the legal framework for their preservation and protection. Indeed, the Council for Conservation of Heritage Sites in Israel is active in Be'er Sheva alongside private initiatives, following other cities that have instigated the creation of preservation plans and protocols.[60] The work of preservation and the lessons – both positive and negative – learned from the early projects in Be'er Sheva should be studied to serve as references for contemporary designs in the arid regions of Israel.

Acknowledgements

Much of the work included in this chapter was developed with graduate students who worked under Professor Isaac A. Meir's supervision over the past fifteen years. These projects were part of their thesis research and/or research papers for courses on Modern Bioclimatic Design, Green Architecture, Energy Aspects of Design, Desert Architecture, and Desert Settlements through Time. We are thankful to all of them for the stimulating discussions, insights, and creativity. We especially acknowledge Assaf Kessler for his research on the retrofit potential of low-cost apartment blocks in Be'er Sheva; Anat Folkman Biller for her research on the microclimatic aspects of internal courtyards, especially those of the Old City of Be'er Sheva; and Fabio Scheinkman for his research on the environmental conditions of urban spaces in a desert town. Part of this research originated in our involvement as climate and green construction consultants on numerous master, detailed, and other plans commissioned by the Israel Ministry of Construction and Housing.

Bibliography

Amir, Tula. *Nahum Zolotov / Architect and Planner*. Tel Aviv: Israeli Center for Libraries, 2011 (In Hebrew).

Ben Shalom (Itzhak), Hofit, Oded Potchter, and Haim Tsoar. 'The Effect of the Urban Heat Island and Global Warming on the Thermal Discomfort in a Desert City – The Case of Beer Sheva, Israel'. In *Proceedings 7th International Conference on Urban Climate*, Yokohama, Japan, June 29–July 3, 2009. Accessed Jan.6, 2019. http://www.ide.titech.ac.jp/~icuc7/extended_abstracts/pdf/375974-1-090521051217-003.pdf.

Bitan, Arie and Sara Rubin. 'Be'er Sheva'. In *Climatic Atlas of Israel for Physical and Environmental Planning and Design*. Tel Aviv: Ramot Publishing Co., Tel Aviv University, 1991 (In Hebrew).

Central Bureau of Statistics (CBS). *Population, by Population Group*. Jerusalem: Central Bureau of Statistics, 2017. Accessed Jan.6, 2019, https://www.cbs.gov.il/he/publications/DocLib/2013/shnaton65_all.pdf.

Efrat, Zvi. *The Israeli Project: Building and Architecture 1948–1973*. Tel Aviv: Tel Aviv Museum of Art, 2004 (In Hebrew).

Elhanani, Abba. *The Struggle for Independence: Israeli Architecture in the Twentieth Century*. Tel Aviv, Israel: Ministry of Defense, 1998 (In Hebrew).

Folkman Biller, Anat. 'The General Performance of Internal Courtyards – Beer Sheva's Patio Houses as a Case Study'. M.Sc. thesis, Ben-Gurion University of the Negev, 2007.

Givoni, Baruch. *Man, Climate & Architecture*. 2nd ed. New York: Van Nostrand Reinhold, 1969.

Gitai, Amos. 'Architecture in Israel. The "Carpet" as Housing – Nahum Zolotov, Israel Broadcasting Corporation, Education Channel (23)', March 27, 2013. Accessed Jan. 6, 2019, https://www.youtube.com/watch?v=DS-2nuBSyWI (In Hebrew).

Golani, Yehonathan and Dieter Gershom von Schwarze, eds. *Israel Builds 1970*. Jerusalem: Israel Ministry of Construction and Housing, 1970.

Heschong Mahone Group. *Windows and Offices: A Study of Office Worker Performance and the Indoor Environment*. California Energy Commission, Final report, P500-03-082-A-9; CEC Contract No. 400-99-013, 2003.

Hemu Kharel Kafle and Hendrik J. Bruins. 'Climatic Trends in Israel 1970–2002: Warmer and Increasing Aridity Inland'. *Climatic Change* 96 .1-2 (2009): 63–77.

Milo Hoffman and Menahem Gideon, *The Psychiatric Hospital in Be'er Sheva: Examination of the Climatic Operation of Passively Cooled Buildings*. Haifa: Technion – Israel Institute of Technology, Faculty of Civil Engineering, Building Research Station, 1985.

Karmi, Ram. *Lyric Architecture*. Tel Aviv: Israel Ministry of Defense, 2001 (In Hebrew).

Kessler, Assaf. 'Could There Be a Green Future for Gray Buildings?' MA thesis, Ben-Gurion University of the Negev, 2011.

Mathews, Edward H. and P. G. Richards. 'A Tool for Predicting Hourly Air Temperatures and Sensible Energy Loads in Buildings at Sketch Design Stage'. *Energy and Buildings* 14.1 (1989): 61–80.

Mathews, Edward H., P. G. Richards, and C. Lombard. 'A First-Order Thermal Model for Building Design'. *Energy and Buildings* 21.2 (1994): 133–45.

Mathews, Edward H., Yair Etzion, E. van Heerden, S. Wegelaar, Evyatar Erell, David Pearlmutter, Isaac A. Meir. 'A Novel Thermal Simulation Model and Its Application on Naturally Ventilated Desert Buildings'. *Building and Environment* 32.5 (1997): 447–56.

Meir, Isaac A. 'Climatic Sub-Regions and Design Contextualism'. *Building and Environment* 24.3 (1989): 245–51.

——— 'Courtyard Microclimate: A Hot Arid Region Case Study'. In *Architecture-City-Environment. Proc. 17th PLEA Int. Conf.*, eds K. Steemers and S. Yannas, 218–22. Cambridge: James & James, 2000.

——— 'Urban Space Evolution in the Desert – The Case of Beer-Sheva'. *Building and Environment* 27.1 (1992): 1–11.

Meir, Isaac A., Yair Etzion, and David Faiman. *Energy Aspects of Design in Arid Zones*. Sede Boqer Campus: Desert Architecture Unit/Applied Solar Calculations Unit, BIDR; & Jerusalem: State of Israel, Ministry of Energy and Infrastructure, Research and Development Division, RD-04-90, 1998.

Meir, Isaac A., David Pearlmutter, and Yair Etzion. 'On the Microclimatic Behavior of Two Semi-Enclosed Attached Courtyards in a Hot Dry Region'. *Building and Environment* 30.4 (1995): 563–72.

Meir, Isaac A. and Susan C. Roaf. 'Thermal Comfort – Thermal Mass: Housing in Hot Dry Climates'. In *Indoor Air 2002, Proc. 9th Int. Conf. Indoor Air Quality and Climate*, (Monterey, CA) ed. H. Levin, vol. 1 (Santa Cruz, CA: Indoor Air, 2002), 1050–55.

MOCH (Israel Ministry of Construction and Housing). *Engineering Research Abstracts for the Years 1971–1988*. Jerusalem: Israel Ministry of Construction and Housing 1988. Accessed March 2018. http://www.moch.gov.il/SiteCollectionDocuments/research/mehkarimhandasimpart1. pdf.

Negev, Avraham, ed. 'Beer Sheba'. In *Beer Sheba: The Archaeological Encyclopedia of the Holy Land*. 3rd ed., 53–54. New York: Prentice Hall Press, 1990.

Pearlmutter, David, Pedro Berliner, and Edna Shaviv. 'Integrated Modeling of Pedestrian Energy Exchange and Thermal Comfort in Urban Street Canyons'. *Building and Environment* 42.6 (2007): 2396–409.

Pearlmutter, David, Dixin Jiao, and Yaakov Garb. 'The Relationship Between Bioclimatic Thermal Stress and Subjective Thermal Sensation in Pedestrian Spaces'. *International Journal of Biometeorology* 58.10 (2014): 2111–2127.

Santamouris, Mattheos, C. Cartalis, and Afroditi Synnefa. 'Local Urban Warming, Possible Impacts and a Resilience Plan to Climate Changes for the Historical Center of Athens, Greece'. *Sustainable Cities and Society* 19 (2015): 281–91.

Shadar, Hadas. *Beer Sheva: Brutalist and Neo-Brutalist Architecture*. Tel Aviv: Bauhaus Center, 2014.

Shashua Bar, Limor, Evyatar Erell, and David Pearlmutter. 'The Cooling Efficiency of Urban Landscape Strategies in a Hot Dry Climate'. *Landscape and Urban Planning* 92.3–4 (2009): 179–86.

Sharon, Arieh. *Kibbutz+Bauhaus: An Architect's Way in a New Land*. Stuttgart and Tel Aviv: Karl Kraemer Verlag and Massada, 1976.

——— *Physical Planning in Israe*l. Jerusalem: HaMadpis HaMemshalti, 1951 (In Hebrew).

Standards Institute of Israel *(SII)*. *Standard of Israel SI 1045: Thermal Insulation of Buildings*. Tel Aviv: Standards Institute of Israel, 2011.

Notes

1 All translations from Hebrew to English are the author's own, unless otherwise specified.

2 Arieh Sharon, *Physical Planning in Israel* (Jerusalem: HaMadpis HaMemshalti, 1951) (In Hebrew).

3 Bauhaus concepts and principles guided the construction of both public institutional and private residential buildings.

4 Amos Gitai, 'Architecture in Israel. The "Carpet" as Housing – Nahum Zolotov, Israel Broadcasting Corporation, Education Channel (23)', March 27, 2013, accessed Jan. 6, 2019, https://www.youtube.com/watch?v=DS-2nuBSyWI (In Hebrew).

5 Tula Amir, *Nahum Zolotov / Architect and Planner* (Tel Aviv: Israeli Center for Libraries, 2011) (In Hebrew); Zvi Efrat, *The Israeli Project: Building and Architecture 1948–1973* (Tel Aviv: Tel Aviv Museum of Art, 2004) (In Hebrew).

6 Baruch Givoni, *Man, Climate & Architecture*, 2nd ed. (New York: Van Nostrand Reinhold, 1969).

7 Arie Bitan and Sara Rubin, 'Be'er Sheva', in *Climatic Atlas of Israel for Physical and Environmental Planning and Design* (Tel Aviv: Ramot Publishing Co., 1991) (In Hebrew).

8 Ibid.

9 Hofit Ben Shalom (Itzhak), Oded Potchter, and Haim Tsoar. 'The Effect of the Urban Heat Island and Global Warming on the Thermal Discomfort in a Desert City – The Case of Beer Sheva, Israel'. In *Proceedings 7th International Conference on Urban Climate*, Yokohama, Japan, June 29–July 3, 2009, accessed Jan. 6, 2019, http://www.ide.titech.ac.jp/~icuc7/extended_abstracts/pdf/375974-1-090521051217-003.pdf.

10 Ibid.

11 Hemu Kharel Kafle and Hendrik J. Bruins, 'Climatic Trends in Israel 1970–2002: Warmer and Increasing Aridity Inland', *Climatic Change* 96.1–2 (2009): 63–77.

12 Avraham Negev, 'Beer Sheba', in *Beer Sheba: The Archaeological Encyclopedia of the Holy Land*, 3rd ed. (New York: Prentice Hall Press, 1990), 53–54.

13 Isaac A. Meir, 'Urban Space Evolution in the Desert: The Case of Beer-Sheva', *Building and Environment* 27.1 (1992): 1–11.

14 Ibid.

15 Ibid.; Negev, 'Beer Sheva', 53–54.

16 Ibid.

17 Ibid.

18 Ibid.

19 Sharon, *Physical Planning*; Sharon was a Bauhaus graduate and planner of the first Israel master plan.

20 Ibid.

21 Ibid.

22 Ibid.

23 Central Bureau of Statistics (CBS), *Population, by Population Group* (Jerusalem: Central Bureau of Statistics, 2017): 40, accessed Jan.6, 2019, https://www.cbs.gov.il/he/publications/DocLib/2013/shnaton65_all.pdf.

24 Spot measurements: DELTA OHM HD8802 digital thermometer with thermocouple K sensor (S110) and Kurz 441-M-A-X air velocity meter; MRC LM-8102 handheld combined thermometer, anemometer, humidity metre, light metre, and sound level metre; longer

period monitoring: Onset HOBO data loggers with various sensors (air temperature, RH, light intensity, assorted external sensors) were used both for indoor and outdoor spaces; infrared thermography: FLIR B335 camera. All microclimatic measurements were made at a height of approximately 1.5 m above ground/floor.

25 Edward H. Mathews, Yair Etzion, E. van Heerden, S. Wegelaar, Evyatar Erell, David Pearlmutter, Isaac A. Meir, 'A Novel Thermal Simulation Model and Its Application on Naturally Ventilated Desert Buildings', *Building and Environment* 32.5 (1997): 447–56; Mathews, Edward H., P. G. Richards, and C. Lombard, 'A First-Order Thermal Model for Building Design', *Energy and Buildings* 21.2 (1994): 133–45.

26 Meir, 'Urban Space', 1–11.

27 David Pearlmutter, Dixin Jiao, and Yaakov Garb, 'The Relationship Between Bioclimatic Thermal Stress and Subjective Thermal Sensation in Pedestrian Spaces', *International Journal of Biometeorology* 58.10 (2014): 2111–2127.

28 Abba Elhanani, *The Struggle for Independence: Israeli Architecture in the Twentieth Century* (Tel Aviv: Tel Aviv Israel Ministry of Defense, 1998) (In Hebrew).

29 David Pearlmutter, Pedro Berliner, and Edna Shaviv, 'Integrated Modeling of Pedestrian Energy Exchange and Thermal Comfort in Urban Street Canyons', *Building and Environment* 42.6 (2007): 2396–409.

30 Yehonathan Golani and Dieter Gershom von Schwarze, eds, *Israel Builds 1970* (Jerusalem: Israel Ministry of Construction and Housing, 1970), 4.72–4.82.

31 Ram Karmi, *Lyric Architecture* (Tel Aviv: Israel Ministry of Defense, 2001), 92–103 (In Hebrew).

32 Heschong Mahone Group, *Windows and Offices: A Study of Office Worker Performance and the Indoor Environment* (California Energy Commission, Final report, P500-03-082-A-9; CEC Contract No. 400-99-013, 2003), 138.

33 Isaac A. Meir, Yair Etzion, and David Faiman, *Energy Aspects of Design in Arid Zones* (Sede Boqer Campus: Desert Architecture Unit/Applied Solar Calculations Unit, BIDR; & Jerusalem: State of Israel, Ministry of Energy and Infrastructure, Research and Development Division, RD-04-90, 1998).

34 Anat Folkman Biller, 'The General Performance of Internal Courtyards – Beer Sheva's Patio Houses as a Case Study' (M.Sc. thesis, Ben-Gurion University of the Negev, 2007), 218–22; Isaac A. Meir, David Pearlmutter, and Yair Etzion, 'On the Microclimatic Behavior of Two Semi-Enclosed Attached Courtyards in a Hot Dry Region', *Building and Environment* 30.4 (1995): 563–72.

35 Ibid.

36 Meir et al., 'On the Microclimatic Behavior', 563–72.

37 Folkman Biller, 'General Performance', 218–22; Limor Shashua Bar, Evyatar Erell, and David Pearlmutter, 'The Cooling Efficiency of Urban Landscape Strategies in a Hot Dry Climate', *Landscape and Urban Planning* 92.3–4 (2009): 179–86.

38 Folkman Biller, 'General Performance', 218–22.

39 Ibid.

40 Ibid.

41 Ibid.

42 The term 'Brutalist architecture' originates in the French word for raw (*brut*), used to describe exposed concrete (*beton brut*) buildings.

43 Gitai, 'Architecture in Israel'.

44 Standards Institute of Israel(SII), *Standard of Israel SI 1045: Thermal Insulation of Buildings* (Tel Aviv: Standards Institute of Israel, 2011).

45 Assaf Kessler, 'Could There Be a Green Future for Gray Buildings?' (MA thesis, Ben-Gurion University of the Negev, 2011).

46 Milo Hoffman and Menahem Gideon, *The Psychiatric Hospital in Be'er Sheva: Examination of the Climatic Operation of Passively Cooled Buildings* (Haifa: Technion – Israel Institute of Technology, Faculty of Civil Engineering, Buidling Research Station, 1985).

47 Ibid.

48 Meir, 'Urban Space', 1–11.

49 Isaac A. Meir and Susan C. Roaf, 'Thermal Comfort – Thermal Mass: Housing in Hot Dry Climates', in *Indoor Air 2002, Proc. 9th Int. Conf. Indoor Air Quality and Climate*, (Monterey, CA) ed. H. Levin, vol. 1 (Santa Cruz, CA: Indoor Air, 2002), 1050–55; Meir, Etzion and Faiman, 1998.

50 Arieh Sharon, *Kibbutz+Bauhaus: An Architect's Way in a New Land* (Stuttgart and Tel Aviv: Karl Kraemer Verlag and Massada, 1976).

51 Meir, 'Urban Space', 1–11; Meir and Roaf, 'Thermal Comfort', 1050–55; Meir et al., *Energy Aspects*, 1998.

52 Kessler, 'Could There Be', 42–45.

53 Alternately, internal insulation can be used in buildings listed for conservation. Though not ideal, it is better than no insulation at all.

54 Kessler, 'Could There Be', 42–45.

55 Mattheos Santamouris, C. Cartalis, and Afroditi Synnefa, 'Local Urban Warming, Possible Impacts and a Resilience Plan to Climate Changes for the Historical Center of Athens, Greece', *Sustainable Cities and Society* 19 (2015): 281–91.

56 Meir, 'Urban Space', 1–11; Meir and Roaf, 'Thermal Comfort', 1050–55.

57 Ben Shalom et al., 'Effect of the Urban Heat'; Folkman Biller, 'General Performance'; Givoni, *Man, Climate*; Meir, 'Urban Space'; Pearlmutter et al., 'Integrated Modeling'; Shashua Bar et al., 'Cooling Efficiency'.

58 Isaac A. Meir, 'Climatic Sub-Regions and Design Contextualism', *Building & Environment* 24.3 (1989): 245–51.

59 *Golani* and von Schwarze, *Israel Builds*, 4.72–4.82.

60 Hadas Shadar, *Beer Sheva: Brutalist and Neo-Brutalist Architecture* (Tel Aviv: Bauhaus Center, 2014). For example, Tel Aviv, with its modern movement areas known as the White City, was declared in 2003 a UNESCO World Heritage Site.

The Other Side of Climate: The Unscientific Nature of Climatic Architectural Design in Israel[1]

Or Aleksandrowicz

Climate has played an elusive role in the history of Israeli architecture, as a concept that was talked about and considered, but never fully grappled with, nor confronted. This dual nature towards climate resulted in architectural designs that, while alluding to climatic themes, refrained from analytical design solutions and rigorous, evidence-based design practices, thus limiting their ability to produce intelligent climatic solutions. It seems that Israeli architects preferred talking about the weather to doing anything about it.

From the 1920s, if not before, overheating indoor spaces was perceived as the main climatic challenge facing the professional builders of Palestine.[2] During the 1930s, a belief in the thermal advantages of natural ventilation became almost the only pillar of local climatic design.[3] Following that common belief, which did not emerge out of systematic scientific exploration, the spatial layout of buildings was designed by following prevailing wind patterns. In Tel Aviv, for example, architects persistently recommended the orientation of living rooms westwards for catching the afternoon sea breeze, while placing bedrooms on the eastern side of the apartment, opened to the cooling night-time eastern winds.[4]

The architectural preoccupation with the virtues of the sea breeze and prevailing winds was a far stretch from a complete understanding of the major climatic variables that affected buildings. Architecture in British Palestine and later in Israel lacked scientific rigour in analysing the thermal performance of buildings in different climatic conditions, and its reference to climate was based only on vague understanding of the complex effects of the elements on the built environment.[5] Typical apartment buildings, especially in the hot and humid Coastal Plain region, continually failed to deliver desirable thermal comfort levels: the apartments tended to overheat, leaving a common impression of summertime night incarceration in unbearably hot and humid interiors, with new, modernist buildings attracting more criticism than older structures.[6] The local version of the 1930s International Style may have been regarded by its local representatives as an 'acclimatized' version of what was built at the same time in Europe,[7] but in the eyes of contemporary critics this 'acclimatization' failed to produce a basic level of thermal comfort.[8]

A new, scientific approach to climatic building design first emerged in British Palestine in the early 1940s through the sporadic efforts of a handful of professional enthusiasts.[9] Yet, it was only after the establishment of the State of Israel in 1948 that research in the field began to gain momentum, mainly through a close cooperation between the Israeli government and the Building Research Station (BRS) at the Technion (Israel Institute of Technology).[10] The availability of new climatic data and understanding, though, did not transform the design habits of architects, and the effect of the emerging science on local architecture was generally marginal.[11] The reasons behind this discrepancy are analysed in this chapter based on two exemplary case studies of 1960s university buildings, each one reflecting different, and sometimes contradicting, approaches of architects towards building climatology and climate.

The Scientific Turn in Local Building Climatology

It seems that the undesirable climatic effects of local design norms and habits during the 1930s left most of the architects of the time indifferent. One architect, though, was an exception: Werner Joseph Wittkower (1903–1997), who should be considered as the unrecognized founder of Israeli building climatology. His analytical and practical works in the field during the 1940s and the first half of the 1950s had no precedent, as well as no contemporaneous equivalents in British Palestine and later in Israel.[12] As an active architect, Wittkower was aware of the need for scientifically sound guidelines for climatic building design, focusing on a limited set of major research questions, like building orientation, building massing, window size and orientation, shading design, and wall and roof composition. He was the first to argue, based on meticulous and quantitative analyses, that exposure to solar radiation is the main climatic element to be considered in the orientation of buildings in Palestine, and not the exploitation of wind.[13]

Wittkower's pioneering work in building climatology began with the preparation of an 83-page manuscript for a book (that was never published) on climatic building design in Palestine, written in German and completed probably in 1942.[14] In its opening pages, he expressed his views on the relation between science and architecture, arguing that science was the only viable way by which clear and rigorous answers to pressing design problems of modern construction could be obtained.[15] Wittkower's own interpretation of this idea included the publication of several theoretical papers on climate and building,[16] and the promotion of two monitoring experiments.[17] The first of them, executed in 1946, was the first local attempt to use controlled monitoring of buildings to answer a specific design question (that of a preferable building orientation), leading to the conclusion that a preferable orientation of the main façades should be to the north and south (because of their much lesser exposure to solar radiation during summer), in sharp contrast to the common practice at that time, which favoured the wind-oriented eastern and western façades.[18] The study transformed local design habits, and a north–south orientation of buildings thus became the common norm among local architects, irrespective of prevailing wind directions.[19]

During the years of the British Mandate (1920–48), scientific research on the interrelations between climate and building concerned the growing Jewish population of the country much more than its British governors.[20] While the British administration created a new system of modern planning administration in the country, their involvement in building activities and building research, especially in respect to housing, was negligible.[21] The situation changed after 1948. Due to the state's proclaimed responsibility for the execution of mass-housing projects for its fast-growing population, the Israeli government had a clear interest in a continued and reliable promotion of building research, with a special emphasis on building climatology.

During the first half of the 1950s, building research was coordinated and funded mainly through the Research Council of Israel (RCI), founded in 1949.[22] Though it managed to promote a couple of building climatology studies until the mid-1950s,[23] the RCI's dwindling resources meant that research efforts in this field remained scattered and sporadic, lacking a coherent approach and centralized coordination. This failure in providing a reliable framework for building research activities coincided with the Technion's increased involvement in promoting building research. Since Yaakov Dori's appointment as its president in February 1951, the Technion attempted to secure a leading position as a research institute.[24] In late 1952, it opened the BRS, headed by civil engineering professor Rahel Shalon.[25]

The BRS's first study on indoor climate was on the 'influence of ceiling height on dwelling houses', published in 1957.[26] It was funded by the Housing Division at the Ministry of Labor that was responsible at that time for the design and construction of public housing in Israel.[27] The Housing Division wished to examine whether the lowering of the typical height of ceilings, which could have potentially reduced building costs, would negatively affect indoor climate. Monitoring took place between July 1955 and March 1956 in test houses in Tirat Hacarmel near Haifa. Results showed that lowering the standard ceiling height from 3.0 to 2.5 metres (10 to 8 feet) would not compromise indoor thermal comfort, while enabling to cut 5 per cent of total building costs in typical housing projects.[28]

The successful results of the study probably convinced Shalon to open a new department for building climatology at the BRS. In 1958, after concluding another ceiling-height study in the desert town of Be'er Sheva,[29] Shalon appointed her assistant, architect Baruch Givoni (b.1920), who was involved in the two ceiling-height studies, as the head of the department. Having only limited experience in building climatology research, Givoni was sent for one year's training at the Research Laboratory of the American Society of Heating and Ventilating Engineers (ASHVE) in Cleveland. He remained in the United States for another year, completing a Master's degree in environmental physiology at the University of Pittsburgh, after which he returned to Israel.[30]

Givoni's return to Israel can be described as the opening page of a new chapter in local building climatology research. For the first time, a permanent research body dedicated its activities to questions of climate and building. Givoni's own varied personal experience, which combined architecture, physiology, and climatology, as well as his close cooperation with the Ministry of Housing (which replaced the Housing Division in 1961), directed indoor climate research towards practical problems of building design.[31] Asher Allweil (1908–1994), the director of the Engineering Department at the Ministry of Housing, commissioned most of these studies,[32] and effectively became a key figure in the promotion of Israeli building research.

Although the first steps in local indoor climate research focused on residential buildings, the methodology itself was relevant for all building types and functions. By the mid-1960s, research work done at the BRS's Department of Indoor Climate (which changed its name to the Department of Building Climatology in 1966) enabled local architects to acquire a better and fuller understanding of the climatic implications of their designs, in residential and public buildings alike. Benefitting from Allweil's practical approach to research questions, Givoni's work (mainly in cooperation with physicist Milo Hoffman) focused on answering basic design questions, which could have had a direct effect on indoor climate. Among the studies commissioned by Allweil were projects on the orientation of walls and openings, the massing of building volumes, the articulation of shading devices, the use of external colour, and the physical composition of walls.[33] The answers, though, were never formulated in a fully prescriptive (not to say dogmatic) manner, but promoted a holistic approach where the architect was encouraged to consciously choose between several design alternatives, each with its own positive and negative climatic aspects.

Surprisingly, the rapid development of local building climatology research during the 1960s, after almost two decades of limited public support, did not made architects more attentive to climatic knowledge. In a meeting dedicated to the relations between the Ministry of Housing and the BRS's Department of Indoor Climate, held in January 1965, Givoni expressed a clear sense of frustration with the reluctance of the Ministry's planners to integrate the knowledge produced by his department into their routine work.[34] He concluded that only legally binding regulations could make the desired transformation in architects' attitudes towards climatic considerations in design. In interviews to the press during the 1960s, Givoni recurrently expressed discontent with local design habits.[35] The picture remained the same during the 1970s and 1980s, even after Givoni's department produced comprehensive sets of guidelines for climatic building design in Israel.[36] In one instance, Givoni remarked, '[U]nfortunately, local architecture is perceived mainly as art, and its scientific sides are almost entirely ignored.'[37] Like a voice crying in the wilderness, research continued to produce knowledge while its application kept lagging far behind.

This discrepancy between the potential and actual application of climatic knowledge by architects is exemplified in this chapter by tracing the design process of two university buildings in 1960s Israel: the Gilman Building (Tel Aviv University) and the Eshkol Tower (University of Haifa). In both cases, architects explicitly considered elements of climatic design, though in different ways. Comparing two university buildings enables a focus on a design process where the clients are also the potential users of the building, thus having a clear interest in improving the building's indoor climate. The uncommon setting of a university campus may also create a design process where architects are encouraged to produce representative, exemplary, or even experimental buildings to promote the university's reputation as a progressive institution. Both elements make university campuses an almost ideal environment for pushing forward the integration of scientific knowledge in design, including in matters of climate. As the two historical cases show, this almost ideal environment was not always enough to secure the integration of climatic considerations into architectural design.

Climatic Design by the Book: Gilman Building, Tel Aviv University Campus (1963–65)

Among Werner Joseph Wittkower's many realized projects, the Gilman Building on the Tel Aviv University campus is one of the finest examples of building climatology integration into architectural design. Designed in 1963 by Wittkower and his partner, Erich Baumann, with architect Israel Stein (b.1934) as the office's architect-in-charge, the project evolved around the concept of solar protection, which, as is demonstrated below, manifested itself along all stages of the design process.

Building orientation posed the first challenge for Wittkower and Stein. The university campus master plan, conceived in the late 1950s by Wittkower, Dov Karmi, Arieh El-Hanani, and Nahum Salkind, mandated that the main façades of the Gilman Building had to be oriented to the east and west.[38] This orientation was in complete contrast to Wittkower's own teachings since the early 1940s, and was probably the result of a need to use the building mass to spatially define the surrounding outdoor areas.

Facing this problematic orientation, Wittkower and Stein came up with a creative solution. They divided the building into two detached rectangular wings, each one arranged around two courtyards [Figure 1]. This enabled to orient the most important spaces of the building (the lecture halls and classrooms) to the north and south, while arranging the service areas and smaller rooms (seminar rooms and offices) along the eastern and western façades. The arrangement of spaces around courtyards also facilitated their cross ventilation. Yet, even with this clever massing of the building, the smaller rooms along the eastern and western

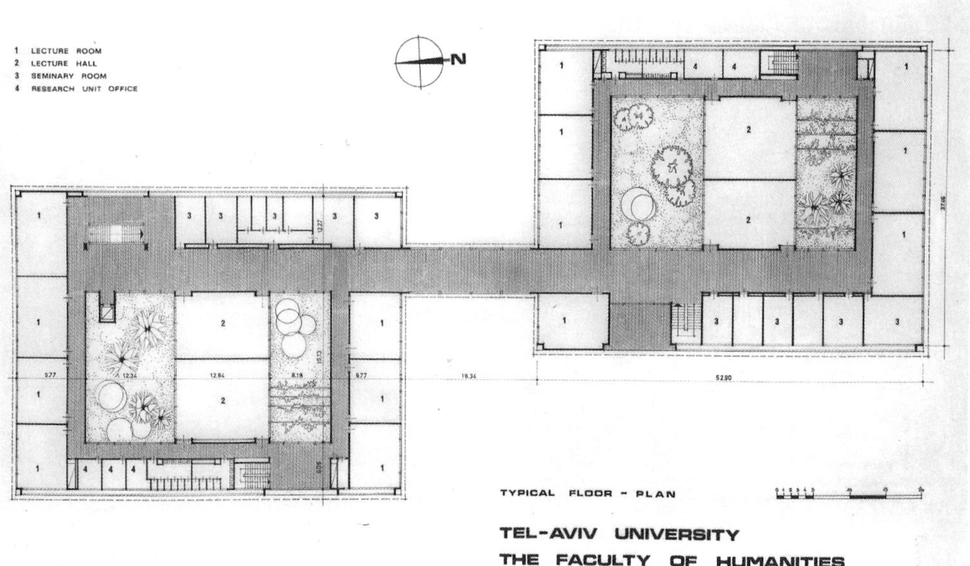

Figure 1: Typical floor plan of the Gilman Building, 1963. Israel Stein Collection, Tel Aviv, Israel.

façades still had to be protected from the effect of direct solar exposure. Solar protections from direct sunlight and glare were also required in the northern and southern lecture halls, especially because Wittkower and Stein decided to enhance their use of natural light by designing them with relatively large windows.[39]

The Gilman Building was designed in an era when a plethora of shading options and styles were regularly applied by Israeli architects. Israel of the 1950s and 1960s was an effervescent field of experimentation and innovation in shading elements of different kinds and effects, and local architects were keen on exploiting the field of solar protections for developing a new local architectural idiom (despite consciously borrowing ideas from abroad, and especially from Brazil).[40] Wittkower and Stein used the rich variety of available prefabricated shading elements in three different ways: fixed hollow precast concrete elements that formed an external shading screen masking almost entirely the eastern and western façades; fixed horizontal aluminium louvered elements that were installed in the northern and southern façades; and sliding PVC-aluminium shutters with rotatable slats that screened some of the façades overlooking the courtyards [Figures 2–5].

Based on thermal simulations of the building,[41] it can be argued that while the eastern and western precast screens of shading elements were very effective in lowering the indoor temperatures of the eastern and western rooms, the southern horizontal louvers were not highly effective in blocking direct solar radiation. The northern louvers, which had practically no thermal effect on the northern rooms, were originally designed only for glare prevention.[42] The positive effect of the eastern and western façades' shading screens had its price, both in the permanent blocking of the view from the eastern and western rooms, and in lowering indoor winter temperatures. These undesirable effects could have only been resolved by using non-fixed shading elements, but this, in turn, would have probably created additional maintenance issues that the architects tried to avoid.[43]

Figure 2: Gilman Building, the western façade, *c.*1965. Photograph by Isaac Berez. Tel Aviv University Archive, Tel Aviv, Israel.

Figure 3: Gilman Building, the south-western corner of the southern wing, showing the different solar protections applied to the southern (right) and western (left) façades. Photograph by Isaac Berez. Tel Aviv University Archive, Tel Aviv, Israel.

Figure 4: Gilman Building, the concrete sun breakers of the eastern façade of the northern wing used as an external screen of the glazed wall behind them, 2012. Photograph by the author Or Aleksandrowicz.

Figure 5: Gilman Building, the smaller courtyard of the southern wing, looking east, *c.*1966. The corridor façades, here facing north and west, were originally screened with sliding aluminium panels of rotatable PVC slats. Israel Stein Collection, Haifa, Israel.

More than with any other building component, the application of shading elements in the Gilman Building exposed an inherent tension between aesthetics and performance. Stein acknowledged that his shading solution for the eastern and western façades also had an aesthetic role, which was to 'unify' the expression of the façades while concealing a less attractive arrangement of windows behind the shading screen.[44] Since the design proved to work well, at least during the hot season, it should be regarded as a noteworthy achievement of coupling optimal performance with preferable aesthetics.

While the horizontal shadings of the southern façades provided adequate (although not fully optimal) protection against the summer sun almost without blocking the welcomed solar radiation during winter, the full glazing of the same façades created a problem of overheating that made the southern rooms remarkably warmer than all the other rooms. Thus, the ingenuity of the spatial scheme of the building, which enabled the orientation of some of its main spaces to the preferable south, was not exploited to its fuller potential because of the decision to use large glazing surfaces in the southern façades. In addition, since the applied shadings did not perfectly block direct south-eastern and south-western solar radiation, the negative effect of glazing was further aggravated by the application of shadings of non-optimal capacities.

Despite these minor shortcomings, the Gilman Building is exemplary in the way it demonstrates that conscious application of knowledge in building climatology can produce an architectural design that has an aesthetic appeal as well as satisfactory thermal performance. The achievement depended not only on Wittkower's and Stein's unique attitude towards climatic building design, but also on their ability to integrate climatic considerations from the very first stages of conceptual design up to the final stages of envelope detailing.

Aesthetics over Climatic Performance: Eshkol Tower, University of Haifa (1964–77)

Ever since the *Brazil Builds* exhibition at the Museum of Modern Art (MoMA) in 1943, Brazilian architecture was an international synonym for creative and intelligent application of external shading devices.[45] Oscar Niemeyer (1907-2012), arguably the most renowned Brazilian architect of his time, produced some of the finest examples of the shading idiom developed and extensively used in Brazil.[46] Many Israeli architects of the 1950s and early 1960s embraced Brazilian architecture and Niemeyer's design idiom as new sources of conscious inspiration, justifying their unrestrained mimicry in alleged climatic similarities between Israel and Brazil.[47] It was therefore almost natural for Yekutiel Federmann, an Israeli businessman, to hire Niemeyer for designing several of his large-scale projects in Haifa and Tel Aviv, hoping that Niemeyer's reputation would help to expedite their approval by the municipal authorities.[48]

Niemeyer's name had also attracted the attention of Eliezer Rafaeli, who, as the administrative manager of the newly founded University of Haifa, was looking for a renowned architect to design the university campus.[49] Like Federmann, Rafaeli was interested in Niemeyer because his reputation and experience were expected to reduce opposition to the university project, which many saw as a deplorable quasi-megalomaniac fit conceived by Abba Hushi, the powerful socialist mayor of Haifa.[50] Niemeyer arrived in Haifa in mid-April 1964 and set his base in Federmann's Dan Hotel in Tel Aviv.[51] Federmann invited Niemeyer to stay in Israel for several months, during which he was expected to produce designs for Federmann's own projects.[52] In addition, Federmann, interested in maintaining excellent relations with Haifa Municipality, allowed Niemeyer to simultaneously work on the design of the city's university campus.[53] By August, a preliminary design for the campus was completed.[54]

Rafaeli's own determination to build the new campus as 'a university under a single roof' led Niemeyer to propose a campus composed of a long rectangular slab on top of a mountain ridge that contained all the lecture halls, classes, and labs, as well as a central library, cafeterias, and an auditorium.[55] On top of this massive slab Niemeyer designed additional geometric volumes, the most conspicuous of all was a box-like 28-floor tower

Figure 6: Oscar Niemeyer, proposal for the University of Haifa campus, a model, 1964. Abba Hushi Archive LG 341. H28 U45 1960 L'université de Haifa, Haifa, Israel.

which was originally intended to host researchers from all the university's departments [Figure 6].[56] The composition resembled the configuration of Niemeyer's previous design of the National Congress of Brazil in Brasília (1957–64), despite the great differences in function between the two projects.

Leaving Israel in late September 1964, Niemeyer left behind a small team that was supposed to take care of the university's detailed design.[57] In a few months' time, though, Haifa Municipality decided to appoint Shlomo Gilead, a prominent Israeli architect, to oversee the project.[58] Gilead accepted the commission based on an explicit condition that

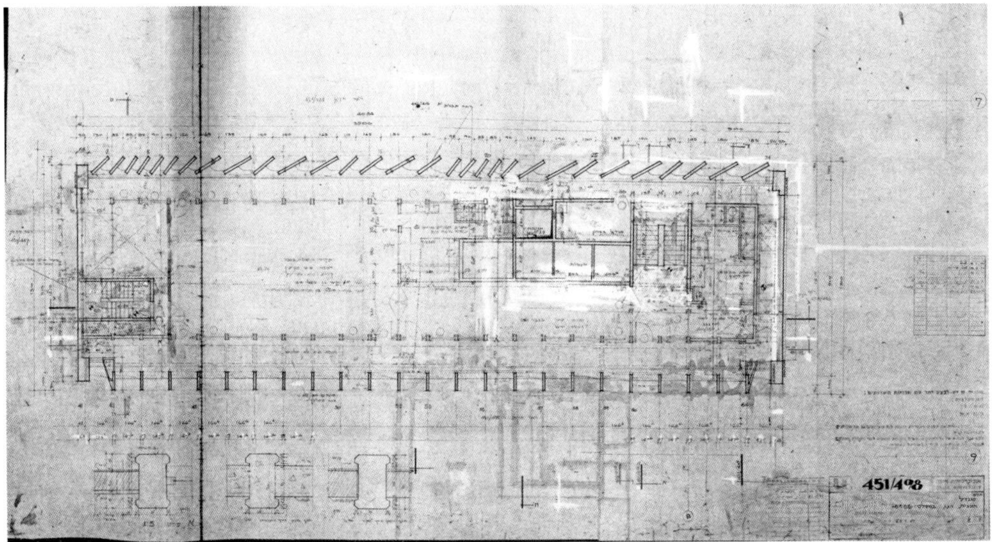

Figure 7: Early roof plan drawing of the Eshkol Tower showing the original design of the sun breakers, signed by Niemeyer, Müller, and Gilead and dated from January 23, 1969. University of Haifa Archive 0735, Haifa, Israel.

the future design would follow Niemeyer's concept, and the project continued to bear the names of both architects, Niemeyer and Gilead.[59]

Niemeyer designed the university tower as an almost generic rectangular slab, whose most remarkable feature was the elongated vertical concrete 'fins' running to the tower's full height and functioning as both structural columns and sun breakers protecting all-glazed south-eastern and north-western curtain walls [Figure 8]. In the south-eastern façade, the 'fins' were designed as perpendicular to the façade, while the north-western façade was screened by diagonal 'fins' of different angles. Similar diagonal 'fins' appeared also in Niemeyer's Ministry of Justice Building in Brasília (designed 1962).

Infrastructure works on the site of the university's main building began in October 1967.[60] Detailed design of the tower was already completed by that time, since the tower's basement floors were structurally an integral part of the main building. During the later stages of detailed design, in November 1967, Joseph Koen, Haifa City Engineer, approached Baruch Givoni and asked him whether the tower could function without installing an air-conditioning system. Givoni took the opportunity and in his written expert opinion criticized Niemeyer's design, focusing on the tower's sun breakers.[61] Givoni argued that Niemeyer's design would create a considerable rise in indoor temperatures and glare in the

Figure 8: Eshkol Tower, the sun breakers system as realized, the south-eastern facade, 2013. Photograph by the author Or Aleksandrowicz.

south-eastern façade, while preventing sufficient natural light in the north-western façade. As a result, he concluded, 'uncomfortable indoor conditions, which cannot be avoided without considerable modifications of the building design, are expected'.[62] Simulations of the original design, conducted by the author, support Givoni's analysis.[63] Bearing in mind the awkward design of the sun breakers, a newspaper report on Givoni's expert opinion hypothesized that Niemeyer might have forgotten he was not designing in Brazil but in the northern hemisphere.[64] Gilead, who was asked by the reporter to comment on Givoni's critique, replied that there were times when aesthetic considerations might be more significant than considerations of savings and functionality.[65]

Givoni's expert opinion did not change the tower's design, and the basement floors were built during 1968 according to the original plans.[66] Despite publicly backing Niemeyer's work, Gilead was probably impressed by Givoni's arguments and attempted to prevent the imminent functional failure of the building by approaching Niemeyer and suggesting to add horizontal shading elements to the south-eastern façade.[67] All his proposals were rejected.[68] To make things worse, Hans Müller, Niemeyer's assistant, proposed to copy the gloom-inducing diagonal sun breakers of the north-western façade on the south-eastern side of the tower,[69] and the option was even seriously considered during 1969.[70]

Delays in the execution of the entire project halted any attempts to modify the original design. In December 1971, the Israeli government stopped funding the construction of public buildings, including Haifa's university campus, and construction of the tower was put on hold.[71] The university was determined to bypass this unexpected obstacle, and in 1973 convinced the government to resume funding of the project after an alternative construction method was suggested.[72] Instead of the reinforced concrete structure designed by Niemeyer,

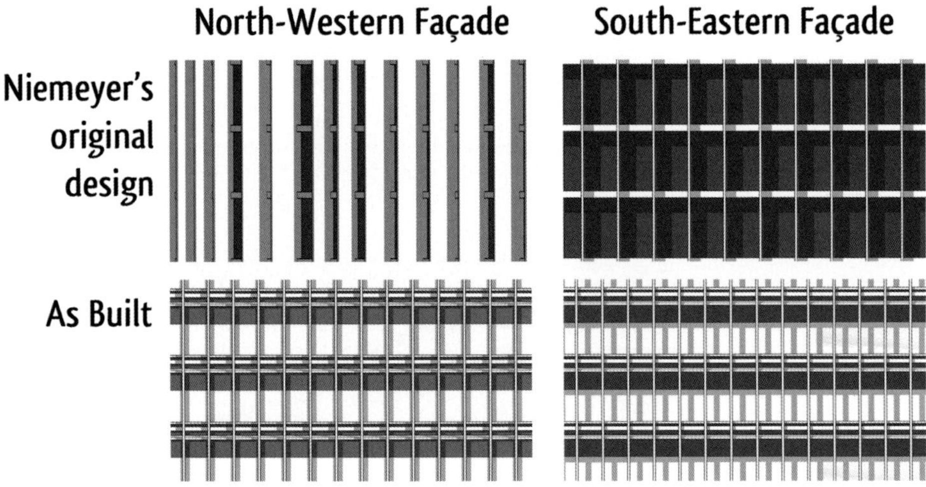

Figure 9: Schematic comparison of the two sun breakers systems of the Eshkol Tower, as designed by Niemeyer in 1968 and as realized. Drawing by the author Or Aleksandrowicz.

the university reached a deal with an Italian company named IRON, a subsidiary of the aluminium manufacturer FEAL (Fonderia Elettrica Alluminio e Leghe), for the manufacturing and construction of a prefabricated steel structure, including its curtain walls, modular indoor partitions, doors, and recessed ceilings. What convinced the government was mainly the attractive financing scheme that the Italian company offered the university.[73]

The transformation of the design to match IRON's prefabricated aluminium systems created an unexpected opportunity for Gilead to rethink the original sun breakers design, and especially to make better-performing horizontal sun breakers the main shading component of both main façades. Gilead insisted on substantially modifying the original design despite the sun breakers' high costs, which amounted to a fifth of all of IRON's construction works,[74] arguing at one point that he was 'giving the utmost importance to the shading of the rooms since without it he [Gilead] thinks that the building is unusable'.[75] The final design retained only a faint echo of Niemeyer's original design, using a thin aluminium version of Niemeyer's vertical façade elements for securing the main shading elements: three horizontal bent aluminium sheets on each floor that provided protection against a relatively wide range of sun angles [Figures 7–10]. Unlike Niemeyer's design, similar sun breakers

Figure 10: Eshkol Tower, the north-western façade, 2013, showing the realized sun breakers system in its entirety. Photograph by the author Or Aleksandrowicz.

were installed in both main façades. Niemeyer was not consulted about the new design, which proved to be far more effective in providing agreeable indoor lighting conditions than his original sun breakers. Yet several other features of Niemeyer's design, including the building's orientation and the use of lightweight and highly glazed façades, nevertheless survived and negatively affected the overall thermal performance of the building.[76] In that sense, the long shadow of Niemeyer could not have been entirely avoided.

In its early stages, the design of the Eshkol Tower exposed a head-on collision between building climatology imperatives and 'starchitect' dogma. Gilead, representing Niemeyer, first favoured sticking with Niemeyer's design even after confronted with Givoni's climatic analysis, only 'because Niemeyer did so, as something to be obeyed to the letter'.[77] Yet as time passed and Niemeyer's involvement in the project faded, Gilead became confident enough to redesign the main façades anew in a way that directly addressed the functionality issues raised by Givoni. This, however, happened only because accidental circumstances mandated the redesign of the façades to accommodate a different construction method.

Conclusion

Building climatology in Israel emerged because of concrete concerns over the thermal dysfunctionality of modern buildings that were built in Palestine from the 1920s. After the establishment of the Technion's BRS in 1952 and the return of Givoni to Israel in 1960 to assume the position of the head of its Department of Indoor Climate, the ground was prepared for the emergence of building climatology as a comprehensive body of knowledge that could be widely applied by architects. By the mid-1960s, Givoni and his team were able to provide concrete answers to questions of thermal comfort, building orientation, building massing, window size and orientation, shading design, and to some extent wall and roof compositions. However, Givoni was disappointed with the reluctance of architects to take advantage of his findings, especially since many of the studies conducted at the BRS were initiated and financed by Israel's Ministry of Housing and were meant to support the design of its numerous housing projects.

The two case studies presented here not only demonstrate the different approaches of architects to the integration of building climatology into architectural design, but also the different effects this integration has when applied during different stages of design. Arguably, the use of climatic data becomes less effective if it is not considered throughout all design stages (conceptual, preliminary, and detailed). In the Gilman Building, evidence-based knowledge in building climatology, based on the personal findings of the main architect, was utilized from the early stages of conceptual design up to the last stages of detailed design. The result was an almost optimal solution. Conversely, in the Eshkol Tower, climatic knowledge was absent from the conceptual and preliminary design stages, and had only a limited, though positive, effect on the building's thermal and visual performance when it was eventually considered during the detailed redesign of the façades.

The historical cases also demonstrate that Israeli architects could have benefited more from scientific climatic research. The superficial and amateurish approach of many of them to questions of building and climate cannot be explained by the lack of a proper knowledge base, or by the complexity of the climatic challenges. Scientific research in the field was always attentive to its application prospects and its products were usually presented in a form of relatively simple design guidelines. What was almost always missing was an honest consideration of the performance of buildings as equal to their formal expression. In that sense, one might wonder whether much has changed since.

Bibliography

Aleksandrowicz, Or. 'Appearance and Performance: Israeli Building Climatology and Its Effect on Local Architectural Practice (1940–1977)'. *Architectural Science Review* 60.5 (2017): 371–81.

——— 'Architecture's Unwanted Child: Building Climatology in Israel, 1940–1977'. Doctoral diss., Vienna University of Technology, 2015.

Aleksandrowicz, Or and Israel Architecture Archive. *Daring the Shutter: The Tel Aviv Idiom of Solar Protections*. Tel Aviv: Public School Editions, 2015.

Aleksandrowicz, Or and Ardeshir Mahdavi. 'The Impact of Building Climatology on Architectural Design: A Simulation-Assisted Historical Case Study' (Paper presented at the *Building Simulation 2015*, Hyderabad, India, December 7–9, 2015).

Aleksandrowicz, Or, and Ardeshir Mahdavi. 'The Application of Building Performance Simulation in the Writing of Architectural History: Analysing Climatic Design in 1960s Israel'. *Frontiers of Architectural Research* 7.3 (2018): 367–82.

Allweil, Asher. 'Building Research in the State of Israel and Its Achievements'. *Davar*, April 24, 1961 (In Hebrew).

Awin, Józef. 'On the Art of Building in Eretz Israel'. *Binyan VeḤaroshet (Construction and Industry)* 6.3–4 (1927): 12 (In Hebrew).

Baerwald, Alexander. 'The Art of Homeland'. *Misḥar VeTa'asiya (Commerce and Industry)* 3.3–4 (1925): 3 (In Hebrew).

Barber, Daniel A. 'Le Corbusier, the Brise-Soleil, and the Socio-Climatic Project of Modern Architecture, 1929–1963'. *Thresholds* 40 (2012): 22–32.

'Building Training Department Opens at the Technion'. *Davar*, 11 June, 1953 (In Hebrew).

M. B., 'Towards Reform in the Consturction of Houses in Tel Aviv'. *Haaretz*, October 15, 1935 (In Hebrew).

'Construction of the Haifa University Campus Expected to Begin This Year'. *Davar*, August 2, 1964.

El-Eini, Roza I. M. *Mandated Landscape: British Imperial Rule in Palestine, 1929–1948*. London: Routledge, 2006.

Elhyani, Zvi. 'Horizontal Ideology, Vertical Vision: Oscar Niemeyer and Israel's Height Dilemma'. In *Constructing a Sense of Place: Architecture and the Zionist Discourse*, edited by Haim Yacobi, 94–96. Aldershot, UK: Ashgate, 2004.

——— 'Oscar Niemeyer and the Outset of Speculative Urbanism in Israel after 1960'. Master's thesis, Technion, 2002 (In Hebrew).

Eliezer Rafaeli to Avraham Shekhterman, June 24, 1975. 133/75. University of Haifa Archive (UHA), Haifa.

Eliezer Rafaeli to Moshe Neudorfer, August 9, 1973. 25/25. University of Haifa Archive (UHA), Haifa.

Eliezer Rafaeli to Pinchas Sapir, January 6, 1972. 25/25. University of Haifa Archive (UHA), Haifa.

Eshel, Tzadok. *Abba Hushi – Man of Haifa*. Tel Aviv: Israel Ministry of Defence, 2002 (In Hebrew).

'Expert Opinion on the "Tower" Building at the University of Haifa', January 9, 1968. 684/21. University of Haifa Archive (UHA), Haifa.

Feige, Rudolf, Walter Koch, Jehuda Neumann, and Werner Joseph Wittkower. *Report on the Indoor Climate of Two Apartments*. Jerusalem: Israel Meteorological Service, 1952.

Givoni, Baruch. *Climatic Design Guidelines for the Different Regions of Israel.* Haifa: Building Research Station, the Technion, 1968 (In Hebrew).

——— 'Identifications of Research Needs in the Field of Problems of Climate and Energy in Building'. In *Identification of Building Research Needs for the Israeli Economy*, 43–45. Haifa: Building Research Station, the Technion, 1983.

Givoni, Baruch. Personal interview with Or Aleksandrowicz, Tel Aviv, December 23, 2012.

——— 'Review of the Relation in Issues of Climatic Problems Between the Building Research Station and the Ministry of Housing'. Gimel-Lamed-863/2. Israel State Archives (ISA), Jerusalem.

Givoni, Baruch and Milo Hoffman. *Climatic Design Recommendations for the Different Regions in Israel.* Haifa: Building Research Station, the Technion, 1972.

——— *Effect of Orientation of Walls and Windows on Indoor Climate.* Haifa: Building Research Station, the Technion, 1965 (In Hebrew).

——— *Effectiveness of Shading Devices.* Haifa: Building Research Station, the Technion, 1964 (In Hebrew).

——— *The Effect of Thermal Properties of Building Materials on Indoor Temperature.* Haifa: Building Research Station, the Technion, 1968 (In Hebrew).

——— *The Effect of Thermal Properties of Building Materials on the Thermal Response of Buildings to Solar Heat Gain through a Window.* Haifa: Building Research Station, the Technion, 1968 (In Hebrew).

——— *Effectiveness of Shading Devices.* Haifa: Building Research Station, the Technion, 1964 (In Hebrew).

——— *Preliminary Study of Cooling of Houses in Desert Regions by Utilizing Outgoing Radiation.* Haifa: Building Research Station, the Technion, 1968 (In Hebrew).

Givoni, Baruch and Rahel Shalon. *Influence of Ceiling Height on Thermal Conditions in Dwelling Houses in Be'er Sheva*. Haifa: Building Research Station, the Technion, 1962 (In Hebrew).

——— *Preliminary Study of the Influence of Window Orientation on Indoor Climate in Beer Sheva.* Haifa: Building Research Station, the Technion, 1963 (In Hebrew).

Givoni, Baruch and Michael Strumpf. *Building Orientation in Eilat.* Haifa: Building Research Station, the Technion, 1962 (In Hebrew).

Goodovitch, Israel M. *Architecturology: An Interim Report*. Tel Aviv: George Allen & Unwin, 1967.

Goodwin, Philip L. *Brazil Builds: Architecture New and Old 1652–1942*. New York: Museum of Modern Art, 1943.

Hans Müller to Shlomo Gilead, October 11, 1968. Shlomo Gilead Collection. Israel Architecture Archive, Tel Aviv.

Hashimshoni, Avia. 'Climatic Problems from the Architect's Point of View'. In *Climate and Man in Israel*, ed. Human Environmental Physiology Group, 124–35. Jerusalem: National Council for Research and Development, 1962 (In Hebrew).

Haelyon, Yaakov. '"Good" Orientation – Not Yet a Comfortable Climate', *Maariv*, March 8, 1966 (In Hebrew).

Karmi, Dov. 'Apartment Orientation in Tel Aviv'. *HaBinyan BaMizraḥ HaQarov* 1.9–10 (1936): 5 (In Hebrew).

——— 'The Sun Breakers'. *Journal of the Association of Engineers and Architects in Israel* 10.3 (1953): 14–15 (In Hebrew).

Magen, Arnon. 'Our Houses Are Not Built Properly'. *Davar*, March 31, 1974 (In Hebrew).

Meeting minutes of Eshkol Tower Design Team, June 21, 1973. 1/685. University of Haifa Archive (UHA), Haifa.

Meeting minutes of the Planning Coordination Committee of the University of Haifa, May 4, 1969. 684/21. University of Haifa Archive (UHA), Haifa.

Mindlin, Henrique E. *Modern Architecture in Brazil*. Rio de Janeiro: Colibris Editora, 1956.

Mirkin, Dan. 'The Tall Tower of the University of Haifa'. *Maariv*, April 4, 1968 (In Hebrew).

Nesher, Arie. 'Climate, Building and Man'. *Haaretz*, January 5, 1962 (In Hebrew).

Neumann, Heinrich, Mordechai Peleg, and Nathan Robinson. *Research on Indoor Climate: Thermal Measurements on Objects in the Jordan Valley: Publication Number 4*. Haifa: Station for Technical Climatology, the Tehnion, 1952 (In Hebrew);

Olgyay, Victor and Aladár Olgyay. *Solar Control and Shading Devices*. Princeton, NJ: Princeton University Press, 1957.

Oz, Yehuda. '"Revolution" on the Carmel – with Height of 25 Floors'. *Maariv*, June 4, 1964 (In Hebrew).

Posner, Julius. 'One-Family Houses in Palestine'. *Habinyan* 1.2 (1937): 1–3 (In Hebrew).

Promotional booklet, 1962. 362(48)/5-2-1962-1. Tel Aviv Municipality Historical Archive, Tel Aviv University, Tel Aviv (In Hebrew).

Pundak, Nahum. 'Science Prolongs Our Lives but We Make Them Shorter'. *Davar*, April 8, 1963 (In Hebrew).

Rafaeli, Eliezer. Personal interview with Or Aleksandrowicz, Haifa, December 27, 2013.

Ratner, Yohanan (Eugen). 'Towards the Original Style'. In *Palestine Building Annual 1934–1935*, 34–36, 75. Tel Aviv: Mischar w'Taasia, 1935.

'Research Council of Israel', *Nature*, August 6, 1949.

Shadar, Hadas. *The Building Blocks of Public Housing*. Tel Aviv: Israel Ministry of Construction and Housing, 2014 (In Hebrew).

Shalon, Rahel, Asher Allweil, Rudolf Landsberg, Alfred Mansfeld, Heinrich Neumann, R. C. Reinitz, and Baruch Givoni. *A Study of the Influence of Ceiling Height on Dwelling Houses*. Haifa: Building Research Station, 1957 (In Hebrew).

Sharon, Arieh. 'Architecture and Planning'. *Lantern* 6.1 (1956): 55.
——— 'Planning of Cooperative Houses'. *Habinyan* 1.1 (1937): 2–3 (In Hebrew).
——— 'Public Buildings in Palestine'. In *Twenty Years of Building: Workers' Settlements, Housing and Public Institutions*, 115–17. Engineers', Architects' and Surveyors' Union, 1940 (In Hebrew).
Stein, Israel. Personal interview with Or Aleksandrowicz, Tel Aviv, September 12, 2012.
Strauss, Walter. 'The Apartment as a Shelter from the Climate, Part 2'. *Yedi'ot LeInyeney Higyena UVri'ut (Hygiene and Health Chronicles)* 1.11 (1941): 45–46 (In Hebrew).
Tel Aviv Municipality. *Yearbook for the Jewish Year 5699*. Tel Aviv: Tel Aviv Municipality, 1939 (In Hebrew).
'The Technion Will Be Involved in Research Too'. *Herut*, May 24, 1951 (In Hebrew).
'The University of Haifa – into Its New Home'. *Davar*, October 25, 1967 (In Hebrew).
Wittkower, Werner Joseph. 'Bauliche Gestaltung Klimatisch Gesunder Wohnräume in Palästina', 1942(?). G.F.0341/23. German-Speaking Jewry Heritage Museum, Tefen.
——— 'Climate-Adapted Building in Israel: How Far Has Our Knowledge Influenced Building Practice?'. *Energy and Buildings* 7.3 (1984): 269–80.
——— 'Climate and Industrial Buildings in Palestine'. *Journal of the Association of Engineers and Architects in Palestine* 7.6 (1946): 2–6 (In Hebrew)
——— 'The Climate and Town Planning'. In *Engineering Survey*, 16–18. Tel Aviv: Engineers', Architects' and Surveyors' Union of Palestine, 1944 (In Hebrew).
——— 'Plan for Tel Aviv University'. *Handasa VeAdrikhalut (Journal of the Association of Engineers and Architects in Israel)* 23.6 (1965): 37–45 (In Hebrew).
——— 'Towards Reform of Town and House Planning in Palestine'. *Journal of the Association of Engineers and Architects in Palestine* 4.6 (1943): 1–4 (In Hebrew).
——— 'Ventilation and Insulation'. *Journal of the Association of Engineers and Architects in Israel* 13.1 (1955): 26–27 (In Hebrew).
Wittkower, Werner Joseph, Joseph Frenkiel, and Jehuda Neumann. *Effects of Some Types of Roof Construction Upon Air Temperatures Close to the Ceiling in the Late Summer Months in Israel*. Jerusalem: Research Council of Israel, 1953 (In English).
Zandberg, Esther. 'Corner of Niemeyer and Israel'. *Ha'ir*, August 12, 1988 (In Hebrew).

Notes

1 All translations from Hebrew to English are the author's own, unless otherwise specified.
2 Alexander Baerwald, 'The Art of Homeland', *Misḥar VeTa'asiya (Commerce and Industry)* 3.3–4 (1925): 3; Józef Awin, 'On the Art of Building in Eretz Israel', *Binyan VeḤaroshet (Construction and Industry)* 6.3–4 (1927): 12 (In Hebrew).
3 Avia Hashimshoni, 'Climatic Problems from the Architect's Point of View', in *Climate and Man in Israel [in Hebrew]*, ed. Human Environmental Physiology Group (Jerusalem: National Council for Research and Development, 1962), 128 (In Hebrew).
4 Dov Karmi, 'Apartment Orientation in Tel Aviv', *HaBinyan BaMizraḥ HaQarov* 1.9–10 (1936): 5 (In Hebrew); Arieh Sharon, 'Planning of Cooperative Houses', *Habinyan* 1.1 (1937):

2–3 (In Hebrew); Tel Aviv Municipality, *Yearbook for the Jewish Year 5699* (Tel Aviv: Tel Aviv Municipality, 1939), 70 (In Hebrew); Arieh Sharon, 'Public Buildings in Palestine', in *Twenty Years of Building: Workers' Settlements, Housing and Public Institutions* (Engineers', Architects' and Surveyors' Union, 1940), 116 (In Hebrew).

5 Hashimshoni, 'Climatic Problems', 127–30.

6 M. B., 'Towards Reform in the Consturction of Houses in Tel Aviv', *Haaretz*, October 15, 1935 (In Hebrew); Walter Strauss, 'The Apartment as a Shelter from the Climate, Part 2', *Yedi'ot LeInyeney Higyena UVri'ut (Hygiene and Health Chronicles)* 1.11 (1941): 45–46 (In Hebrew); Ibid.

7 Yohanan (Eugen) Ratner, 'Towards the Original Style', in *Palestine Building Annual 1934–1935* (Tel Aviv: Mischar w'Taasia, 1935), 35; Julius Posner, 'One-Family Houses in Palestine', *Habinyan* 1.2 (1937): 1–2 (In Hebrew).

8 M. B., 'Towards Reform'; Strauss, 'Apartment'.

9 Or Aleksandrowicz, 'Appearance and Performance: Israeli Building Climatology and Its Effect on Local Architectural Practice (1940–1977)', *Architectural Science Review* 60.5 (2017): 372–73.

10 Ibid., 374–76.

11 Ibid., 377–78.

12 Or Aleksandrowicz, 'Architecture's Unwanted Child: Building Climatology in Israel, 1940–1977' (doctoral diss., Vienna University of Technology, 2015), 69–111.

13 Werner Joseph Wittkower, 'Towards Reform of Town and House Planning in Palestine', *Journal of the Association of Engineers and Architects in Palestine* 4.6 (1943): 1–4 (In Hebrew); Werner Joseph Wittkower, 'Climate-Adapted Building in Israel: How Far Has Our Knowledge Influenced Building Practice?', *Energy and Buildings* 7.3 (1984): 269.

14 Probably the only surviving copy of the manuscript was discovered by the author in the Rudolf Feige collection at the German-speaking Jewry Heritage Museum, Tefen, Israel. See: Werner Joseph Wittkower, 'Bauliche Gestaltung Klimatisch Gesunder Wohnräume in Palästina', 1942(?), G.F.0341/23, German-Speaking Jewry Heritage Museum, Tefen.

15 Ibid.

16 Wittkower, 'Towards Reform'; Werner Joseph Wittkower, 'The Climate and Town Planning', in *Engineering Survey* (Tel Aviv: Engineers', Architects' and Surveyors' Union of Palestine, 1944), 16–18 (In Hebrew); Werner Joseph Wittkower, 'Climate and Industrial Buildings in Palestine', *Journal of the Association of Engineers and Architects in Palestine* 7.6 (1946): 2–6 (In Hebrew); Werner Joseph Wittkower, 'Ventilation and Insulation', *Journal of the Association of Engineers and Architects in Israel* 13.1 (1955): 26–27 (In Hebrew).

17 Feige, Rudolf, Walter Koch, Jehuda Neumann, and Werner Joseph Wittkower, *Report on the Indoor Climate of Two Apartments* (Jerusalem: Israel Meteorological Service, 1952); Werner Joseph Wittkower, Joseph Frenkiel, and Jehuda Neumann, *Effects of Some Types of Roof Construction Upon Air Temperatures Close to the Ceiling in the Late Summer Months in Israel* (Jerusalem: Research Council of Israel, 1953) (In English). See also: Wittkower, 'Climate-Adapted'.

18 Karmi, 'Apartment'; Sharon, 'Planning'; Sharon, 'Public Buildings'.

19 Hashimshoni, 'Climatic Problems', 128.
20 Aleksandrowicz, 'Appearance', 373.
21 Ibid.; Roza I. M. El-Eini, *Mandated Landscape: British Imperial Rule in Palestine, 1929–1948* (London: Routledge, 2006), 94–103; Aleksandrowicz, 'Appearance'.
22 'Research Council of Israel', *Nature*, August 6, 1949, 214.
23 Heinrich Neumann, Mordechai Peleg, and Nathan Robinson, *Research on Indoor Climate: Thermal Measurements on Objects in the Jordan Valley: Publication Number 4* (Haifa: Station for Technical Climatology, the Tehnion, 1952) (In Hebrew); Wittkower et al. *Effects.*
24 'The Technion Will Be Involved in Research Too', *Herut*, May 24, 1951, 4 (In Hebrew).
25 'Building Training Department Opens at the Technion', *Davar*, 11 June, 1953, 10 (In Hebrew).
26 Rahel Shalon, Asher Allweil, Rudolf Landsberg, Alfred Mansfeld, Heinrich Neumann, R. C. Reinitz, and Baruch Givoni, *A Study of the Influence of Ceiling Height on Dwelling Houses* (Haifa: Building Research Station, 1957) (In Hebrew).
27 Hadas Shadar, *The Building Blocks of Public Housing* (Tel Aviv: Israel Ministry of Construction and Housing, 2014), 15 (In Hebrew).
28 Shalon et al., *Study*.
29 Baruch Givoni and Rahel Shalon, *Influence of Ceiling Height on Thermal Conditions in Dwelling Houses in Be'er Sheva* (Haifa: Building Research Station, the Technion, 1962 (In Hebrew).
30 Baruch Givoni, personal interview with Or Aleksandrowicz, Tel Aviv, December 23, 2012.
31 Aleksandrowicz, 'Appearance', 377.
32 Asher Allweil, 'Building Research in the State of Israel and Its Achievements', *Davar*, April 24, 1961, 5 (In Hebrew).
33 Baruch Givoni and Michael Strumpf, *Building Orientation in Eilat* (Haifa: Building Research Station, the Technion, 1962) (In Hebrew); Baruch Givoni and Rahel Shalon, *Preliminary Study of the Influence of Window Orientation on Indoor Climate in Beer Sheva* (Haifa: Building Research Station, the Technion, 1963) (In Hebrew); Baruch Givoni and Milo Hoffman, *Effectiveness of Shading Devices* (Haifa: Building Research Station, the Technion, 1964) (In Hebrew); Baruch Givoni and Milo Hoffman, *Effect of Orientation of Walls and Windows on Indoor Climate* (Haifa: Building Research Station, the Technion, 1965) (In Hebrew); Baruch Givoni and Milo Hoffman, *The Effect of Thermal Properties of Building Materials on the Thermal Response of Buildings to Solar Heat Gain through a Window* (Haifa: Building Research Station, the Technion, 1968) (In Hebrew); Baruch Givoni and Milo Hoffman, *Preliminary Study of Cooling of Houses in Desert Regions by Utilizing Outgoing Radiation*. Haifa: Building Research Station, the Technion, 1968 (In Hebrew); Baruch Givoni and Milo Hoffman, *The Effect of Thermal Properties of Building Materials on Indoor Temperature*. Haifa: Building Research Station, the Technion, 1968 (In Hebrew).
34 Baruch Givoni, 'Review of the relation in issues of climatic problems between the Building Research Station and the Ministry of Housing', Gimel-Lamed-863/2, Israel State Archives (ISA), Jerusalem.

35 Arie Nesher, 'Climate, Building and Man', *Haaretz*, January 5, 1962 (In Hebrew); Nahum Pundak, 'Science Prolongs Our Lives but We Make Them Shorter', *Davar*, April 8, 1963, 4 (In Hebrew); Yaakov Haelyon, '"Good" Orientation – Not Yet a Comfortable Climate', *Maariv*, March 8, 1966, 10 (In Hebrew).

36 Baruch Givoni, *Climatic Design Guidelines for the Different Regions of Israel* (Haifa: Building Research Station, the Technion, 1968) (In Hebrew); Baruch Givoni and Milo Hoffman, *Climatic Design Recommendations for the Different Regions in Israel* (Haifa: Building Research Station, the Technion, 1972).

37 Arnon Magen, 'Our Houses Are Not Built Properly', *Davar*, March 31, 1974, 8 (In Hebrew). See also: Baruch Givoni, 'Identifications of Research Needs in the Field of Problems of Climate and Energy in Building', in *Identification of Building Research Needs for the Israeli Economy* (Haifa: Building Research Station, the Technion, 1983), 43–45.

38 Promotional booklet published by Tel Aviv University, 1962, 362(48)/5-2-1962-1, Tel Aviv Municipality Historical Archive, Tel Aviv (In Hebrew); Israel Stein, personal interview with Or Aleksandrowicz, Tel Aviv, September 12, 2012.

39 Stein, personal interview.

40 Or Aleksandrowicz and Israel Architecture Archive, *Daring the Shutter: The Tel Aviv Idiom of Solar Protections* (Tel Aviv: Public School Editions, 2015), 36–43.

41 Or Aleksandrowicz and Ardeshir Mahdavi, 'The Impact of Building Climatology on Architectural Design: A Simulation-Assisted Historical Case Study' (Paper presented at the *Building Simulation 2015*, Hyderabad, India, December 7–9, 2015); Or Aleksandrowicz and Ardeshir Mahdavi, 'The Application of Building Performance Simulation in the Writing of Architectural History: Analysing Climatic Design in 1960s Israel', *Frontiers of Architectural Research* 7.3 (2018).

42 Stein, personal interview; Werner Joseph Wittkower, 'Plan for Tel Aviv University', *Handasa VeAdrikhalut (Journal of the Association of Engineers and Architects in Israel)* 23.6 (1965): 41 (In Hebrew).

43 Stein, personal interview.

44 Ibid.

45 Philip L. Goodwin, *Brazil Builds: Architecture New and Old 1652–1942* (New York: Museum of Modern Art, 1943), 81–84; Henrique E. Mindlin, *Modern Architecture in Brazil* (Rio de Janeiro: Colibris Editora, 1956), 10–12; Daniel A. Barber, 'Le Corbusier, the Brise-Soleil, and the Socio-Climatic Project of Modern Architecture, 1929–1963', *Thresholds* 40 (2012): 22–32.

46 A telling indication of Niemeyer's reputation as a master designer of solar protections is the fact that eight of his designs, more than of any other architect, were chosen by the Olgyay brothers as case studies for their seminal work on shading devices, published in 1957. See Victor Olgyay and Aladár Olgyay, *Solar Control and Shading Devices* (Princeton, NJ: Princeton University Press, 1957).

47 Dov Karmi, 'The Sun Breakers', *Journal of the Association of Engineers and Architects in Israel* 10.3 (1953): 14–15 (In Hebrew); Arieh Sharon, 'Architecture and Planning', *Lantern* 6.1 (1956): 55; Israel M. Goodovitch, *Architecturology: An Interim Report* (Tel

Aviv: George Allen & Unwin, 1967), 10; Zvi Elhyani, 'Horizontal Ideology, Vertical Vision: Oscar Niemeyer and Israel's Height Dilemma', in *Constructing a Sense of Place: Architecture and the Zionist Discourse*, ed. Haim Yacobi (Aldershot, UK: Ashgate, 2004), 94–96.

48 Zvi Elhyani, 'Oscar Niemeyer and the Outset of Speculative Urbanism in Israel after 1960' (Master's thesis, Technion, 2002), 100–01 (In Hebrew).

49 Eliezer Rafaeli, personal interview with Or Aleksandrowicz, Haifa, December 27, 2013.

50 Tzadok Eshel, *Abba Hushi – Man of Haifa* (Tel Aviv: Israel Ministry of Defence, 2002), 276–81 (In Hebrew).

51 Yehuda Oz, '"Revolution" on the Carmel – with Height of 25 Floors', *Maariv*, June 4, 1964, 13 (In Hebrew).

52 Elhyani, 'Horizontal Ideology', 90.

53 Rafaeli, personal interview; Esther Zandberg, 'Corner of Niemeyer and Israel', *Ha'ir*, August 12, 1988, 38–39 (In Hebrew).

54 'Construction of the Haifa University Campus Expected to Begin This Year', *Davar*, August 2, 1964, 8.

55 Rafaeli, personal interview.

56 The tower was named after Israel's third prime minister, Levi Eshkol, shortly after his death in February 1969. Until then it was referred to only as 'the tower' or as a part of 'Niemeyer's building'.

57 The team's main members were two of Niemeyer's closest assistants, the (Jewish) structural engineer Samuel Rawet and the German architect Hans Müller, as well as Haim Tibon, a local architect who was later appointed by Niemeyer to be his official representative in Israel.

58 Elhyani, 'Oscar Niemeyer', 104–05.

59 Ibid.

60 'The University of Haifa – into Its New Home', *Davar*, October 25, 1967, 10 (In Hebrew).

61 'Expert Opinion on the "Tower" Building at the University of Haifa', January 9, 1968, 684/21, University of Haifa Archive (UHA), Haifa.

62 Ibid.

63 Aleksandrowicz, 'Architecture's Unwanted Child', 400–23.

64 Dan Mirkin, 'The Tall Tower of the University of Haifa', *Maariv*, April 4, 1968 (In Hebrew).

65 Ibid., 25.

66 This is also evident from the inspection of three historical aerial photographs that documented the building of the main university building, kept at the University of Haifa Archive (scan numbers 0003, 0007, and 0010), Haifa.

67 Hans Müller to Shlomo Gilead, October 11, 1968, Shlomo Gilead Collection, Israel Architecture Archive, Tel Aviv.

68 Ibid.

69 Ibid.

70 Meeting Minutes of the Planning Coordination Committee of the University of Haifa, May 4, 1969, 684/21, University of Haifa Archive (UHA), Haifa.

71 Eliezer Rafaeli to Pinchas Sapir, January 6, 1972, 25/25,

72 Eliezer Rafaeli to Avraham Shekhterman, June 24, 1975, 133/75, University of Haifa Archive (UHA), Haifa.
73 Ibid.
74 Eliezer Rafaeli to Moshe Neudorfer, August 9, 1973, 25/25, University of Haifa Archive (UHA), Haifa.
75 Meeting Minutes of Eshkol Tower Design Team, June 21, 1973, 1/685, University of Haifa Archive (UHA), Haifa.
76 Aleksandrowicz, 'Architecture's Unwanted Child', 400–23.
77 Mirkin, 'Tall Tower', 25.

Section IV

Reflections Abroad

Building and Re-Building a Nation's Identity: Israeli and Italian Architectural Culture, Their Representation and the Role of Bruno Zevi (1918–2000)

Matteo Cassani Simonetti

In Italy, following the end of World War II, continuity or discontinuity with the experiences of the interwar period represented two main routes on which to base new architecture. Post-war reconstruction and the complex legacies of twenty years of Fascist rule created opportunities needed for, on the one hand, cultural renewal that questioned Italian identity and, on the other hand, the assimilation of new concepts from abroad.

In this context, Italian awareness of Israeli architectural experiments in the framework of building a new state, emerged as a contribution that was initially episodic, and later, from the mid-1950s, more structured. In those years, architecture built in the 1930s and 1940s in Palestine was presented as a significant example of the modern tradition, wherein language, technology, and social demands were at the core of all development. Within this framework, the heritage of modern architecture was embraced, yet its formalism was relinquished in favour of placing the needs of man and society at the centre of architectural planning. However, from the mid-1950s the work of the 'statehood generation' of Israeli architects, the first trained directly in Israel after the founding of the new state, was widely presented in Italian architectural journals for its pragmatism and its questioning of an established modernist vocabulary, which departed from the consolidated International Style and the legacy of the older masters of modern architecture.

The presentation of Israeli architecture in major Italian journals may appear simply as one of many cultural exchanges in the post-war search of alternatives for Italian renewal. However, the chief proponent of Israeli architecture was the Jewish architectural critic and historian Bruno Zevi (1918–2000), who embraced the Zionist cause both politically and culturally.[1] Zevi presented projects developed in Israel in *L'architettura. Cronache e storia*, the periodical founded by him in 1955, attempting an analysis that would illustrate Jewish thought regarding architecture: thus, the contribution of Jewish architectural culture, in the work of one of its protagonists, plays a decisive role in the historiography of Italian architecture. For Zevi, identity was intrinsically linked to historiographic research, which expanded beyond Italian geographical boundaries so as to acquire an international perspective.

Alongside Zevi's publications, Israeli architecture was extensively publicized in architecture journals between 1945 and 1978; its presence was significant enough to convey an architectural language, especially during the second half of the 1960s and in the 1970s, when the legacy of modernism was being criticized and reassessed.

The diverse Italian interpretations of Israeli architecture, as well as Zevi's role in these, are key to understanding their cultural context and, above all, their producers. This essay researches 30 years of this published discourse, addressing three central aspects. First, the use of Zionist Palestinian architecture as a model, in the reconstruction of Italy during the first decade following World War II. During this period, there existed a conjunction between the Italian debate and new theories of organic and Zionist Palestinian architectures as possible alternatives to modernism. Second, this chapter analyses what Jewish identities meant for Italian architecture, concentrating upon Zevi's central contribution. Finally, I discuss Zevi's role in promoting new architectural concepts, and his demonstration of the lessons that Italian architecture could learn from Israeli architecture.

Reconstruction in Italy and Zionist Palestinian Architecture as a Model for Organic Architecture, 1945–1955

The March 1943 issue of the journal *Costruzioni Casabella*, edited by Giuseppe Pagano, displayed a photograph depicting a landscape destroyed by bombing – one of many such instances in a war-torn Italy. In this image, a backlit man with his back turned to the camera stares motionless and overwhelmed at the ruins of a city, wondering, perhaps, how an entire country might be rebuilt [Figure 1].

ANNO XVI - NUMERO 183
MARZO 1943 - XXI

COSTRUZIONI

RIVISTA MENSILE • DIRETTORE ARCHITETTO GIUSEPPE PAGANO • VICE DIRETTORE ARCHITETTO GIANCARLO PALANTI
DIREZIONE E REDAZIONE: MILANO, CORSO SEMPIONE 6 TELEF. 95042 • EDITORE PROPRIETARIO: GRUPPO EDITORIALE DOMUS S. A. MILANO, CORSO SEMPIONE 6 TELEF. 95-041
Concessionaria esclusiva per la pubblicità: UNIONE PUBBLICITÀ ITALIANA S. A. - MILANO, PALAZZO DELLA BORSA - PIAZZA DEGLI AFFARI (Telefoni da 12-451 a 12-457) e sue succursali
Una copia: Italia lire 18, estero lire 21 • Abbonamento per un anno: Italia lire 190, estero lire 226 • Conto Corrente Postale 3-5690 (Gruppo 3°)

LA RICOSTRUZIONE DELL'EUROPA: CAPITALE PROBLEMA DI ATTUALITÀ NEL CAMPO EDILIZIO
(G. PAGANO - A. AALTO)

UN ALBERGO SULLA COSTA LIGURE
(ANDREANI - BUCCI)

UN PROGETTO DI SCUOLA ALL'APERTO
(ANDREANI - BUCCI)

PARTICOLARI COSTRUTTIVI
(DIOTALLEVI E MARESCOTTI)

LA CASA LITTORIA DI PINÈ
(ASTENGO - BAIRATI - BIANCO - BURSI)

INDICE DELLE ARTI
IL QUADRO NON È UNA FIGURINA
(R. GIOLLI)

DUE PAGINE DI NOTE BIBLIOGRAFICHE - 2°

L'ARCHITETTURA MONDIALE

PREZZI D'ABBONAMENTO PER L'ITALIA, IMPERO E COLONIE

Figure 1: Cover of *Costruzioni Casabella*, March 1943. Photograph by Giuseppe Pagano. Source: *Costruzioni Casabella* 183 (1943).

At the end of World War II, Italy, liberated in April 1945, had to rebuild its political structure, physical structure (most of the major cities had suffered heavy bombings), social structure, and, last but not least, cultural structure.[2] Reconstruction was therefore a compendium of all aspects of human life: architecture and the city were placed at the centre of this process.

Given that many modernist architects fought within the resistance, two aspects weighed on the subsequent debate: liberating the experiences of modern architecture from its ambiguous and sinister connivance with Fascism, on the one hand; and, on the other, reviving the legacy of Italian modernists who had been the victims of Fascism, such as Edoardo Persico, Giuseppe Terragni, and Giuseppe Pagano. The list of martyrs would be much longer if the Jewish architects who were either killed or had escaped, such as Ernesto Nathan Rogers, were included. Dealing with this heritage and with these 'political difficulties' – the word *political* including all aspects of human activity – became one of the main issues facing post-war Italian architectural culture.[3]

Italian architectural culture was revived by the re-establishment of the architectural press, as well as architects' associations. The journals *Metron* and *La nuova città* were established, while *Casabella* and *Domus* were slowly resuming publication; in April 1945 in Milan, the Movimento Studi per l'Architettura (MSA – Architectural Studies Movement) was founded, its founders including some of the greatest architects of the modern era – e.g., Franco Albini, Piero Bottoni, Ignazio Gardella, and Enrico Peressutti. In Rome, a group of architects associated with the journal *Metron*, founded the Associazione per l'Architettura Organica (APAO – Association for Organic Architecture), which established the School of Organic Architecture, an alternative to the Faculty of Architecture of Rome that still employed professors who had enjoyed prominent roles during the Fascist regime.[4] 'Vitality', 'happiness', and 'focusing on the future' were the recurring mottos in the debate and the propositions put forward for the country's moral reconstruction, and a new democratic spirit was adopted.

The idea of organic architecture began penetrating Italian architectural discourse in 1945, also with Zevi's 1945 *Verso un'architettura organica. Saggio sullo sviluppo del pensiero architettonico negli ultimi cinquant'anni.*[5] This volume significantly impacted the national debate in Italy, and eventually constituted an alternative to modernist, International Style orthodoxy. In the same years the pages of *Metron* introduced Italian architects to debates on the meaning of the adjective 'organic' and the problems of reconstruction, by featuring projects from all over Europe and North America (for example, by Richard Neutra and Frank Lloyd Wright), as well as essays written by Alvar Aalto, Walter Gropius, and Hannes Meyer. *Metron's* eleventh issue, published in 1946, was devoted to architecture in Palestine [Figure 2].

Architect Guido Zevi and others selected projects from Tel Aviv and texts from *Habinyan* journal, presenting the Palestinian experience of the Zionist pioneers. The issue included examples of single-family houses, workers cooperatives' dwellings in Tel Aviv, and significant emphasis was placed upon the planning of the Zionist agricultural colonies and their establishment, as well as Alexander Klein's project for Haifa Bay and urban planning

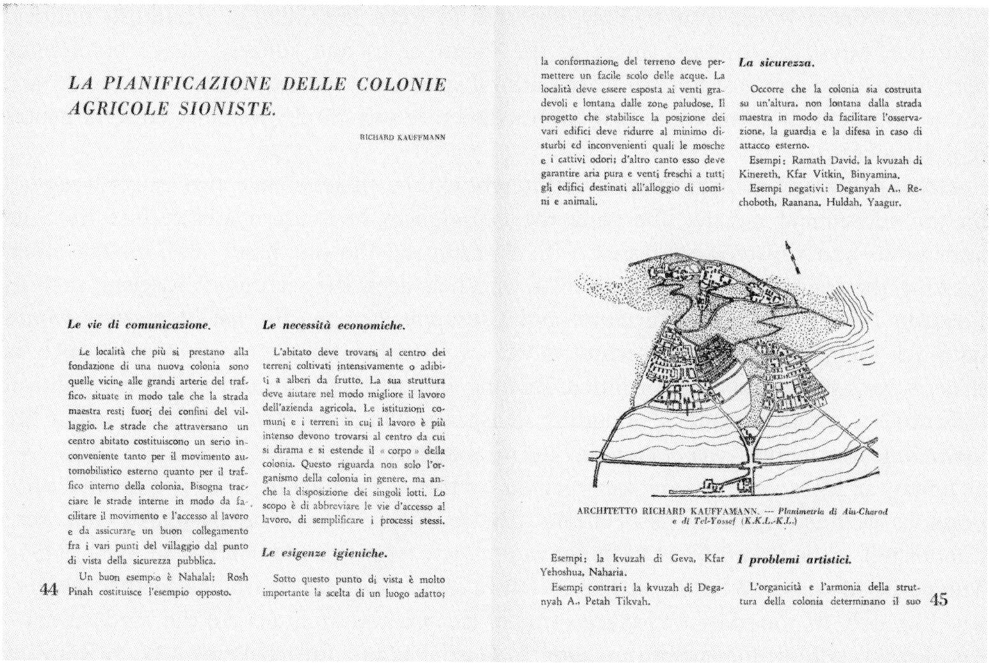

LA PIANIFICAZIONE DELLE COLONIE AGRICOLE SIONISTE.

RICHARD KAUFFMANN

Le vie di comunicazione.

Le località che più si prestano alla fondazione di una nuova colonia sono quelle vicine alle grandi arterie del traffico, situate in modo tale che la strada maestra resti fuori dei confini del villaggio. Le strade che attraversano un centro abitato costituiscono un serio inconveniente tanto per il movimento automobilistico esterno quanto per il traffico interno della colonia. Bisogna tracciare le strade interne in modo da facilitare il movimento e l'accesso al lavoro e da assicurare un buon collegamento fra i vari punti del villaggio dal punto di vista della sicurezza pubblica.

Un buon esempio è Nahalal: Rosh Pinah costituisce l'esempio opposto.

44

Le necessità economiche.

L'abitato deve trovarsi al centro dei terreni coltivati intensivamente o adibiti a alberi da frutto. La sua struttura deve aiutare nel modo migliore il lavoro dell'azienda agricola. Le istituzioni comuni e i terreni in cui il lavoro è più intenso devono trovarsi al centro da cui si dirama e si estende il « corpo » della colonia. Questo riguarda non solo l'organismo della colonia in genere, ma anche la disposizione dei singoli lotti. Lo scopo è di abbreviare le vie d'accesso al lavoro, di semplificare i processi stessi.

Le esigenze igieniche.

Sotto questo punto di vista è molto importante la scelta di un luogo adatto; la conformazione del terreno deve permettere un facile scolo delle acque. La località deve essere esposta ai venti gradevoli e lontana dalle zone paludose. Il progetto che stabilisce la posizione dei vari edifici deve ridurre al minimo disturbi ed inconvenienti quali le mosche e i cattivi odori; d'altro canto esso deve garantire aria pura e venti freschi a tutti gli edifici destinati all'alloggio di uomini e animali.

La sicurezza.

Occorre che la colonia sia costruita su un'altura, non lontana dalla strada maestra in modo da facilitare l'osservazione, la guardia e la difesa in caso di attacco esterno.

Esempi: Ramath David, la kvuzah di Kinereth, Kfar Vitkin, Binyamina.

Esempi negativi: Deganyah A., Rechoboth, Raanana, Huldah, Yaagur.

ARCHITETTO RICHARD KAUFFAMANN. — *Planimetria di Ain-Charod e di Tel-Yossef (K.K.L.-K.L.)*

Esempi: la kvuzah di Geva, Kfar Yehoshua, Naharia.

Esempi contrari: la kvuzah di Deganyah A., Petah Tikvah.

I problemi artistici.

L'organicità e l'armonia della struttura della colonia determinano il suo

45

Figure 2: Page from the article by Richard Kauffmann in *Metron*. Source: Richard Kauffmann, 'La pianificazione delle colonie agricole sioniste', *Metron* 11 (1946): 4.

in general. These were among the first accounts of Zionist architecture and urban planning presented to European readers since the publication of Eric Mendelsohn's and Josef Neufeld's work, which had been published in the *Architectural Review* during the 1930s and 1940s.[6] *Metron* focused not only on architectural vocabulary and technology, but also underscored its social achievements: 'the system of life and the social features of Jewish colonisation is interesting', the editorial observed, while the entire issue made no reference to 'historical precedents of Palestinian architecture').[7] What the review sought in this experience was the pragmatic dimension of design associated with a social purpose. In Italy, this implied linking democracy directly with the subject of organic architecture, presented consistently in all issues of the magazine.[8] In the issue's texts, 'Organic' and 'Jewish' were paired, describing experiences based on shared pragmatic solutions, which were intended to realize a common ideal. In addition, the relationships between public and private were discussed, for example, with regard to the 'the assignment of land: the example of Jewish Palestine shows the creative abilities of a spontaneous popular movement, guided towards constructive goals by a broad human and social vision'.[9]

Similar to *Metron*, Bruno Zevi connected the communal Zionist settlement forms of the *moshav*, the *kibbutz* and the *kvutzah* (a small kibbutz) to the idea of 'organic' (as interpreted by him). These new settlement types could thus serve as a model for the creation of new neighbourhoods in Italy. In *Verso un'architettura organica*, Zevi argues that 'organic architecture is defined [...] in contrast with the theoretical, the geometric, the artificial standards, the white boxes and cylinders of so much of early modern architecture; in contrast with the "nudism" of the latter').[10] For Zevi, organic architecture was above all grounded in 'a social idea, not a figurative one. In other words, [organic refers] to an architecture that wants to be human, before being humanistic'.[11] In ceding the predominance of the figurative – a topic that Zevi would take up again later to establish a connection between architecture and Judaism – he emphasized his concern with process and the social aspects of architecture, rather than with the exceptional building. For Zevi, the difference between an eminently rational design process and one more open to empiricism, reality, and the sensitivity of the architect, lies not in the formal results of architecture but in a 'mental and psychological attitude'[12]. A distinction is thus made between two different ways of understanding the world 'between the Greek and the Gothic, between Le Corbusier and Aalto'.[13]

Returning to *Metron*, the projects presented in this journal, apart from the Jewish and Zionist culture that distinguished them, possessed similarities relevant to the Italian debate: for example, proposals by Bottoni for a public housing unit (1945), which evolved from an Italian modern tradition that began in the fifth Triennale di Milano (1933), presented such similarities. It is perhaps symbolic that the issue of *Metron* presenting the similarities between these Italian public housing designs and the Palestinian ones, also included one of the first publications of the plans for Milan's QT8 district, designed by Bottoni and his team.[14] Bottoni's plan for the QT8 district involved social and architectural premises similar to Palestinian ones, but filtered through his communist ideology.[15]

Italian publications continued to present Israeli projects following the establishment of the State of Israel in 1948. These were now devoted to presenting new Israeli regional planning ideas. This new architectural era in Israel was introduced to Italian architects by Vito A. Volterra (1921–2013), a correspondent in Haifa for the journal *Urbanistica*, edited by Adriano Olivetti.[16] These were examples whose significance lay not in their final architectural product, but in the social and developmental model they proposed [Figure 3].

From the mid-1950s, Israel's architecture became the subject of extensive studies in major architecture journals – *Domus*, directed by Gio Ponti; *L'architettura. Cronache e storia*; and *Zodiac*. These critiques included formal, social, or identity-related interpretations. Moreover, Zevi became a leading figure in Israeli architectural discourse by intervening cyclically as a member of the International Technical Cooperation Centre and the World Committee for Jerusalem, as well as in many other activities in Israel. His presence, however, cannot be explained and contextualized without looking into attempts to define Jewish Italian architecture, an attempt that prompted the Roman scholar to establish an intensive engagement with Israeli culture.

Notiziario estero

Israel

La Valle del Giordano, le prime realizzazioni e la nuova pianificazione regionale.

La Valle del Giordano, che è situata nella parte settentrionale e orientale di Israel, era considerata, nell'antichità biblica, la porta del Paradiso terrestre.

Il fiume Giordano (in ebraico Yarden) è formato dal confluire di tre corsi d'acqua, Yor, Dan, Banyas, che scaturiscono dalle pendici meridionali della montagna dello Hermon (1).

Dopo un percorso di circa 350 km in direzione N-S, il Giordano si getta nel Mar Rosso, all'altitudine di m. 394 sotto il livello del Mediterraneo.

La parte settentrionale della vallata di questo fiume si chiama Emek Hule; ed è caratterizzata dalla presenza dell'omonimo Lago di Hule, che una volta aveva contorni instabili ed era causa di impaludamenti e quindi d'infestazioni malariche.

Dal 1928 al 1947 venne messo in atto un piano di bonifica dello Emek Hule, che permise la fondazione e lo sviluppo di ventun colonie, sicchè tale zona divenne una tra le più densamente popolate delle zone rurali in Israel.

Poco dopo l'uscita dal Lago di Hule, il Giordano entra in una stretta gola, intagliata in dure rocce, e con un poderoso salto discende dall'altitudine di +2 m. a quella di —208 m. Il fiume entra quindi nel Lago Kinereth o Lago Tiberiade (2).

A N-O del Lago Kinereth, presso la costa, vi sono: gli avanzi di Kfar Nahum (Cafarnao), località menzionata nei Vangeli, e il Monte delle Beatitudini, pure menzionato nei Vangeli, la cui sommità non raggiunge il livello del mare! Sempre a N-O del Lago, ma abbastanza lontano dalla costa, sui monti della Galilea (che raggiungono una discreta altitudine), sorge la città di Zfad (Safed), costituita da un nucleo antico, ricco di monumenti religiosi ebraici, e da un contiguo nucleo moderno, realizzato conformemente a un ottimo piano regolatore. La popolazione di Zfad, che ammontava appena a 10.000 abitanti al termine del Mandato Britannico in Palestina, tende ora a raddoppiare. Presso questa città, all'altitudine di circa m 1000 s. m., è stato creato un moderno e razionale villaggio sanatoriale, circondato da una pineta di recente impianto e in continuo incremento, in una località dotata delle migliori caratteristiche climatiche. Sulle pendici orientali della montagna di Zfad venne fondato, nel secolo scorso, uno dei primi centri della colonizzazione ebraica, Rosh Pinà (Pietra Angolare), non collettivistico.

Sulla riva occidentale del Lago Kinereth sorge la città di Tiberya (Tiberiade), così chiamata in onore dell'imperatore romano Tiberio. Anche questa città è costituita da un vecchio nucleo con monumenti religiosi ebraici antichi e medioevali e da un nucleo moderno in continuo sviluppo, soprattutto per l'importanza del luogo quale centro di commerci e quale stazione di soggiorno e cura (vi è una buona spiaggia e vi sono sorgenti termali nei dintorni). La popolazione di Tiberya, che pochi anni fa ammontava a 13.000 abitanti, tende anch'essa a raddoppiare.

Procedendo verso l'estremità meridionale del Lago Kinereth, s'incontrano i *kibbutzim* (colonie rurali collettive) di Kinereth, di Degania Alef e di Degania Beth. Degania Alef è la più antica colonia rurale collettiva fondata in Terra d'Israel, datando dal 1909.

Sulla sponda orientale del Lago Kinereth sorge un tipico villaggio di pescatori, Ein Ghev.

Uscendo dal Lago Kinereth, il Giordano riceve a sinistra le acque del suo principale affluente, lo Yarmuk, il cui corso si svolge per la maggior parte in territorio transgiordano.

Presso la confluenza dello Yarmuk con il Giordano è situato uno dei più bei *kibbutzim* d'Israel, Ashdoth Ya'akov, costituito da un nucleo residenziale con le caratteristiche della città-giardino e da un nucleo agricolo-industriale (fabbrica di conserve, estratti e sciroppi di frutta, ecc.). Il piano regolatore particolareggiato di Ashdoth Ya'akov ha considerato scrupolosamente le caratteristiche del terreno e i venti regnanti e dominanti nella zona, per cui i collegamenti esterni del nucleo agricolo-industriale avvengono al di fuori dell'abitato e le esalazioni delle fabbriche vengono sospinte dalle correnti aeree lontano dall'abitato stesso.

Procedendo ancora verso Sud il Giordano scorre incassato tra rive dirupate e tortuose. La vallata discende sempre più sotto il livello del mare. In tale zona è notevole una centrale elettrica.

Alla latitudine 32° 30' s'incontra a destra del Giordano,

Dall'alto al basso: **DEGANIA B - Una delle prime colonie collettive sul lago di Galilea. - NAHALAL - la prima colonia agricola cooperativa. - Un Kibbutz della Valle del Giordano; con i simboli sono indicati: la scuola, il dormitorio, e le attrezzature zootecniche.**

59

Figure 3: Page from the article by Vito A. Volterra about Israel in *Urbanistica*. Source: Vito A. Volterra, *'Israel'*, *Urbanistica* 4 (1950): 59.

Architecture and Judaism in Italy: Attempts at Definition and the Research of Bruno Zevi

Due to the small number of Jews in Italy and their desire to be assimilated by Italian culture, any discussion of the contribution of Jewish architects to the local architectural culture of the 1900s must remain qualitative and tentative, as is the case with other aspects of Jewish contribution to Italian cultural history.[17] However, the presence and centrality of Jews in Italian architectural discourse – Rogers, post-war director of the magazine *Casabella-Continuità*; Zevi, first involved in *Metron* and then director of *L'architettura. Cronache e storia* and the entrepreneur Olivetti, promoter of *Comunità* and from 1950 *Metron* as well, just to mention some of the better-known names – underscore the importance of this cultural matrix within the goings-on of Italian architecture.[18]

In pre-war Italy, very few Jews chose architecture as a profession, a phenomenon arguably prompted by the desire to assimilate.[19] As Francesco Tentori writes, most Jewish Italian architects favoured a policy of 'integration within individual, different nationalities', preferring to 'minimize or camouflage their own Jewish condition'.[20]

In 1912, however, Italian Rabbi Dante Lattes stated that 'the only visible monument that expresses the vitality of the people and the idea of Israel in the eyes of the world' is the Temple.[21] This claim questioned architecture's ability to represent Jewish culture. Lattes's position denies all possibilities other than those related to the construction of Jewish culture's main edifice, in which representative needs, associated with rite and culture, are manifested to the utmost degree while neglecting all other typologies. Such iterations should also be seen in the context of Italian synagogue architecture from the latter part of the nineteenth-century that, as in most Western European countries, was characterized by orientalist eclecticism.[22] Some of these solutions, however, sought to blend in the Italian urban landscape. For example, in the Israeli Temple of Rome (1904), planned by Osvaldo Armanni and Vincenzo Costa, the architects applied an eclectic ornamentation that integrated oriental and Roman designs, stating that those 'severe, simple forms, nevertheless possess a moderate richness, and perfectly harmonise, in our view, with those of other monuments in our city'.[23] Adherence to eclecticism was complete but the call for tenders for the project lacked articulation, laconically prescribing only a 'monumental and severe character […] [the Temple must] be suitably decorated, with absolute exclusion of any figure of man or animal'.[24]

In support of an 'architectural' assimilation during the period of Fascism, the engineer and writer Augusto Bachi (1906–1970) argued that 'a Jewish architecture, a Jewish artistic trend in construction, never existed';[25] therefore, the Jews 'relied entirely on the technique and taste of builders of the place' in which they lived.[26] Such contentions were widely shared and partially confirmed by the prohibitions on practising architecture to which the Jews were subjected.

Concurrently, however, attempts were made at the first definitions of Jewish architecture unrelated to sacred buildings: Amedeo Revere, while asserting that the Jews had for 'centuries

Figure 4: Manfredo D'Urbino, Jarach grave, Cemetery of Milano, Milan. Source: Amedeo Revere, 'Manfredo D'Urbino ed il problema di un'architettura ebraica', *La Rassegna Mensile di Israel* 6–7 (1937): 298.

been in a state of meditation that was not the most suitable for architectural achievements, and much less for the creation of one's own architecture', recognized in the work of Manfredo D'Urbino – who at the time was among the most renowned Jewish architects – 'certain Jewish characteristics, however indefinable. There can be no doubt that the spirit, qualities, and hereditary tastes do affect an art which is architecture' [Figure 4].[27]

In this respect, therefore, it was better for Revere to seek the blend of culture and architecture not so much in 'defining or discovering a Jewish style' but rather in expressing 'the intimate tendencies of the Jewish artist', thus avoiding any generalization in rediscovering an intimate and personal dimension within the creative process. For the author it was therefore inconceivable to have 'Jewish architectural art made by non-Jews'.[28] D'Urbino was rather active during the Fascist period, and Revere compared his work to the 'rational cubist style of today', positioning the architect's experience within the Jewish roots of modernity that 'share the Jewish mindset, as it tends to the *essential* by overcoming the superfluous or the *illusory*'.[29] D'Urbino himself sought this identity in architecture realized in Palestine, writing that the German roots of architectural modernity were fulfilled in the Holy Land:

> rationalism and functionalism have never found a better opportunity for affirming their principles. One could say that it was born in the west, it grew up in the cold countries of northern Europe, and finally found its place and full expression under the beautiful blue sky of the east.[30]

D'Urbino broadened his reflection, saying that

> the appearance of construction of sacred places are the same as civilian ones, since today's Jew wants religious thought to pervade the life of every day and every moment, so that every house, every garden becomes a temple, and God becomes an entity to be built with creative activity.[31]

Beyond affirmations that appear very general, these seminal critiques were interrupted in the late 1930s with the tragedy of the Shoah and could only be resumed after the end of the war.

Attempts to define Jewish architectural identity were halted and resumed after the war: one of the strongest promoters of a definition of Jewish architectural identity was Zevi. For Zevi, research on architecture and Judaism was part of a long-lasting and wide-ranging commitment. In 1998, he recalled how his Jewish identity guided his every choice:

> I identify with this subject, in which my proud Jewish and passionate Zionist being coincides with the anti-fascist struggle, of 'Giustizia e libertà' and the Partito d'Azione, which has characterised my entire life, and with the daily battles for organic architecture for an environment that promotes human happiness.[32]

This expression has become famous as a testimony of his experience of the connection between Jewish culture and architecture.[33] Over a 30-year period, Zevi returned to the topic of Judaism and architecture, alongside his public activities and those related to the Israeli community in Rome. In fact, on the occasion of the Hebrew translation of his *Saper vedere l'architettura* in 1958, Zevi wrote a preface wherein he referred to the themes that initially characterized his work:

> the specific value of architecture [consists of] spaces, enclosed cavities of buildings and urban environments, as these spaces reflect social life, the customs and aspirations of an era; finally, how the creative personality of architects is [expressed] through them.[34]

This reflection was largely permeated by research directed primarily at promoting the State of Israel. Although he recalled the position according to which 'in the history of architecture there is no Jewish chapter, because the Jews, especially in their dispersal and the ghettos, could not architecturally represent their chosen civilisation, their system of life',[35] he asserted that those who

> visited European ghettos, especially those in Italy, saw in the narrow streets and miserable houses a poem that spatially projects the aspirations of a people; and in their synagogues, schools, and community buildings one sees significant architectural episodes, strong and delicate figurative accents.[36]

While this text was published in 1958, it cannot be said that it was written only for that moment in time. On the contrary, its contents warrant a re-examination of Zevi's earlier theoretical and historiographical work, which reveals that his being a Jewish Zionist significantly contributed to the text as well.[37] Zevi concurrently addressed the relationship between space and time in architecture, a theme recurring in his works, as well as in his next attempt at exegesis of Jewish culture: 'Ebraismo e concezione spazio-temporale nell'arte' (1974). In this text, Zevi emphasizes and praises the unsystematic nature – and especially the elaboration – of memory and the meaning of time : 'anxiety of time'[38] and 'daily'[39] are read as founding principles of this Jewish culture.

Zevi often cites Abraham Joshua Heschel's 1951 *The Sabbath: Its Meaning for Modern Man*, in which the Polish rabbi and philosopher argues for the predominance of time in Judaism as opposed to the hegemony of space in the modern world.[40] Zevi also refers to Thorleif Boman's lesser-known *Hebrew Thought Compared with Greek* (1960), which discusses the different concepts of space and time in Hebrew and Greek thought.[41] Zevi's understanding transcends art and architecture to reflect in a more general manner on a peculiar way of understanding space and time and its subsequent impact upon non-Jewish artists and authors. It is not surprising to find in the Hebrew edition of *Saper vedere l'architettura* an additional text by the great Zionist thinker Martin Buber, who stresses the importance of the perception and experience of traversing space for perceiving architectural form, a topic that will recur in the work of Zevi:

> Those facing a cathedral, [standing] before the façade or in any other place, perceive what can be seen from there, extrapolating only an allusion [in Hebrew – *remez*] – though a very refined allusion – to the essence of the building. If you want to have something more you should cross the entire building, observing every part of it from the outside and from the inside and thus getting to know the whole reality of this impressive image, as if it could be obtained […], with the soles of the feet, until all the impressions are fused into a single view of the entire building. Architecture forces one to observe in a special way. It requires a fusion of points of view and an overall vision.[42]

Buber, whose fresh approach perceived art as a major means of education and of constructing identity in the new Israeli State, observed that

> Jewish character was also deeply embedded in the perception and form of these [visual art] works [...]. Pay attention to the peculiar appropriation of light and shadow, the play of the atmosphere around objects, the integration of an individual object with its surrounding environment, the broad concept of space, the strange inward movement. Everywhere you will recognise elements of Jewish perception and formation.[43]

More precisely, he recognized in other dimensions, besides space, a significant contribution to Jewish culture that seems very important for following Zevi's work:

> Of course, his soul was not yet developed to the point where he could turn suffering into virtue – to be able to see the world as time, as happening, as flowing, as movement, even as soul. He was, therefore, satisfied with a world that was more impressions of experiences than actual experiences. His space was impoverished, nearly two-dimensional. In literature, our only document, we find little physical representation. The descriptions, if they appeal to the eye at all, encompass movement and size, almost nowhere is there colour and form.[44]

If the vision of space appears to be secondary for the thinkers who influenced Zevi, many scholars have argued that associating space with time is one of Judaism's major contributions to modern culture.[45] The rejection of all preconceived dogma and theory and being open to the exception rather than the norm, whose outcomes are found in the form of an articulated and dynamic language, constitute the two main themes with which Zevi interpreted architecture. In particular he supported the expressionist school (especially the work of Mendelsohn) and then, in the 1980s, deconstructionism, as essentially products of the Jewish culture strongly linked to Mendelsohn's work.[46] This cultural affinity characterizes Zevi's historicity, wherein the topicality, vitality, and operability of history in the present can be attributed, in large measure, to a Jewish tradition.

In addition to his contribution to defining Jewish architectural identity, Zevi ardently promoted collaboration with the Israeli Association of Engineers and Architects. The International Technical Cooperation Centre (ITCC), of which he was president, was a key instrument in this. Architecture was a central arena in materializing the humanistic and social objectives of ITCC, which aspired for 'modern technology to satisfy an atavistic need for justice and a humanistic aim'.[47] The centre's conferences were held on an annual basis (the second conference was held in Rome in 1968, and the third in Tel Aviv the following year), and were attended by renowned architects from Europe, America, India, and, of course, Israel, such as Louis Kahn, Moshe Safdie, and Arieh Sharon.

During these years, and for over a decade afterwards, Zevi served as a member of the World Committee for Jerusalem (WCJ), established following the controversy over the new city plan.[48] While the ITCC was engaged with a range of issues pertaining to the development of the entire country, the WCJ was charged with presenting a scheme for preserving the Old City of Jerusalem while developing its new zones, and was required to develop a city plan capable of meeting its religious, political, and cultural needs.[49] With regard to the conservation of ancient architecture and its relationship with new construction, Zevi had played an important role in a similar Italian debate, and this affected his proposal for Jerusalem. He advised avoiding what had happened in Venice (i.e., the expulsion of the population from the ancient city for the creation of an environment specifically tailored for tourists), and advocated a direct comparison between the ancient city centre and modern architecture. Zevi advocated the search for a style capable of giving identity to the State of Israel – a style that would establish a dialogue between the ancient city and the modern one, rather than a mimesis of Arab and traditional forms. He therefore supported Israeli architecture's 'lack of an original figurative translation in the civilisation of the Eastern Jewish communities [and] the loathing to give new towns, villages and houses a middle eastern appearance that would have been substantially false, maybe picturesque, certainly immoral'.[50] This approach remained at the centre of his reflection, by which he connected a political vision to an architectural one.

Regarding this last issue, Zevi certainly did not imply his alignment with what the culture of restoration had drawn up in 1964 in Venice by promoting the International Charter for the Conservation and Restoration of Monuments and Sites ("The Venice Charter"). More likely, he supported the solution proposed in an ensuing conference, *Gli architetti moderni e l'incontro tra antico e nuovo*, which also took place in Venice the following year. In his congress speech, he uncompromisingly defended the comparison and contrast between ancient and modern architecture, an approach consistent with his historiographic methodology. He argued that both ancient and modern can find their expression in urban space: the first through preservation and the second by reflecting contemporary culture in a manner that eschews any form of 'modernised classical' or 'camouflaged modern in the old city'.[51]

Zevi also participated in organizing the exhibition *Contemporary Architecture in Israel* held at the Palazzo Taverna in Rome at the end of the 1960s, as part of projects promoted by In/Arch (National Institute of Architecture).[52] This event sought to retrace Israeli architecture from the days of the pioneers. Inspired by Zevi's historiographical angle, Massimo Dalla Torre, the exhibition's curator, mused over the origins of Israeli architecture, on whether they began 2000 years ago or twenty years ago, arguing that 'one cannot speak of "Jewish art", but it is fair to recognise a Jewish perspective in art'.[53] That the exhibition was officially promoted by the Israeli State is demonstrated by the inclusion of catalogue texts by M. Bentov, the Israeli Minister of Construction, and D. Tenne, the Ministry of Construction's General Director. The catalogue included major public architectural projects, attesting to the young state's commitment to solving social and practical problems and to constructing identity.

All of Zevi's activities reflect his continued commitment to searching for a Jewish and Israeli identity, a search that was intrinsically grounded in his interpretations of architecture and the city. An additional key aspect of his research was his presentation of Israeli projects in *L'architettura. Cronache e storia*, which was central in the range of Italian publications devoted to this theme.

Israeli architecture as portrayed in Italian publications (1948–78)

In 1964, Manfredo Tafuri reviewed a competition for designing a central area between Tel Aviv and Jaffa, for *Casabella-Continuità*. In an article entitled 'Razionalismo critico e nuovo utopismo', the critic, with his usual flair, interpreted Israel's internationally renowned architectural products and compared them with a similar competition for the Italian city of Turin [Figure 5].[54]

Figure 5: Cover of *Casabella-Continuità* with the project by J. H. van den Broek and J. B. Bakema for Tel Aviv–Jaffa. Source: *Casabella-Continuità* 293 (1964).

The Israeli case, therefore, provided Tafuri with the opportunity to reflect on the process of overcoming the legacy of the modern in a broad international context. While Tafuri was carrying on a wide-ranging ideological reading of the project, one of the competitors, Jan Lubicz-Nycz, reflected on the identity of Jewish architecture:

> The intention of the architect was to create a part of the city [...] in which to intimately insert the spirit of Jewish tradition, the birth of a new nation (in this biblical land of Israel) and a new way of life, of life conditioned by the history of Judaism, by eternal exile, by persecution and suffering, by the constant search for the Promised Land, of drama, vitality and Hope.[55]

L'architettura. Cronache e storia, was founded by Zevi in 1955 after the closure of *Metron*. It ran for more than twenty years, during which about forty presentations – entrusted to various scholars – discussed major Israeli architects and their work, initially focusing on their social commitment to constructing the new state, and subsequently their formal approaches.

The vision of Jewish architecture is understood in these journals as the overcoming of rationalism, oneness with nature, and the social practice of 'two generations of architects, one of pioneering Zionists and another of militants in the war of independence'.[56] This political vision of Israeli architecture was manifested by Zevi in the social experiment of the kibbutz (Zevi himself wrote the introduction to the 1976 book by Sharon, *Kibbutz + Bauhaus*) [Figure 6].[57]

The experience of the kibbutz revealed an expressive engagement with architectural plasticity, interpreted by Zevi as a symbol of conjugation between personal liberty and architectural identity. To this end the periodical included works by Sharon, by the Rechter–Zarhy–Rechter office, and projects by Ram Karmi, which for Zevi represented these ideas [Figure 7].

A different and relevant interpretation of Israeli architecture can be seen in the dozens of articles that appeared in *Domus*. Here, Israeli architecture was displayed primarily for its formal aspects. One issue, as an example, presented architectural works termed by Pierre Restany as 'spatial art',[58] and was demonstrated by projects such as the Bat Yam City Hall, designed by Zvi Heker, Alfred Neumann, and Eldar Sharon. Restany interpreted the building as 'geometric acrobatics, seeking to create an image'.[59]

The architecture of Israel was described in *Domus* through its aesthetic manifestations, while downplaying its social aspects and representation of identity. Israeli experiments with Brutalism, prefabrication and megastructural architecture, all considered innovative during the 1960s and 1970s, were enlisted by the magazine for suggesting an alternative language within the Italian debate that, as noted by Tafuri and Dal Co in 1976, was suspended in an 'isolated and intimating study, often absorbed by cultured or autobiographical memories'.[60]

Profilo di un architetto israeliano:

Arieh Sharon, dalla Bauhaus ad una terra mediterranea

presentazione di Fabrizio Cocchia

Figure 6: Works by Arieh Sharon illustrated in *L'architettura: Cronache e storia*. Source: 'Profilo di un architetto israeliano: Arieh Sharon, dalla Bauhaus ad una terra mediterranea', *L'architettura. Cronache e storia* 23 (1957): 302–303.

The projects published in *Domus* demonstrated a shared desire for technological and linguistic development, linked to geometric forms. This interest was reflected in additional publications: *Zodiac*, for example, devoted an entire issue in 1969 to geometric research in architecture, publishing works by Frederick Kiesler, R. Buckminster Fuller, Alfred Neumann, Anne Griswold Tyng, Walter Kuhn, and Moshe Safdie. In the editorial, Maria Bottero interpreted this architecture as transcending the technological and geometric dimension, and addressed the common symbolic intent, as well as the deep cultural roots of the work of Kiesler and Fuller. She conceived the differences between them as superficial, and although she did not state this clearly, she perhaps identified a common Jewish matrix that underlay their choices: 'the man-universe congruity and the reference of every particular event to the totality that includes it'.[61] According to Bottero, 'the field of spatial consideration is the cosmos; the field of psychic consideration is the memory'.[62] Thus, in discussing the Shrine of the Book at the Israel Museum, Jerusalem, planned by Kiesler and Armand Phillip Bartos, the building's symbolic aspect is addressed, and its function as the crucible for the Dead Sea Scrolls is presented alongside Fuller's utopian projects, wherein the symbolic dimension is

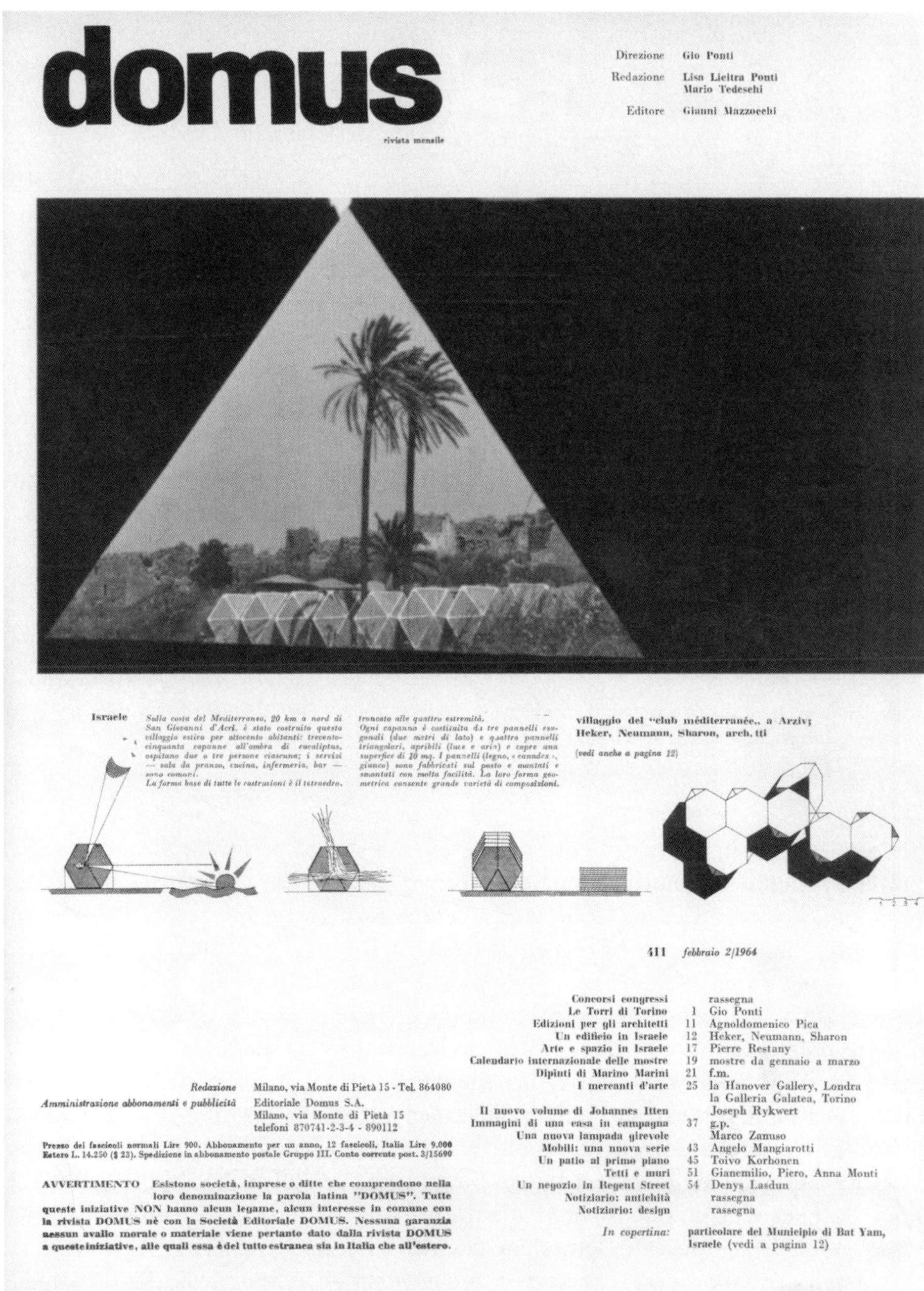

domus

rivista mensile

Direzione Gio Ponti
Redazione Lisa Licitra Ponti, Mario Tedeschi
Editore Gianni Mazzocchi

Israele *Sulla costa del Mediterraneo, 20 km a nord di San Giovanni d'Acri, è stato costruito questo villaggio estivo per ottocento abitanti: trecentocinquanta capanne all'ombra di eucaliptus, ospitano due o tre persone ciascuna; i servizi — sala da pranzo, cucina, infermeria, bar — sono comuni. La forma base di tutte le costruzioni è il tetraedro, troncato alle quattro estremità. Ogni capanna è costituita da tre pannelli esagonali (due metri di lato) e quattro pannelli triangolari, apribili (luce e aria) e copre una superfice di 10 mq. I pannelli (legno, «canadex», giunco) sono fabbricati sul posto e montati e smontati con molta facilità. La loro forma geometrica consente grande varietà di composizioni.*

villaggio del "club méditerranée", a Arziv; Heker, Neumann, Sharon, arch. tti

(vedi anche a pagina 12)

411 *febbraio 2/1964*

Concorsi congressi		rassegna
Le Torri di Torino	1	Gio Ponti
Edizioni per gli architetti	11	Agnoldomenico Pica
Un edificio in Israele	12	Heker, Neumann, Sharon
Arte e spazio in Israele	17	Pierre Restany
Calendario internazionale delle mostre	19	mostre da gennaio a marzo
Dipinti di Marino Marini	21	f.m.
I mercanti d'arte	25	la Hanover Gallery, Londra la Galleria Galatea, Torino
Il nuovo volume di Johannes Itten		Joseph Rykwert
Immagini di una casa in campagna	37	g.p.
Una nuova lampada girevole		Marco Zanuso
Mobili: una nuova serie	43	Angelo Mangiarotti
Un patio al primo piano	45	Toivo Korhonen
Tetti e muri	51	Gianemilio, Piero, Anna Monti
Un negozio in Regent Street	54	Denys Lasdun
Notiziario: antichità		rassegna
Notiziario: design		rassegna

In copertina: particolare del Municipio di Bat Yam, Israele (vedi a pagina 12)

Redazione Milano, via Monte di Pietà 15 - Tel. 864080
Amministrazione abbonamenti e pubblicità Editoriale Domus S.A. Milano, via Monte di Pietà 15 telefoni 870741-2-3-4 - 890112

Prezzo dei fascicoli normali Lire 900. Abbonamento per un anno, 12 fascicoli, Italia Lire 9.000 Estero L. 14.250 ($ 23). Spedizione in abbonamento postale Gruppo III. Conto corrente post. 3/15690

AVVERTIMENTO Esistono società, imprese o ditte che comprendono nella loro denominazione la parola latina "DOMUS". Tutte queste iniziative NON hanno alcun legame, alcun interesse in comune con la rivista DOMUS nè con la Società Editoriale DOMUS. Nessuna garanzia nessun avallo morale o materiale viene pertanto dato dalla rivista DOMUS a queste iniziative, alle quali essa è del tutto estranea sia in Italia che all'estero.

Figure 7: First page of *Domus* with project by Zvi Heker, Alfred Neumann, and Eldar Sharon in Achziv. Source: *Domus* 411 (1964).

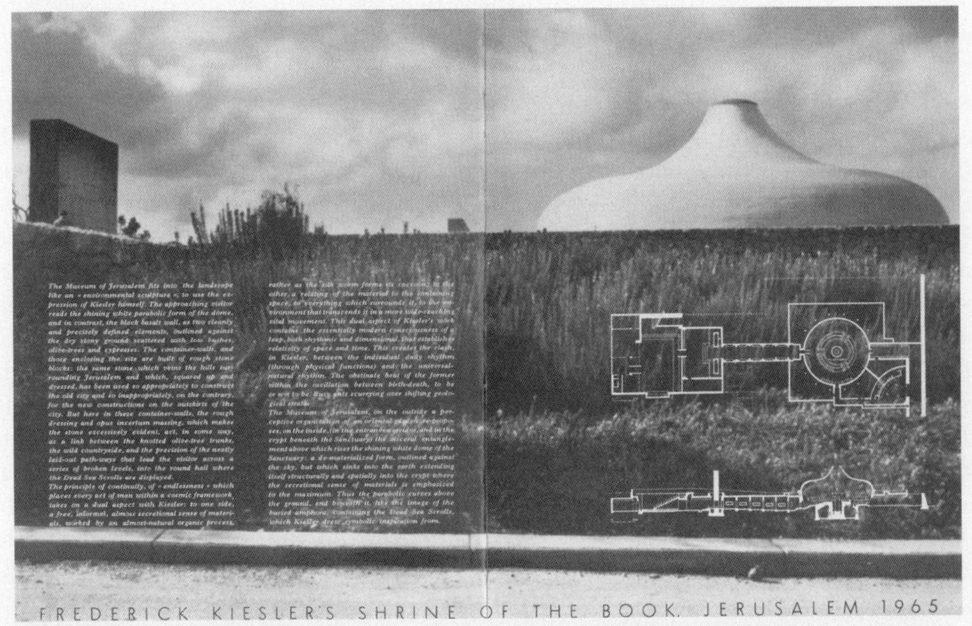

The Museum of Jerusalem fits into the landscape like an « environmental sculpture », to use the expression of Kiesler himself. The approaching visitor reads the shining white parabolic form of the dome, and in contrast, the black basalt wall, as two cleanly and precisely defined elements, outlined against the dry stony ground scattered with low bushes, olive-trees and cypresses. The container-walls, and those enclosing the site are built of rough stone blocks: the same stone which veins the hills surrounding Jerusalem and which, squared up and dressed, has been used to appropriately to construct the old city and to inappropriately, on the contrary, for the new constructions on the outskirts of the city. But here in these container-walls, the rough dressing and opus incertum massing, which makes the stone excessively evident, act, in some way, as a link between the knotted olive-tree trunks, the wild countryside, and the precision of the neatly laid-out path-ways that lead the visitor across a series of broken levels, into the round hall where the Dead Sea Scrolls are displayed.
The principle of continuity, of « endlessness » which places every act of man within a cosmic framework, takes on a dual aspect with Kiesler: to one side, a free, informal, almost secretional sense of materials, worked by an almost-natural organic process, rather as the silk worm forms its cocoon; to the other, a relating of the material to the containing space, to everything which surrounds it, to the environment that transcends it in a more wide-reaching vital movement. This dual aspect of Kiesler's work contains the essentially modern consciousness of a leap, both rhythmic and dimensional, that establishes relativity of space and time. This creates the clash, in Kiesler, between the individual daily rhythm (through physical functions) and the universal-natural rhythm. The obstinate beat of the former within the oscillation between birth-death, to be or not to be. Busy [illegible] scurrying over shifting geological strata.
The Museum of Jerusalem, on the outside a perceptive organization of an oriental [illegible] sequences, on the inside (in the entrance corridor, and in the crypt beneath the Sanctuary) the mineral entanglement above which rises the shining white dome of the Sanctuary: a de-materialized form, outlined against the sky, but which sinks into the earth extending itself structurally and spatially into the crypt where the secretional sense of materials is emphasized to the maximum. Thus the parabolic curves above the ground, and beneath it, like the image of the buried amphora, containing the Dead Sea Scrolls, which Kiesler drew symbolic inspiration from.

FREDERICK KIESLER'S SHRINE OF THE BOOK. JERUSALEM 1965

Figure 8: The presentation of Frederick Kiesler's Shrine of the Book in Jerusalem. Source: 'Frederick Kiesler's Shrine of the Book, Jerusalem 1965', *Zodiac* 17 (1969): 6–7.

present in what he calls the 'Law of Structure' – a law capable of ordering all phenomena in the universe [Figure 8].[63]

Thus, *L'architettura. Cronache e storia, Domus*, and *Zodiac* provided a discussion on the identity of Jewish architecture, and regularly presented the best-known projects in Israel, while engaging formal, technological, social, and identity issues.

Conclusion

In Italy between 1945 and 1978, an attempt was made to define the identity of Jewish architecture (not just in an Italian context), and major journals presented what was taking place in the young State of Israel.

The frequent presence of Israeli architecture across the pages of periodicals, can initially be understood as an attempt to collect the most lively and *organic* inheritance of the modern movement. Subsequently, its presentation can be interpreted as the search for alternatives to modernism, and the quest for an updated architectural vocabulary, which ensued the crisis of the modern style. The many interpretations provided for this architecture testify to the lasting interest that it aroused, and demonstrate Italian culture's self-reflexivity. However, such a variegated image of Israeli architecture in Italy clashes with an even greater problem: the question of Jewish identity, which remains an unresolved issue that is general, rather than only historiographical. In this respect, any attempt to define general categories encounters several difficulties, the least of them being hypotheses so vast, that they transcend the purely Jewish sphere. When attempting to define Jewish identities in architecture, the lack of documents hinders the full reconstruction of their history: architects, architectural historians, and critics are generally reticent to describe these personal aspects, rendering historiographical hypotheses as largely based on broad and very general considerations. While there was a noticeable presence and participation of renowned Jewish practitioners and clients in Italian architecture in the late twentieth century, the task of defining a common identity remains difficult. In considering them as individuals, in exploring their mutual relationships, as well as in understanding their multiple identities and cultures, it is possible to recount separate episodes and examine different figures; the effort to generalize can even seem pernicious or occasional. In this story, Zevi's role is essential: he was one of the main theorists of Jewish architectural identity of the twentieth century and, in addition, one of the key figures in the making of the relationship between Italian and Israeli architectural culture. Furthermore, these two perspectives are paramount for recognizing the central role that Jewish culture had in his work and criticism, thus serving as a reminder of the centrality of Jewish identity in the post-war architectural discourse.

Acknowledgements

This research was made possible in part by a postdoctoral scholarship from the EDEN (Erasmus Mundus Academic Network) programme in the Department of Art History – at the University of Haifa, Israel. I want to thank Ron Fuchs from the Department of Art History, University of Haifa and Giovanni Leoni from the Department of Architecture, University of Bologna. I am also grateful to David Cassuto, Giovanni Chiaramonte, Marcello De Masi, Adachiara Zevi, and, as always, Ramona Loffredo. This text is dedicated to the memory of Leonardo Wolovsky.

Bibliography

'All'Ordine degli architetti di Roma'. *Metron* 2 (1945): 73–74.

Architettura contemporanea in Israele. Roma: Officina edizioni, 1969.

Bachi, Augusto. 'Appunti sulla architettura della Sinagoga'. *La Rassegna Mensile di Israel* 1–2 (1933): 25–46.

Baffa, Matilde, Corinna Morandi, Sara Protasoni, and Augusto Rossari. *Il Movimento di studi per l'architettura: 1945–1961*. Roma-Bari: Laterza 1995.

Bedoire, Fredric. *The Jewish Contribution to Modern Architecture, 1830–1930*. Jersey City: KTAV Pub. House, 2004.

M. Bill, R. Buckminster Fuller, P. Johnson, L. Kahn, R. Meier, N. Pevsner, L. Piccinato, and M. Safdie. *The Jerusalem Committee. Town planning Subcommittee, December 19–21, 1970. Participants from Abroad*. 'Associazioni, istituti e comitati (1945–1999)'. b. 11, folder 9 'World Committee for Jerusalem'. ABZ (Archivio Bruno Zevi), Rome.

Boman, Thorleif. *Hebrew Thought Compared with Greek*. New York: W.W. Norton & Co., 1960.

Bottero, Maria. 'Introduction'. *Zodiac* 17 (1969): 5.

Braiterman, Zachary. *The Shape of Revelation: Aesthtics and Modern Jewish Thought*. Stanford: Stanford University Press, 2007.

Buber, Martin. 'Eine jungjüdische Bühne'. *Die Welt*, November 8, 1901.

——— 'Ein Wort zum funften Kongress', *Jüdische Volksstimme* 3, February 15, 1902.

——— 'Prefazione all'edizione ebraica di *Saper vedere l'architettura* di Bruno Zevi [1957]'. *La Rassegna Mensile di Israel* 1 (2000): 2–4

Buckminster Fuller, Richard. 'Comprehensive Thinking'. In *World Design Science Decade, 1965–1975. Five Two-Year Phases of a World Retooling Design Proposed to the International Union of Architects for Adoption by World Architectural Schools. Phase 1, Document 3*, edited by John McHale. Carbondale, IL: Southern Illinois University, 1965.

Casciato, Maristella. 'Wright and Italy: The Promise of Organic Architecture'. In *Frank Lloyd Wright: Europe and Beyond*, edited by Anthony Alofsin, 79–99. Berkeley, Los Angeles and London: University of California Press, 1999.

Cassuto, David. 'Il vano architettonico della sinagoga barocca in Italia'. In *Italia Judaica*, 467–81. Roma: Ministero per i Beni Culturali e Ambientali, 1983.

Dalla Torre, Massimo. 'Introduction'. In *Architettura contemporanea in Israele*, 5. Roma: Officina edizioni, 1969.

De Felice, Renzo. *Storia degli ebrei italiani sotto il fascismo*. Torino: Einaudi, 1962.

Dulio, Roberto. *Introduzione a Bruno Zevi*. Roma-Bari: Laterza, 2008.

D'Urbino, Manfredo. 'La nuova architettura di un'antica civiltà: l'ebraica'. *Rassegna di Architettura* 1 (1933): 16–25.

D'Urbino, Manfredo. Letter to the Ministry of the Interior, Milan, March 20, 1939. *Ministero dell'Interno, Direzione generale Demografia e Razza, Divisione razza, Fascicoli personali*. b. 228, folder 15703 'D'Urbino Manfredo'. ACS (Archivio Centrale dello Stato), Rome.

Falbel, Anat. 'Introdução'(Introduction). In Bruno Zevi, *Arquitetura e judaísmo: Mendelsohn*, IX–XXX. São Paulo: Perspectiva, 2002.

——— 'Lewis Mumford and the Quest for a Jewish Architecture'. In *Nationalism and Architecture*, edited by Raymond Quek, Darren Deane, and Sarah Butler, 67–79. Farnham: Ashgate, 2012.

Giedion, Sigfried. *Space, Time and Architecture: The Growth of a New Tradition*. Cambridge, MA and London: Harvard University Press and H. Milford, Oxford University Press, 1941.

'Gli Ebrei e l'Architettura. Prefazione all'edizione ebraica del volume *Saper vedere l'architettura*'. *La Rassegna Mensile di Israel* 7 (1958): 314.

Heschel, Abraham Joshua. *The Sabbath: Its Meaning for Modern Man*. New York: Farrar, Straus and Young, 1951.

Kauffmann, Richard. 'La pianificazione delle colonie agricole sioniste'. *Metron* 11 (1946): 45–51.

Krinsky, Carol Herselle. *Synagogues of Europe: Architecture, History, Meaning*. New York: Architectural History Foundation, 1985.
'Il finanziamento dell'attività edilizia in Palestina'. *Metron* 11 (1946): 25.
'In Israele: il municipio di Bat Yam, Tel Aviv'. *Domus* 411 (1964): 14.
Lattes, Dante. 'Il nuovo tempio israelitico di Trieste'. *Il corriere israelitico* 2 (1912), 35.
Morgan, Giulio. 'Un Convalescenziario sul panorama di Nazareth'. *L'architettura. Cronache e storia* 87 (1963): 610.
Nitzan-Shiftan, Alona. 'Capital City or Spiritual Center? The Politics of Architecture in Post-1967 Jerusalem'. *Cities* 3 (2005): 229–40.
——— 'The Walled City and the White City: The Construction of the Tel Aviv/Jerusalem Dichotomy'. *Perspecta* 39 (2007): 92–104.
——— *Seizing Jerusalem: The Architectures of Unilateral Unification*. Minneapolis: University of Minnesota Press, 2017.
Prefazione di 'Saper vedere l'architettura' di Bruno Zevi. 'Martin Buber Archive, General and philosophical material'. ARC. Ms. Var, 350 02 160. National Library of Israel, Jerusalem.
Programma di concorso per il progetto di un tempio israelitico con accessori ed altri locali annessi da erigersi in Roma a cura ed uso dell'Università israelitica, 1889. 'Pratiche per la costruzione del nuovo Tempio'. b. 60 – 07 inf. 01. ASCER (Archivio storico della Comunità ebraica di Roma), Rome.
Racheli, Alberto Maria. 'Architettura e architetti delle sinagoghe italiane nel periodo eclettico'. In *Italia Judaica*, 483–97. Roma: Ministero per i Beni Culturali e Ambientali, 1983.
Restany, Pierre. 'Arte e spazio in Israele'. *Domus* 411 (1964): 13.
Revere, Amedeo. 'Manfredo D'Urbino ed il problema di un'architettura ebraica'. *La Rassegna Mensile di Israel* 6–7 (1937): 299–301.
Rosenfeld, Gavriel D. 'Postwar Jewish Architecture and the Memory of the Holocaust'. In *Jewish Dimensions in Modern Visual Culture: Antisemitism, Assimilation, Affirmation*, eds Rose Carol Long, Matthew Baigell, and Milly Heyd, 285–302. Waltham, MA: Brandeis University Press, 2010.
——— *Building After Auschwitz: Jewish Architecture and the Memory of the Holocaust*. New Haven: Yale University Press, 2011.
Sachs Angeli and Edward van Voolen, eds. *Jewish Identity in Contemporary Architecture*. München: Prestel, 2004.
Sharon, Arieh. *Planning Jerusalem: The Master Plan for the Old City of Jerusalem and Its Environs*. New York: McGraw-Hill, 1974.
——— *Kibbutz + Bauhaus: An Architect's Way in a New Land*. Stuttgart: Kramer, 1976.
'Sviluppo edilizio e urbanistico in Palestina'. *Metron* 11 (1946): 4.
Tafuri, Manfredo and Francesco Dal Co. *Architettura contemporanea*. Milano: Electa, 1976.
Tafuri, Manfredo. 'Razionalismo critico e nuovo utopismo'. *Casabella-Continuità* 293 (1964): 18–41.
——— *History of Italian Architecture, 1944–1985*, translated by Jessica Levine. Cambridge, MA and London: MIT Press, 1989.
Tedeschi, Eugenio. Review of *La casa a chi lavora*, by Piero Bottoni. *Metron* 2 (1945): 47.
Tentori, Francesco. 'Un grande architetto ebreo'. *Rassegna di architettura* 115–16 (2005): 11–15.

Tonon, Graziella. 'QT8: urbanistica e architettura per una nuova civiltà dell'abitare'. In *Le case nella Triennale. Dal Parco al QT8*, eds Graziella Leyla Ciagà and Graziella Tonon, 141–53. Milano: Electa, 2005.
Veronesi, Giulia. *Difficoltà politiche dell'architettura in Italia: 1920–1940*. Milano: Politecnica Tamburini, 1953.
Volterra, Vito A. 'Israel'. *Urbanistica* 4 (1950): 59.
——— 'Israel – Città di Tiberiade'. *Urbanistica* 8 (1951): 70–72.
Yacobi, Haim, ed. *Constructing a Sense of Place: Architecture and the Zionist Discourse*. Florence: Taylor and Francis, 2004.
Zevi, Bruno. *Verso un'architettura organica. Saggio sullo sviluppo del pensiero architettonico negli ultimi cinquant'anni*. Torino: Einaudi, 1945.
——— *Saper vedere l'architettura. Saggio sull'interpretazione spaziale dell'architettura*. Torino: Einaudi, 1948.
——— 'Gli Ebrei e l'Architettura. Prefazione all'edizione ebraica del volume "Saper vedere l'architettura"'. *La Rassegna Mensile di Israel* 7 (1958).
——— *L'architettura moderna israeliana*, 1965. 'Attività editoriale, Saggi, articoli, discorsi e interviste (1943–1999)'. b. 17, folder 23 '1965'. ABZ (Archivio Bruno Zevi), Rome.
——— '[Speech]'. *Archicollegio* 7–8 (1965): 24.
——— 'International Technical Cooperation Centre'. *L'architettura. Cronache e storia* 152 (1968): 73.
——— *Erich Mendelsohn. Opera completa. Architettura e immagini architettoniche*. Milano: Etas Kompass, 1970.
——— 'Ebraismo e concezione spazio-temporale nell'arte'. *La Rassegna Mensile di Israel* 6 (1974): 207–22.
——— 'Introduction'. In *Kibbutz + Bauhaus: An Architect's Way in a New Land*, 6–7. Stuttgart: Kramer, 1976.
——— *Ebraismo e architettura*. Firenze: La Giuntina, 1993.
——— *Spazio e non-spazio ebraico. Confronto del compositore jazz Uri Caine con la musica di Mahler*, Jewish Community of Venice, November 29, 1998. 'Partecipazione a eventi (1935–1999)'. b. 65, folder 50. ABZ (Archivio Bruno Zevi), Rome.
——— *Ebraismo e architettura*, edited by Manuel Orazi. Firenze: La Giuntina, 2018.

Notes

1 The relationship with Israeli culture had a central place in Zevi's life. For the following period of his life, not discussed in the present research, see the collection of documents, keep in Archivio Bruno Zevi–Roma, titled *Bruno con noialtri* composed by Leo Guido B. Sonnino in 2002.

2 See: Manfredo Tafuri, *History of Italian Architecture, 1944–1985*, trans. Jessica Levine (Cambridge, MA and London: MIT Press, 1989).

3 See: Giulia Veronesi, *Difficoltà politiche dell'architettura in Italia: 1920–1940* (Milano: Politecnica Tamburini, 1953). All translations from Italian to English are the author's own, unless otherwise specified.

4 See: 'All'Ordine degli architetti di Roma', *Metron* 2 (1945): 73–74; Matilde Baffa, Corinna Morandi, Sara Protasoni, and Augusto Rossari, *Il Movimento di studi per l'architettura: 1945–1961* (Roma-Bari: Laterza 1995), 115–47.

5 Zevi, Bruno, *Verso un'architettura organica. Saggio sullo sviluppo del pensiero architettonico negli ultimi cinquant'anni* (Torino: Einaudi, 1945).

6 For Mendelsohn's works in Palestine, see Ita Heinze-Mühleib, *Erich Mendelsohn. Bauten und Projekte in Palästina (1934–1941)* (Munchen: Scaneg, 1986).

7 'Sviluppo edilizio e urbanistico in Palestina', Metron 11 (1946): 4.

8 For a discussion of the connection between organic architecture and democratic life in Italy, see Maristella Casciato, 'Wright and Italy: The Promise of Organic Architecture', in *Frank Lloyd Wright: Europe and Beyond*, ed. Anthony Alofsin (Berkeley, Los Angeles and London: University of California Press, 1999), 79–99.

9 'Il finanziamento dell'attività edilizia in Palestina', *Metron* 11 (1946): 25.

10 Zevi, *Verso*, 71.

11 Ibid., 75.

12 Ibid., 69.

13 Ibid., 69.

14 See Eugenio Tedeschi, review of the *La casa a chi lavora*, by Piero Bottoni, *Metron* 2 (1945): 47. About Zionism and architecture, see: *Constructing a Sense of Place: Architecture and the Zionist Discourse,* edited by Haim Yacobi (Florence: Taylor and Francis, 2004).

15 See: Graziella Tonon, 'QT8: urbanistica e architettura per una nuova civiltà dell'abitare', in *Le case nella Triennale. Dal Parco al QT8*, eds Graziella Leyla Ciagà and Graziella Tonon (Milano: Electa, 2005), 141–53.

16 Vito A. Volterra, 'Israel – Città di Tiberiade', *Urbanistica* 8 (1951): 70–72.

17 Several studies dealing with modern architecture and Judaism in the broader sense have been published in recent years, most notably: Fredric Bedoire, *The Jewish Contribution to Modern Architecture, 1830–1930* (Jersey City: KTAV Pub. House, 2004); Angeli Sachs and Edward van Voolen, eds, *Jewish Identity In Contemporary Architecture* (München: Prestel, 2004); Gavriel D. Rosenfeld, *Building After Auschwitz. Jewish Architecture and the Memory of the Holocaust* (New Haven: Yale University Press, 2011); Anat Falbel, 'Lewis Mumford and the Quest for a Jewish Architecture', in *Nationalism and Architecture*, eds Raymond Quek, Darren Deane, and Sarah Butler (Farnham: Ashgate, 2012), 67–79. For the presence of Jewish culture in modernity, see: Zachary Braiterman, *The Shape of Revelation: Aesthetics and Modern Jewish Thought* (Stanford: Stanford University Press, 2007) and the considerations of Gavriel D. Rosenfeld, 'Postwar Jewish Architecture and the Memory of the Holocaust', in *Jewish Dimensions in Modern Visual Culture: Antisemitism, Assimilation, Affirmation*, eds Rose Carol Long, Matthew Baigell, and Milly Heyd (Waltham, MA: Brandeis University Press, 2010), 285–302.

18 See: Anat Falbel, 'Introdução' (Introduction), in Bruno Zevi, *Arquitetura e judaísmo: Mendelsohn* (São Paulo: Perspectiva, 2002), IX–XXX.

19 In 1938 only 23 architects were counted in Italy. For Italian census, see: Archivio Centrale dello Stato–Roma, *Ministero dell'Interno, Direzione generale Demografia e Razza, Divisione razza, Fascicoli personali*; Renzo De Felice, *Storia degli ebrei italiani sotto il fascismo* (Torino: Einaudi, 1962), 5–30.

20 Francesco Tentori, 'Un grande architetto ebreo', *Rassegna di architettura* 115–16 (2005): 11–15.

21 Dante Lattes, 'Il nuovo tempio israelitico di Trieste', *Il corriere israelitico* 2 (1912): 35.

22 Of the extensive literature on synagogue architecture, see: David Cassuto, 'Il vano architettonico della sinagoga barocca in Italia', in *Italia Judaica* (Roma: Ministero per i Beni Culturali e Ambientali, 1983), 467–81; Carol Herselle Krinsky, *Synagogues of Europe: Architecture, History, Meaning* (New York: Architectural History Foundation, 1985).

23 Vincenzo Costa and Osvaldo Armanni, cited in Alberto Maria Racheli, 'Architettura e architetti delle sinagoghe italiane nel periodo eclettico', in *Italia Judaica* (Roma: Ministero per i Beni Culturali e Ambientali, 1983), 495.

24 *Programma di concorso per il progetto di un tempio israelitico con accessori ed altri locali annessi da erigersi in Roma a cura ed uso dell'Università israelitica*, 1889, Archivio storico della Comunità ebraica di Roma, *Pratiche per la costruzione del nuovo Tempio*, b. 60–07/01.

25 Augusto Bachi, 'Appunti sulla architettura della Sinagoga', *La Rassegna Mensile di Israel* 1–2 (1933): 25–46

26 Ibid., 25–46.

27 D'Urbino was trained at the School of Fine Arts in Modena until 1910, in Lucca in 1911, in Florence in 1912, and then graduated from the School of Architecture of the Royal Academy of Brera in Milan in 1914. Letter by D'Urbino to the Ministry of the Interior, Milan, March 20, 1939, Archivio Centrale dello Stato–Roma, *Ministero dell'Interno, Direzione generale Demografia e Razza, Divisione razza, Fascicoli personali*, b. 228, f. 15703 'D'Urbino Manfredo'.

28 Amedeo Revere, 'Manfredo D'Urbino ed il problema di un'architettura ebraica', *La Rassegna Mensile di Israel* 6–7 (1937): 299–301.

29 Ibid.

30 Ibid.

31 Manfredo D'Urbino, 'La nuova architettura di un'antica civiltà: l'ebraica', *Rassegna di Architettura* 1 (1933): 16–25.

32 Bruno Zevi, *Spazio e non-spazio ebraico. Confronto del compositore jazz Uri Caine con la musica di Mahler*, Jewish Community of Venice, November 29, 1998, Archivio Bruno Zevi–Roma, *Partecipazione a eventi (1935–1999)*, b. 65, f. 50.

33 Bruno Zevi, *Ebraismo e architettura* (Firenze: La Giuntina, 1993). See the new edition with the essay by Manuel Orazi: Bruno Zevi, *Ebraismo e architettura*, ed. Manuel Orazi (Firenze: La Giuntina, 2018).

34 Bruno Zevi, 'Gli Ebrei e l'Architettura. Prefazione all'edizione ebraica del volume *Saper vedere l'architettura*', *La Rassegna Mensile di Israel* 7 (1958): 314. Bruno Zevi, *Saper vedere l'architettura. Saggio sull'interpretazione spaziale dell'architettura* (Torino: Einaudi, 1948).

35 Zevi, 'Gli Ebrei', 314.

36 Ibid., 314.

37 For a review of the influences of art criticism on *Saper vedere l'architettura*, see: Roberto Dulio, *Introduzione a Bruno Zevi* (Roma-Bari: Laterza, 2008), 66–75

38 Bruno Zevi, 'Ebraismo e concezione spazio-temporale nell'arte', *La Rassegna Mensile di Israel* 6 (1974): 207–22. The text takes up the inaugural speech of the *9th Congress of Jewish*

Communities in Italy, delivered in Roma in Protomoteca Hall of the Campidoglio on June 8, 1974

39 Ibid., 207–22.

40 Abraham Joshua Heschel, *The Sabbath: Its Meaning for Modern Man* (New York: Farrar, Straus and Young, 1951), 12.

41 Thorleif Boman, *Hebrew Thought Compared with Greek* (New York: W.W. Norton & Co., 1960), 123–83.

42 Martin Buber, 'Prefazione all'edizione ebraica di *Saper vedere l'architettura* di Bruno Zevi [1957]', *La Rassegna Mensile di Israel* 1 (2000): 2–4. See also: *Prefazione di 'Saper vedere l'architettura' di Bruno Zevi*, Martin Buber Archive, National Library of Israel, Jerusalem, *General and philosophical material*, ARC. Ms. Var, 350 02 160,

43 Martin Buber, 'Eine jungjüdische Bühne', *Die Welt*, November 8, 1901. On the relationship between nationalism and Jewish identity, see: Anat Falbel, 'Lewis Mumford', 67–79.

44 Martin Buber, 'Ein Wort zum funften Kongress', *Jüdische Volksstimme* 3, February 15, 1902.

45 Zevi founded this thought on the interpretation of Albert Einstein's thinking. In this sense, see also the work of another Jewish intellectual, Sigfried Giedion. See: Sigfried Giedion, *Space, Time and Architecture: The Growth of a New Tradition* (Cambridge, MA and London: Harvard University Press and H. Milford, Oxford University Press, 1941).

46 Bruno Zevi, *Erich Mendelsohn. Opera completa. Architettura e immagini architettoniche* (Milan: Etas Kompass, 1970). The 1997 edition has a new chapter, 'Action architects. L'espressionismo oggi', dedicated to the work of Reima Pietilä, Jörn Utzon, Jean Renaudie, Zvi Hecker, Daniel Libeskind, and Frank Owen Gehry.

47 Bruno Zevi, 'International Technical Cooperation Centre', *L'architettura. Cronache e storia* 152 (1968): 73.

48 Participants in the 1970 meeting included M. Bill, R. Buckminster Fuller, P. Johnson, L. Kahn, R. Meier, N. Pevsner, L. Piccinato, and M. Safdie, *The Jerusalem Committee. Town planning Subcommittee, December 19–21, 1970. Participants from Abroad*, Archivio Bruno Zevi–Roma, *Associazioni, istituti e comitati (1945–1999)*, b. 11, f. 9 'World Committee for Jerusalem'.

49 See: Arieh Sharon, *Planning Jerusalem: The Master Plan for the Old City of Jerusalem and Its Environs* (New York: McGraw-Hill, 1974); Alona Nitzan-Shiftan, 'Capital City or Spiritual center? The Politics of Architecture in Post-1967 Jerusalem', *Cities* 3 (2005): 229–40; Alona Nitzan-Shiftan, *Seizing Jerusalem. The Architectures of Unilateral Unification* (Minneapolis: University of Minnesota Press, 2017), 19–44.

50 Bruno Zevi, *L'architettura moderna israeliana*, 1965, Archivio Bruno Zevi–Roma, *Attività editoriale, Saggi, articoli, discorsi e interviste (1943–1999)*, b. 17, f. 23 '1965'.

51 Bruno Zevi, '[Speech]', *Archicollegio* 7–8 (1965): 24.

52 *Architettura contemporanea in Israele* (Roma: Officina edizioni, 1969). Zevi founded the In/Arch in 1959.

53 Massimo Dalla Torre, 'Introduction', in *Architettura contemporanea in Israele* (Roma: Officina edizioni, 1969), 5.

54 Manfredo Tafuri, 'Razionalismo critico e nuovo utopismo', *Casabella-Continuità* 293 (1964): 18–41. See: Alona Nitzan-Shiftan, 'The Walled City and the White City: The Construction of the Tel Aviv/ Jerusalem Dichotomy', *Perspecta* 39 (2007): 92–104.

55 Tafuri, 'Razionalismo critico', 20.
56 Giulio Morgan, 'Un Convalescenziario sul panorama di Nazareth', *L'architettura. Cronache e storia* 87 (1963): 610.
57 Bruno Zevi, 'Introduction', *Kibbutz + Bauhaus: An Architect's Way in a New Land* (Stuttgart: Kramer 1976), 6–7.
58 Pierre Restany, 'Arte e spazio in Israele', *Domus* 411 (1964): 13.
59 'In Israele: il municipio di Bat Yam, Tel Aviv', *Domus* 411 (1964): 14.
60 Manfredo Tafuri and Francesco Dal Co, *Architettura contemporanea* (Milan: Electa, 1976), 385.
61 Maria Bottero, 'Introduction', *Zodiac* 17 (1969): 5.
62 Ibid., 5.
63 See: Richard Buckminster Fuller, 'Comprehensive Thinking', in *World Design Science Decade, 1965–1975. Five Two-Year Phases of a World Retooling Design Proposed to the International Union of Architects for Adoption by World Architectural Schools. Phase 1, Document 3*, ed. John McHale (Carbondale, IL: Southern Illinois University, 1965).

Prefabricating Nativism: The Design of the Israeli Knesset, 1956–1966, and the Sierra Leone Parliament, 1960–1964[1]

Ayala Levin

Characterizing Israel as 'prosperous modern villa in the jungle' in 1996, Foreign Minister Ehud Barak portrayed it as an isolated outpost of enlightenment in the midst of Middle Eastern 'wilderness'.[2] By symbolizing Israel with this architectural image, Barak constituted a sharp dichotomy between a western modern villa and an untamed natural and supposedly primitive environment. In the late 1950s, however, this was not the image Israel wished to present internationally, when it was seeking diplomatic relations with Africa's and Asia's decolonizing states and offering development aid. By contrast, Israel wished to present itself as a bridgehead between East and West, or between the developing and developed countries.

These relationships coincided with optimistic development plans that African governments carried out with the support of foreign aid. The new development narrative postulated the postcolonial latecomers' ability 'to catch up' with the West via the omnipotence of science and technology. A tangible example of such a 'leap', Israel demonstrated to African visitors a test case that proved the theory. If Europe offered a fait-accompli image of a distant desired future, Israel presented a moving image of development in the making; an acceleration of history that can be emulated and repeated elsewhere. The shared sense of urgency is exemplified in the fact that one of the most prestigious projects that Israeli architects undertook abroad, the design and construction of the Sierra Leone parliament, was concurrent with the design and construction of the Israeli parliament, the Knesset. This was one of the first projects Israeli architects and engineers undertook as part of Israeli aid during the 'golden age' of the Israeli–African relationship from 1958 to 1973.[3] The design of the Knesset by architect Joseph Klarwein instigated a heated public debate that led to commissioning prominent architect Dov Karmi to revise it. Following his and his son Ram Karmi's revisions, they were commissioned to design the Sierra Leone parliament.

This chapter focuses on the debate over the proper design for the Israeli Knesset and Ram Karmi's vision of Zionist nativity, which he hoped to materialize in the design of the Knesset but could only fully express in Sierra Leone, away from the Israeli public debate and the series of compromises that surrounded the design of the Knesset. In this sense, the Sierra Leone parliament is an early manifestation of the turn to locality in Israeli architecture, which architectural historian Alona Nitzan-Shiftan identified in the architects of the 'generation of the state', of which Ram Karmi was arguably the most dominant figure.[4] Not unlike colonial projects, where architects were free to implement their designs while circumventing the hurdles of public opinion and bureaucracy back home,[5] this project presented Karmi's 'solutions' to the Israeli conflict between modernity and tradition, universalism and nationalism.

By comparing the design of the Knesset with that of the Sierra Leone parliament, this chapter brings to the fore the predicament of post-war national representation via modern architecture. The functionalist 'international' aesthetic of the modernist architectural idiom conveyed the image of postcolonial nations' desired modernity, as key to participation in the international community diplomatically, culturally, and economically.[6] However, it also presented the challenge of how to render this aesthetic nationally representative. At the heart of this predicament was the double temporality of the nation-state that, as Benedict Anderson has famously argued, draws its youthful vitality from its ostensibly primordial past.[7] In the case of Israel – a 'post-colonial colony', to use intellectual historian Joseph Masaad's apt phrase – the problem was of asserting a historical continuity and belonging in the so-called land of the patriarchs.[8] Reminiscent of Israel's dual society of Jewish settlers and the local Palestinian population, Sierra Leone's society was historically based on a social, cultural, and economic divide between the Krio, descenders of the freed slaves who settled in Freetown, which was conceived in 1787 as an enlightenment colony for repatriated Africans, and the indigenous population.[9] British indirect rule fixated this divide by granting Freetown peninsula, mostly comprised of Krio, the status of a colony, while dividing the indigenous hinterland into administrative provinces, governed by customary law and purportedly timeless traditions.[10] Adding to the problem of representing the multiple ethnicities and cultures that postcolonial states typically faced with independence was the deep cultural chasm between the two societies, with the first identifying with western culture and the second with local traditions.

This chapter considers the design of the Sierra Leone parliament by Ram Karmi as a mirror image of his desires for the design of the Knesset. It poses the question of what their respective design concepts can teach us about the problem of modernist representation of national belonging in Israel as in other post-war states. As this chapter demonstrates, it was the tension between the conflicting temporalities of the nation-state – between rapid technical development, on the one hand, and the manifestation of deep-rooted historical belonging, on the other – that was at the heart of the debate in Israel and that Ram Karmi wished to resolve in his design for the Sierra Leone parliament.

The Knesset Controversy

As in Ghana and Nigeria, where Israel had already established relations prior to Sierra Leone, Israel's foreign ministry offered the assistance of the country's largest construction company, Solel Boneh, in the setting-up of a joint Israeli–Sierra Leonean national construction company.[11] Unlike competing British firms, who claimed that there was not enough time to construct a parliament in time for the independence celebrations, scheduled in the summer of 1960 for April 27, 1961, Solel Boneh's management promised to deliver the parliament in time for the occasion.[12] The ability to do so was predicated partly on the commission of the same architects who had been working on the Knesset design, father and son Dov and Ram Karmi of the office of Karmi–Meltzer–Karmi, to design the parliament.

The Karmis became involved in the latter stages of the design process of the Knesset in the late 1950s, following the heated debate that the 1956 design competition for the parliament roused. Sharing the Euro-American post-war sentiment that associated neoclassicism with fascist regimes,[13] the architectural community in Israel protested against the winning entry, whose neoclassical style, they claimed, was unfitting for a young democratic state.[14] The contested winning entry by the architect Joseph Klarwein was a stripped classicist rectangular structure, with the assembly hall flanked on both sides by courtyards and the exterior surrounded by a colonnade.[15] Before immigrating to Palestine in 1933, the Poland-born architect was educated at the Munich Polytechnic, trained at the studio of the German expressionist architect and set designer Hans Poelzig in Berlin, and worked for ten years at the expressionist architect Fritz Hoger's Hamburg office. In Palestine, however, Klarwein turned to the prevalent modernist idiom that served well both the hegemony of Labor Zionism as well as the urban bourgeoisie, while selectively imbuing it with classicism in representative buildings such as the Knesset.[16]

While a Greek temple would have been a fitting, albeit conservative, model for a modern acropolis, Klarwein denied this was his primary reference. In one interview, the Jerusalem-based architect traced his inspiration to Jerusalem's Old City Walls, as well as to his studies of the archaeological sites of the Roman king Herod the Great's family tomb and of the Old City built in the sixteenth century under the Ottoman ruler Suleiman the Magnificent. When confronted with the question of the influence of Greek temples, he admitted that there was some resemblance but instead of referring to it as a distinct style, he situated Greek architecture within the *long durée* traditions of the Orient.[17] In another interview he stated that while he was not seeking a particular oriental style, he was perhaps inspired by ancient Egyptian temples. Yet the style he came up with for the Knesset, he stressed, 'does not belong to any period – it belongs to all periods'.[18] Similarly, regarding the Jerusalem Wall he said: 'It is built with simple straight lines. Simple and arid stones like the rocky ground around it. It is always beautiful. Modern and beautiful.'[19] The reference to simplicity of lines, whether Egyptian, Greek, or sixteenth-century Ottoman, as embodying eternal beauty, and therefore 'modern', can be interpreted as reminiscent of the synthetic, yet contradictory approaches of British colonial architects such as Sir Edwin Landseer Lutyens in New Delhi and Austen St Barbe Harrison in Mandatory Palestine.[20] Similarly to Lutyens, Klarwein identified in the simplicity of stripped classicism a key to what he perceived as a universal language of forms; similarly to Harrison, he turned to a wide range of 'regional' sources of inspiration – divested of history and politics – for that timeless 'modernity' that he found in his objectified Orient.

The situating of the State of Israel within this colonial lineage, or conversely, as part of an imagined *long durée* of the Orient, was one of the causes of the ardent response that the winning entry instigated among the architectural community. Arguing that the building did not embody the spirit of the time like the prevalent modernist idiom, Klarwein's contemporaries deemed it unfit to represent a young dynamic state.[21] The competition for the Knesset, therefore, exposed the problem of imbuing architectural modernism, which was promoted on principles of functionalism and internationalism, with monumentality and representation that would provide a distinct sense of identity and community. This dilemma was particularly acute in the context of crafting a modern yet national identity for the new states that emerged after World War II.

To appease the local architectural community, and following architect Shimon Povsner's unsuccessful appointment to rework the design in collaboration with Klarwein,[22] Dov Karmi, who was awarded the Israel Prize in 1957, was invited as a consultant in early 1960.[23] His son Ram, who joined his office in 1956, collaborated on the project. The main changes they introduced were turning the rectangular shape of the building into a square, removing the courtyards, and locating the assembly hall off centre. Moreover, the architects added terraces for offices in the south slope, rather than locating them at the perimeter of the assembly hall, where they were situated in Klarwein's original design. Since Klarwein continued to have some control over the final design, one of the limitations placed on their revisions was that the colonnade surrounding the representative part of the building must remain.[24] The young Karmi, who had a notoriously vehement temper, presented an uncompromising position regarding the columns. First, he suggested five large partitions in a portico in the spirit of the parliament in Chandigarh,[25] the new Punjabi capitol designed by the renowned Swiss architect Le Corbusier. Later, he amended it to seven concrete columns, following the number of columns in the Parthenon, claiming that the eye cannot grasp more than seven elements at once.[26] His persistence regarding the columns resulted in a severe clash that led his father to remove him from the project. According to Ram Karmi, his father sent him away to design the Sierra Leone parliament, where he could build 'a Knesset without columns'.[27]

Rootedness and Expansion

The Sierra Leone parliament design demonstrates that the columns were merely a symptom of a deeper conflict embedded in the very materiality of the Israeli Knesset. Like the Knesset, it was divided into two parts according to their function: the assembly hall served the representative function, while the sloping terraces served for offices and future functions such as the government's archive [Figures 1–2]. However, whereas in Sierra Leone the two parts are unified by the coating of a local stone on their surfaces, in the Knesset they are divided by the different materials employed: the assembly hall is coated with stone while the terraces are faced with glass [Figure 3]. The designers' choice to materially juxtapose the two

Figure 1: Aerial view of the Knesset's north facade, Jerusalem, contemporary view (2010). Photograph by Moshe Milner. Courtesy of the Israel Government Press Office.

Figure 2: Ram Karmi, Sierra Leone parliament, Freetown, 1960, model. Courtesy of Azrieli Architectural Archive: Ram Karmi Collection.

Figure 3: The Knesset's south façade under construction, Jerusalem, early 1960s. Photograph by Moshe Fridan. Courtesy of Israel Government Press Archive.

parts of the structure emphasized the topographical and functional division between the representative and the administrative spaces. This structural and material juxtaposition was part of a contemporaneous international trend exemplified in projects such as Lina Bo Bardi's Sao Paulo Museum of Art (1956–68) and Mies van der Rohe's Neue Nationalgalerie in Berlin (1962–68). Yet the Knesset structure presented a curious inversion of their material and tectonic logic: unlike these two buildings, where an accentuated structural frame supports the airy glass box of the representational space, at the Knesset the stone-coated main structure visually rests on glass terraces.

This curious decision – to have a stone-coated building rest on concrete, steel, and glass terraces – perplexed contemporary commentators in Israel. They pointed out the tectonic incongruity, which failed to give a sense of structural unity or continuity between the two parts.[28] Against Klarwein's original insistence on a unitary image, which he hoped to achieve by referring to the Old City Walls,[29] the addition of the glass-faced terraces presented a competing logic that marked a radical departure from the original design. According to the Karmis, the reason they chose steel and glass for the terraces' addition was to allow structural flexibility for further extension of the offices.[30] Intended to accommodate growth and change, this horizontal expansion logic was influenced by the mid-century European revisionist modernist group Team X, particularly by the ideas of Dutch architect Aldo van Eyck, as articulated in his Amsterdam Orphanage (1955–60). It may also have been inspired by American architect Louis Kahn's contemporary design for the Jewish Community Center in Trenton, New Jersey (1954–59). While Klarwein's and Karmi's approaches may seem structurally and visually incompatible, both derive from a similar desire to connect the structure to the ground. If for Klarwein this was via the material but timeless connection to the local stone, which he associated with various building traditions in the region, for Ram Karmi the connection to the ground was rendered through the grading terraces that may reference agricultural terraces, a vernacular form of cultivation practised by the Arab fellahin.

Through this reference to Palestinian vernacular, the design of the Knesset heralded the generational watershed that, as mentioned at the outset of this chapter, has been termed by Nitzan-Shiftan the 'turn to locality' in Israeli architecture. While Nitzan-Shiftan emphasizes this turn by referring to the emulation of Arab architecture following the conquering of East Jerusalem in the 1967 War, she traces the shift back to the late 1950s, when a generation of architects, born and raised in Palestine, was influenced by Team X's turn to vernacular architecture as source of inspiration, and borrowed from the Arab vernacular to assert a more authentic relationship to the Israeli territory than that of their modernist émigré predecessors.[31] It was their desire to gain a degree of nativity, comparable with the Arab population, that motivated this generation of the first 'natives' (sabra) of the Israeli State to seek inspiration in the Arab vernacular.[32] Ram Karmi, who studied at the Architectural Association in London from 1951 to 1956, and was therefore one of the earliest Israeli architects to be exposed to Team X's influence and the Brutalist approach of some of its leading members, became, by the late 1960s, the most dominant architect of this 'generation of the state'.[33]

In their search for an image of Israeli belonging to the land, the 'generation of the state' architects turned to the figure of the Arab fellah as a model for emulation. As Nitzan-Shiftan demonstrates, the relationship of 'the *fellah* to his house, which he builds and maintains with his own hands' was perceived as 'a relationship of belonging, of identification, and of strong emotional attachment'.[34] Karmi, too, employed the figure of the fellah in his writings, only to offer a modern alternative to his traditional form of belonging:

> The modern building ceased being a stable mass resting on the ground in the corporeal expansiveness of a fellah sitting confidently on his land. The building becomes transparent, thin, and muscular: its skeleton is like a tree trunk that is not laid on the ground but planted in it, nailing its roots deeply. And the deeper the roots, so is the foliage vaster, since it does not depend on its weight but on its strength, to its dynamic muscularity that reaches its long lean arms to the sides, as if hanging by a thread, similar to the outward extending cantilevers in Frank Lloyd Wright's Fallingwater.[35]

In this retrospective theorization of his work, Karmi juxtaposed the 'corporeal expansiveness', which he associated with the fellah's confident relationship with the land, with an image of a transparent and thin muscular tissue supported by a skeletal infrastructure. While Karmi referred to Frank Lloyd Wright's Fallingwater house of 1935, this description is reminiscent more of Hungarian-born architect Yona Friedman's Ville Spatiale multi-storey space-frame of the late 1950s, which is another example of a horizontal expansion logic inspired by Team X's revisionist modernism, with its light modular infrastructure and flexible enveloping materials.[36] Karmi's image, however, differs from Friedman's raised structures, which could have been potentially superimposed over any given territory. Instead, he emphasized the structure's rootedness in the terrain. Karmi metaphorically replaced the massive rock that serves as the vertical axis in Fallingwater with a slender tree trunk, and Wright's extending reinforced concrete cantilevers with the image of vast delicate foliage. 'Muscular' yet airy, Karmi located the source of strength of this imagined structure in its motion downwards and upwards, vertically and horizontally, where the passive confidence he associated with the fellah was replaced by tension, 'as if hanging by a thread'.

Similarly, instead of 'sitting confidently on the land', the stone-faced concrete structure of the Knesset assembly hall is placed on Karmi's seemingly fragile glass terraces, creating a visual tension between the two. The dynamic relationship is achieved not only by material juxtaposition and tectonic inversion but also via the metaphoric logic it conveys. The allusion to agriculture in the technically advanced structure refers to the Zionist modernization of agriculture, which provided the economic basis for the realization of a Jewish nation-state. The terraces thus embody the modern basis for the seemingly archaic assembly hall. By creating a hybrid between vernacular agriculture and a glass and steel rhizome-like structure, the Israeli modern linkage to the ground is performed as an inorganic organism, a technologically advanced base for the monumental, allegedly timeless, presence of the nation.[37]

While Karmi stated that it was the 'Mediterranean' Le Corbusier who was his true inspiration,[38] he nonetheless related to Frank Lloyd Wright, whose model of organic architecture he interpreted as quintessentially American, and appropriate for settler-colonial societies such as Israel:

> A Full-fledged American symbolizes the true force of primordial nature – a deep interior impulse, liberated from the European-based architectural tradition […] Wright identified with the pioneer that conquers the vast prairies; we, the Sabras – that knew this character from American movies – felt like him […] we, like the Americans, are leaves on a tree, immigrant-refugees that began a new life in a new country; but as the sons of one place they are also united, since these leaves are tied to each other as a tree, planted in water creeks.[39]

The image of the tree is evoked again as a metaphor for unison in difference and dispersal, and the perseverance of a central constant core, despite the course of history, is symbolized by the running water. Against Karmi's figurative consistency, as manifested in his repeated employment of the tree trope, the wording he used to invest the tree with his desired symbolism betrays irreconcilable contradictions between settler-colonialism and nativism, and between the dispersed places of origin of immigrants and their supposed shared unitary primordial source. In an essay on Esther Raab, known as 'the first Sabra poet', literary theorist Hannan Hever explains Zionist desire for nativism as an attempt to naturalize Jewish presence in the territory and the effacement of its colonial character.[40] This desire was pregnant with the temporal paradox of radical beginning, on the one hand, and with time immemorial of continuous ownership of the land, on the other.[41] Born in the territory of the ancients, explains historian Yael Zerubavel, the sabras or 'New Hebrews' were considered as an authentic continuation of the ancients *and* as a 'radically transformed breed' of their Jewish immigrant parents.[42] Despite this seemingly privileged and secure position in comparison with their immigrant parents, Karmi, like Raab, desired to identify with the settler-pioneers in their 'conquest' of the territory.[43] By identifying with the Labor Zionist pioneer, while at the same time claiming a new 'native' understanding of the place, Karmi sought to maintain the pioneering zeal and perpetuate its creative energy, even after the establishment of the state.

The attempt to reconcile the temporal schism between the sabras' supposed primordial belonging and the radical beginning they represent was the driving force behind their creative process, whose ultimate referent was the territory itself. As Hever demonstrates, Raab's poetic act became 'a primary tool for the colonialist appropriation of space, appearing as an endless motion that nourishes the appropriative desire over and over'.[44] For Karmi, Israeli architects who turned to Brutalism in the 1960s

> [a]spired to an authentic locality and saw in concrete a local material. They felt that the work of the architect and the artist is equal, by the force of faith that throbs in it, to the work of the fellah who diligently cultivates his land.[45]

Associating concrete with the land, Karmi coalesced the land as an object of desire with the material medium of his artistic production.

The burden of 'proof' of native belonging is located principally in the visual realm. Since nativism is constructed as a natural 'biological fact', in order for it to seem apparent it needs to be clearly recognizable. This could not be carried out by a simple borrowing of forms from the Arab vernacular or the use of local stone in a timeless oriental fashion, as suggested by Klarwein. It had to be created anew, while undermining its own newness, since, as Hever explains, the idea of a 'new beginning' also portends Zionism's impending end. This duality had to be sublimated to perpetuate a sense of indefinite continuity from time immemorial.[46]

In the first, and, to my knowledge, only study to date of the history of the design and construction of the Knesset, Sheila Hattis-Rolef writes that its site was proclaimed as a hub of Jewish stonemasons during the Second Temple era.[47] This proclamation served well Karmi's narrative of material reappropriation. Beyond the meaning attached to the stones by Klarwein, used as markers of the oriental traditions shared by the different peoples that inhabited the region, the association of the location of the building specifically with an ancient Hebraic material practice, was part of a general trend characteristic of Zionist narration that linked antiquity and national rejuvenation. In the 1950s, this narrative focused on creating a direct correspondence between the Bible, the Jewish people, and state territory. This narrative must have appealed especially to the architects of the 'Generation of the State' in their search for an authentic relation with the land. In pre-state Israel, where the Jewish unskilled workforce competed with cheap and experienced Arab labour, the Jewish building industry depended on industrialized techniques in the training of the Jewish builder. The archaeological identification of stonemasonry as a Hebraic tradition concealed the anxiety over the loss of this craft among the majority of the Jewish population, and the fact that the trade had become almost exclusively a Palestinian Arab domain, including the quarries from which the stone for building the Knesset eventually arrived.[48]

To compensate for this loss, the Knesset's stone-clad façade was conceived as a non-bearing detached screen [Figure 4], denoting that the building was in fact constructed using the most advanced technology of that time. The vertically divided screens create an illusion of folding, with each pair of vertical strips bending slightly inward, facing each other. Rather than mimicking a heavily laid stone structure, the screen emphasizes the fact that it is a

Figure 4: Knesset north façade and main entrance, Jerusalem, contemporary view (2013). Photograph by Ayala Levin.

nonbearing wall, thus asserting its employment of industrial building techniques and adherence to modernist aesthetics. In this architectural statement, the Knesset joins a few generations of modernist architecture in Jerusalem that followed British regulations mandating the use of stone façades for construction in Jerusalem, especially in the Old City environs, by using increasingly thinner cladding, emphasizing that it is in fact merely that.[49] Rather than functioning as a construction material, the stone cladding exposes itself as an ornament that does not necessitate the application of traditional masonry, and thus joined the industrial image of the concrete, iron and glass rendering of the agricultural terraces.[50] However, as we learnt from the Knesset's contemporary critics, the modernized treatment of the stone did not ameliorate the tectonic incongruity between the two parts. It was only in Sierra Leone that Ram Karmi could project his image of modern nativism, free from the compromises and contradictions that led to its tectonic incongruity at the Knesset.

Fixing Nationalism in Stone

Considering the chosen site of the Sierra Leone parliament in Freetown as comparable to that of Givat Ram, Karmi reworked his design for the Knesset and projected onto the West African postcolonial nation his image of a desired nativity – a building that 'grows from the

Figure 5: Dov Karmi, Ram Karmi, and Zvi Meltzer, Sierra Leone parliament, early 1960s. Courtesy of Azrieli Architectural Archive: Ram Karmi Collection.

ground' [Figure 5].[51] In a curiously classical gesture, he topped the parliament building with a faintly golden shallow dome recalling that of the Capitol Building in neighbouring Liberia, which had been completed in 1956. However, when observed from the historical nucleus of the city and the main approaching road, the dome is hardly discernible, while the building's terraces gain prominence as the visual lead-up to the main building. In contrast with the Israeli Knesset, the integration of the terraces with the main building creates an effect of organic continuity between the two parts – an effect achieved by the repeating horizontal lines of the cantilevers that hang over the window strips. Their perspectival rendering unequivocally recalls Frank Lloyd Wright's Fallingwater [Figure 6]. According to Karmi's drawings and model, a pedestrian route leading up the slope would have extended these horizontal lines down the hill in accordance with the site's topography. Projecting surfaces

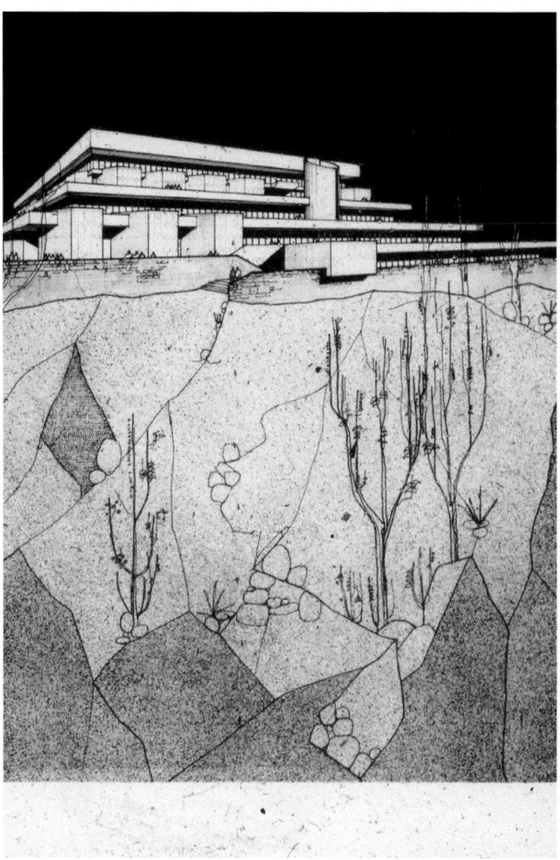

Figure 6: Ram Karmi, Sierra Leone parliament, Freetown, 1960, perspective. Courtesy of Azrieli Architectural Archive: Ram Karmi Collection.

Figure 7: Dov Karmi, Ram Karmi, and Zvi Meltzer, Sierra Leone parliament under construction, Freetown, early 1960s. Courtesy of Azrieli Architectural Archive: Ram Karmi Collection.

coated with white plaster were interleaved between the laterite stones whose earthy reddish tones dominate the building's façade to create a sense of visual dynamism, and accentuate the projected massing [Figure 7]. This interplay of surfaces is echoed in the foyer surrounding the assembly hall, where it is imbued with metaphoric meaning by literalizing Karmi's tree-trunk metaphor: the columns are divided into wooden fluted trunks at the base, growing white trunks at the top, denoting the dynamic young elements of the nation and symbolizing the process of organic rejuvenation. This sense of dynamism is accentuated with the symmetrical ramps that frame the building's entrance.

While Klarwein's use of stone in Jerusalem served to denote a linear continuum between the state and an ancient Hebrew civilization, in Freetown Karmi carved out an image of nativity from the ground, bypassing any reference to local history, recent or ancient.[52] Following their professional experience in Israel, where modernist Jewish architects had difficulty borrowing directly from Palestinian building crafts without undermining their Zionist claims over the territory, Karmi and Zvi Meltzer, the architect on site, did not consider the wooden-slat multistory houses of repatriated Africans and British colonial administrators in Freetown, or the mud structures of the country's rural areas, as sources for their design. Karmi and Meltzer instead 'invented' a tradition by converting the local laterite stone into cladding.

Whereas it had been used as building material for contemporaneous multistory office buildings and houses, the architects elevated the laterite stone to become the parliament façade's most dominant feature. While they also used laterite blocks in the interior to clad the assembly chamber, it was the crushed stone that they embedded in concrete plates on the cantilevered exteriors that symbolized more than anything Karmi's autochthonous vision of a building that 'grows from the ground'. A manual technique that can be performed by unskilled labour, the embedding of the crushed laterite stone into concrete plates was carried out *in situ*, and created an open-air makeshift prefabrication plant that involved hundreds of workers. The architects were quite stunned by the image of the mass of workers performing manual labour, comparable to an ancient civilization's monumental undertaking.[53]

The autochthonous effect became more pronounced over time as the iron-rich stone on the building's exterior gradually deepened its rusty shade due to its perpetual exposure to the elements. By crushing the stone and fixing it into concrete plates, the architects both pre-empted the stone's tendency to corrode and disintegrate and hastened its colour transformation by increasing its surface area.[54] Like the contemporaneous parliament buildings designed by Louis Kahn in Dakha and Le Corbusier in Chandigarh, the weathering of the stone instilled an aura of archaism and authenticity while also asserting the building's modernity.[55] Through this method, the architects ensured that the parliament would convey the paradoxical temporality of the postcolonial nation-state, in which autochthony converges not only with the newness of the present but also with the future, when the building's surface would increasingly merge with the land's rusty shade. That the excavated stone, an ostensibly unequivocal symbol of autochthony, was nonetheless subjected to a process of acclimatization, undermines assertions of nativity as a given autochthonic fact, and emphasizes instead that it is subject to becoming.

The architects' aesthetic of nativism was inflected with Zionist anxieties, in which connection with the ground and the environment at large was imagined as part of a process of cultural unification under the banner of shared territory and natural belonging. Not fully aware of the social divide that historically characterized Sierra Leone,[56] it can be assumed that the architects attributed this novel use of stone the symbolism of a new national aesthetic that offered an alternative to the British colonial neoclassical language of representation, on the one hand, and could bypass ethnic, cultural, and religious rivalries, on the other.

However, not everyone in the Sierra Leone government was equally enthusiastic about this image of nativism. One of the parliament's highest clerks, most probably a Krio, asked Karmi, while touring the construction site, when the Carrara marble was expected to arrive. As interpreted by Karmi, implicit in this comment was a critique that the parliament was incomplete without the finish of luxurious marble.[57] No doubt informed by colonial architecture, this expectation demonstrates that the historical divide between the Krio and the indigenous population continued until the very days of independence. While this chapter focused on the Israeli side of this exchange, suffice it to say that the predicaments and inherent contradictions of postcolonial national representation were not resolved by their displacement from the Israeli parliament building to the Sierra Leone one.

Conclusion

The adaptation of the design for the Israeli parliament in the Sierra Leonean context was a projection of Karmi's desire for a modern nativism, one that encapsulated Zionist yearnings and anxieties, but that could paradoxically only be materialized on, and by means of, foreign grounds. As this chapter has demonstrated, the Knesset design was built, literally, on contradictions. A result of a series of compromises between Klarwein's original design and the revisions suggested later by Dov and Ram Karmi, the building conveys a tectonic incongruity between its two parts: the representative assembly hall, and the office terraces that serve as its base. As I have argued in this chapter, the young Karmi found in the Sierra Leone parliament project an opportunity to design not only a 'Knesset without columns', but a building that 'grows from the ground' – where its two parts, the assembly hall and the office terraces, presented a unified image, in contrast with the Israeli Knesset.

The Knesset's design controversy was about the proper image for the young nation – a dilemma that could not be solved simply in the marriage of modern techniques of construction, the use of local stone, and references to classical traditions. At stake was conveying the modernity of the Israeli State, while linking it to an Hebraic archaic origin. The modernized use of local stone for the facing of its entrance's façade encapsulates this duality, but it also reveals the contradictions in the attempt to present a continuity between archaic and modern Israeli culture. These contradictions stem from the fact that in order to compete with the experienced Palestinian building trade, Jewish construction in the pre-state period depended on industrialization. In this sense, industrialization became the Israeli vernacular.[58] Sierra Leone's non-industrialized context freed the architects from dependence on industrial production and made it possible for Karmi to project the fantasy of the revival of ancient Hebrew masonry. In Sierra Leone, the marrying of novel techniques with the use of the easily recognizable local stone, along with the employment of masses of unskilled labour, culminated in the foundation of a prefab modern (yet non-industrialized) tradition. While the design of the Sierra Leone parliament projected an image of timeless autochthony, it also presented the building as a symbol for an ongoing project of national becoming. However, this new national aesthetic could not bypass the conflicts embedded in such attempts, in Sierra Leone, as in Israel.

Bibliography

Aleksandrowicz, Or. 'Kurkar, Cement, Arabs, Jews: How to Construct a Hebrew City'. *Theory and Criticism* 36 (Spring 2010): 61–87 (In Hebrew).

Amir, Yonatan. 'Owner of Plan Number 13'. *Ma'ariv*, July 26, 1957 (In Hebrew).

'An Experts' Committee Approved Klarwein's Plan for the Knesset Building'. *Davar*, April 17, 1958 (In Hebrew).

Avermaete, Tom. 'The Discovery of the Everyday: Team 10's Re-Visioning of C.I.A.M.'s Modern Project'. In *ACSA International Conference, Contribution and Confusion: Architecture and the Influence of Other Fields of Inquiry, Helsinki, July 27–30, 2003*, edited by Scott Poole and Pia Sarpaneva, 2–8, accessed January 7, 2019, http://apps.acsa-arch.org/resources/proceedings/indexsearch.aspx?txtKeyword1=%22Avermaete%2C+Tom%22&ddField1=1.

Bar-Yosef, Eitan. *A Villa in the Jungle: Africa in Israeli Culture*. Jerusalem: Van Lear Jerusalem Institute and Hakibbutz Hameuchad, 2013 (In Hebrew).

Ben-Asher Gitler, Inbal. 'Campus Architecture as Nation Building: Israeli Architect Arieh Sharon's Obafemi Awolowo University Campus, Ile-Ife, Nigeria'. In *Third World Modernism: Architecture, Development and Identity*, edited by Duanfang Lu, 112–40 (New York and London: Routledge, 2011).

Ben-Shaul, Haim. 'On the Delay in the Plan'. *Ma'ariv*, February 11, 1960 (In Hebrew).

Bhabha, Homi K. *The Location of Culture*. New York and London: Routledge, 1994.

Brinker, Menachem. 'The Generation of the State: A Cultural or Political Concept?' In *Wars, Revolutions, and Generational Identity*, edited by Joseph Mali, 143–57. Tel Aviv: Am Oved, 2001 (In Hebrew).

Celik, Zeynep. *Urban Forms and Colonial Confrontations: Algiers under French Rule*. Berkeley: University of California Press, 1997.

Curtis, William J. R. 'Authenticity, Abstraction and the Ancient Sense: Le Corbusier's and Louis Kahn's Ideas of Parliament'. *Perspecta* 20 (1983): 181–94.

Efrat, Zvi. *The Israeli Project: Building and Architecture, 1948–1973*. Tel Aviv: Tel Aviv Museum of Art, 2004 (In Hebrew).

Elhanany, Abba, Abraham Erlik, Shlomo Gilad, Nahum Zolotov, Yitzhak Yashar, Michael Nadler, Emanuel Friedman, Moshe Rosetti, David Reznik. 'Monumental Construction in the Twentieth Century: Symposium'. *Tvai* 3 (Spring 1967): 14–22 (In Hebrew)

'An Experts' Committee Approved Klarwein's Plan for the Knesset Building'. *Davar*, April 17, 1958 (In Hebrew).

Fuchs, Ron and Gilbert Herbert. 'Representing Mandatory Palestine: Austen St. Barbe Harrison and the Representational Buildings of the British Mandate in Palestine, 1922–37'. *Architectural History* 43 (2000): 281–333.

Fyfe, Christopher and Eldred Jones, eds, *Freetown: A Symposium*. Freetown: Sierra Leone University Press, 1968.

Gideon, Siegfried. 'The Need for a New Monumentality'. In *New Architecture and City Planning: A Symposium*, edited by Paul Zucker, 549–68. New York: Philosophical Library, 1944.

Hattis-Rolef, Sheila. 'The Knesset Building in Givat Ram: Planning and Construction'. *Cathedra* 96 (2000): 131–170 (In Hebrew).

——— 'The Planning of the Knesset: Additions and Amendments'. *Cathedra* 105 (2002): 171–80 (In Hebrew).

Hever, Hannan. *Nativism, Zionism, and Beyond*. Syracuse and New York: Syracuse University Press, 2014.

Hitchcock, Henry-Russel and Phillip Johnson. *The International Style: Architecture Since 1922*. New York: W. W. Norton & Co., 1932.

'The House of Seniors'. *Davar*, August 2, 1957.

Karmi, Ram. Interview in Meira Yagid-Haimovich, *Dov Karmi: Architect-Engineer Public Domestica*. Tel Aviv: Tel Aviv Museum of Art, 2011, DVD and Book.

——— Interview with Ayala Levin. Herzliya Pituach, Israel, August 4, 2011.

——— *Lyric Architecture*. Tel Aviv: Israeli Ministry of Defense, 2001 (In Hebrew).

Kroyanker, David. *Jerusalem Architecture – Periods and Styles: The Modern Construction Outside the Old City Walls, 1948–1990*. Jerusalem: Keter, 1991 (In Hebrew).

Levey, Zach. 'The Rise and Decline of a Special Relationship: Israel and Ghana, 1957–1966'. *African Studies Review* 46.1 (2003): 155–77.

Levin, Ayala. 'Exporting Architectural National Expertise: Arieh Sharon's Ile-Ife University Campus in West Nigeria (1962–1976)'. In *Nationalism and Architecture*, edited by Raymond Quek and Darren Deane, 53–66. Aldershot, UK and Burlington, VT: Ashgate, 2012.

——— 'Exporting Zionism: Architectural Modernism in Israeli-African Technical Cooperation, 1958–1973'. Ph.D. diss., Columbia University, 2015.

Levin, Michael. 'Regional Aspects of the International Style in Tel Aviv and Jerusalem'. In *Critical Regionalism: The Pomona Meeting Proceedings*, edited by Spyros Amourgis, 240–57. Pomona, CA: College of Environmental Design, California State Polytechnic University, 1991.

Mamdani, Mahmood. *Citizen and Subject: Contemporary Africa and the Legacy of Late Colonialism*. Princeton, NJ: Princeton University Press, 1996.

Massad, Joseph. 'The "Post-Colonial" Colony: Time, Space, and Bodies in Palestine/Israel'. In *The Pre-Occupation of Postcolonial Studies*, edited by Fawzia Afzal-Khan and Kalpana Seshadri-Crooks, 311–46. Durham; London: Duke University Press, 2000.

Meltzer, Zvi. Interview with Ayala Levin. Rishon LeZion, Israel, August 16, 2011.

Mitchell, Timothy. *Rule of Experts: Egypt, Techno-Politics, Modernity*. Berkeley and Los Angeles: University of California Press, 2002.

Nasr, Joe and Mercedes Volait, eds. *Urbanism: Imported or Exported*. Chichester, UK: Wiley-Academy, 2003.

Nitzan-Shiftan, Alona. 'Seizing Locality in Jerusalem'. In *The End of Tradition?* edited by Nezar AlSayyad, 231–55. London and New York: Routledge, 2004.

Nolan, Ginger. 'Savage Mind to Savage Machine: Techniques and Disciplines of Creativity, c. 1880–1985'. Ph.D. diss., Columbia University, 2015.

Porter, Arthur T. *Creoledom: A Study of the Development of Freetown Society*. London: Oxford University Press, 1963.

Rotbard, Sharon. 'Wall and Tower: The Mould of Israeli Architecture'. In *A Civilian Occupation*, edited by Rafi Segal and Eyal Weizman, 39–56. Tel Aviv and New York: Babel and Verso, 2003.

Sabatino, Michelangelo. 'Spaces of Criticism: Exhibitions and the Vernacular in Italian Modernism'. *Journal of Architectural Education* 62, 3 (2009): 35–52.

Shekhori, Shlomo. 'Sierra Leone's Parliament Opened in Time', *Davar*, May 11, 1961.

Weizman, Eyal. *Hollow Land: Israel's Architecture of Occupation*. London and New York: Verso, 2007.

Wright, Frank Lloyd. *An Autobiography*. New York: Horizon Press, 1977.

Wright, Gwendolyn. *The Politics of Design in French Colonial Urbanism*. Chicago and London: University of Chicago Press, 1991.

Wyse, Akintola. *The Krio of Sierra Leone: An Interpretative History*. London: C. Hurst and Company, 1989.

Yacobi, Haim. *Israel and Africa: A Genealogy of Moral Geography*. Abingdon, Oxon and New York: Routledge, 2016.

——— 'The Architecture of Foreign Policy: Israeli Architects in Africa'. *OASE* 82 (2010): 35–54.

Yagid-Haimovich, Meira. *Dov Karmi: Architect-Engineer Public Domestica*. Tel Aviv: Tel Aviv Museum of Art, 2011. DVD and book.

Zerubavel, Yael. *Recovered Roots: Collective Memory and the Making of Israeli National Tradition*. Chicago: University of Chicago Press, 1994.

Notes

1 All translations from Hebrew to English are the author's own, unless otherwise specified.

2 Ehud Barak, cited in Eitan Bar-Yosef, *A Villa in the Jungle: Africa in Israeli Culture* (Jerusalem: Van Lear Jerusalem Institute and Hakibbutz Hameuchad, 2013), 10 (In Hebrew). As Bar-Yosef notes, this statement is particularly ironic given that Prime Minister Yitzhak Rabin's assassination had occurred just a few months prior.

3 For a review of Israeli architectural projects as part of this aid, see: Zvi Efrat, *The Israeli Project: Building and Architecture, 1948–1973* (Tel Aviv: Tel Aviv Museum of Art, 2004), 607–30 (In Hebrew); Haim Yacobi, 'The Architecture of Foreign Policy: Israeli Architects in Africa', *OASE* 82 (2010), 35–54; Haim Yacobi, *Israel and Africa: A Genealogy of Moral Geography* (Abingdon and New York: Routledge, 2016). For in-depth discussions of specific projects, see: Inbal Ben-Asher Gitler, 'Campus Architecture as Nation Building: Israeli Architect Arieh Sharon's Obafemi Awolowo University Campus, Ile-Ife, Nigeria', in *Third World Modernism: Architecture, Development and Identity*, ed. Duanfang Lu (New York and London: Routledge, 2011), 112–40; Ayala Levin, 'Exporting Architectural National Expertise: Arieh Sharon's Ile-Ife University Campus in West Nigeria (1962–1976)', in *Nationalism and Architecture*, eds Raymond Quek and Darren Deane (Aldershot, UK and Burlington, VT: Ashgate, 2012), 53–66; Ayala Levin, 'Exporting Zionism: Architectural Modernism in Israeli-African Technical Cooperation, 1958–1973' (Ph.D. diss., Columbia University, 2015).

4 Alona Nitzan-Shiftan, 'Seizing Locality in Jerusalem', in *The End of Tradition?* ed. Nezar AlSayyad (London and New York: Routledge, 2004), 231–55. The term 'generation of the state' was first coined by literary theorist Menachem Brinker to define a literary generation. See: Menachem Brinker, 'The Generation of the State: A Cultural or Political Concept?' in *Wars, Revolutions, and Generational Identity*, ed. Joseph Mali (Tel Aviv: Am Oved, 2001), 143–57 (In Hebrew).

5 See, for example, Gwendolyn Wright, *The Politics of Design in French Colonial Urbanism* (Chicago and London: University of Chicago Press, 1991); Zeynep Celik, *Urban Forms and Colonial Confrontations: Algiers under French Rule* (Berkeley: University

of California Press, 1997). Sometimes local agencies initiated these experiments. See: Joe Nasr and Mercedes Volait, eds, *Urbanism: Imported or Exported* (Chichester, UK: Wiley-Academy, 2003).

6 Modernist architecture was famously dubbed as the 'International Style' in an eponymous exhibition at the MoMA in 1932. See Henry-Russel Hitchcock and Phillip Johnson, *The International Style: Architecture Since 1922* (New York: W. W. Norton & Co., 1932).

7 See discussion in Timothy Mitchell, *Rule of Experts: Egypt, Techno-Politics, Modernity* (Berkeley and Los Angeles: University of California Press, 2002), 179–83.

8 Joseph Massad, 'The "Post-Colonial" Colony: Time, Space, and Bodies in Palestine/Israel', in *The Pre-Occupation of Postcolonial Studies*, eds Fawzia Afzal-Khan and Kalpana Seshadri-Crooks (Durham; London: Duke University Press, 2000), 311–46.

9 For a comprehensive history of Freetown's establishment as an enlightenment colony, see: Christopher Fyfe and Eldred Jones, eds, *Freetown: A Symposium* (Freetown: Sierra Leone University Press, 1968). For the history of the Krio, and the social divide of the indigenous population, see: Akintola Wyse, *The Krio of Sierra Leone: An Interpretative History* (London: C. Hurst and Company, 1989); Arthur T. Porter, *Creoledom: A Study of the Development of Freetown Society* (London: Oxford University Press, 1963). Throughout the twentieth century, the cultural and political hegemony of the Krio has gradually decreased.

10 In 1808, Britain declared Freetown a Crown Colony, and in 1896 annexed the hinterland. This annexation created what African political scholar Mahmood Mamdani has characterized as the colonial bifurcated state, legally and administratively divided between direct and indirect rule: in Sierra Leone, the Freetown peninsula was under the direct rule of the Colony and exemplified a form of 'urban civil power', while the hinterland provinces were under the indirect rule of the Protectorate and exemplified a 'rural tribal authority'. Mahmood Mamdani, *Citizen and Subject: Contemporary Africa and the Legacy of Late Colonialism* (Princeton, NJ: Princeton University Press, 1996), 18.

11 On Israel's first diplomatic steps in Africa, see: Zach Levey, 'The Rise and Decline of a Special Relationship: Israel and Ghana, 1957–1966', *African Studies Review* 46.1 (2003): 155–77.

12 Shlomo Shekhori, 'Sierra Leone's Parliament Opened in Time', *Davar*, May 11, 1961, 5.

13 Siegfried Gideon, 'The Need for a New Monumentality', in *New Architecture and City Planning: A Symposium*, ed. By Paul Zucker (New York: Philosophical Library, 1944), 549–68.

14 See: Sheila Hattis-Rolef, 'The Knesset Building in Givat Ram: Planning and Construction', *Cathedra* 96 (2000), 138 (In Hebrew).

15 'The House of Seniors', *Davar*, August 2, 1957, 23 (In Hebrew).

16 The Dagon Silos in Haifa is probably Klarwein's most expressionist project in Israel (1953–66).

17 Yonatan Amir, 'Owner of Plan Number 13', *Ma'ariv*, July 26, 1957, 2 (In Hebrew).

18 'House of Seniors', 23.

19 Amir, 'Owner', 2.

20 Ron Fuchs and Gilbert Herbert, 'Representing Mandatory Palestine: Austen St. Barbe Harrison and the Representational Buildings of the British Mandate in Palestine, 1922–37', *Architectural History* 43 (2000): 281–333, especially 284–85.
21 Hattis-Rolef, 'Knesset Building', 140; David Kroyanker, *Jerusalem Architecture – Periods and Styles: The Modern Construction Outside the Old City Walls, 1948–1990* (Jerusalem: Keter, 1991), 106–08 (In Hebrew).
22 'An Experts' Committee Approved Klarwein's Plan for the Knesset Building', *Davar*, April 17, 1958, 4 (In Hebrew); Hattis-Rolef, 'Knesset Building', 141; Kroyanker, *Jerusalem Architecture*, 108–09.
23 Haim Ben-Shaul, 'On the Delay in the Plan', *Ma'ariv*, February 11, 1960, 3 (In Hebrew); Sheila Hattis-Rolef, 'The Planning of the Knesset: Additions and Amendments', *Cathedra* 105 (2002), 171–80 (In Hebrew).
24 Hattis-Rolef, 'Knesset Building', 147.
25 Ram Karmi, interview in Meira Yagid-Haimovich, *Dov Karmi: Architect-Engineer Public Domestica* (Tel Aviv: Tel Aviv Museum of Art, 2011), DVD and book.
26 Hattis-Rolef, 'Knesset Building', 147.
27 Ibid.; Ram Karmi, interview in Meira Yagid-Haimovich, *Dov Karmi*. According to Ram Karmi, he was the sole author of the Sierra Leone parliament's design. Ram Karmi, interview with Ayala Levin, Herzliya Pituach, Israel, August 4, 2011. However, Zvi Meltzer, the architect on site, contributed to the project as well. Zvi Meltzer, interview with Ayala Levin, Rishon LeZion, August 16, 2011.
28 Abba Elhanany, Abraham Erlik, Shlomo Gilad, Nahum Zolotov, Yitzhak Yashar, Michael Nadler, Emanuel Friedman, Moshe Rosetti, David Reznik, , 'Monumental Construction in the Twentieth Century: Symposium', *Tvai* 3 (Spring 1967): 14–22 (In Hebrew); Bill Gillit, a British architect and Ram Karmi's classmate who joined the design team of the Knesset in its later stages, also expressed this criticism. See Hattis-Rolef, 'Planning', 174.
29 'House of Seniors', 23.
30 Hattis-Rolef, 'Knesset Building', 145. The terraces were completed in 1991.
31 Nitzan-Shiftan, 'Seizing Locality', 231–55. On Team X's interest in vernacular architecture, see: Tom Avermaete, 'The Discovery of the Everyday: Team 10's Re-Visioning of C.I.A.M's Modern Project', *ACSA International Conference, Contribution and Confusion: Architecture and the Influence of Other Fields of Inquiry, Helsinki, July 27–30, 2003*, eds Scott Poole and Pia Sarpaneva, 2–8, accessed January 7, 2019, http://apps.acsa-arch.org/resources/proceedings/indexsearch.aspx?txtKeyword1=%22Avermaete%2C+Tom%22&ddField1=1.
32 Nitzan-Shiftan, 'Seizing Locality', 238–41.
33 See note 3.
34 Cited in Nitzan-Shiftan, 'Seizing Locality', 238 (original emphasis).
35 Ram Karmi, *Lyric Architecture* (Tel Aviv: Israeli Ministry of Defense, 2001), 46 (In Hebrew), author's translation.
36 For a discussion of Yona Friedman's Ville Spatiale in the context of Team X's turn to the vernacular, see: Ginger Nolan, 'Savage Mind to Savage Machine: Techniques and Disciplines of Creativity, c. 1880–1985' (Ph.D. diss., Columbia University, 2015), 136–44.

37 Since the terraces represent a different temporality than the representative building, they are relegated to the back. The tension between these two temporalities is similar to what postcolonial theorist Homi K. Bhabha identifies as the conflicting temporalities of the nation between 'the accumulative temporality of the pedagogical, and the repetitious, recursive strategy of the performative'. See: Homi K. Bhabha, *The Location of Culture* (London; New York: Routledge, 1994), 209.
38 Karmi, *Lyric Architecture*, 53.
39 Ibid, 48–49, author's translation.
40 Hannan Hever, *Nativism, Zionism, and Beyond* (Syracuse and New York: Syracuse University Press, 2014), 3–4.
41 Ibid., 4–5.
42 Yael Zerubavel, *Recovered Roots: Collective Memory and the Making of Israeli National Tradition* (Chicago: University of Chicago Press, 1994), 25–27. However, both Zerubavel and Hever maintain that Zionism rejected a total rupture between the New Hebrew and Jewish continuity. For this reason, Hever differentiates between Zionist nativism and Zionism.
43 Hever, *Nativism*, 12.
44 Ibid., 11.
45 Karmi, *Lyric Architecture*, 63–64, author's translation.
46 Hever, *Nativism*, 7.
47 Hattis-Rolef, 'Knesset Building', 136. In Zionist culture, the Second Temple symbolizes the period of Hebraic heroism. See: Zerubavel, *Recovered*, 23.
48 Or Aleksandrowicz, 'Kurkar, Cement, Arabs, Jews: How to Construct a Hebrew City', *Theory and Criticism* 36 (Spring 2010): 61–87 (In Hebrew); Eyal Weizman, *Hollow Land: Israel's Architecture of Occupation* (London and New York: Verso, 2007), 33.
49 Michael Levin, 'Regional Aspects of the International Style in Tel Aviv and Jerusalem', in *Critical Regionalism: The Pomona Meeting Proceedings*, ed. Spyros Amourgis (Pomona, CA: College of Environmental Design, California State Polytechnic University, 1991), 248–54. Weizman, *Hollow*, 27–30.
50 In Daniel Karavan's mural inside the assembly hall, on the other hand, the artist collaborated with Palestinian stonemasons, whose names he wanted to include on the wall next to his. He was denied this and consequently withdrew his name from the wall.
51 Karmi's formulation is reminiscent of Frank Lloyd Wright's statement: 'I knew well that no house should ever be *on* a hill or *on* anything. It should be *of* the hill. Belonging to it'. Frank Lloyd Wright, *An Autobiography* (New York: Horizon Press, 1977), 191–200, cited in Michelangelo Sabatino, 'Spaces of Criticism: Exhibitions and the Vernacular in Italian Modernism', *Journal of Architectural Education* 62, 3 (2009), 49 (original emphasis).
52 The 'traditional' house in Sierra Leone is a clay and earth structure topped with a thatch roof. It tends to be constructed either of 'wattle and daub' (in which a 'wattle', or frame of poles secured by intertwined twigs and vines, is 'daubed' or plastered with soft earth to cover it), or of clay and earth blocks that have been dried and hardened in the sun.
53 Karmi, interview with Ayala Levin.

54 Ibid.
55 William J. R. Curtis, 'Authenticity, Abstraction and the Ancient Sense: Le Corbusier's and Louis Kahn's Ideas of Parliament', *Perspecta* 20 (1983): 181–94.
56 Karmi, interview with Ayala Levin; Meltzer, interview.
57 Karmi, interview with Ayala Levin.
58 Sharon Rotbard makes a similar claim regarding prefabrication. See Sharon Rotbard, 'Wall and Tower: The Mould of Israeli Architecture', in *A Civilian Occupation*, eds Rafi Segal and Eyal Weizman (Tel Aviv and New York: Babel and Verso, 2003), 39–56.

Conclusion

Inbal Ben-Asher Gitler and Anat Geva

In 2002, architectural historian Zvi Efrat curated an exhibition at the Tel Aviv Museum, titled *The Israeli Project*. The exhibition presented Israeli architecture and, to a lesser extent, urban planning created between 1948 and 1973. Efrat's seminal book of the same name, published in 2004, undertook the compilation and critique of that extensive group of works.[1] He did not explain his closing with the year 1973. We assume the year was selected since it marked the 1973 War, identified as a turning point in Israeli politics and society. As such, Efrat proposed yet another temporal boundary, in addition to those discussed in our introduction and by our book's authors. His premise was that

> nearly all architecture built during Israel's first two decades [...] represented a social-realist hegemony that succeeded in dictating a regime of taste, and activated an efficient mechanism of planned culture while producing a new surface-image [...] remarkably different from that of the *Yishuv* and the [pre-state British] mandatory establishment.[2]

Even Efrat described his research as a process that unsettled earlier assumptions. He states that what had initially seemed as a 'dogmatic building operation', gradually revealed itself as a built environment rich with iterations, whose 'parts make up for more than one whole'.[3]

The studies presented in this volume do more than unravel this 'whole' and its components. They expose and uncover the complexity of the tenets of late modernism. In this, they support the epistemological and methodological demand for a reassessment of the modern movement, promoted by architectural historians in recent years. We will address this issue further in the closing paragraphs of this conclusion.

The structure and content of this book underscore the multiple avenues and themes implicit in the discussion and study of Israeli architecture. The chapters explore the motivations, challenges, and requirements faced by architects in Israel, whether working in the country or outside its borders, whether in consensual or contested territory. Furthermore, this book examines the diverse discourses – local and international – that dealt with the Israeli built environment. The book's four sections illustrate architecture's role in social transformations, technological approaches, and climatic considerations, revealing the Israeli case of modern architecture as an excellent example of modernism's international expansion.

Each of the chapters in the book's first section, 'Modern Experiments in Rural and Urban Design', presents a novel interpretation of the settlement types with which they engage. The essays by Yair Barak, Oryan Shachar, and Yael Allweil, problematize the role of new settlements in different parts of Israel, and vis-à-vis Palestinian presence or absence. Barak discusses the settling of Kiryat-Gat and its surrounding Lakhish region as a result of the forced expulsion of its Palestinian population in the aftermath of the 1948 War. Shachar considers the selection of Israel's northern region, the Galilee, and the specific town of Hatzor HaGlilit as a national site for densifying Jewish settlement as a response to a growing Arab-Israeli population. Barak and Shachar's chapters, while not directly engaging the memory of Palestinian space, open an exploratory dimension for its investigation. Their examination of how vernacular elements – defined as either Mediterranean or Palestinian – were subtly integrated into modernist dwellings, presents a possible point of departure for examining architecture as a site for the creation or reiteration of cultural memory. Allweil researches new communal settlements in the West Bank, an Israeli-occupied territory with a Palestinian majority. There, an Israeli-Jewish political movement, often opposing national policies, embarked upon a settlement project spanning decades. These projects intended to create a Jewish presence in a contested region. Allweil's chapter discusses the enduring and significant role assigned to architecture and spatial planning in attempts for political strategic gains. These three chapters also illustrate the transformations in the policy of social uniformity, demonstrating the shift from the concept of 'one dwelling type fits all' to diversified approaches tailored to different communities.

The fourth chapter in this section is by Elissa Rosenberg. Her research of Shmuel Bickels's kibbutz landscape designs, that provided an excellent example of innovation produced by the periphery rather than by the state's centre. While paying tribute to western modernist landscape planning, of which Bickels was well-informed, Rosenberg reveals the contingency of architecture and landscape in this unique rural settlement type.

As argued by both Allweil and Shachar, and as exemplified in Efrat's above-cited description, research has interpreted the Israeli architecture and planning of the first three decades primarily as state-sponsored and controlled operations, or a 'top-down planning model of progress and development'.[4] However, the case studies presented here challenge these accepted paradigms. The kibbutz community usually had full and exclusive control of the planning and design of its communal space; the Gur community and the Elon-More movement are also examples of projects where the community, rather than the state, dictated ideological planning according to their own needs. The chapters in this section therefore propose alternative perceptions of nation building and its agents, of its typological evolvement, as well as of its temporal and modernist frameworks.

The second section of the book, titled 'Public Architecture as a Testing Ground', discusses three different typologies: exhibition spaces, youth villages, and synagogues. Eliyahu Keller examines in his chapter the question, 'what is the Jewish state if not a type of national orphanage for those whose homes and ancestors have been taken away?'[5] He investigates this metaphorical question by comparing the Israel Museum in Jerusalem (1965) with Aldo van Eyck's Amsterdam Orphanage in the Netherlands (1955–60). This comparison explores the engagement of post-war modernism with symbolic content, and the impact of structuralist theory on the design of the Israel Museum.

In Sigal Davidi's chapter about Genia Averbuch's youth village projects, the orphanage is no longer a metaphor. As Davidi demonstrates, this architecture, intended for orphaned youth and teenaged new immigrants, reinterpreted the rural tradition crystalized in Zionist pre-state architecture. Averbuch's plans conveyed a regional identity and were a remarkable expression of the state ideology of uniformity. They provided the spatial complement to an educational curriculum intended to transform the youthful newcomers into 'Israelis'. In addition, this chapter addresses gender issues, as it reveals the impact of women architects and women's organizations on the Israeli built environment. Additional chapters in this volume also highlight the role of prominent women architects practising in Palestine and Israel – Dora Gad, Shulamit Nadler, Ada Karmi-Melamed, and Bracha Chyutin. These women architects made important strides even from an international perspective but, as in other locales, they are still relatively absent from architectural historiography.

A different building type is discussed by Naomi Simhony in her chapter on modern synagogues in Israel. Specifically, she looks at the role of synagogues in a new nation founded upon secular ideals. The chapter demonstrates that these buildings were conceived as modern houses of worship, which were imbued with national and religious symbolism that produced novel sacred architecture. Over time, these synagogues became iconic structures and symbolize new Jewish identity.

The last chapter of this section by Jeremy Kargon, focuses on a design competition for a technological centre, the Technodea (1978). While the completed Israel Museum became what is arguably one of Israel's 'national icons', the significant Technodea competition remained on paper and as a model. Kargon identifies the winning project, designed by Schocken, Shaviv, and Margalit-Gerstein, as a turning point in Israeli architecture. It introduced postmodernism to Israeli architectural discourse, applying it both stylistically and functionally.

The four case studies of this section demonstrate that typologies of public architecture indeed served as a testing ground for an expansion of their conceptual limits, in their social function, modern aesthetic, use of new building materials, and the construction of national identity.

The issue of climate, to which the third section of this book is dedicated, has bearings on modernism as an agent of progress. As the authors of these chapters show, using up-to-date climatic solutions for the creation of thermal comfort was a direct expression of technological and scientific advancements. Not all these experiments were successful, and many designs were based on architects' intuition, or on vernacular architecture, rather than being a result of *in situ* testing. Nonetheless, they reflected an awareness of developments in the field. The projects discussed by Binder and Kofman in the first chapter were progressive in their modernist, modular approach and in their informed engagement with the Dead Sea's hostile extreme environment. Different passive measures were used to adapt to the harsh terrain and climate (e.g., orientation to capture the prevailing breezes and views; shading devices; compact buildings; etc.). In this respect, these projects represented a complete integration of local vernacular – both traditional and contemporary – with modernism, as emblems of the pioneering spirit of the 'conquest of the desert'.[6]

The chapter by Isaac A. Meir, Rachel Bernstein, and Keren Shalev demonstrates how the Negev desert served as grounds for thermal experimentation. As architects acted on preconceptions rather than upon scientific data accumulation, they created architecture that was, in fact, unsuitable for desert conditions. In addition to these conclusions, the chapter's thermal analyses contribute an important aspect to the stylistic and ideological uses of concrete, so common in the Israeli adaptation of Brutalism in design. Meir et al. further explain the interrelationship between Be'er Sheva's urban plan and its architecture in light of changing approaches to environmentally conscious planning. In all these aspects, the experimental architecture built in the Negev desert inherently manifested the idea that arid land could become productive with the aid of spatial transformations that included the introduction of progressive measures in architecture.

In the last chapter of this section, Or Aleksandrowicz discusses the use of campus buildings – the civic architecture that is perhaps the most symbolic of progress – as a testing ground for introducing late modernism along with climate solutions. Aleksandrowicz identifies different approaches to science-based climate consideration design. These include shading apparatuses made from concrete, applied as precast blocks or poured-on-site elements, which presented innovative solutions for dealing with the high radiation of the Mediterranean region. These shading devices are also discussed by Binder and Kofman, as well as by Meir et al., as related to desert conditions. Taken together, the research presented in this section reaffirms the empirical approach as the rule, rather than the exception, among Israeli architects searching for building climatology solutions. It demonstrates that progress usually remained a formal and structural approach that often failed to apply the products of scientific research. In extreme conditions the integration of vernacular passive cooling was utilized to provide thermal comfort before air conditioning was introduced to Israel. Beyond climate considerations, the new university campuses and settling of desert terrains embodied the pioneer identity, an identity inherent in the creation of the Israeli forward-looking image of progress.

'Reflections Abroad' – the final section of the book – looks at the exportation of Israeli architecture abroad by studying key examples of civic architecture, and the impact of the media. Architecture and the media are examined in the first chapter of this section by Matteo Cassani Simonetti, who studies new Israeli projects as published in Italian architectural periodicals. In the next chapter of this section, Ayala Levin addresses the parliament building of Sierra Leone, an Israeli architectural exportation inspired by the Israeli parliament in Jerusalem (the Knesset), that intended to construct the African country's national image. Both Simonetti and Levin recruit their respective comparisons – Israel and Italy, Israel and Africa – to conduct a critical re-examination of issues of identity in architecture. It seems that these parallelisms have problematized our interpretations of the formation of distinct national identities. In addition, they suggest that such processes are part of a global process.

Simonetti demonstrates how Italian critics emphasized the modernism of Zionist and Israeli architecture. He argues that this was done in order to advocate the introduction of modern architecture to Italy, which was conceived by critics as signifying progress and democracy. Levin's analysis of Karmi's design for both the Knesset and the Sierra Leone parliament, demonstrates how the architect harnessed modernism's pliability to create a distinct identity for each of the locales in which he planned. In reflecting abroad, Karmi's Sierra Leone parliament makes for a key case study in the wider compendium of projects by Israeli architects executed in Third World countries.[7] Both chapters add to the growing body of research demonstrating that modernism, to a great extent, was tested and developed beyond Europe and became a multi-directional world phenomenon.[8]

The book's studies undermine additional premises relating to the modern movement in general and to its Middle-Eastern examples. First, they challenge the stringent separation between pre-World War II and post-war modernism. They adopt a more nuanced approach to early modernist heritage as negotiated by its first 'descendants'. Second, the assumption that modernism always meant progress is also called into question by these studies.[9] This can be seen, for example, in the development of the communal settlement, in which strategies of spatial intervention and accumulative growth both undermined and circumvented the totality of state-planning mechanisms and their application. Modern design with climate solutions was also often integrated with traditional design, and was imbued with a cultural, rather than scientific, perception of the desert as an empty wilderness. Perhaps the clearest evidence of the disentanglement of modernism from progress lies in the discourse created with the vernacular – not only by way of adopting form or material, but by the ideological position that the vernacular implied.

Architectural historian Mark Crinson has described the appropriation of the vernacular as 'an apotropaic device by which much of modernism, and much of the management of its past, could disavow not just the differences that make cultural form meaningful but the relations of economic or military dominance that structure colonial encounter'.[10] The issue of whether or not Israeli architectural encounters with the vernacular can be defined as colonial is a contentious one, especially due to the question: whose vernacular architecture is it? Because these encounters were significantly impacted by the Arab–Israeli and Palestinian–Israeli conflicts, issues such as economic or military dominance, weakness, or struggle, nonetheless remain relevant. In post-1948 Israel, the vernacular was often inspired by, and evoked, Arab or Palestinian architecture, intended to create a notion of locality. However, it was sometimes Jewish or archaeological, and thus often emerged as a memory of the biblical and historical Jewish past. In this capacity, it served to manifest Zionist identity. The vernacular was also a reworking of pre-state Jewish, Zionist, and even Mediterranean forms. Hence, multiple interpretations of the vernacular influenced architects' choices, which were at times indeed a 'disavowal', but in other instances – just the opposite. Thus, Crinson's concept of a 'dynamic vernacular', used by him to describe the complex junctures between 'high' modernist architecture and its vernacular sources,[11] can be used to describe the phenomena revealed in the analyses of the role and context of the vernacular in modern Israeli architecture, presented in the case studies in this volume.

These phenomena underscore the simultaneous existence of different expressions of modernism in varying spheres of architectural production. In the Israeli case, instances where modernism did not necessarily imply progress were contradicted in its enlistment by the state as an idea that indeed reflected the productions of an 'advanced' and 'unified' Israeli society. Progress and unification were both central aspects of Zionist ideology, continued by the post-1948 nation-state. The new state sought to affirm national – Zionist – claims for the land by *progressive* development and settlement. The immediacy demanded by nation building was achieved by modernist planning, design and technology, thereby turning architecture into a key political tool in forming and disseminating these ideologies.

Finally, while more than a decade ago Efrat enlisted 'marginality' as a key characteristic of Israeli architecture,[12] the research presented in this volume demonstrates that experiments, even when carried in the periphery, of which Israel is but one example, can indeed be cutting-edge, celebratory, and appreciated. As such, they undermine the accepted premise that architecture built in the West or the *Metropole* is necessarily more advanced than that which is produced outside its established geographical and ideological boundaries. Thus, it suggests a dialectical process, rather than a unidirectional transfer of knowledge.

While this book puts forth new research, it also reveals how much is yet to be discovered. More research is needed with regard to the social and political implications of the massive Jewish immigration into Israel from other Middle Eastern countries, as well as the impact and effects of Palestinian displacement upon architectural culture. There are under-explored topics to be developed, such as the discourse of Brutalism and Structuralism and their application, as well as their direct bearing on the investigation of regionalism and locality. The wider Middle Eastern perspective merits investigation as well, and studies comparing Israel with other Middle Eastern countries have yet to be carried out.

We hope that this compilation will serve as a stepping stone to a continuing investigation of ideology, agency, and production in Israeli architectural culture. Shedding light upon these themes was the object of this volume, which exposes the palimpsest of nation building as an experimental laboratory and reveals its conceptual and physical building blocks.

Bibliography

Avermaete, Tom, Serhat Krakayali, and Marion von Osten, eds. *Colonial Modern: Aesthetics of the Past – Rebellions for the Future*. London: Black Dog Publishing, 2010.

Ben-Asher Gitler, Inbal. 'Campus Architecture as Nation Building: Israeli Architect Arieh Sharon's Obafemi Awolowo University Campus in Ile-Ife, Nigeria, 1962–1976'. In *Third*

World Modernism: Architecture, Development and Identity, edited by Duanfang Lu, 112–40. Abingdon and New York: Routledge, 2010.

Carranza, Luis E. and Fernando Luiz Lara. *Modern Architecture in Latin America: Art, Technology, and Utopia*. Austin: University of Texas Press, 2015.

Crinson, Mark. 'Dynamic Vernacular – An Introduction'. *ABE Journal: Architecture Beyond Europe* 9–10 (2016). Accessed January 18, 2019. https://journals.openedition.org/abe/3002?lang=en.

Efrat, Zvi. *The Israeli Project: Architecture and Building 1948–1973*, co-edited by Zvi Elhyani. Tel Aviv: Tel Aviv Museum of Art, 2004 (In Hebrew).

Feniger, Neta and Rachel Kallus. 'Building a "New Middle East": Israeli Architects in Iran in the 1970s'. *Journal of Architecture* 22.4 (2017): 765–85.

James-Chakraborty, Kathleen. 'Beyond Postcolonialism: New Directions for the History of Nonwestern Architecture'. *Frontiers of Architectural Research* 3, no. 1 (2014): 1–9.

Lu, Duanfang, ed. *Third World Modernism: Architecture, Development and Identity*. Abingdon and New York: Routledge, 2010.

Yacobi, Haim. *Israel and Africa: A Genealogy of Moral Geography*. Abingdon and New York: Routledge, 2015.

Notes

1 Zvi Efrat, *The Israeli Project: Architecture and Building 1948–1973*, co-ed. Zvi Elhyani (Tel Aviv: Tel Aviv Museum of Art, 2004) (In Hebrew).

2 Efrat, *The Israeli Project*, 26.

3 Ibid.

4 Oryan Shachar's chapter in this book, 47.

5 Eliyahu Keller's chapter in this book, 134.

6 Daphne Binder and Theodore Kofman's chapter in this book.

7 Inbal Ben-Asher Gitler, 'Campus Architecture as Nation Building: Israeli Architect Arieh Sharon's Obafemi Awolowo University Campus in Ile-Ife, Nigeria, 1962–1976', in *Third World Modernism: Architecture, Development and Identity*, ed. Duanfang Lu (Abingdon and New York: Routledge, 2010), 112–40; Haim Yacobi, *Israel and Africa: A Genealogy of Moral Geography* (Abingdon and New York: Routledge, 2015); Neta Feniger and Rachel Kallus, 'Building a "New Middle East": Israeli Architects in Iran in the 1970s', *Journal of Architecture* 22.4 (2017): 765–85.

8 See, for example, Tom Avermaete, Serhat Krakayali, and Marion von Osten, eds. *Colonial Modern: Aesthetics of the Past – Rebellions for the Future* (London: Black Dog Publishing, 2010); Duanfang Lu, ed. *Third World Modernism: Architecture, Development and Identity*, (Abingdon and New York: Routledge, 2010); Luis E. Carranza and Fernando Luiz Lara, *Modern Architecture in Latin America: Art, Technology, and Utopia* (Austin: University of Texas Press, 2015).

9 Kathleen James-Chakraborty, 'Beyond Postcolonialism: New Directions for the History of Nonwestern Architecture', *Frontiers of Architectural Research* 3, no. 1 (2014): 3.

10 Mark Crinson, 'Dynamic Vernacular – An Introduction', *ABE Journal: Architecture Beyond Europe* 9–10 (2016): par. 7. Accessed January 18, 2019. https://journals.openedition.org/abe/3002?lang=en.

11 Ibid.

12 Efrat, *The Israeli Project*, 29–30.

Author Biographies

Inbal Ben-Asher Gitler is a senior lecturer of modern art, architecture, and visual culture at Sapir Academic College and adjunct lecturer at Ben Gurion University of the Negev, Israel. She received her Ph.D. from Tel Aviv University. She researches modern and contemporary Israeli architecture and visual culture. Her recent publications include 'Visualizing Democracy, Difference and Judaism in Israeli Posters, 1948–1978', published in *Israel Studies* in 2017, and the edited volume *Monuments and Site-Specific Sculpture in Urban and Rural Space* (Cambridge Scholars, 2017). She is presently researching the architecture of Jerusalem during the British Mandate, and is investigating the implementation and assimilation of Brutalism and Structuralism in Israel from the 1950s until the 1970s.

Anat Geva, Ph.D., registered architect and a professor of architecture at Texas A&M University, teaches design, history of building technology, sacred architecture, and preservation. She has published two books with Routledge: *Frank Lloyd Wright Sacred Architecture: Faith, Form and Building Technology* (2012) and the edited volume *Modernism and American Mid-20th Century Sacred Architecture* (2019). Her forthcoming book on the modern American synagogue is under contract with Texas A&M University Press. She has previously been the editor of two journals (ARRIS and PER), and a book review editor for *APT Bulletin*. She was one of the founders of the ACS Forum, served as a board member for SAH, as the president of SESAH, vice chair of CHSA, and secretary of NCPE.

Yair Barak is a Ph.D. candidate at the Cohn Institute for the History and Philosophy of Science and Ideas, Tel Aviv University. His main academic interests are economic history, history of economic thought, and social and cultural perspectives of time and space. His research topics include the effect of the monetary revolution of the thirteenth and fourteenth centuries on theology; German Cameralism of the eighteenth century; Adam Smith's social-economic philosophy; global and Israeli processes of privatization in the twentieth century; tax reforms in Israel; the queue as an economic-cultural phenomenon; and the 65-year-long Israeli social-religious battle over the implementation of daylight savings time. His research on the Glikson Neighborhood in Kiryat Gat (IHU) integrates his interests, as this economic-social-architectural episode is a chapter in the political-economic history of Israel that aimed at achieving national goals by increasing ethnic integration through a detailed and calculated architectural structure.

Oryan Shachar is an architect and graduate of Bezalel (2002). She completed her MA and doctoral studies at the Faculty of Architecture and Town Planning, Technion Israel Institute of Technology (2012). Her doctorate dissertation engages in modern architectures, urban communities, and historical narratives in Hatzor Haglilit. She was a postdoctoral scholarship recipient at Yad Ben-Zvi Institute and today researches the history of architectural preservation in Israel within the framework of the Technion IIT, the Israel Antiquities Authority and Daat Ha'makom Center for the Study of Cultures of Place in the Modern Jewish World. Oryan teaches history of Israeli and modern architecture and architectural conservation at the faculty of Architecture at the Technion, and at WIZO School of Design, Haifa. Oryan is the publication house manager of the Avie and Sarah Arenson Built Heritage Research Center in the Faculty of Architecture and Town Planning at the Technion.

Yael Allweil, Ph.D., is an architect and assistant professor in the Faculty of Architecture and Town Planning at the Technion, Israel, and associate fellow at the Truman Institute, Hebrew University. She completed her Ph.D. in architecture history at UC Berkeley, exploring the history of Israel-Palestine as one of the gain and loss of citizen housing. She is head of the *Housing Architecture, History and Theory* research group at the Technion. Her research was published in the monograph *Homeland: Zionism as Housing Regime 1860–2011* (Routledge, 2017) and a number of journal articles in *Urban Studies, Footprint, Architecture Beyond Europe, City, TDSR,* and *IJIA*. Yael's work involves academic research and activism in the context of the Israeli housing social movement.

Elissa Rosenberg is associate professor in the urban design graduate programme at the Bezalel Academy of Arts and Design, Jerusalem. She is also associate professor emerita at University of Virginia, where she served as chair of the Landscape Architecture Department. Her research has focused on contemporary landscape architecture and urban design including issues of gender and urban space, post-industrial landscapes, urban infrastructure, and landscapes of commemoration. Her work on the kibbutz has argued for its role as a laboratory of landscape design, specifically in the development of landscape modernism, as well as other areas of innovation, such as the experimental use of native plants and the invention of a unique secular Jewish cemetery typology.

Eliyahu Keller is an architect from Jerusalem, Israel. He is a Ph.D. candidate in the history, theory and criticism of architecture and art programme at the Massachusetts Institute of Technology. Eliyahu was the co-editor of *Thresholds 46: SCATTER!*, the departmental peer-reviewed journal published by the MIT Press in May 2018. He holds a bachelor of architecture from Israel and a master's in design studies with distinction from the Harvard Graduate School of Design, where he was awarded the Dimitris Pikionis Award. He has served as a research assistant for the Harvard-Mellon Urban Initiative and was a member of the Berlin Portal Research Group. His research has been supported by the David Rockefeller Institute for Latin-American Studies, the MIT Presidential Fellowship and several MISTI Global Seed fund grants. His current work investigates the various modalities of architectural imagination in relation to the appearance of nuclear weapons, and apocalyptic thinking in the Cold War.

Sigal Davidi is an architect and architectural historian. She holds a Ph.D. from Tel Aviv University (2015) and lectures at the Azrieli School of Architecture at Tel Aviv University. Davidi received the Leo Baeck Institute Jerusalem Ph.D. Dissertation Prize (2017) and the Goldberg Prize for an Outstanding Manuscript by the Open University of Israel (2018). She was a Minerva postdoctoral fellow at the Technische Universität Berlin, Institute of Architecture (2018) and is currently a visiting scholar at the Katz Center for Advanced Judaic Studies at the University of Pennsylvania (2019-2020). She writes and lectures on the history of architecture in Israel, with a special interest in modern architecture and women architects in pre-state Israel. Her book on the work of women architects in pre-state Israel will be published in Hebrew in 2019.

Naomi Simhony is an architect and researcher who holds a Bachelor of Architecture (B. Arch.) and an MA in philosophy from Tel-Aviv University. Her MA thesis examined the relationship between theology and aesthetics in Franz Rosenzweig's *The Star of Redemption*. Her doctoral studies at The Hebrew University of Jerusalem focus on modern synagogue architecture in the state of Israel over the first decades of statehood. Her research aims to uncover the means by which modern Israeli synagogue defines a new Jewish-national identity that weaves together liturgical tradition, symbolism, and memory on one hand, and a Zionist, modern, national ideology on the other. The research is based upon architectural-historical analysis of a defined corpus across three disciplines: history and theory of architecture, Jewish thought, and Jewish history.

Jeremy Kargon is associate professor at Morgan State University's School of Architecture and Planning (SA+P). A licensed architect from 1991 onwards, Kargon worked professionally in the US and in Israel. Since joining Morgan in 2007, he has explored architecture's representation and its different manifestations over time, across changing geographies, and within diverse cultures. Kargon's recent publications have dealt with visual depictions of urban landscapes, the use of graphic notation to represent non-visual experience, and the history of Baltimore's architecture after World War II. Other interests include the architecture of student religious centres on American college campuses, regional water management practices, and the history of Israeli architectural competitions. Between 2014 and 2018, Jeremy Kargon served as the SA+P's director for the graduate program in architecture.

Daphne Binder received her bachelor of architecture at the Cooper Union in 2011 and her master of architecture at the Yale School of Architecture in 2016. Daphne's research endeavours have ranged from the study of the Dead Sea's built environment, culminating in the exhibition 'Circumnavigating the Dead Sea' (The Cooper Union, 2010), to the study of urbanism in New England tourist towns. Daphne is a practicing architect in New York and Boston, has taught at The Cooper Union and Northeastern University, and is the co-founder of Space O.D.T, a multidisciplinary design firm.

Theodore 'Teddy' Kofman received his bachelor of architecture from the Cooper Union and his master of urban design from the Harvard Graduate School of Design. Previously, he studied in the David Azrieli School of Architecture at Tel Aviv University. Teddy has conducted extensive research focused on urbanization, co-organizing the symposium 'In the Shadow of the Megacity', which dealt with urban transformation in rural territories (The Cooper Union, 2015). Focusing on institutions, performing arts, and exhibition spaces, Teddy has designed both independently and at various practices in New York and Tel Aviv, and is the co-founder of Space O.D.T, a multidisciplinary design firm. He has taught design studios at the Harvard Graduate School of Design, Pratt Institute and The Cooper Union.

Isaac A. Meir holds B.Arch.T.Pl. and M.Sc. degrees from the Technion-I.I.T., and a Ph.D. from the Archeology Division of Ben-Gurion University of the Negev (BGU). He joined the BGU faculty in 1986 and is affiliated with the Desert Architecture & Urban Planning Unit, and the Dept. of Structural Engineering, Faculty of Engineering Sciences. He participates in the design of environmentally conscious and experimental projects in the Israeli deserts. Consultant to the Israel Ministries of Construction and Housing, Energy Water and Infrastructures, Israel Land Administration, and the Standards Institute of Israel. Heads multidisciplinary teams focusing on green technologies and sustainable development. His research interests include sustainable design in arid zones; Post Occupancy Evaluation (POE); Indoor Environment Quality (IEQ); microclimate of open spaces; Life Cycle Energy Analysis (LCEA); retrofit and upgrade of vernacular prototypes; proactive contingency planning. In 2016 he received the Israel Green Building Council Award for Leadership in Green Building.

Rachel Bernstein is originally from Maryland, USA, where she spent several years as a reporter in Baltimore and Washington, DC. Her M.A. research in Desert Studies focused on refugee camps in arid environments. She continued as a Ph.D. candidate at The Kreitman School of Advanced Graduate Studies, BGU, studying desert communities in Late Antiquity, and their architectonic and urban contexts. She has won several fellowships, including the Koenen Fellowship for Training in Papyrology (2017) and the Albright Institute of Archaeological Research Fellowship (2019-2020). Rachel currently resides in Jerusalem and is an editor at *The Jerusalem Post*.

Keren Shalev is a landscape architect and a Ph.D. candidate at The Kreitman School of Advanced Graduate Studies, BGU. Keren completed her B.L.Arch. studies at the Technion Israel Institute of Technology. Her master's and Ph.D. studies at BGU have been dedicated to the research of rural communities in Israel. She has won a number of distinctions, among them the Pratt Foundation Scholarship. Keren's research is multidisciplinary as her interests focus on the areas of evolution of spatial living patterns and the geographic, socioeconomic and demographic factors influencing the character of new rural development. More topics of interest are the social challenges of rural evolution aspects, such as sense of place and sense of belonging. Keren lives with her partner, an ecologist, and their two daughters in a small village in the Negev Desert, Israel. She teaches courses in landscape architecture, sustainable development and urban planning.

Or Aleksandrowicz is an architect, researcher, editor, translator, and assistant professor at the Faculty of Architecture and Town Planning, the Technion Israel Institute of Technology. Aleksandrowicz graduated from Tel Aviv University (2002) and wrote his master's (2012) and doctoral (2015) theses at TU Wien. His doctoral study focused on the history of building climatology in Israel and its effects on Israeli architecture. Since 2006, Aleksandrowicz has been the editor-in-chief of the *Architectures* series at Babel Publishers (Tel Aviv), the leading Hebrew book series on architecture and town planning. His book, *Daring the Shutter: The Tel Aviv Idiom of Solar Protections* (Israel Architecture Archive, 2015), recounts the technological history of shading devices in Tel Aviv.

Matteo Cassani Simonetti received his Ph.D. in architecture from the Dipartimento di Architettura of Università di Bologna, where he is presently a junior researcher. He won an Erasmus-Mundus postdoctoral fellowship for research at the University of Haifa and, recently, was member of the scientific committee of international congress, 'How to Narrate the History of Architecture? Centenary of Birth of Architectural Historian Bruno Zevi (1918-2000)' (Technion IIT, 2018). His fields of studies deal mainly with Italian architecture during the nineteenth and twentieth centuries. He curated the exhibition 'Biagio Rossetti secondo Bruno Zevi' (Rome, 2018-2019, with F. Ceccarelli and A. Zevi). Among his publications are the articles 'Word, Image, Architecture: Vittorio Savi and Luigi Ghirri' (2017); '"Architecture" (1921) e "Eupalinos ou l'Architecte": Note sulla Compagnie des Arts Français, un testo di Paul Valéry e un "recueil" curato da Louis Süe e André Mare' (2019) and the books *Piero Bottoni: Architecture and Design in Milan – Finzi House History* (2018) and *Architettura moderna e centri antichi: Piero Bottoni e Ferrara (1932-1970)* (2016).

Ayala Levin is assistant professor in the Art History Department at Northwestern University. Her research is concerned with north-south and south-south architectural knowledge exchange, with a focus on building and urban planning projects in post-independence African states. She is currently completing a monograph on the export of Israeli architectural and planning models to Sierra Leone, Nigeria, Ethiopia, and the Ivory Coast in the 1960s–1970s. Levin completed her Ph.D. at Columbia University. Before joining Northwestern University, she was a fellow at the Princeton-Mellon Initiative in Architecture, Urbanism and the Humanities and a postdoctoral researcher in the European Research Council project 'Apartheid: The Global Itinerary'.

Index

***Bold** numbers denote illustrations.*

H

O

S